Lecture Notes in Computer Science 7942

Commenced Publication in 1973
Founding and Former Series Editors:
Gerhard Goos, Juris Hartmanis, and Jan van Leeuwen

Margus Veanes   Luca Viganò (Eds.)

Tests and Proofs

7th International Conference, TAP 2013
Budapest, Hungary, June 16-20, 2013
Proceedings

 Springer

Volume Editors

Margus Veanes
Microsoft Research
Redmond, WA 98052-5321, USA
E-mail: margus@microsoft.com

Luca Viganò
Università di Verona
37134 Verona, Italy
E-mail: luca.vigano@univr.it

ISSN 0302-9743   e-ISSN 1611-3349
ISBN 978-3-642-38915-3   e-ISBN 978-3-642-38916-0
DOI 10.1007/978-3-642-38916-0
Springer Heidelberg Dordrecht London New York

Library of Congress Control Number: 2013939782

CR Subject Classification (1998): D.2.4, D.2, D.1, D.3, F.3, F.4.1

LNCS Sublibrary: SL 2 – Programming and Software Engineering

Typesetting: Camera-ready by author, data conversion by Scientific Publishing Services, Chennai, India

Printed on acid-free paper

Springer is part of Springer Science+Business Media (www.springer.com)

Preface

This volume contains the papers presented at the 7th International Conference on Tests and Proofs (TAP 2013), held during June 16–20, 2013, in Budapest, Hungary, as part of the Software Technologies: Applications and Foundations (STAF) federated event.

TAP 2013 was the seventh event in a series of conferences devoted to the synergy of proofs and tests, to the application of techniques from both sides and their combination for the advancement of software quality. Testing and proving seem to be contradictory techniques: once you have proved your program to be correct then additional testing seems pointless; on the other hand, when such a proof in not feasible, then testing the program seems to be the only option. This view has dominated the research community since the dawn of computer science, and has resulted in distinct communities pursuing the seemingly orthogonal research areas. In the past few years an increasing number of research efforts have encountered the need for combining proofs and tests, dropping earlier dogmatic views of incompatibility and taking instead the best of what each of these software engineering domains has to offer.

The first TAP conference (held at ETH Zurich in February 2007) was an effort to provide a forum for the cross-fertilization of ideas and approaches from the testing and proving communities. For the 2008 edition, the Monash University Prato Centre near Florence provided a stimulating environment. The third TAP was again held at ETH Zurich in July 2009. Since 2010, TAP has been co-located with TOOLS, and its instance for 2010 therefore took place at the School of Informatics (E.T.S. de Ingenieria Informatica) of the University of Malaga, while TOOLS 2011 took place at ETH Zurich again. In 2012, TAP was part of TOOLS again, this time held at the Czech Technical University in Prague. TAP 2013 was hosted in Budapest, the capital of Hungary, as part of STAF (the follow-up of TOOLS) and was held on the south campus of the Budapest University of Technology and Economics.

We wish to sincerely thank all authors who submitted their work for consideration. Although, we initially received 29 submissions, five were withdrawn. Out of the 24 remaining submissions, we finally accepted 12 papers, after a formal refereeing process requiring at least three reviews from the Program Committee or by a reviewer appointed by the Program Committee. The overall quality of the submissions was very high. The accepted papers are contributions related to the following four research topics that also form the sessions of the final program: test generation, model-based testing and mutants, declarative debugging, and tool testing.

We are very proud that TAP 2013 featured a keynote given by Andrei Voronkov on EasyChair, who, besides being the inventor and main developer of EasyChair, is also a leading expert on theorem proving, which is a field closely related to the theme of TAP. EasyChair was used to manage the TAP 2013 conference proceedings, and made the whole chairing process as easy as it can possibly get. Moreover, we were very happy to host two tutorials, one on Frama-C for specifying and proving program correctness, and the other one on Pex4Fun that uses symbolic execution to provide a gaming environment for learning and teaching programming. We also invited the keynote speaker and the tutorial authors to contribute a paper; the first tutorial authors did so, which is also indicated in the title of that paper. We would like to thank the Program Committee members as well as the additional reviewers for their energy and their professional work in the review and selection process. Their names are listed on the following pages. The lively discussions during the paper selection were vital and constructive.

We thank the organizers of the STAF event, in particular the Conference Chair Daniel Varro and the local Organizing Chair Akos Horvath, for their hard work and their support in making the conference a success, we thank the Budapest University of Technology and Economics for providing the facilities, and we thank Springer for publishing these proceedings.

June 2013   Margus Veanes
                                                            Luca Viganò

Organization

Program Committee

Paul Ammann	George Mason University, USA
Dirk Beyer	University of Passau, Germany
Achim D. Brucker	SAP AG, SAP Research, Germany
Robert Clarisó	Universitat Oberta de Catalunya, Spain
Marco Comini	University of Udine, Italy
Catherine Dubois	ENSIIE-CEDRIC, France
Juhan Ernits	Tallinn University of Technology, Estonia
Gordon Fraser	University of Sheffield, UK
Angelo Gargantini	University of Bergamo, Italy
Christoph Gladisch	Karlsruhe Institute of Technology, Germany
Martin Gogolla	Database Systems Group, University of Bremen, Germany
Arnaud Gotlieb	INRIA Rennes - Bretagne Atlantique, France
Reiner Hähnle	Technical University of Darmstadt, Germany
Bart Jacobs	Katholieke Universiteit Leuven, Belgium
Jacques Julliand	Université de Franche-Comté, France
Thierry Jéron	INRIA Rennes - Bretagne Atlantique, France
Gregory Kapfhammer	Department of Computer Science, Allegheny College, USA
Nikolai Kosmatov	CEA, LIST, Software Reliability Laboratory, France
Victor Kuliamin	Institute for System Programming, Russian Academy of Sciences, Russia
Michael Leuschel	University of Düsseldorf, Germany
Karl Meinke	Royal Institute of Technology (KTH) Stockholm, Sweden
Alexandre Petrenko	CRIM, Canada
Holger Schlingloff	Fraunhofer FIRST and Humboldt University, Germany
T.H. Tse	The University of Hong Kong, SAR China
Margus Veanes	Microsoft Research, USA
Luca Viganò	University of Verona, Italy
Burkhart Wolff	Université Paris-Sud, France
Fatiha Zaidi	Université Paris-Sud, France

Additional Reviewers

Baruzzo, Andrea
Bobot, Francois
Bubel, Richard
Giorgetti, Alain
Hentschel, Martin
Krieger, Matthias

Schmitt, Peter
Titolo, Laura
Torella, Luca
Ulbrich, Mattias
Williams, Nicky

Table of Contents

Incremental Refinement Checking
for Test Case Generation

Bernhard K. Aichernig, Elisabeth Jöbstl, and Matthias Kegele

Institute for Software Technology, Graz University of Technology, Austria
{aichernig,joebstl}@ist.tugraz.at, matthias.kegele@student.tugraz.at

Abstract. We combine model-based testing and mutation testing to automatically generate a test suite that achieves a high mutation adequacy score. The original model representing the system under test is mutated. To generate test cases that detect whether a modelled fault has been implemented, we perform a refinement check between the original and the mutated models. Action systems serve as formal models. They are well-suited to model reactive systems and allow non-determinism. We extend our previous work by two techniques to improve efficiency: (1) a strategy to efficiently handle a large number of mutants and (2) incremental solving. A case study illustrates the potential of our improvements. The runtime for checking appr. 200 mutants could be reduced from 20s to 3s. We implemented our algorithms in two versions: one uses a constraint solver, the other one an SMT solver. Both show similar performance.

Keywords: model-based testing, mutation testing, action systems, conformance, refinement, constraint solving, SMT solving.

1 Introduction

We combine model-based testing [28] and mutation testing [20,16] to automatically generate test cases that achieve a high mutation adequacy score. As pointed out by Jia and Harman in their recent survey on mutation testing [22], *"practical software test data generation for mutation test adequacy remains an unresolved problem"*. Furthermore, they identified a *"pressing need"* to address this problem. One particular issue is scalability, which is the main topic of this paper.

Fig. 1 gives an overview of our approach. The left-hand side (non-grey parts) refers to model-based testing: it is assumed that the source code of the system under test (SUT) is not accessible (black-box testing). Therefore, a tester develops a formal model describing the expected behaviour of the SUT. This model is assumed to be correct with respect to some properties derived from the requirements. This can be assured, e.g. via model checking. It serves as input for our test case generation tool, where it is used to generate the input stimuli and as a test oracle for the expected behaviour. The resulting tests are automatically executed. If all tests pass, we have conformance between the model and the SUT. However, since exhaustive testing is impractical, we have to select a proper subset of the possible test cases. We accomplish this by combining this model-based

M. Veanes and L. Viganò (Eds.): TAP 2013, LNCS 7942, pp. 1–19, 2013.

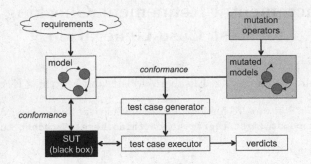

Fig. 1. Model-based mutation testing

testing approach with mutation testing. As we have no access to the source code of the SUT, we mutate our model of the SUT (cf. grey parts in Fig. 1). Then, given the original model and a set of mutated models, we automatically generate test cases that *kill* the model mutants, i.e., reveal their non-conforming behaviour. The generated tests are then executed on the SUT and will detect if a mutated model has been implemented. Hence, our model-based mutation testing approach is fault-centred. It tests against non-conformance rather than for conformance - we are aiming for falsification rather than for verification.

In our approach, equivalent model mutants are singled out automatically. In contrast to the original idea of program mutation [20,16], where a given set of test cases is analysed, here we generate a test suite that will kill all (non-equivalent) model mutants. This is non-trivial, since it involves an equivalence (conformance) check between original and mutated models (cf. Fig. 1), which we focus on in this paper. Since, equivalence is undecidable in general, we restrict ourselves to bounded domains.

Though the problem of checking for equivalence of two systems is hard enough already, we do also allow non-determinism in our models. In a non-deterministic model, a given (sequence of) input stimuli may cause several possible output observations. Non-determinism arises due to abstraction that is frequently required in good test models. When comparing two non-deterministic models (an original and a mutant in our case), equivalence is not sufficient any more. Hence, the conformance relation needs to be an order or preorder relation. Refinement is such an order relation [17]. We implemented a refinement checker for non-deterministic models to enable the generation of test cases that are able to detect whether a faulty model has been implemented in the SUT.

In principle, this model-based mutation testing approach could be implemented with existing tools, like model checkers [18]. We refrained from that as they are more general and therefore more complex than necessary. Thus, adaptations to optimise existing model checkers for our particular needs would probably not be beneficial. Furthermore, for generating test cases we need access to the internals of the state space. The counterexample trace is insufficient for non-deterministic models.

Previous Work. A first implementation of our model-based mutation testing approach has been implemented in our tool *Ulysses* [2]. It is basically checking input-output conformance [27] of two action systems and performs an explicit forward search of the state spaces. Our experience with the tool shows that the performance of explicit enumeration of the state space involves high memory consumption and runtimes. In [5] we illustrated that this is even the case for rather small models involving parameters. To overcome this and facilitate the handling of complex models, we work on an efficient tool that treats data symbolically. We already presented some aspects of our work previously: we explained the basic refinement checking approach [5], pointed out problems that need to be handled [6], and presented techniques that considerably improved the efficiency of our approach [4]. The main contributions of this paper are two further important improvements on efficiency: the efficient handling of a large number of mutants and the implementation of incremental solving in constraint logic programming. We implemented our approach and our improvements in two different ways: one uses Prolog and a constraint solving library, the other one an SMT solver. Both perform equally well. A first case study on a car alarm system shows the benefits of our improvements: the execution time could be reduced from approximately 20 to about 3 seconds. This is a reduction of about 85%.

The rest of this paper is organised as follows: In Section 2, we introduce preliminaries, i.e., our modelling language and our notion of refinement. In Section 3, we explain our refinement checking approach and present two techniques to increase its efficiency in Section 4. Their implementations are discussed in Section 5. In Section 6, we report on our case study. In Section 7, we cover related work and we conclude in Section 8.

2 Preliminaries

2.1 Action Systems

Our chosen modelling formalism are action systems [9], which are well-suited to model reactive and concurrent systems. They have a formal semantics with refinement laws and are compositional [10]. Recently, action systems have been adopted in the B-method [1]. The main idea is that a system state is updated by guarded actions that may be enabled or not. If no action is enabled, the action system terminates. If several actions are enabled, one is chosen non-deterministically. Hence, concurrency is modelled in an interleaving semantics. We use an example to introduce action systems. The formal syntax and semantics have been presented earlier [6,4].

Example 1. Listing 1.1 shows code snippets from an action system modelling a car alarm system. It defines the action *'AlarmOn'*, which turns on the flash lights and the signal-horn in case an alarm has been triggered.

All data types in our action systems are integers with restricted ranges. Line 1 defines the type 'bool' with two possible values: 0 or 1. Line 2 declares two variables with name f and s which are of type *bool*. They are used to indicate

Listing 1.1. Code snippet of an action system modelling a car alarm system

```
1   type(bool , X) :- X in  0..1.
2   var([f , s], bool).
3   state_def([f , s, ...]).
4   init([0, 0, ...]).
5   as :-
6     actions (
7       'AlarmOn'::( f #= 0 #/\ s #= 0) => (
8         (( f := 1 ; s := 1)      % (( f := 0) ; s := 1)
9         []
10         (s := 1 ; f := 1)),
11       ...) ,
12     dood ( 'AlarmOn' [] ... ).
```

whether the flash lights and the sound (signal horn) are turned on. Line 3 defines the list of variables representing the state of the action system. The initial values for the state are defined in Line 4. The *actions*-block (Lines 6–11) defines named actions, which consist of a name, a guard and a body (*name* :: *guard* => *body*). The action *'AlarmOn'* (Lines 7–10) models the activation of the alarms. This is only possible if both alarms are turned off before (guard in Line 7). It is not specified in which order the two alarms are turned on. This is modelled by the non-deterministic choice ([]) of two sequential compositions (;). Either, Line 8 turns on the flash first and afterwards the sound or Line 10 first turns on the sound and then the flash. The *do-od* block (Line 12) connects previously defined actions via non-deterministic choice. Basically, the execution of an action system is a continuous iteration over the do-od block.

Our overall goal is to generate a test case that is able to detect certain faults. For this purpose, we mutate our models and perform a refinement check between the original and the mutated model. The comment (%) in Line 8 represents a possible mutation. It assigns the variable f the value 0 instead of 1. This leads to a difference in the behaviour of the original action system (the specification) and the mutated one. The original activates both alarms. The mutant cannot always establish this behaviour. Although it results in the correct post-state by choosing Line 10, it might also end up in a wrong post-state by executing the mutated statement of Line 8. In this case, the flash will not be activated. This scenario is a counterexample to refinement. It allows us to derive a test case that is able to identify whether the modelled fault has been implemented in a SUT.

Semantics. The formal semantics of action systems is typically defined in terms of weakest preconditions. However, we found a relational predicative semantics being more suitable for our constraint-based approach. Its formal definition can be found in [6], where we also motivate our choice.

Example 2. The predicative semantics of the action *'AlarmOn'* in Example 1 is:

$$f = 0 \wedge s = 0 \wedge \tag{1}$$

$$(\exists f_0, s_0 : (f_0 = 1 \wedge s_0 = s \wedge f' = f_0 \wedge s' = 1) \vee \tag{2}$$

$$\exists f_0, s_0 : (f_0 = f \wedge s_0 = 1 \wedge f' = 1 \wedge s' = s_0)) \wedge \tag{3}$$

$$act' = 1 \tag{4}$$

Our relational semantics for an action is defined as $g \wedge B \wedge tr' = tr \,\widehat{}\, [l]$. Equation 1 represents the guard g. Equations 2 and 3 represent the action's body B. Equation 2 refers to Line 8 of Example 1, Equation 3 to Line 10. Each represents a sequential composition: there must exist an intermediate state $\overline{v_0}$ (here f_0 and s_0) that can be reached from the first body predicate and from which the second body predicate can lead to its final state (f', s'). Assignments update one variable with the value of an expression and leave the rest unchanged, e.g., the semantics of $f := 1$ (Line 10, Example 1) is $f' = 1 \wedge s' = s_0$. Equation 2 and 3 are connected via disjunction, which represents the non-deterministic choice between the sequential compositions. Finally, Equation 4 deals with the executed action (act'). To make this formal semantics processable by constraint solvers, the action labels are encoded as integers, i.e., the label *'AlarmOn'* is represented by the constant 1. For the same reason, quantifiers are eliminated by substitutions (see [4] for details) resulting in the following constraints:

$$f = 0 \wedge s = 0 \wedge ((f' = 1 \wedge s' = 1) \vee (f' = 1 \wedge s' = 1)) \wedge act' = 1$$

This is how our tool generates the constraints. Further simplifications are possible, but currently not implemented: as both cases of the disjunction are equivalent, they may be reduced to one:

$$C^o = (f = 0 \wedge s = 0 \wedge f' = 1 \wedge s' = 1 \wedge act' = 1)$$

This expresses what was intended to be modelled: the action *'AlarmOn'* is executed if neither sound nor flash is activated yet and turns on both alarms. In disjunction with the semantics of the other actions, which are only indicated by …in Example 1, C^o represents the transition relation of the action system.

Analogously, the simplified semantics of the mutation given in Example 1 is:

$$C^m = (f = 0 \wedge s = 0 \wedge ((f' = 0 \wedge s' = 1) \vee (f' = 1 \wedge s' = 1)) \wedge act' = 1)$$

2.2   Conformance Relation

Once the modelling language with a precise semantics is fixed, we can define what it means that a SUT conforms to a given reference model, i.e. if the observations of a SUT confirm the theory induced by a formal model. This relation between a model and the SUT is called conformance relation.

In model-based mutation testing, the conformance relation plays an additional role. It defines if a syntactic change in a mutant represents an observable fault, i.e. if a mutant is equivalent or not. However, for our non-deterministic models an equivalence relation is not suitable as pointed out in [6]. An abstract non-deterministic model may allow more than its concrete counterpart. Hence, useful conformance relations are relations relying on some ordering from abstract to more concrete models. One of these order relations is refinement, which uses implication to define conformance. A concrete implementation I refines an abstract model M, iff the implementation implies the model. The following definition of refinement relies on the Unifying Theories of Programming (UTP) of Hoare and He [21] giving M and I a predicative semantics.

Definition 1. *(Refinement) Let $v = \langle x, y, \dots \rangle$ be the set of variables denoting observations before execution and $v' = \langle x', y', \dots \rangle$ denoting the observations afterwards. Then*

$$M \sqsubseteq I \ =_{df} \ \forall v, v' : \ I(v, v') \ \Rightarrow \ M(v, v')$$

In [3] we developed a mutation testing theory based on this notion of refinement. The key idea is to find test cases whenever a mutated model M^M does not refine an original model M^O, i.e. if $M^O \not\sqsubseteq M^M$. Hence, we are interested in counterexamples to refinement. From Definition 1 follows that such counterexamples exist if and only if implication does not hold:

$$\exists v, v' : \ M^M(v, v') \wedge \neg M^O(v, v')$$

This formula expresses that there are observations in the mutant M^M that are not allowed by the original model M^O. We call a state, i.e. a valuation of all variables, *unsafe* if such an observation can be made.

Definition 2. *(Unsafe State) A pre-state u is called unsafe if it shows wrong (not conforming) behaviour in a mutated model M^M with respect to an original model M^O. Formally, we have:*

$$u \in \{ v \mid \exists \ v' : M^M(v, v') \wedge \neg M^O(v, v') \}$$

We see that an unsafe state can lead to an incorrect next state. In model-based mutation testing, we are interested in generating test cases that cover such unsafe states. Hence, our fault-based testing criteria are based on unsafe states. How we search for unsafe states in action systems is discussed in the next section.

3   Refinement Checking

In [5] we already gave an overview of our refinement checking approach. Fig. 2 depicts our process to find an unsafe state. The inputs are the original action system model AS^O and a mutated version AS^M. Each action system consists of a set of actions AS^O_i and AS^M_j respectively, which are combined via the non-deterministic choice operator. The observations in our action system language

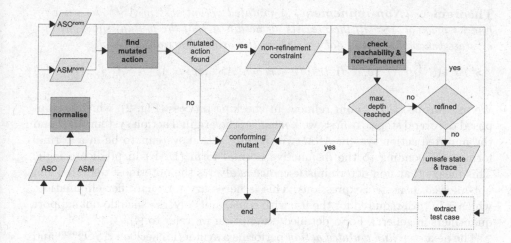

Fig. 2. Process for finding an unsafe state

are the event traces and the system states before $(\overline{v}, tr)$ and after one execution $(\overline{v}', tr')$ of the do-od block. Then, a mutated action system AS^M refines its original version AS^O if and only if all observations possible in the mutant are allowed by the original. Hence, our notion of refinement is based on both, event traces and states. However, in an action system not all states are reachable from the initial state. Therefore, reachability has to be taken into account.

We reduce the general refinement problem of action systems to a step-wise simulation problem only considering the execution of the do-od block from reachable states:

Definition 3. (Refinement of Action Systems) *Let AS^O and AS^M be two action systems with corresponding do-od blocks P^O and P^M. Furthermore, we assume a function "reach" that returns the set of reachable states for a given trace in an action system. Then*

$$AS^O \sqsubseteq AS^M =_{df} \forall \overline{v}, \overline{v}', tr, tr' : ((\overline{v} \in reach(AS^O, tr) \wedge P^M) \Rightarrow P^O)$$

This definition is different to Back's original refinement definition based on state traces [10]. Here, also the possible event traces are taken into account. Hence, also the action labels have to be refined.

Negating this refinement definition and considering the fact that the do-od block is a non-deterministic choice of actions A_i leads to the non-refinement condition for two action systems:

$$\exists \overline{v}, \overline{v}', tr, tr' : (\overline{v} \in reach(AS^O, tr) \wedge (A_1^M \vee \cdots \vee A_n^M) \wedge \neg A_1^O \wedge \cdots \wedge \neg A_m^O)$$

By applying the distributive law, we bring the disjunction outwards and obtain a set of constraints for detecting non-refinement.

Theorem 1. *(Non-refinement) A mutated action system AS^M does not refine its original AS^O iff there exists an action A_i^M of the mutant showing trace or state-behaviour that is not possible in the original action system:*

$$AS^O \not\sqsubseteq AS^M \text{ iff } \bigvee_{i=1}^{n} \exists \overline{v}, \overline{v}', tr, tr' : (\overline{v} \in reach(AS^O, tr) \wedge A_i^M \wedge \neg A_1^O \wedge ... \wedge \neg A_m^O)$$

We use this property in our refinement checking process (Fig. 2), which is composed of several steps. At first, we *normalise* the original action system ASO and the mutated action system ASM. We require action systems to be in a normal form corresponding to the disjunctive normal form (DNF) in predicate logic. This means that non-deterministic choice is always the outermost operator and not allowed in nested expressions. This is necessary for quantifier elimination, which is in turn required for the use with constraint solvers which do not support quantifiers in general. For a detailed description we refer to [4].

The next step *find mutated action* performs a syntactic check on ASO^{norm} and ASM^{norm} to find out which action has been mutated. We then use Theorem 1 for which only one of the sub-constraints of the form $A_i^M \wedge \neg A_1^O \wedge \cdots \wedge \neg A_m^O$ can be fulfilled: the one where A_i^M is the encoding of the just found mutated action. Hence, we are able to construct a *non-refinement constraint*, which is the sub-constraint containing the mutated action. It describes the set of unsafe states. Finally, the step *check reachability and non-refinement* performs a reachability analysis on the original action system and uses the non-refinement constraint to test each reached state whether it is an unsafe state. Note that the syntactic check fails to identify mutants that are syntactically non-equivalent but behaviourally equivalent. These mutants could be skipped for reachability analysis and could be detected via a semantic analysis using Theorem 1. However, this semantic check has turned out to be more costly than the syntactic check followed by a reachability analysis [4].

Our process either results in the verdict *conform*, which means that the mutated action system conforms to the original, or in an unsafe state and a sequence of actions leading to this state. In the latter case it is possible to derive a test case. As test case extraction is out of the scope of this paper it is only indicated by a dotted box in Fig. 2. For more details on our individual process steps and the used algorithms, we refer to [5,4].

Example 3. We continue Example 1 to illustrate our refinement checking process. The action 'AlarmOn' is already in normal form. Non-deterministic choice is the outermost operator and not nested in any other expressions. Our syntactic comparison reveals that the action 'AlarmOn' has been mutated. The semantics of the original (C^o) and the mutant (C^m) have already been constructed in Example 2. By combining them, we get the non-refinement constraint:

$$C^m \wedge \neg C^o = (f = 0 \wedge s = 0 \wedge ((f' = 0 \wedge s' = 1) \vee (f' = 1 \wedge s' = 1)) \wedge act' = 1) \wedge$$

$$\neg(f = 0 \wedge s = 0 \wedge f' = 1 \wedge s' = 1 \wedge act' = 1)$$

Note that existential quantification of the state variables is implicitly performed by the constraint solver. The next step is the reachability analysis starting from the action system's initial state. By setting $f = 0$ and $s = 0$ in the above non-refinement constraint and by simplification, we get:

$$(((f' = 0 \wedge s' = 1) \vee (f' = 1 \wedge s' = 1)) \wedge act' = 1) \wedge \neg(f' = 1 \wedge s' = 1 \wedge act' = 1)$$

This constraint has one solution: $f' = 0, s' = 1, act' = 1$. It reveals wrong observations after the initial state. Originally, both f' and s' should be set, but the mutant only sets s'. Hence, already the initial state ($f = 0, s = 0$) is an unsafe state and no further reachability analysis is required in this simplified example. In the original model the action is only triggered if additional conditions hold.

4   Efficiency

We presented techniques to improve the efficiency of our approach before [4]. Two of them are already incorporated in the description of our process in the previous section. The first one regards quantifier elimination. The second concerns the syntactic analysis to identify the mutated action. In the following, we present two newly implemented techniques to save computation time.

4.1   Pre-computation of Reachable States

So far, our refinement check between one original action system and a set of corresponding mutants has been implemented as described in Alg. 1. The input is one original action system (*as*) and a set of corresponding mutated action systems (*mutants*). Note that all action systems are supposed to be in normal form. The result is a map *unsafes* linking the mutants and their unsafe states. The algorithm iterates over the set of mutants (Line 4). For each mutant, it explores the state space of the original action system *as* (Line 6). The procedure *findNextState* implements a breadth-first search for successor states of state *s*, whereas it does not explore any state more than once (by maintaining a list of visited states). To ensure termination, it stops exploration at a user-specified depth limit. At each call, it returns the next reached state. This state is then tested whether it is an unsafe state (Line 8). If this is the case, the state space exploration is stopped and the next mutant is processed, where again state space exploration is performed. Note that we omitted the recording of the traces leading to the unsafe states for the sake of simplicity.

An advantage of Alg. 1 is that the state space is explored on demand, i.e., it is only explored until an unsafe state is found and not further. Given a small set of mutants, this algorithm is appropriate. When dealing with a large set of mutants, it is not that clever any more as the same state space is explored again and again. An alternative is to pre-compute all reachable states up to a given depth and then search for unsafe states in this set. Exploring the full state space to the maximum bound is not really an overhead as it has to be done for each equivalent mutant anyway. Given a large set of mutants, the probability that it contains at least one equivalent mutant is rather high.

Alg. 1. *chkRef*(*as*, *mutants*) : *unsafes*	**Alg. 2.** *chkRef1*(*as*, *mutants*) : *unsafes*
1: *unsafes* := [ ]	1: *unsafes* := [ ]
2: *visited* := {}	2: *states* := *findAllStates*(*as*)
3: **for all** *asm* ∈ *mutants* **do**	3: **for all** *asm* ∈ *mutants* **do**
4: *s* := *getInitState*(*as*)	4: **for all** *s* ∈ *states* **do**
5: **repeat**	5: **if** *unsafe*(*s*, *as*, *asm*) **then**
6: *s* := *findNextState*(*as*, *s*, *visited*)	6: *unsafes.add*(*asm*, *s*)
7: *visited* := *visited* ∪ *s*	7: **break**
8: **until** *unsafe*(*s*, *as*, *asm*)	8: **end if**
9: *unsafes.add*(*asm*, *s*)	9: **end for**
10: **end for**	10: **end for**
11: **return** *unsafes*	11: **return** *unsafes*

Alg. 2 describes the refinement check with a pre-computed state space. It takes the same input as Alg. 1 and results in the same output. Again, all action systems are supposed to be in normal form. In contrast to Alg. 1, Alg. 2 only explores the state space once and then reuses the reached states during mutation analysis. The procedure *findAllStates* (Line 2) works analogously to the *findNextState* procedure of Alg. 1, but does not return one reachable state after the other. Instead, it returns the full set of reachable states at once. Afterwards, iteration over the mutants starts (Line 3), where each of the reached states (Line 4) is tested whether it is an unsafe state (Line 5). Once an unsafe state is found, we save the result (Line 6), stop searching for unsafe states (Line 7), and proceed with the next mutant without exploring the state space again.

4.2   Incremental Solving

Incremental solving is a technique to efficiently solve several constraints $c_1, ..., c_n$ that have large parts in common. The constraints are related to each other by the adding and/or the removal of small parts. Incremental solving exploits the findings made during solving the constraint c_i for solving the subsequent constraint c_{i+1} [29].

Our refinement checking process (Fig. 2) is well suited to exploit incremental solving. Alg. 2_incr is a more detailed version of Alg. 2 and gives additional information on the application of incremental solving. In Line 1, the original action system is translated. The resulting constraint system represents its transition relation (*trans_rel*). It is posted to the constraint/SMT solver's store (Line 2). The used interface for posting and retracting constraints acts as a stack, where constraints can be pushed or popped. Additionally, the interface provides a *solve* method. If the current store is satisfiable, it succeeds and a model may be retrieved. Otherwise, the constraints in the store are unsatisfiable and it returns false. The *solve* method is used in *findAllStates* (Line 3), where the transition relation of *as* is already in the solver's store. The procedure *findAllStates* starts at the initial state of *as* and recursively searches for all possible successor states.

Alg. 2_incr. *chkRefIncremental(as, mutants) : unsafes*

```
 1: trans_rel := trans(as)                    13:     solver.push(v = s) // s = unsafe?
 2: solver.push(trans_rel)                     14:     if solver.solve() then
 3: states := findAllStates(as, solver)        15:         u := s
 4: solver.pop()                               16:         solver.pop()
 5: solver.push(¬trans_rel)                    17:         break
 6: unsafes := []                              18:     end if
 7: for all asm ∈ mutants do                   19:     solver.pop()
 8:     u := nil                               20:   end for
 9:     aᵐ := findMutatedAction(as, asm)       21:   unsafes.add(asm, u)
10:     mut_act := trans(aᵐ)                   22:   solver.pop()
11:     solver.push(mut_act)                   23: end for
12:     for all s ∈ states do                  24: return unsafes
```

As the state space is now fully explored (up to a given depth limit), the transition relation is not needed any more and can be removed from the store (Line 4). In exchange, the negated transition relation is required for each refinement check with a mutant (cf. Theorem 1). It is added to the store in Line 5. The actual refinement check starts in Line 7. It iterates over the set of mutants. In Line 9, *findMutatedAction* syntactically compares the original and the mutated action system. Thereby, it identifies the mutated action a^m, which represents the second part of our non-refinement constraint (cf. Section 3). It is translated into constraints (Line 10) and added to the solver's store (Line 11), which now contains the complete non-refinement constraint for the current mutant. Lines 12 to 20 search for an unsafe state in the list of reachable states. Each state s is used as the pre-state v of the non-refinement constraint (Line 13). If it is satisfiable, we just found an unsafe state - a state from which the mutant behaves in a way that is not specified by the original (Lines 14 and 15). In this case we stop iterating over the states (Line 17). In any case, the constraint $v = s$ is removed from the store (Line 16 and Line 19 respectively). Line 21 inserts the mutant *asm* and the found unsafe state into the map *unsafes*. If no unsafe state could be found, *nil* is inserted and the mutant is considered to be equivalent up to the specified depth limit. To process the next mutant, the part of the non-refinement constraint that is specific to the current mutant has to be removed from the store (Line 22).

Alg. 2_incr shows that both the reachability analysis and the check for unsafe states are well suited to exploit incremental solving. During reachability, the transition relation is solved again and again - only the pre-states change (Line 3). While testing states whether they are unsafe, the non-refinement constraint has to be solved repeatedly - again with changing pre-states (Line13). Each non-refinement constraint contains the negated original (Line 5). Thus, when processing several mutants, there is a common part remaining in the store.

Incremental solving in Alg. 1 works analogously. Hence, we do not go into detail here. Note that we will use *Alg. 1_incr* to refer to the incremental version of Alg. 1 in the following.

5   Implementations

We implemented two versions of our refinement checking process (Fig. 2). The first version implements the repeated exploration of the state space, the second the pre-computation of the state space. Both incorporate incremental solving techniques. Hence, they implement Alg. 1_incr and Alg. 2_incr.

Our implementations are highly depending on the used solvers as they consume a large amount of our overall execution time. There is a strong competition within the constraint solving and SMT solving communities. Consider for example the yearly SMT competition[1]. Therefore, the solvers are constantly enhanced to outperform others. For this reason, we followed two parallel tracks in terms of solving techniques and also programming languages. The first implements the two algorithms in SICStus Prolog[2] (version 4.1.2) and uses the integrated constraint solver *clpfd* (Constraint Logic Programming over Finite Domains) [15]. The second track is implemented in the Scala programming language[3] and uses an SMT solver (Z3[4], version 4.0 for Mac OS X). While *clpfd* uses a specific input language, Z3 allows the use of SMT-LIB v2[5]. It is supported by most SMT solvers and hence facilitates the use of different solvers. We also experimented with CVC3[6], MathSAT 5[7] and SMTInterpol[8], but Z3 was the most efficient for our problem. We restrict ourselves to linear integer arithmetic (QF_LIA logic in SMT-LIB).

In SICStus Prolog, the use of the constraint solver is very simple as its functionality is provided as a library. In order to use Z3 in Scala, we use JNA (Java Native Access)[9] to make the C API of Z3 accessible in Java. As Scala code is compiled to Java byte code, there is a strong interoperability with Java. Within Scala, Java libraries may be called directly and vice versa.

Incremental solving is directly supported by Z3. Its C API offers methods to push and pop clauses and to solve the clauses in the store. In Prolog, the *clpfd* library does not directly offer such an interface, but we could implement incremental solving using constraint logic programming and enforced backtracking.

---

[1] smtcomp.sourceforge.net
[2] http://www.sics.se/sicstus/
[3] http://www.scala-lang.org/
[4] http://research.microsoft.com/projects/z3/
[5] http://www.smtlib.org/
[6] http://www.cs.nyu.edu/acsys/cvc3/
[7] http://mathsat.fbk.eu/
[8] http://ultimate.informatik.uni-freiburg.de/smtinterpol/
[9] https://github.com/twall/jna

6   Case Study: A Car Alarm System

To test our implementations, we used a simplified version of a car alarm system (CAS) by Ford. It already served as an industrial demonstrator in the MO-GENTES project[10]. It can be considered as representative for embedded systems and has become a benchmark example within our research group.

Requirements. The following requirements served as the basis for our model:

R1   *Arming.* The system is armed 20 seconds after the vehicle is locked and the bonnet, luggage compartment, and all doors are closed.

R2   *Alarm.* The alarm sounds for 30 seconds if an unauthorised person opens the door, the luggage compartment, or the bonnet. The hazard flasher lights will flash for five minutes.

R3   *Deactivation* The anti-theft alarm system can be deactivated at any time, even when the alarm is sounding, by unlocking the vehicle from outside.

Fig. 3 shows a UML state machine of our CAS. From the state *OpenAndUnlocked* one can traverse to *ClosedAndLocked* by closing all doors and locking the car. Actions of closing, opening, locking, and unlocking are modelled by corresponding signals *Close*, *Open*, *Lock*, and *Unlock*. As specified in requirement R1, the alarm system is armed after 20 seconds in *ClosedAndLocked*. Upon entry of the *Armed* state, the model calls the method *AlarmArmed.SetOn*. Upon leaving the state, which can be done by either unlocking the car or opening a door, *AlarmArmed.SetOff* is called. Similarly, when entering the *Alarm* state, the optical and acoustic alarms are enabled. When leaving the alarm state, either via a timeout or via unlocking the car, both acoustic and optical alarm are turned off. Note that the order of these two events is not specified, neither for enabling nor for disabling the alarms. Hence the system is not deterministic. When leaving the *Alarm* state after a timeout (cf. requirement R2) the system returns to the *Armed* state only in case it receives a *Close* signal. Turning off the acoustic alarm after 30 seconds, as specified in requirement R2, is reflected in the time-triggered transition leading to the *Flash* sub-state of the *Alarm* state. Here, the elapsing of time is modelled by explicit transitions using time triggers.

Mutations. We modelled the CAS described above as an action system and then manually created first order mutants of the model. We applied three mutation operators: (1) We set all possible guards to true (34 mutants). (2) We swapped equal and unequal operators (56 mutants). (3) We incremented all integer constants by 1, whereas we took the smallest possible value at the upper bound of a domain to avoid domain violations (116 mutants). Additionally, we added the original action system as an equivalent mutant (207 mutants in total).

---

[10] https://www.mogentes.eu

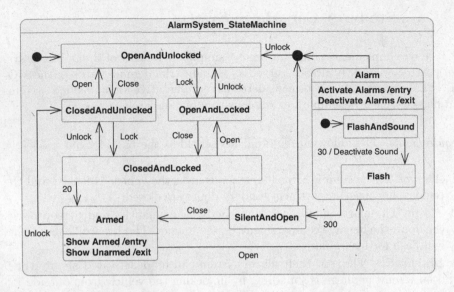

Fig. 3. UML state machine of the car alarm system

Variants. As in our previous works [5,4], we use four slightly different versions of our CAS model: (1) *CAS_1*: the CAS as introduced above with parameter values 20, 30, and 270 for waiting, (2) *CAS_10* with parameter values multiplied by 10 (200, 300, and 2700), (3) *CAS_100* with parameters multiplied by 100, and (4) *CAS_1000* with parameters multiplied by 1000. These extended parameter ranges shall test the capabilities of our symbolic approach.

Extended Model. Additionally, we built another extended version of the basic car alarm system (*CAS_1*). We parameterised the *Lock* and *Unlock* events with a PIN code. If the PIN is correct when (un)locking the car, everything behaves as usual. If someone tries to (un)lock the car with an incorrect PIN, the same mechanisms as when opening the car in the *Armed* state are triggered. This means that the system traverses to the *Alarm* state and the flash and sound alarms are turned on. Again, this state is left via timeouts or via unlocking the car with the correct PIN. For this *CAS_PIN* version, the timeouts are always 20, 30 and 270 seconds. Nevertheless, there are also two variants: one with a Boolean PIN and one with a PIN consisting of three digits (0-999). Again, we applied our three mutation operators explained above and added the original as an equivalent mutant resulting in 246 mutants.

Technical Details. Below, we present results on these six versions of the car alarm system obtained by (a) our Prolog implementation using constraint solving and (b) our Scala implementation using the Z3 SMT solver. All of our experiments were conducted on a machine with a dual-core processor (2.8 GHz Intel Core i7) and 8 GB RAM with a 64-bit operating system (Mac OS X v10.7).

Table 1. Runtimes (sec) for the CAS obtained by our two implementations

		CAS				CAS_PIN	
		1	10	100	1000	Bool	0-999
Prolog & Constraint Solving	Alg. 1	19	19	23	20	19	26
Prolog & Constraint Solving	Alg. 1_incr	2.82	2.84	3.38	8.55	3.52	5.93
	Alg. 2_incr	2.63	2.62	2.66	2.69	3.28	3.27
Scala & SMT Solving	Alg. 1_incr	18.13	17.60	17.69	17.72	21.05	22.23
	Alg. 2_incr	4.18	4.15	4.13	4.11	5.28	5.33

6.1 Results

Table 1 shows the runtimes for our CAS case study. All values are given in seconds and state the time needed for refinement checking of the original action system with all of its mutants. It gives numbers for the Prolog implementation using a constraint solver and the Scala implementation using an SMT solver.

The Prolog implementation yields the following results. Alg. 1_incr achieves runtimes from 2.82 to 8.55 seconds for the four CAS versions each with 207 mutants. For the two CAS versions with a PIN code (245 mutants in each case), it needs 3.52 and 5.93 seconds respectively. Hence, the runtimes are not constant with increasing domains of the parameters. Alg. 2_incr performs better. It is faster and the runtime is constant. Note that during constraint solving the most-constrained heuristic has been used for variable selection. The values for these variables were selected in ascending order. Our experiments in [4] indicate that this combination is a reasonable choice.

For the Prolog implementation, Table 1 also lists runtimes without our two optimisations. This corresponds to Alg. 1. For CAS_1 to CAS_1000, these earlier results were already reported in [4]. The computation times for refinement checking of 207 mutants were about 20 seconds for each CAS version. These numbers show that we achieved a significant performance gain by our latest improvements (see Section 4). The execution time could be improved from approximately 20 seconds to less than 3 seconds, which is a reduction by 85%. For CAS_PIN, Alg. 1 achieved a runtime of 19 seconds for the Boolean PIN and 26 seconds for the three-digit PIN. With our optimisations, the Prolog runtime is a bit more than 3 seconds for both CAS_PIN versions. Again, the performance gain is considerable. The runtimes could be reduced by 84% and 88% respectively.

Using the Scala implementation of Alg. 1_incr and the Z3 SMT solver, it takes approximately 18 seconds for CAS_1 to CAS_1000. The two CAS versions extended with a PIN code require about 22 seconds each. For Alg. 2_incr, we have runtimes of 4 seconds for CAS_1 to CAS_1000 and 5 seconds for the two CAS_PIN versions. In contrast to the implementation based on constraint solving, the SMT-solver-based implementation always shows constant runtime. Again, Alg. 2_incr performs better than Alg. 1_incr.

Using Alg. 2_incr, both implementations achieve almost equally fast runtimes. For Alg. 1_incr, the SMT-solver-based implementation is slower, but still reasonable. This cannot solely be explained by the use of different solving techniques (constraint vs. SMT solving) as we discuss in the following.

6.2   Discussion

We implemented two refinement checking tools for action systems and compared their runtimes. Both tools result in the same counterexamples and unsafe states, but are implemented differently. They use different techniques for problem solving. One relies on constraint solving, the other one on SMT solving. Nevertheless, the comparison cannot only be reduced to this. There are other factors influencing the performance of the implementations. They are written in different programming languages. On the one hand, the logic programming language Prolog was used. Its main advantage for our application is the native support for constraint solving. Due to its backtracking facilities, also incremental solving could be implemented quite efficiently. On the other hand, Scala is used. It is a functional, object-oriented programming language based on the Java Virtual Machine (JVM). In contrast to the Prolog implementation, the program written in Scala depends on an external SMT solver that is only accessible via non-Java APIs (C, Python, ...). This introduces some overhead compared to the native constraint solving support in Prolog. Additionally, the implementations were written by different programmers. The individual styles of programming may also have influenced the comparability of the results.

We are aware that the results from our case study may not generalise. We reported on our experience with this kind of models, which we think are representative for many typical embedded systems. Nevertheless, the scalability of our approach on the CAS does not necessarily have to be representative for other types of models. Yet, our first results are certainly promising.

7   Related Work

To our knowledge, our test case generation approach is the first that deals with non-deterministic systems, uses mutations, and is based on constraint solving techniques. Nevertheless, there exist various works overlapping in one or several aspects. There are constraint-based test case generation approaches on the source code level, where no non-determinism has to be considered. A mutation-based approach is [30] for example. Java-like programs are mutated and transformed into constraints via SSA form to generate distinguishing test cases. [19] does not use mutations, but structural criteria for test data generation via SSA form.

Regarding black-box techniques, one of the first models to be mutated were predicate-calculus specifications [14] and formal Z specifications [26]. Later on, model checkers were available to check temporal formulae expressing equivalence between original and mutated models. In case of non-equivalence, this leads to counterexamples that serve as test cases [8]. Most test case generation approaches using model checkers deal with deterministic systems. Nevertheless, there also exist works considering non-determinism and the involved difficulties. [24] suggests to synchronise non-deterministic choices in the original and the mutated model via common variables to avoid false positive counterexamples. [13] proposes two approaches that cope with non-determinism: modular model checking of a composition of the mutant and the specification, and incremental test generation via observers and traditional model checking. [23] also considers non-determinism. It uses the model checker/refinement checker FDR (Failures-Divergence Refinement) for the CSP process algebra [25] to generate test cases. However, this approach is not mutation-based.

Other model-based mutation testing techniques considering non-determinism include two ioco (input-output conformance [27]) checkers for LOTOS specifications [7] and action systems [2]. Both are not symbolic, but rely on explicit state space enumeration. In our symbolic approach, we use constraint/SMT solvers that support incremental solving. Incremental solving has already been applied to many problem domains, e.g., bounded model checking [29].

8 Conclusion

We enhanced our refinement checking approach for non-deterministic action systems in two ways. Firstly, we presented a more efficient way of processing a large number of mutants. Secondly, we exploited incremental solving techniques. We implemented both improvements in two implementation tracks: the first one uses Prolog and constraint solving, the second Scala and the SMT solver Z3. First case studies with a car alarm system showed that our two improvements significantly reduced runtime. Previous results [4] could be improved by up to 85%. Our case study also indicates that both SMT and constraint solvers are able to cope with refinement checking problems.

The ultimate goal of our work is to enable test case generation that targets specific faults. Thereby, a mutation adequacy score that is as high as possible shall be achieved. This paper dealt with the necessary, underlying conformance check. Future work will attach to this and generate the desired test cases.

Of course, we are aware that our results may not generalise. To give further evidence for the effectiveness and scalability of our approach, we already work on further case studies. Regarding effectiveness, one very important aspect of our model-based mutation testing approach are the used fault models. So far, we only applied three manual mutation operators for action systems. We aim for integrating our refinement checking implementations into an already existing framework. It uses UML models, which are mutated and then translated into action systems. In [2], this framework has already been used successfully with an explicit conformance checking tool. Nevertheless, scalability was an issue and motivated this work. Regarding scalability of our new approach, also counterexample-guided abstraction refinement techniques similar as in SLAM [11] or BLAST [12] may be an interesting topic for future work.

Acknowledgments. Research herein was funded by the Austrian Research Promotion Agency (FFG), program line "Trust in IT Systems", project number 829583, TRUst via Failed FALsification of Complex Dependable Systems Using Automated Test Case Generation through Model Mutation (TRUFAL).

References

1. Abrial, J.R.: Modeling in Event-B: System and Software Engineering. Cambridge University Press (2010)
2. Aichernig, B.K., Brandl, H., Jöbstl, E., Krenn, W.: Efficient mutation killers in action. In: ICST, pp. 120–129. IEEE (2011)
3. Aichernig, B.K., He, J.: Mutation testing in UTP. Formal Aspects of Computing 21(1-2), 33–64 (2009)
4. Aichernig, B.K., Jöbstl, E.: Efficient refinement checking for model-based mutation testing. In: QSIC, pp. 21–30. IEEE (2012)
5. Aichernig, B.K., Jöbstl, E.: Towards symbolic model-based mutation testing: Combining reachability and refinement checking. In: MBT. EPTCS, vol. 80, pp. 88–102 (2012)
6. Aichernig, B.K., Jöbstl, E.: Towards symbolic model-based mutation testing: Pitfalls in expressing semantics as constraints. In: ICST, pp. 752–757. IEEE (2012)
7. Aichernig, B.K., Peischl, B., Weiglhofer, M., Wotawa, F.: Protocol conformance testing a SIP registrar: An industrial application of formal methods. In: SEFM, pp. 215–224. IEEE (2007)
8. Ammann, P., Black, P.E., Majurski, W.: Using model checking to generate tests from specifications. In: ICFEM, pp. 46–54. IEEE (1998)
9. Back, R.J., Kurki-Suonio, R.: Decentralization of process nets with centralized control. In: PODC, pp. 131–142. ACM (1983)
10. Back, R.J., Sere, K.: Stepwise refinement of action systems. Structured Programming 12, 17–30 (1991)
11. Ball, T., Rajamani, S.K.: Automatically validating temporal safety properties of interfaces. In: Dwyer, M.B. (ed.) SPIN 2001. LNCS, vol. 2057, pp. 103–122. Springer, Heidelberg (2001)
12. Beyer, D., Henzinger, T.A., Jhala, R., Majumdar, R.: The software model checker BLAST. STTT 9, 505–525 (2007)
13. Boroday, S., Petrenko, A., Groz, R.: Can a model checker generate tests for nondeterministic systems? Electr. Notes Theor. Comput. Sci. 190(2), 3–19 (2007)
14. Budd, T.A., Gopal, A.S.: Program testing by specification mutation. Computer Languages 10(1), 63–73 (1985)
15. Carlsson, M., Ottosson, G., Carlson, B.: An open-ended finite domain constraint solver. In: Hartel, P.H., Kuchen, H. (eds.) PLILP 1997. LNCS, vol. 1292, pp. 191–206. Springer, Heidelberg (1997)
16. DeMillo, R., Lipton, R., Sayward, F.: Hints on test data selection: Help for the practicing programmer. IEEE Computer 11(4), 34–41 (1978)
17. Dijkstra, E., Scholten, C.: Predicate Calculus and Program Semantics. Texts and Monographs in Computer Science. Springer (1990)
18. Fraser, G., Wotawa, F., Ammann, P.E.: Testing with model checkers: a survey. Softw. Test. Verif. Reliab. 19(3), 215–261 (2009)
19. Gotlieb, A., Botella, B., Rueher, M.: Automatic test data generation using constraint solving techniques. In: ISSTA, pp. 53–62 (1998)

20. Hamlet, R.G.: Testing programs with the aid of a compiler. IEEE Trans. Software Eng. 3(4), 279–290 (1977)
21. Hoare, C., He, J.: Unifying Theories of Programming. Prentice-Hall (1998)
22. Jia, Y., Harman, M.: An analysis and survey of the development of mutation testing. IEEE Trans. Software Eng. 37(5), 649–678 (2011)
23. Nogueira, S., Sampaio, A., Mota, A.M.: Guided test generation from CSP models. In: Fitzgerald, J.S., Haxthausen, A.E., Yenigun, H. (eds.) ICTAC 2008. LNCS, vol. 5160, pp. 258–273. Springer, Heidelberg (2008)
24. Okun, V., Black, P.E., Yesha, Y.: Testing with model checker: Insuring fault visibility. In: 2002 WSEAS Int. Conf. on System Science, Applied Mathematics & Computer Science, and Power Engineering Systems, pp. 1351–1356 (2003)
25. Roscoe, A.W.: Model-checking CSP, ch. 21. Prentice-Hall (1994)
26. Stocks, P.A.: Applying formal methods to software testing. Ph.D. thesis, Department of computer science, University of Queensland (1993)
27. Tretmans, J.: Test generation with inputs, outputs and repetitive quiescence. Software - Concepts and Tools 17(3), 103–120 (1996)
28. Utting, M., Pretschner, A., Legeard, B.: A taxonomy of model-based testing approaches. Softw. Test. Verif. Reliab. (2011)
29. Whittemore, J., Kim, J., Sakallah, K.: SATIRE: A new incremental satisfiability engine. In: DAC, pp. 542–545. ACM (2001)
30. Wotawa, F., Nica, M., Aichernig, B.K.: Generating distinguishing tests using the Minion constraint solver. In: ICST, pp. 325–330. IEEE (2010)

Time for Mutants —Model-Based Mutation Testing with Timed Automata

Bernhard K. Aichernig[1], Florian Lorber[1], and Dejan Ničković[2]

[1] Institute for Software Technology
Graz University of Technology, Austria
{aichernig,florber}@ist.tugraz.at
[2] AIT Austrian Institute of Technology
Vienna, Austria
dejan.nickovic@ait.ac.at

Abstract. Model-based testing is a popular technology for automatic and systematic test case generation (TCG), where a system-under-test (SUT) is tested for conformance with a model that specifies its intended behavior. Model-based mutation testing is a specific variant of model-based testing that is fault-oriented. In mutation testing, the test case generation is guided by a *mutant*, an intentionally altered version of the original model that specifies a common modeling error.

In this paper, we propose a mutation testing framework for real-time applications, where the model of the SUT and its mutants are expressed as a variant of timed automata. We develop an algorithm for mutation-based real-time test case generation that uses symbolic bounded model checking techniques and incremental solving. We present an implementation of our test case generation technique and illustrate it with a non-trivial car alarm example, providing experimental results.

1 Introduction

A common practice to show that a system meets its requirements and works as expected consists in *testing* the system. Historically, testing has been predominantly a manual activity, where a human designs a test experiment, by choosing inputs that are fed to the SUT, and observing its reactions and outputs. Traditional testing suffers from two pitfalls: (1) due to a finite number of experiments, testing activity can only reveal presence of safety errors in the system, but not their absence; and (2) the testing process is manual, hence ad-hoc, time and human resource consuming and error-prone.

The first short-coming of testing was addressed by formal verification and theorem proving, which consist in providing rigorous evidence in the form of a mathematical proof that a system always behaves according to its specification. The automation of the verification technology was enabled with *model checking* [28,12], a technique that consists in exhaustive exploration of the system's underlying state space. Although model checking resolves in theory the issues present in classical testing, it suffers from the so-called state-space explosion

M. Veanes and L. Viganò (Eds.): TAP 2013, LNCS 7942, pp. 20–38, 2013.

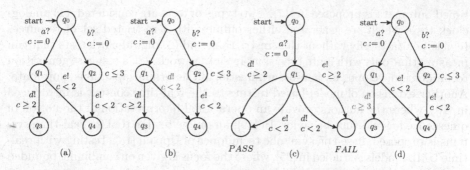

Fig. 1. Timed mutants example: (a) TA model A; (b) mutant M_1; (c) a test case generated from M_1 and (d) mutant M_2

problems. In the past decades, large part of the effort invested by the verification research community went into developing methods that fight the state-space explosion problem (see for example [11,7,13]).

Model-based testing [31] was introduced as a pragmatic compromise between the conceptual simplicity of classical testing, and automation and exhaustiveness of model checking. In model-based testing, test suites are automatically generated from a mathematical *model* of the SUT. The main advantage of this technique is the full test automation that provides effective means to catch errors in the SUT. The aim of model-based testing is to check conformance of the SUT to a given specification, where the SUT is often seen as a "black-box" with unknown internal structure, but observable input/output interface. Model-based testing is commonly combined with some coverage criteria, with the aim to generate test cases that cover most possible use cases of the SUT.

Model-based mutation testing is a specific type of model-based testing, in which faults are deliberately injected into the specification model. The aim of mutation-based testing techniques is to generate test cases that can detect the injected errors. This means that a generated test case shall fail if it is executed on a (deterministic) system-under-test that implements the faulty model. The power of this testing approach is that it can guarantee the absence of certain specific faults. In practice, it will be combined with standard techniques, e.g. with random test-case generation [1]. Mutation-based testing was studied in [2,29] in the context of UML models, and in [9,15] in the context of Simulink models. Model-based mutation testing is also known as specification-based mutation testing. A recent survey by Jia and Harman [16] documents the growing interest in mutation testing and points out the open problem of generating test cases by means of mutation analysis. The present work contributes to this line of research.

In embedded systems, models are often derived from real-time requirements, resulting in extensions of model-based testing to the real-time context. This includes usage modeling the SUT with a timed formalism and adaptation of conformance relations to real-time. A comprehensive overview and comparison of real-time conformance relations is presented in [30]. A framework for black-box conformance testing based on the model of partially-observable, non-deterministic timed automata is proposed in [17]. Two types of tests are considered: (1) analog-clock tests which are generated either offline with a restricted set of resources (clocks) or on-the-fly without that restriction; and (2) digital-clock tests that can measure time only with finite precision. In similar work [22], a test case generation technique is developed for non-deterministic, but determinizable timed automata. Another extension of model-based testing to the real-time context is introduced in [10], where the authors provide an operational interpretation of the notion of quiescence for real-time behavior. In [19], an online testing tool for real-time systems is proposed, based on symbolic techniques of Uppaal [18]. Testing with real-time UML models is studied in [25], where the focus is given on combining bounded model checking techniques with abstract interpretation for test case generation.

In this paper, we propose a framework for mutation testing of real-time systems modeled using a deterministic class of timed automata (TA) [3]. Given a TA specification, we first propose *mutation operators* which mimic common modeling errors. Given a specification model of an SUT and its mutant, we develop a technique for automatic generation of a real-time test case which exactly tries to "drive" the SUT to the error inserted by the mutation operator, as illustrated by the following example.

Example 1. Consider the TA model A from Figure 1 (a) and its timed mutants M_1 and M_2, shown in Figure 1 (b,d). The mutant M_1 alters the original specification by changing the output action of the transition $q_1 \to q_4$ from $e!$ to $d!$. In model-based mutation testing, we generate a test case leading to an error introduced by the mutant, resulting in the test case shown in Figure 1 (c). Note that not every mutant of a real-time specification introduces errors. The mutant M_2 is such an example: since location q_1 has no invariant, delaying is allowed.

In contrast to [17,22,10,19], we propose a *symbolic* test generation procedure based on bounded model checking (BMC) techniques and which uses a Satisfiability Modulo Theories (SMT) solver to generate test cases. The bounded model checking approach for test case generation is promising in the context of mutation testing, which is fault oriented and focuses on finding finite witnesses exposing faults resulting from mutating a specification. In addition, SMT solvers provide support for future extensions such as handling unbounded data domains. Our test case generation framework combines existing results on TA decision problems [3], real-time conformance relations [17] and symbolic solving of TA decision problems [21,5,4] and applies them in a novel setting of mutation-based test case generation. We are not aware of other work which applies BMC techniques for generating real-time test cases from timed automata.

The survey [14] gives an extensive overview of existing test case generation approaches via model checking. [8] investigates problems and solutions for test case generation via model checkers for non-deterministic specifications. The work in [24,23] proposes a mutation-based testing framework for real-time systems using TA with Tasks. In contrary to our work, they generate test cases for mutants that violate task deadlines, while we check the real-time conformance between a specification and its mutants. While some of the mutation operators we propose are specific to timed automata, most of them can be related to the state chart operators introduced in [27].

2 Timed Automata with Inputs and Outputs

The time domain that we consider is the set $\mathbb{R}_{\geq 0}$ of non-negative reals. We denote by Σ the finite set of actions, partitioned into two disjoint sets Σ_I and Σ_O of input and output actions, respectively. A *time sequence* is a finite non-decreasing sequence of non-negative reals. A *timed trace* σ is a finite alternating sequence of actions and time delays of the form $t_1 \cdot a_1 \cdots t_k \cdot a_k$, where for all $i \in [1, k]$, $a_i \in \Sigma$ and $(t_i)_{i \in [1,k]}$ is a time sequence.

Let $\mathcal{C}$ be a finite set of *clock* variables. Clock *valuation* $v(c)$ is a function $v : \mathcal{C} \to \mathbb{R}_{\geq 0}$ assigning a real value to every clock $c \in \mathcal{C}$. We denote by $\mathcal{H}$ the set of all clock valuations and by $\mathbf{0}$ the valuation assigning 0 to every clock in $\mathcal{C}$. Let $v \in \mathcal{H}$ be a valuation and $t \in \mathbb{R}_{\geq 0}$, we then have $v + t$ defined by $(v + t)(c) = v(c) + t$ for all $c \in \mathcal{C}$. For a subset ρ of $\mathcal{C}$, we denote by $v[\rho]$ the valuation such that for every $c \in \rho$, $v[\rho](c) = 0$ and for every $c \in \mathcal{C} \backslash \rho$, $v[\rho](c) = v(c)$. A *clock constraint* φ is a conjunction of predicates over clock variables in $\mathcal{C}$ defined by the grammar

$$\varphi ::= c \circ k \mid \varphi_1 \wedge \varphi_2,$$

where $c \in \mathcal{C}$, $k \in \mathbb{N}$ and $\circ \in \{<, \leq, =, \geq, >\}$. Given a clock valuation $v \in \mathcal{H}$, we write $v \models \varphi$ when v satisfies the clock constraint φ. We are now ready to formally define *input/output* timed automata (TAIO):

Definition 1. *A TAIO[1] A is a tuple $(Q, \hat{q}, \Sigma_I, \Sigma_O, \mathcal{C}, I, \Delta)$, where Q is a finite set of* locations, *$\hat{q} \in Q$ is the* initial *location, Σ_I is a finite set of* input actions *and Σ_O is a finite set of* output actions, *such that $\Sigma_I \cap \Sigma_O = \emptyset$ and Σ is the set of actions $\Sigma_I \cup \Sigma_O$, $\mathcal{C}$ is a finite set of* clock *variables, I is a finite set of location* invariants, *that are conjunctions of constraints of the form $c < d$ or $c \leq d$, where $c \in \mathcal{C}$ and $d \in \mathbb{N}$ and each invariant is bound to its specific location, and Δ is a finite set of* transitions *of the form (q, a, g, ρ, q'), where*

- *$q, q' \in Q$ are the* source *and the* target *locations;*
- *$a \in \Sigma$ is the transition action*
- *g is a* guard, *a conjunction of constraints of the form $c \circ d$, where $\circ \in \{<, \leq, =, \geq, >\}$ and $d \in \mathbb{N}$;*
- *$\rho \subseteq \mathcal{C}$ is a set of clocks to be* reset.

We say that a TAIO A is *deterministic* if for all transitions (q, a, g_1, ρ_1, q_1) and (q, a, g_2, ρ_2, q_2) in Δ, $q_1 \neq q_2$ implies that $g_1 \wedge g_2 = \emptyset$. We denote by $\mathcal{A}$ the set of all TAIO and by $\text{Det}(\mathcal{A}) \subset \mathcal{A}$ its deterministic subset. We denote by $\Delta_O \subseteq \Delta$

---

[1] TAIO are similar to UPPAAL TA, which we use to illustrate our examples. One difference is that for simplicity of presentation we do not have *urgent* and *committed* locations. However, these types of locations are just syntactic sugar to make modeling easier, and can be expressed with standard timed automata.

the set $\{\delta = (q, a, g, \rho, q') \mid \delta \in \Delta \text{ and } a \in \Sigma_O\}$ of transitions labeled by an output action and by $\Delta_I = \Delta \backslash \Delta_O$ the set of transitions labeled by an input action. We define $|\mathcal{G}|$ to be the number of basic constraints that appear in all the guards of all the transitions in A, i.e. $|\mathcal{G}| = \Sigma_{\delta \in \Delta} |J_g|$, where $\delta = (q, a, g, \rho, q')$ and g is of the form $\bigwedge_{j \in J_g} c_j \circ d_j$. We define $|\mathcal{I}|$ as the number of basic constraints that appear in all the invariants of all the locations in A.

The *semantics* of a TAIO $A = (Q, \hat{q}, \Sigma_I, \Sigma_O, \mathcal{C}, I, \Delta)$ is given by the *timed input/output transition system* (TIOTS) $[[A]] = (S, \hat{s}, \mathbb{R}_{\geq 0}, \Sigma, T)$, where $S = \{(q, v) \in Q \times \mathcal{H} \mid v \models I(q)\}$, $\hat{s} = (\hat{q}, \mathbf{0})$, $T \subseteq S \times (\Sigma \cup \mathbb{R}_{\geq 0}) \times S$ is the transition relation consisting of *discrete* and *timed* transitions such that:

- **Discrete transitions:** $((q, v), a, (q', v')) \in T$, where $a \in \Sigma$, if there exists a transition (q, a, g, ρ, q') in Δ, such that: (1) $v \models g$; (2) $v' = v[\rho]$ and (3) $v' \models I(q')$; and
- **Timed transitions:** $((q, v), t, (q, v + t)) \in T$, where $t \in \mathbb{R}_{\geq 0}$, if $v + t \models I(q)$.

A *run* r of a TAIO A is the sequence of alternating timed and discrete transitions of the form $(q_1, v_1) \xrightarrow{t_1} (q_1, v_1 + t_1) \xrightarrow{\delta_1} (q_2, v_2) \xrightarrow{t_2} \cdots$, where $q_1 = \hat{q}$, $v_1 = \mathbf{0}$ and $\delta_i = (q_i, a_i, g_i, \rho_i, q_{i+1})$, inducing the timed trace $\sigma = t_1 \cdot a_1 \cdot t_2 \cdots$. We denote by $L(A)$ the set of timed traces induced by all runs of A.

3   Mutation of TAIOs

Mutation of a specification consists in altering the model in a small way, mimicking common implementation errors. In our setting, a mutation is a function $\mu_m : \text{Det}(\mathcal{A}) \to 2^{\mathcal{A}}$ parameterized by a mutation operator m which maps a deterministic TAIO A into a finite set $\mu_m(A)$ of possibly non-deterministic TAIOs , where each $M \in \mu_m(A)$ is called an m-mutant of A. For our experiments we only created first-order mutants, i.e., each mutated TAIO covers only one particular mutation.

We now introduce and define specific mutation operators which are relevant to the TAIO model.

Definition 2. *Given a TAIO $A = (Q, \hat{q}, \Sigma_I, \Sigma_O, \mathcal{C}, I, \Delta)$, its mutants are defined by the following mutation operators:*

1. ***Change action (μ_{ca})*** *generates from A a set of $|\Delta_I|(|\Sigma_O|) + |\Delta_O|(|\Sigma_O| - 1)$ mutants, where every mutant changes a single transition in A by replacing the action labeling the transition by a different output label. This mimics an implementation fault producing wrong output signals. A TAIO $M \in \mu_{ca}(A)$, if M is of the form $(Q, \hat{q}, \Sigma_I, \Sigma_O, \mathcal{C}, I, (\Delta \backslash \{\delta\}) \cup \{\delta_m\})$, such that $\delta = (q, a, g, \rho, q') \in \Delta$, $\delta_m = (q, a_m, g, \rho, q')$, $a_m \in \Sigma_O$ and $a_m \neq a$;*
2. ***Change target (μ_{ct})*** *generates from A a set of $|\Delta|(|Q| - 1)$ mutants, where every mutant replaces the target location of a transition in A, by another location in A. This reflects the behaviour of an implementation fault where a signal leads to a wrong internal state. A TAIO $M \in \mu_{ct}(A)$, if M is of the form $(Q, \hat{q}, \Sigma_I, \Sigma_O, \mathcal{C}, I, (\Delta \backslash \{\delta\}) \cup \{\delta_m\})$, such that $\delta = (q, a, g, \rho, q') \in \Delta$, $\delta_m = (q, a, g, \rho, q'_m)$, $q'_m \in Q$ and $q'_m \neq q'$;*

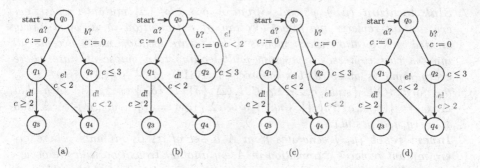

Fig. 2. Mutant M of model A resulting from: (a) $\mu_{ca}(A)$; (b) $\mu_{ct}(A)$; (c) $\mu_{cs}(A)$; (d) $\mu_{cg}(A)$;

3. **Change source**[2] (μ_{cs}) *generates from A a set of $|\Delta|(|Q| - 1)$ mutants, where every mutant replaces the source location of a transition in A, by another location in A. This expresses an implementation fault where a signal can be triggered from a state where it should be disabled. A TAIO $M \in \mu_{cs}(A)$, if M is of the form $(Q, \hat{q}, \Sigma_I, \Sigma_O, \mathcal{C}, I, (\Delta \backslash \{\delta\}) \cup \{\delta_m\})$, such that $\delta = (q, a, g, \rho, q') \in \Delta$, $\delta_m = (q_m, a, g, \rho, q')$, $q_m \in Q$ and $q_m \neq q$;*

4. **Change guard** (μ_{cg}) *generates from A a set of $4|\mathcal{G}|$ mutants, where every mutant replaces a transition in A with another one which changes the original guard by altering every equality/inequality sign appearing in the guard by another one. This covers implementation faults with faulty enabling conditions. A TAIO $M \in \mu_{cg}(A)$, if M is of the form $(Q, \hat{q}, \Sigma_I, \Sigma_O, \mathcal{C}, I, (\Delta \backslash \{\delta\}) \cup \{\delta_m\}))$, such that $\delta = (q, a, g, \rho, q') \in \Delta$, $\delta_m = (q, a, g_m, \rho, q')$, $g = \bigwedge_{i \in I} c_i \circ_i d_i$, $g_m = \bigwedge_{i \in I} c_i \circ_i^m d_i$, $\circ, \circ_i^m \in \{<, \leq, =, \geq, >\}$, $\circ_i \neq \circ_i^m$ for some $i \in I$ and $\circ_j = \circ_j^m$ for all $j \neq i$;*

5. **Negate guard** (μ_{ng}) *generates from A a set of $|\Delta|$ mutants, where every mutant replaces the guard in a transition in A, by its negation. This covers implementation faults where the programmer forgot negating a condition. A TAIO $M \in \mu_{ng}(A)$, if M is of the form $(Q, \hat{q}, \Sigma_I, \Sigma_O, \mathcal{C}, I, (\Delta \backslash \{\delta\}) \cup \{\delta_m\})$, such that $\delta = (q, a, g, \rho, q') \in \Delta$ and $\delta_m = (q_m, a, \neg g, \rho, q')$*[3];

6. **Change invariant** (μ_{ci}) *generates from A a set of $|\mathcal{I}|$ mutants, where every mutant replaces the invariant of a location with another invariant with 1 added to the right side of the invariant. This mimics an "off by one"-fault allowing to stay longer in a state than intended. A TAIO $M \in \mu_{ci}(A)$, if M is of the form $(Q, \hat{q}, \Sigma_I, \Sigma_O, \mathcal{C}, I_m, \Delta)$, and there exists $q \in Q$ such that $I(q) = \bigwedge_{i \in I} c_i \circ d_i$, $\circ \in \{<, \leq\}$, $I_m(q) = \bigwedge_{i \in I} c_i \circ d_i^m$, $d_i^m = d_i + 1$ for some $i \in I$, $d_j^m = d_j$ for all $j \neq i$ and $I(q') = I_m(q')$ for all $q' \neq q$;*

---

[2] Note that change source and target mutation operators also generate mutants where a self-loop transition is created, hence there is no need for a separate "self-loop" mutation operator.

[3] For the sake of simplicity, we represent δ_m as a single transition even though $\neg g$ may also have disjunctions. The guard $\neg g$ can be represented in DNF and every disjunction of the guard can be used as a guard of a separate transition.

7. **Sink location** *(μ_{sl})* *generates from A a set of $|\Delta|$ mutants, where every mutant replaces the target location of a transition in A, by a newly created sink location which models a don't care location which accepts all inputs. This expresses a program fault leading to a quiescent state where every input is accepted, but ignored. A TAIO $M \in \mu_{sl}(A)$, if M is of the form $(Q \cup \{sink\}, \hat{q}, \Sigma_I, \Sigma_O, C, I, (\Delta\backslash\{\delta\}) \cup \{\delta_m\} \cup \Delta_{sink})$, such that $\Delta_{sink} = \{(sink, a, true, \{\}, sink) \mid a \in \Sigma_I\}$, $\delta = (q, a, g, \rho, q') \in \Delta$ and $\delta_m = (q, a, g, \rho, sink)$;*

8. **Invert reset** *(μ_{ir})* *generates from A a set of $|\Delta||C|$ mutants, where every mutant replaces a transition in A, by another transition with the occurrence of one clock flipped compared to the original set of clocks. This reflects different timing errors, e.g. the incorrect reseting of a timer. A TAIO $M \in \mu_{cs}(A)$, if M is of the form $(Q, \hat{q}, \Sigma_I, \Sigma_O, C, I, (\Delta\backslash\{\delta\}) \cup \{\delta_m\})$, such that $\delta = (q, a, g, \rho, q') \in \Delta$, $\delta_m = (q, a, g, \rho_m, q')$, and for some $c \in C$ either $\rho_m = \rho \cup \{c_m\}$ if $c_m \notin \rho$, or $\rho_m = \rho\backslash\{c_m\}$ if $c_m \in \rho$.*

Figure 2 illustrates mutants resulting from applying the above mutation operators to the model A from Figure 1(a). The effectiveness of the mutation operators is analyzed and evaluated in more details in Section 7. For more complex models there might rise the need to reduce the amount of mutants. Here we refer to the survey by Jia and Harmann[16], that describes multiple ways of reducing mutants for mutation testing, which can in general also be applied to model-based mutation testing.

Several different approaches to model mutation have already been published, using Finite State Machines [26,27], Kripke structures [8] or Event Sequence Graphs [6]. [23] introduces mutation operators for Timed Automata with Tasks, yet the mutation operators there concentrate on tasks and timeliness and not the core essence of TA. Our mutation operators 6 and 8 are specific to TA, while the other ones are similar or closely related to the operators described in [27].

4   Conformance Relations for Timed Automata

Different real-time extensions of the input-output conformance relation ioco were studied and compared in [30]. We consider the timed input-output conformance relation introduced in [17] and inspired by ioco. Intuitively, $\mathcal{A}_I$ conforms to $\mathcal{A}_S$ if for each observable behavior specified in $\mathcal{A}_S$, the possible outputs of $\mathcal{A}_I$ after this behavior is a subset of the possible outputs of $\mathcal{A}_S$. In contrast to ioco, tioco does not use the notion of quiescence, but requires explicit specification of timeouts. Since we consider TAIO without silent (τ) transitions, all actions are observable. Hence, we present a simplified version of the tioco definition from [17], first introducing operators illustrated in Equation 1.

$$A \text{ after } \sigma = \{s \in S \mid \hat{s} \xrightarrow{\sigma} s\}$$
$$\text{elapse(s)} = \{t > 0 \mid s \xrightarrow{t}\}$$
$$\text{out}(s) \quad = \{a \in \Sigma_O \mid s \xrightarrow{a}\} \cup \text{elapse(s)} \tag{1}$$
$$\text{out}(S) \quad = \bigcup_{s \in S} \text{out}(s)$$

Given a TAIO A and $\sigma \in L(\Sigma)$, A after σ is the set of all states of A that can be reached by the sequence σ. Given a state $s \in S$, elapse(s) is the set of all delays that can elapse from s without A making any action, and out(s) is the set of all output actions or time delays that can occur when the system is at state s, a definition which naturally extends to set of states S.

Definition 3. *The* timed input-output conformance relation, *denoted by tioco, is defined as*

$$A_I \text{ tioco } A_S \text{ iff } \forall \sigma \in L(A_S) : \text{out}(A_I \text{ after } \sigma) \subseteq \text{out}(A_S \text{ after } \sigma)$$

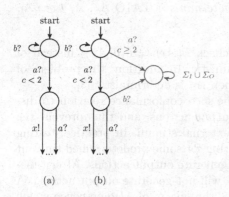

Fig. 3. Demonic completion of TAIO: (a) A; and (b) $d(A)$

In [17], the authors develop a number of theoretical results about the tioco relation. In particular, they establish that given two TAIO A_I and A_S, if A_I tioco A_S, then the set of observable traces of A_I is included in the set of observable traces of A_S, while the converse is not true in general. However, if A_S is input-enabled, then the set inclusion between observable traces of A_I and A_S also implies the tioco conformance of A_I to A_S.

Specification automaton A_S has often intentionally under-specified inputs in order to model assumptions about the environment in which the SUT is designed to operate correctly. Hence, the input-enabledness is not a desired requirement for A_S in this context. In [31,17], the notion of *demonic completion*, illustrated in Figure 3 was introduced to transform automatically a model A_S and make it input-enabled. In essence, all non-specified inputs in all locations of A_S lead to a new *sink* "don't care" location, from which any behavior is possible.

Given a deterministic TAIO $A = (Q, \hat{q}, \Sigma_I, \Sigma_O, C, I, \Delta)$, its demonic completion $d(A)$ is the input-enabled TAIO $d(A) = (Q \cup \{\text{sink}\}, \hat{q}, \Sigma_I, \Sigma_O, C, I_d, \Delta_d)$, where $I_d(q) = I(q)$ and $I_d(\text{sink}) = \text{true}$ and $\Delta_d = \Delta \cup \{(\text{sink}, a, \text{true}, \{\}, \text{sink}) \mid a \in \Sigma\} \cup \{(q, a, \neg g, \{\}, \text{sink}) \mid q \in Q \wedge a \in \Sigma_I\}$, such that for each $q \in Q$ and $a \in \Sigma_I$, $g = (g_1 \vee \ldots \vee g_k) \wedge I(q)$, where $\{g_i\}_i$ are guards of the outgoing transitions of q labeled by a. Strictly speaking, g contains disjunctions of constraints, and thus cannot be directly used as a guard on a transition in a TAIO. In fact, we would need to transform g into a disjunctive normal form, and have a separate copy of the transition for each disjunction labeled by the appropriate guard. We omit the details of this transformation. It is not hard to see that

$$L(d(A)) = L(A) \cup \{\sigma \cdot a \cdot (\mathbb{R}_{\geq 0} \cdot \Sigma)^* \mid a \in \Sigma_I, \sigma \in L(A) \wedge \sigma \cdot a \notin L(A)\}$$

Given an arbitrary TAIO A_I and a deterministic specification TAIO A_S, considering the demonic completion $d(A_S)$ instead of A_S does not affect the conformance relation. Formally, we have the following proposition, proved in [17].

Proposition 1. *Given a deterministic TAIO A_S and its demonic completion $d(A_S)$, for any TAIO A_I, A_I tioco A_S if and only if A_I tioco $d(A_S)$.*

It turns out that given two TAIO A_S and A_I, by applying demonic completion $d(A_S)$ to A_S, checking tioco of A_I to A_S is equivalent to checking the language inclusion $L(A_I) \subseteq L(d(A_S))$, a result stated in the next Proposition, and which follows from Lemma 3 and Proposition 3 in [17].

Proposition 2. *Given a TAIO A_I and a deterministic TAIO A_S, A_I tioco A_S if and only if $L(A_I) \subseteq L(d(A_S))$.*

By Proposition 2, it follows that one can check $L(A_I) \subseteq L(d(A_S))$ instead of checking A_I tioco A_S when A_S is deterministic. In addition, the problem of checking $L(A_I) \subseteq L(d(A_S))$ is decidable when A_S is deterministic [3].

Remark: *Quiescence* was introduced in the ioco conformance relation to distinguish states which do not accept any output actions, and thus prevent the system to autonomously proceed without external stimuli. In practice, testing an SUT in a quiescent state consists in waiting for some predetermined timeout to expire, ensuring that the SUT does not generate output actions. After timeout expiration, it is assumed that the SUT will not generate output actions. A timed extension of ioco from [10] introduces the notion of M-quiescence which makes the timeout an explicit parameter of the definition, resulting in a family of conformance relations. In contrast, tioco does not use quiescence, but rather expects timeouts to be part of the specification model. We believe that the tioco approach is more natural since it exposes timeouts in an explicit way and gives more flexibility to the engineer, while resulting in a more elegant definition of the conformance relation. However, we do not put restrictions on our TAIO model, and allow true invariants and guards. As a consequence, we add an additional global timeout, but defer it to the test driver, as explained in Section 7.

5   Symbolic Test Case Generation from Timed Mutants

In model-based testing, the SUT is often seen as a black box and a conformance relations such as tioco serves to establish soundness of the TCG algorithm, but is not actually computed. In fact, only the specification model is explored in order to generate test cases, and the conformance relation defines the test verdict.

In contrast, mutation testing requires effective conformance checking of the mutated model to the original specification. Mutation testing is a particular instance of fault oriented testing where the test cases are generated in a way that attempts to "steer" the SUT towards failure, due to a common modeling error if one exists. Hence, the rationale behind this approach is that if the mutated model does not conform to its original version, the mutation introduces traces which were not in the original model, and the non-conformance witness trace serves as the basis to generate a test case. In case that the mutated model conforms to its original version, the mutation does not introduce new behavior with respect to the original specification, hence no useful test case is generated. It follows that test cases are generated only if the mutated model does not conform to its original version. We propose a TCG algorithm, summarized as follows:

1. Given a deterministic TAIO A, a mutation operator m and a mutation function μ_m, generate the mutant $M \in \mu_m(A)$;
2. Generate $d(A)$ by demonic completion of A;
3. Check M tioco A, by effectively checking $L(M) \subseteq L(d(A))$;
4. If $L(M) \not\subseteq L(d(A))$, generate a test case based on the trace which witnesses non conformance of M to A.

The steps 1 and 2 were already presented in Section 3 and 4, respectively. In this section, we detail the steps 3 and 4 of our test case generation framework.

5.1 k-Bounded Language Inclusion

We have seen that mutation-based testing is fault-oriented, i.e. test cases are generated only if the mutated model does not conform to its original version. Consequently, symbolic techniques based on BMC are well-adapted to solve this type of problems. In addition, the language inclusion problem between two timed automata A_I and A_S, where A_S is deterministic is PSPACE-complete, hence computationally expensive. In our setting, we are interested in finding finite counter-example traces witnessing violation of language inclusion. Missing such a witness, due to an insufficient bound, results in generating less test cases and is a trade-off between generating a complete test suite and computing it efficiently.

BMC was used in [4,21] for the reachability analysis of TA, and in [5] for checking the language inclusion between two timed automata. We encode the language inclusion problem as a k-bounded language inclusion SMT problem. Intuitively, given two TAIO A_I and A_S such that A_S is deterministic and an integer bound k, we have $L(A_I) \not\subseteq^k L(A_S)$ if there exists a timed trace $\sigma = t_1 \cdot a_1 \cdots t_i \cdot a_i$ such that $i \leq k$, $\sigma \in L(A_I)$ and $\sigma \notin L(A_S)$. We construct a formula $\varphi^k_{A_I,A_S}$ that is satisfiable if and only if $L(A_I) \not\subseteq^k L(A_S)$.

Let $A = (Q, \hat{q}, \Sigma_I, \Sigma_O, \mathcal{C}, I, \Delta)$ be a TAIO. We denote by $\text{loc}_A : Q \to \{1, \ldots, |Q|\}$ and $\text{act}_A : \Sigma \to \{1, \ldots, |\Sigma|\}$ functions assigning unique integers to locations and actions in A, respectively. Given A and a constant k, we denote by X the set of variables $\{x^1, \ldots, x^{k+1}\}$ that range over the domain $\{1, \ldots, |Q|\}$, where x^i encodes the location of A after the ith step. Similarly, let $\mathcal{A} = \{\alpha^1, \ldots, \alpha^k\}$ be the set of variables ranging over $\{1, \ldots, |\Sigma|\}$, where α^i encodes the action in A applied in the ith discrete step. We denote by $D = \{d^1, \ldots, d^k\}$ the set of real-valued variables, where d^i encodes the delay action applied in the ith time step. Let C^i denote the set of real variables obtained by renaming every clock $c \in C$ by c^i. We denote by $C = \bigcup_{i=1}^{k+1} C^i \cup \bigcup_{i=1}^{k+1} C^{*,i}$ the set of real (clock valuation) variables, where $c^{*,i} \in C^{*,i}$ and $c^i \in C^i$ encode the valuation of the clock $c \in C$ after the ith timed and discrete step, respectively.

We express the effect of applying Reset_ρ in the ith step of a run to the set C of clocks in A as follows:

$$\text{doReset}^i_{A,\rho}(C) \equiv \bigwedge_{c \in \rho} c^{i+1} = 0 \wedge \bigwedge_{c \notin \rho} c^{i+1} = c^{*,i}$$

We express the ith passage of time in A as follows:

$$\text{tDelay}^i_A(D, C) \equiv \bigwedge_{c \in C} (c^{*,i} - c^i) = d^i$$

The ith time step in a location $q \in Q$ is expressed with:

$$\text{tStep}^i_{A,q}(D, X, C) \equiv x^i = \text{loc}_A(q) \wedge \text{tDelay}^i_A(D, C) \wedge I(q)[C \backslash C^{*,i}],$$

where $I(q)[C \backslash C^{*,i}]$ is the invariant of q, with every clock $c \in C$ substituted by $c^{*,i}$. The formula for the ith discrete step is:

$$\text{dStep}^i_{A,\delta}(A, X, C) \equiv x^i = \text{loc}_A(q) \wedge \alpha^i = \text{act}_A(a) \wedge g[C \backslash C^{*,i}] \wedge$$
$$\text{doReset}^i_{A,\rho}(C) \wedge x^{i+1} = \text{loc}_A(q')$$

where $g[C \backslash C^{*,i}]$ denotes the guard of δ, where every clock $c \in C$ is substituted by $c^{*,i}$. We express the segment of a path in TAIO A from j to k with the following formula:

$$\text{path}^{j,k}_A(A, D, X, C) \equiv \bigwedge_{i=j}^{k} (\bigvee_{q \in Q} \text{tStep}^i_{A,q}(D, X, C) \wedge \bigvee_{\delta \in \Delta} \text{dStep}^i_{A,\delta}(A, X, C))$$

The initial state of TAIO A is expressed as follows:

$$\text{init}_A(X, C) \equiv x^1 = \text{loc}_A(\hat{q}) \wedge \bigwedge_{c \in C} (c^1 = 0)$$

Let $A_I = (Q_I, \hat{q}_I, \Sigma_I, \Sigma_O, C, I_I, \Delta_I)$ and $A_S = (Q_S, \hat{q}_S, \Sigma_I, \Sigma_O, C, I_S, \Delta_S)$ be two TAIOs such that A_S is deterministic. The general formula $\varphi^k_{A_I, A_S}(i, A, D, X_I, X_S, C_I, C_S)$ specifies the negation of k-language inclusion:

$$\varphi^k_{A_I, A_S} \equiv \bigwedge_{i=1}^{k} (d^i \geq 0 \wedge \alpha^i \geq 1 \wedge \alpha^i \leq |\Sigma|) \wedge i \geq 1 \wedge i \leq k \qquad \wedge$$
$$\text{init}_{A_I}(X_I, C_I) \wedge \text{init}_{A_S}(X_S, C_S) \wedge \text{path}^{1,i}_{A_I}(A, D, X_I, C_I) \wedge$$
$$\text{path}^{1,i-1}_{A_S}(A, D, X_S, C_S) \wedge \neg\text{path}^{i,i}_{A_S}(A, D, X_S, C_S)$$

5.2   Test Case Generation

Given a specification model A and its mutant M, our test case generation algorithm creates a *test* only if M does not conform to A. The generated test follows a *test purpose*, which is in our case the timed trace σ which witnesses the non conformance of M to A and exposes the error caused by the mutation in M. We denote a test by A_T and give it in a form of a deterministic TAIO. The test A_T specifies the execution of real-time traces and provides a *verdict* after observing at most k combined (timed/discrete) steps of a trace. The verdict can be:

- *Pass* (**pass**) - if the test purpose was successfully reached and the error introduced by the mutant was not exposed by the SUT during the test execution;
- *Inconclusive* (**inc**) - if the test purpose covering the fault introduced by the mutant could not be reached by the SUT during the test execution;
- *Fail* (**fail**) - if the fault introduced by the mutant as part of the test purposed was exposed by the SUT during the test execution.

The skeleton of A_T consists of the sequence $q_1 \cdot \delta_1 \cdots q_k \cdot \delta_k$ of locations and transitions in A which are executed while observing the witness trace $\sigma = t_1 \cdot a_i \cdots t_k \cdot a_k$. This skeleton corresponds effectively to the test purpose described above. In addition, A_T is completed according to Algorithm 1 satisfying a number of properties described next. After observing a prefix $\sigma' = t_1 \cdot a_1 \cdots t_i \cdot a_i$ of σ, A_T is in location q_i, where $i < k$, and can do one of the following:

- Wait if the invariant of q_i allows a positive time delay;
- Emit action a if a is an input action equal to a_i and the transition δ_i is enabled, and move to location q_{i+1};
- Accept action a if a is an output action equal to a_i and the transition δ_i is enabled, and move to location q_{i+1};
- Accept action a if a is an output action different from a_i and there exists an enabled transition δ in A with source location q_i and labeled with a, and move to the **inc** verdict location (Line 7);
- Refuse action a if a is an output action and there are no transitions in A with the source location q_i which is both labeled by a and enabled, and move to the **fail** verdict location (Lines 12-18).

Finally, when A_T is in location q_k, it accepts all outputs a such that there exists an enabled transition δ in A with source location q_k and labeled by a, moving to the **pass** location (Line 9), and it rejects all other outputs, moving to the **fail** location (Lines 12-18).

Note that our test A_T follows a fixed qualitative sequence of actions, defined by the witness σ. In particular, it stops following a valid output in the specification A if it differs from the one in the witness σ, and returning **inc** as verdict. It means that the test is not pursued when the SUT deviates from the test purpose. On the other hand, A_T is time adaptive, and the witness σ defines a class of timing constraints which are allowed by the test. In fact, it is unlikely that an expected output action is preceded by the exact time delay as defined by the witness trace. Hence, we need the test to be flexible and accept the expected output in a larger time range defined by the specification model. In addition, if we allow time flexibility for output actions, we cannot use the strict time delay from the witness trace σ, to precede an input action either, since it may violate input assumptions of the specification during some test execution. We illustrate this observation in Figure 4, which depicts model A and its mutant M. The trace $\sigma = 4 \cdot x! \cdot 2 \cdot a? \cdot 2 \cdot y!$ witnesses non-conformance of M to A and is used as the skeleton for the test A_T. During test execution, the test may observe the prefix $\sigma' = 2 \cdot x!$, which is allowed by the specification. In that case, if A_T requires exactly 2 time units to elapse between observing $x!$ and emitting $a?$, the assumptions expressed by A are violated. Hence we keep the time constraints symbolic, with an elapse of time between $x!$ and $a?$ dependent on previous observations.

6   Implementation

In this section, we present the tool that implements the test case generation framework described in Section 5. The implementation of the algorithms is done in Scala (v2.9.1). We use standard Uppaal TA XML format to model TAIO specifications. The (bounded) language inclusion between two TAIOs is computed using the Z3 (v4.0) SMT solver [20]. The communication between our implementation in Scala and the Z3 solver relies on the Scala^Z3 API.

The test case generation framework, depicted in Figure 5, consists of four main steps: (1) parsing and demonic completion of the TAIO model; (2) mutation of the TAIO model; (3) language inclusion between the original model and its mutant; and (4) test case generation. In what follows, we present more details about these steps.

Specification Parsing and Demonic Completion. The TAIO model specified in the Uppaal XML format is parsed with Scala's parser generator. We require the following restrictions on the Uppaal automata in order to guarantee their compliance with the TAIO model: (1) one automaton per file; (2) no urgent nor committed locations. We note that modeling style can have important impact on the number and effectiveness of consecutive generation of mutants and test cases. We implemented demonic completion of the model by direct application of the procedure from Section 4.

Mutation of Models. Our tool supports all mutation operators introduced in Section 3. We store each mutant as a separate Uppaal XML model.

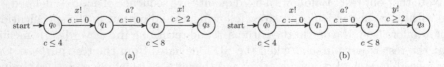

Fig. 4. Necessity of symbolic constraints on inputs in a test

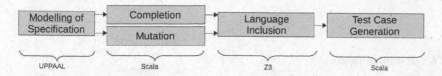

Fig. 5. Test case generation framework

Algorithm 1. Test case generation algorithm

Input: $A = (Q, \hat{q}, \Sigma_I, \Sigma_O, \mathcal{C}, I, \Delta)$ and $\delta_1 \cdots \delta_k$
Output: Test automaton A_T
1: $\Delta_T \leftarrow \bigcup_{i=1}^{k-1} \{\delta_i\}$
2: $Q_T \leftarrow \{q_i | (q_i, a, g, p, q') \in \delta_1 \cdots \delta_k\}$
3: $Q_T \leftarrow Q_T \cup \{\mathbf{pass}, \mathbf{fail}, \mathbf{inc}\}$
4: **for** $i = 1$ to k **do**
5:     **for all** $(q_i, a, g, \rho, q') \in \Delta \backslash \{\delta_i\}$ st. $a \in \Sigma_O$ **do**
6:       **if** $i < k$ **then**
7:         $\Delta_T \leftarrow \Delta_T \cup \{(q_i, a, g, \{\}, \mathbf{inc})\}$
8:       **else**
9:         $\Delta_T \leftarrow \Delta_T \cup \{(q_i, a, g, \{\}, \mathbf{pass})\}$
10:       **end if**
11:     **end for**
12:     **for all** $a \in \Sigma_O$ st. $\exists (q_i, a, g_j, \rho, q') \in \Delta$ **do**
13:       $g_T \leftarrow (g_1 \vee \ldots \vee g_n) \wedge I(q)$ st. $\{g_j\}$ are guards of outgoing transitions from q_T labeled by a
14:       $\Delta_T \leftarrow \Delta_T \cup \{(q_i, a, \neg g_T, \{\}, \mathbf{fail})\}$
15:     **end for**
16:     **for all** $a \in \Sigma_O$ st. $\not\exists (q_i, a, g, \rho, q') \in \Delta$ **do**
17:       $\Delta_T \leftarrow \Delta_T \cup \{(q_i, a, \mathrm{true}, \{\}, \mathbf{fail})\}$
18:     **end for**
19: **end for**
20: **return** $A_T \leftarrow (Q_T, \hat{q}, \Sigma_O, \Sigma_I, \mathcal{C}, I, \Delta_T)$

Language Inclusion. Language inclusion check between a model and its mutant is at core of the TCG framework. We translate an Uppaal model and its mutant to a bounded language inclusion problem expressed as an SMT-LIB2 formula, following the procedure described in Section 5.1. The formula is fed to the Z3 solver, which looks for the existence of a satisfying assignment to the variables representing a witness trace violating the language inclusion property.

In addition, we implemented the same TCG algorithm using Z3's incremental solving feature, with the aim to improve the computation time of the bounded language inclusion check. Given an SMT formula expressing the k-bounded language inclusion problem, we first feed the Z3 solver with the sub-formula for the i-bounded language inclusion problem, for some i smaller than k. Z3 checks the satisfiability of the sub-formula, and if a satisfying assignment is found, the procedure stops. Otherwise, we pop the sub-formula from the Z3 stack and push the sub-formula expressing the step from i to $i + 1$. The procedure is iterated until a witness is found or the k bound is reached.

Test Case Generation. if Z3 generates a counter-example which witnesses violation of language inclusion between the specification and its mutant, we use this counter-example together with the specification model in order to generate a test case. The test case generation implementation closely follows Algorithm 1.

CAS Requirements

Arming: The system is armed 20s after the vehicle is locked and the bonnet, luggage compartment and all doors are closed;

Alarm: The alarm sounds for 30s if an unauthorized person opens the door, the luggage compartment or the bonnet. The hazard flasher lights flashes for 5min;

Deactivation: The anti-theft alarm system can be deactivated at any time, even when the alarm is sounding, by unlocking the vehicle from outside.

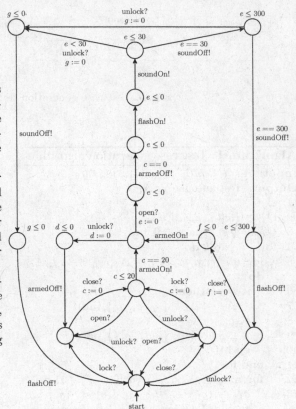

Fig. 6. Car alarm system: requirements and its TAIO model

7   Case Study and Experimental Results

In this section we illustrate our TCG approach with the Car Alarm System (CAS) [2,29] and evaluate the framework. The car alarm system (CAS) is a model inspired by the Ford's demonstrator developed in the EU FP7 project MOGENTES[4]. We developed the TAIO model of the CAS from the requirements provided by Ford, both shown in Figure 6.

We applied our mutation testing tool to the CAS example. We first generated all the mutants (1099) and for each mutant checked whether it tioco-conforms to the original CAS model, by effectively doing the k-bounded language inclusion test. We set the maximal k bound to 20 for the k-bounded language inclusion test. We generated tests from all the non-conformant mutants. The whole procedure took 62.3 minutes and produced a total of 628 test cases. 471 mutants are tioco conformant to the specification and therefore did not produce any test cases. Table 1 shows the run time of the standard and incremental approaches

---

[4] http://www.mogentes.eu

Table 1. Computation time for k-bounded language inclusion check

k	5	10	15	20
Std Solving	0.1s	40.1s	115.2s	279.5s
Inc Solving	0.1s	0.3s	0.6s	1.0s

for the language inclusion applied on the CAS and a single equivalent mutant, indicating the efficiency of the incremental solving.

In order to evaluate our mutation testing framework, we used an existing implementation of CAS [1], developed in Java. The implementation consists of 4 public methods, *open*, *close*, *lock* and *unlock*, and 2 internal methods, *setState* and the constructor. The CAS implementation simulates time elapse with a *tick* method. We also used the 38 implementation mutants of the CAS descibed in [1]. They were produced using the Java mutation tool μJava[5]. Applying all mutation operators of μJava to all methods except *tick* resulted originally in 72 mutants.

Some of the mutants were equivalent to the original implementation or to other mutants. After filtering them out, the total of 38 unique faulty implementations were derived. Table 2 shows the total numbers of implementation mutants and equivalent ones. Both the correct and the 38 faulty CAS implementations were used to evaluate the effectiveness of the test cases we generated.

We developed a test driver in order to execute generated tests on the CAS implementation. We integrated quiescence in the test driver, which is responsible to detect prolonged absence of outputs. We set the maximal timeout that the driver is allowed to wait for an output action to 400 time units. If the timeout is reached without observing an action, the test outputs a verdict **pass** if the test is in the last location with the true invariant or **inc** otherwise. The test driver immediately emits an input action when the associated transition becomes enabled. If the timeout is reached before the transition labeled by the input action becomes enabled, the test driver gives the **inc** verdict. Note that we executed tests on a Java implementation which models time passage as discrete ticks. We can currently interface our test driver to any simulated implementation model with arbitrary model of time, as long as time is simulated and communicated in form of time stamps. However, we do not yet support interfacing the test driver to a physical SUT, where the real passage of time cannot be controlled. In order to allow such support, we would need to model elaborated interfacing delays between the SUT and the test driver (see [17] for a detailed discussion on test execution and "delay automata"). We postpone the extension of our test drivers to physical real-time SUT to future work.

We say that a faulty implementation is *killed* if at least one test case reaches the verdict **fail** during a test execution. We analyzed the effectiveness of our mutation operators with respect to their ability to kill faulty implementations. Table 3 summarizes the results on effectiveness of mutation operators, where each row provides the number of mutants, the number of resulting test cases, the average number of faulty implementations killed per test case and the *mutation score* of a mutation operator. Mutation score is the measure which gives

---

[5] http://cs.gmu.edu/~offutt/mujava/

Table 2. Injected faults into the CAS implementation

	Mutants	Equiv.	Pairwise Equiv.	Different Faults
SetState	6	0	1	5
Close	16	2	6	8
Open	16	2	6	8
Lock	12	2	4	6
Unlock	20	2	8	10
Constr.	2	0	1	1
Total	72	8	26	38

the percentage of faulty implementations killed by mutants resulting of a single mutation operator. We achieved a total of 100% mutation score for the combined mutation operators. The highest mutation score is achieved by the "change target" operator $M2$, at the price of generating 375 mutants and 267 test cases. Evaluation results also show that most of the faulty implementations are killed by $M2$-mutants which contain self-loops. We also observed that 3 faulty implementations were only killed by "sink state" mutants ($M7$).

Following the above observations, we conducted another experiment in which we only applied "sink state" and "self-loop" mutations, resulting in only 50 mutants. All mutants were shown to be non tioco-conformant to original models, generating 50 test cases in just $56s$. In addition, combining these two operators resulted in 100% mutation score. These results indicate that a smart choice of a small subset of mutation operators can achieve high mutation scores while considerably reducing test case generation and execution times.

Table 3. Mutation analysis of mutation operators. The list of mutation operators can be seen in Section 3.

		M1	M2	M3	M4	M5	M6	M7	M8	**Total**
Model Mutants	[#]	139	375	375	24	25	11	25	125	1099
TCs	[#]	139	267	165	6	3	11	25	12	628
av. Kills per TC	[#]	12.5	13.2	12.4	16.3	16.3	17.8	17.8	13.8	13
Mutation Score	[%]	71	94.7	92.1	57.9	47.4	60.5	89.5	57.9	**100**

8   Conclusion

We proposed a novel real-time mutation testing framework. Our TCG technique relies on BMC and uses incremental SMT solving. We illustrated our testing approach on a Car Alarm System and presented promising experimental results, showing that we were able to kill all faulty implementations efficiently.

In the next step, we will apply our framework to other case studies, and study mutation operators effectiveness in more detail, adding more complex mutation operators and identifying a small set of operators which achieve high mutation scores for a larger class of problems. We will extend our test driver to allow test execution on physical real-time SUTs. In the current setting, we generate a test case in a form of a simple timed automaton which is extended from the witness trace and the original specification model. We plan to improve witness to test extension, by considering more refined timing constraints in the test contained in the region automaton of the specification model. We also plan to extend the expressiveness of the TA model with data variables, non-determinism and silent transitions. We finally plan to add support for incremental TCG for real-time systems consisting of multiple components.

Acknowledgements. We would like to thank Rupert Schlick from AIT for fruitful discussions and anonymous reviewers for their useful suggestions.

The research leading to these results has received funding from ARTEMIS Joint Undertaking under grant agreement number 269335 (MBAT) and from national fundings (Federal Ministry for Transport, Innovation and Technology and Austrian Research Promotion Agency) under program line Trust in IT Systems, project number 829583 (TRUFAL).

References

1. Aichernig, B.K., Brandl, H., Jöbstl, E., Krenn, W.: Efficient mutation killers in action. In: ICST, pp. 120–129 (2011)
2. Aichernig, B.K., Brandl, H., Jöbstl, E., Krenn, W.: UML in action: a two-layered interpretation for testing. ACM SIGSOFT SEN 36(1), 1–8 (2011)
3. Alur, R., Dill, D.L.: A theory of timed automata. Theor. Comput. Sci. 126(2), 183–235 (1994)
4. Audemard, G., Cimatti, A., Kornilowicz, A., Sebastiani, R.: Bounded model checking for timed systems. In: Peled, D.A., Vardi, M.Y. (eds.) FORTE 2002. LNCS, vol. 2529, pp. 243–259. Springer, Heidelberg (2002)
5. Badban, B., Lange, M.: Exact incremental analysis of timed automata with an SMT-solver. In: Fahrenberg, U., Tripakis, S. (eds.) FORMATS 2011. LNCS, vol. 6919, pp. 177–192. Springer, Heidelberg (2011)
6. Belli, F., Budnik, C.J., Wong, W.E.: Basic operations for generating behavioral mutants. In: MUTATION, pp. 9–18. IEEE Computer Society Press (2006)
7. Biere, A., Cimatti, A., Clarke, E.M., Strichman, O., Zhu, Y.: Bounded model checking. Advances in Computers 58, 117–148 (2003)
8. Boroday, S., Petrenko, A., Groz, R.: Can a model checker generate tests for non-deterministic systems? ENTCS 190(2), 3–19 (2007); MBT 2007
9. Brillout, A., He, N., Mazzucchi, M., Kroening, D., Purandare, M., Rümmer, P., Weissenbacher, G.: Mutation-based test case generation for simulink models. In: de Boer, F.S., Bonsangue, M.M., Hallerstede, S., Leuschel, M. (eds.) FMCO 2009. LNCS, vol. 6286, pp. 208–227. Springer, Heidelberg (2010)
10. Briones, L.B., Brinksma, E.: A test generation framework for quiescent real-time systems. In: Grabowski, J., Nielsen, B. (eds.) FATES 2004. LNCS, vol. 3395, pp. 64–78. Springer, Heidelberg (2005)
11. Burch, J.R., Clarke, E.M., McMillan, K.L., Dill, D.L., Hwang, L.J.: Symbolic model checking: 10^{20} states and beyond. In: LICS, pp. 428–439 (1990)
12. Clarke, E.M., Emerson, E.A.: Design and synthesis of synchronization skeletons using branching-time temporal logic. In: Engeler, E. (ed.) Logic of Programs 1979. LNCS, vol. 125, pp. 52–71. Springer, Heidelberg (1981)

13. Clarke, E.M., Grumberg, O., Jha, S., Lu, Y., Veith, H.: Counterexample-guided abstraction refinement. In: Emerson, E.A., Sistla, A.P. (eds.) CAV 2000. LNCS, vol. 1855, pp. 154–169. Springer, Heidelberg (2000)
14. Fraser, G., Wotawa, F., Ammann, P.E.: Testing with model checkers: a survey. Softw. Test. Verif. Reliab. 19(3), 215–261 (2009)
15. He, N., Rümmer, P., Kroening, D.: Test-case generation for embedded simulink via formal concept analysis. In: DAC, pp. 224–229 (2011)
16. Jia, Y., Harman, M.: An analysis and survey of the development of mutation testing. IEEE Transactions on Software Engineering 37(5), 649–678 (2011)
17. Krichen, M., Tripakis, S.: Conformance testing for real-time systems. Formal Methods in System Design 34(3), 238–304 (2009)
18. Larsen, K.G., Pettersson, P., Yi, W.: Uppaal in a nutshell. STTT 1(1-2), 134–152 (1997)
19. Mikucionis, M., Larsen, K.G., Nielsen, B.: T-uppaal: Online model-based testing of real-time systems. In: ASE, pp. 396–397 (2004)
20. de Moura, L., Bjørner, N.S.: Z3: An efficient SMT solver. In: Ramakrishnan, C.R., Rehof, J. (eds.) TACAS 2008. LNCS, vol. 4963, pp. 337–340. Springer, Heidelberg (2008)
21. Niebert, P., Mahfoudh, M., Asarin, E., Bozga, M., Maler, O., Jain, N.: Verification of timed automata via satisfiability checking. In: Damm, W., Olderog, E.-R. (eds.) FTRTFT 2002. LNCS, vol. 2469, pp. 225–244. Springer, Heidelberg (2002)
22. Nielsen, B., Skou, A.: Automated test generation from timed automata. STTT 5(1), 59–77 (2003)
23. Nilsson, R., Offutt, J., Andler, S.F.: Mutation-based testing criteria for timeliness. In: COMPSAC 2004, vol. 1, pp. 306–311 (2004)
24. Nilsson, R., Offutt, J., Mellin, J.: Test case generation for mutation-based testing of timeliness. ENTCS 164(4), 97–114 (2006); MBT 2006
25. Peleska, J., Vorobev, E., Lapschies, F.: Automated test case generation with SMT-solving and abstract interpretation. In: Bobaru, M., Havelund, K., Holzmann, G.J., Joshi, R. (eds.) NFM 2011. LNCS, vol. 6617, pp. 298–312. Springer, Heidelberg (2011)
26. Fabbri, S.C.P.F., Delamaro, M.E., Maldonado, J.C., Masiero, P.C.: Mutation analysis testing for finite state machines. In: ICSRE, pp. 220–229 (1994)
27. Fabbri, S.C.P.F., Maldonado, J.C., Sugeta, T., Masiero, P.C.: Mutation testing applied to validate specifications based on statecharts. In: Software Reliability Engineering, pp. 210–219 (1999)
28. Queille, J., Sifakis, J.: Iterative methods for the analysis of petri nets. In: Selected Papers from the First and the Second European Workshop on ICATPN, pp. 161–167 (1981)
29. Schlick, R., Herzner, W., Jöbstl, E.: Fault-based generation of test cases from UML-models - approach and some experiences. In: Flammini, F., Bologna, S., Vittorini, V. (eds.) SAFECOMP 2011. LNCS, vol. 6894, pp. 270–283. Springer, Heidelberg (2011)
30. Schmaltz, J., Tretmans, J.: On conformance testing for timed systems. In: Cassez, F., Jard, C. (eds.) FORMATS 2008. LNCS, vol. 5215, pp. 250–264. Springer, Heidelberg (2008)
31. Tretmans, J.: Model based testing with labelled transition systems. In: Hierons, R.M., Bowen, J.P., Harman, M. (eds.) FORTEST. LNCS, vol. 4949, pp. 1–38. Springer, Heidelberg (2008)

Model-Based Testing for Verification Back-Ends[*]

Cyrille Artho[1], Armin Biere[2], and Martina Seidl[2,3]

[1] National Institute of Advanced Industrial Science and Technology (AIST),
Research Institute for Secure Systems (RISEC), AIST Amagasaki
c.artho@aist.go.jp
[2] Institute for Formal Models and Verification,
Johannes Kepler University, Linz, Austria
{martina.seidl,armin.biere}@jku.at
[3] Business Informatics Group
Vienna University of Technology, Vienna, Austria

Abstract. Many verification tools used in practice rely on sophisticated SAT and SMT solvers. These reasoning engines are assumed and expected to be correct, but, in general, too complex to be fully verified. Therefore, effective testing techniques have to be employed. In this paper, we show how to employ model-based testing (MBT) to test sequences of application programming interface (API) calls and different system configurations. We applied this approach to our SAT solver Lingeling and compared it to existing testing approaches, revealing the effectiveness of MBT for the development of reliable SAT solvers.

1 Introduction

Rigorous formal techniques provide the tools for verifying crucial stability and correctness properties of hardware and software systems in order to increase their reliability as well as the trust of their users. Examples of successful verification techniques include model checking and automated theorem proving (cf. [1] for a survey). For applying these techniques, dedicated software is required which provides (semi-)automatic support during the verification process. Solving verification problems is not a trivial task and therefore, many sophisticated approaches have been developed. Many of these approaches break down the original problem to the problem of deciding the satisfiability of propositional logic (SAT) and extensions (SMT) [2]. For SAT, the prototypical NP-complete problem, not only a myriad of results are available giving a profound understanding of its theoretical properties, but also very efficient tools called SAT solvers [3] have been made available over the last ten years.

When a SAT solver serves as back-end in a verification tool, its correctness and stability is of particular importance, as the trust put in the system to be verified strongly depends on the trust in the verification system, and hence in the

---

[*] This work was partially funded by the Vienna Science and Technology Fund (WWTF) under grant ICT10-018 and by the Austrian Science Fund (FWF) under NFN Grant S11408-N23 (RiSE).

M. Veanes and L. Viganò (Eds.): TAP 2013, LNCS 7942, pp. 39–55, 2013.

SAT solver. Efforts have been made to verify SAT solvers, but since the implementation of modern SAT solvers relies on sophisticated low-level optimizations, complete verification is hardly possible. To ensure robustness of a SAT solver, one has to rely on traditional testing techniques. In particular, grammar-based black-box testing and delta debugging have shown to be of great value [4].

In this paper, we present a *model-based testing framework* for verification back-ends like SAT solvers. This framework allows testing different system configurations and sequences of calls to the application programming interface (API) of the verification back-end. Whereas in previous approaches only the input data has been randomly generated, we suggest to randomly produce valid sequences of API calls. Possible sequences are described by the means of a state machine.

Additionally, we randomly vary the different configurations of the verification back-end. Often, a verification tool implements a huge number of options which enable/disable/configure different pruning techniques and heuristics. The optimal settings for the options is strongly dependent on the problem to be solved, so there is no general optimal setting. We use a model to describe the different configurations of a verification back-end. Guided by this model, we instantiate the verification back-end randomly. If a defect in the verification back-end triggers a failure, we show how to reduce a failure producing trace by *delta debugging*.

The main contribution of this paper is therefore to introduce model-based API testing and model-based option testing, their combination with delta debugging, and an empirical evaluation showing the effectiveness of our framework.

We realize the proposed testing framework for the SAT solver Lingeling [5], which is an advanced industrial-strength SAT solver, with top rankings in recent SAT competitions.[1] It is used in many verification applications both in industry and academia. To evaluate the presented approach, we set up three experiments where we randomly seed some faults in Lingeling and compare the new approach to other well-established testing techniques.

This paper is structured as follows. First, we introduce basic notions of SAT solving and testing techniques in Section 2. Then we introduce a general architecture for model-based testing verification back-ends in Section 3, which is instantiated for the SAT solver Lingeling as described in Section 4. Experiments that underpin the effectiveness of our framework are shown in Section 5. Section 6 discusses related work, and Section 7 concludes with a discussion of related approaches and an outlook to future work.

2   Fuzzing and Delta Debugging for SAT Revisited

Since a detailed discussion of SAT solving is not within the scope of this work, we shortly revisit only the concepts and terminology important for the rest of the paper. A comprehensive introduction to the state-of-the-art in SAT solving is given in [2]. Additionally, we recapitulate the general idea of *grammar-based black-box testing* (vulgo *fuzz testing* or simply *fuzzing*) and *delta debugging*.

---

[1] `http://baldur.iti.kit.edu/SAT-Challenge-2012/`

2.1   Background

In general, SAT solvers implement conceptually simple algorithms to decide the (un)satisfiability of a propositional formula. A propositional formula is a conjunction of clauses. A clause is a disjunction of literals, with a literal being a variable or a negated variable. The task of a SAT solver is to find an assignment to each variable such that the overall formula evaluates to true in case of satisfiability or to show that there is no such assignment in case of unsatisfiability. A variable may be assigned the value true or false. A negated variable $\neg x$ is true (resp. false) if it is assigned false (resp. true). A clause is true if at least one of its literals is true. A formula is true if all of its clauses are true. Propositional formulas of the described structure are said to be in *conjunctive normal form* (CNF), which is the default representation for state-of-the-art SAT solvers.

For solving a propositional formula, most state-of-the-art SAT solvers implement a variant of the algorithm by Davis, Logeman, and Loveland (DLL) [6] which traverses the search space in a depth-first manner until either all clauses are satisfied or until at least one clause is fal-

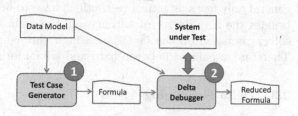

Fig. 1. Fuzzing + Delta Debugging

sified. In the latter case the SAT solver backtracks if not all assignments have been considered. For the application of SAT solvers on reasoning problems of practical relevance, a naive implementation of this algorithm is insufficient. Very sophisticated pruning techniques like learning and effective heuristics and data structures have to be realized within a SAT solver, such that the source code of a SAT solver has thousands lines of code usually written in the programming language C; e. g., the SAT solver Lingeling [5] consists of more than 20,000 lines of code. For making a SAT solver efficient on a certain set of formulas, mostly the right configuration, i. e., a specific combination of the options and parameter settings of the solver, has to be found. Due to very sophisticated pruning techniques and well-thought-out implementation tricks, a SAT solver can be tuned in such a manner that it solves most problems occurring in applications in a reasonable amount of time, although the worst case runtime of course remains exponential.

Brummayer et al. [4] showed that fuzz testing and delta debugging is effective in testing and debugging large SAT solver implementations, with a high degree of automation. The basic workflow is shown in Fig. 1. It consists of the *test case generator* for generating random formulas according to a grammar provided by a data model and the *delta debugger* for reducing the size of the formula such that the failure still occurs. In the following, we shortly review the two components as we will extend this approach in the rest of this paper. Please note that this approach is not restricted to propositional logic, but may be also used for other languages with more complex concepts (cf. [7,8,9]).

2.2 Test Case Generation

In grammar-based black-box testing no knowledge about the internal structure of the system under test (SUT) is available. The SUT is fed with randomly generated input data for automatically testing stability and correctness of the system. In order to ensure that the input data can be parsed, i.e., not only scenarios with malformed input data are tested, a model is provided which describes the set of syntactically valid inputs. This model may be specified by the means of a textual grammar, hard-coded in fuzzing tools like CNFuzz and FuzzSAT [4] or it may follow the approach of [10], where the structure of the formulas to be generated is specified in a domain-specific language.

For propositional formulas, several models have been proposed whose practical hardness may be configured by a few parameters, like the ratio of variables and clauses [11,12]. Since the language of propositional logic is not very complex, in general only few syntactical restrictions have to be considered. As argued in [4], besides the high degree of automation, the main success factor of fuzzing SAT solvers is based on the fact that a high throughput of test cases is achieved. Therefore, a balance between hard and trivial formulas has to be found.

2.3 Delta Debugging

Given an input which observably triggers a failure of the system under test, the delta debugger has the goal to simplify the input while preserving the failure. On this simplified input the analysis of reasons for the failure, i.e., the debugging, becomes easier. In the context of SAT, input formulas often consist of tens of thousands of clauses. For a human developer it is hardly feasible to manually step through the code of the SAT solver when such a huge input is processed. In order to reduce the input to a new syntactically correct test case, and also for the delta debugging process itself, knowledge on the structure of the input data is useful. For SAT formulas in CNF, delta debuggers remove either clauses or some literals of a clause. Delta debuggers for non-CNF formulas like qprodd[2] or for SMT like deltaSMT[3] and ddSMT[4] need more sophisticated reduction techniques, since the underlying data structures are trees instead of lists of lists (see also [13]).

In contrast to the test case generator, the delta debugger has to call the system under test. In order to simplify given input data, the delta debugger goes through the following process: First, the SUT is run on the given input data. Then the delta debugger tries to reduce the size of the input based on some heuristics. The SUT is run again, now with the reduced test case. If the failure is still observed, the delta debugger tries to perform more simplifications. Otherwise, it undoes the changes and applies different reductions. The latter steps are repeated until either a time limit is reached or the obtained test case fulfills some predefined quality criteria.

---

[2] http://fmv.jku.at/qprodd/
[3] http://fmv.jku.at/deltasmt/
[4] http://fmv.jku.at/ddsmt/

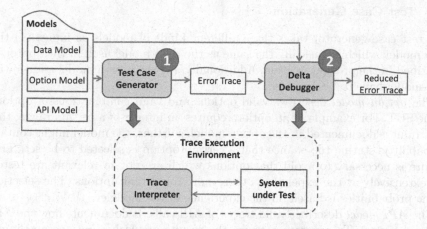

Fig. 2. Extended Workflow for Fuzzing and Delta Debugging

3   General Architecture

The testing approach discussed in the previous section is agnostic of the SUT. Communication with the SUT is done via a file, which is generated by the test case generator and reduced by the delta debugger in the case a failure has been found. For solving propositional formulas, all SAT solvers which are able to process the standard DIMACS format, can be plugged into the testing workflow shown in Fig. 1. In that workflow, the test case generator and delta debugger produce and reduce propositional formulas in CNF. However, little control over the execution behavior of the SUT is possible with the consequence that not all features of the system are covered by the generated test cases.

In particular, incremental SAT solving as implemented in most modern SAT solvers, cannot be tested. Incremental SAT solving is used for many applications, e.g., for enumerating all solutions of a formula. After solving a satisfiable formula, the solver neither terminates nor is reset; instead, additional constraints are provided. The SAT solver checks if the formula is still satisfiable with the new constraints. Furthermore, the SUT is run with certain options set, but there might be defects which only show up under a certain combination of options.

To circumvent these problems, we propose to use a model-based testing approach for verification back-ends like SAT solvers. In particular, we suggest to fuzz not only the input data, but to generate sequences of API calls, to cover more features of a solver. The sequences of valid API calls are described by a state machine. To test different combination of options, setting options is also fuzzed. The range of possible options is also defined by a model. The adopted workflow is shown in Fig. 2. The goal is still to produce syntactically valid input data, which uncovers defects of the SUT. The individual components of the proposed approach are described in the following.

3.1   Test Case Generation

The test case generator takes three different kinds of models as input: (1) the data model, which is basically the same as the data model used in the approach described in the previous section. Additionally, (2) the option model and (3) the API model have to be provided.

The *option model* describes valid options and valid combinations of options of the SUT. For example, if an option requires an integer of a certain range, this constraint is documented in the option model. Further, the model might contain probabilities stating the chance that a certain option is selected to be set. This feature is necessary to avoid that options which are not so relevant are tested too extensively at the expense of other, more important options. The selection of the probabilities is based on the experience of the modeler.

The *API model* describes valid traces of API calls. It documents how the API has to be used. To generate a trace, the results of fuzzing options and input data have to be included. Hence the test case generator has to combine the three models. For example, the input data may be either read from a file or it may be programmatically handed over by dedicated API calls. As the call of certain functions might be optional, also the API model may be equipped with probabilities for the selection of functions which are not mandatory to be called.

Both the API model and the option model contain information specific to the SUT. Since verification back-ends like SAT solvers often have similar functionality and APIs, reuse is achievable by specifying a generic model and appending to each state the API calls to be performed. If another system with similar functionality has to be tested, only the names of API calls have to be changed.

In principle, the test case generator could be used without communicating to the trace execution environment which is described in Section 3.3. If the test case generator has a direct exchange with the SUT while generating the test data, the results of API calls can be directly considered during the search for a trace which triggers a failure.

3.2   Delta Debugging

For the API testing approach, the delta debugger not only has to reduce the input data, i. e., the formula, but the trace itself such that the failure still occurs. As a trace is a linear sequence of API calls, no complicated rewriting is needed when a call is removed as it would be necessary if the internal node of a tree is removed. However, the delta debugger has to obey the description of the API model in order to maintain a valid trace. For example, there might be calls which may not be removed, like the initialization and release routines or the function which starts the actual solving process.

As for the test case generator, the delta debugger communicates with the system under test in order to incorporate the result of a selected action into the reduction process. Since the mere removal of an API call may not be enough to obtain the expected reduction, it might be necessary also to vary the arguments of a call.

3.3   Trace Execution

In our approach, both the test case generator and the delta debugger communicate with the SUT to achieve better results. For the test case generator this means to get a high coverage rate for uncovering defects. For the delta debugger this means to reduce the failure-triggering traces as much as possible. Communication can be achieved in two ways: either the test case generator and delta debugger directly call API functions. Although this is the more direct implementation, it reduces the reusability of the framework. Alternatively, calls could be attached to the transitions of the API model. If a transition is taken, its attached function is invoked as in Modbat [14]. A potential issue of that approach is that such a testing framework may only support certain programming languages. Furthermore, the testing framework has to interpret the output and return values of the SUT; this again makes the testing framework tailored towards a given system.

Alternatively, the SUT may be wrapped into an execution environment, where a trace interpreter interacts with the SUT. The trace interpreter has to be developed for each SUT individually and is able to call the functions of the SUT directly. The output of the SUT may then be translated into a format which can be processed by the testing framework. The trace interpreter allows to replay the trace reduced by the delta debugger which can then undergo manual debugging in order to find and eliminate defects.

Using a trace interpreter to replay a trace has another practical advantage. If a solver is used as a verification back-end in a larger verification system, it might happen that the solver triggers a failure when a certain sequence of API calls is performed. It might be difficult to reproduce the failure by simply dumping the formula and passing it as command line argument, because internally the solver follows another sequence of API calls. In order to report the defect to the solver developer without giving away the whole verification system, the trace of the failing run of the solver might be produced (under the assumption that the solver is equipped with a logging functionality). The solver developer can replay the trace, analyze the undesired behavior, and fix the bug.

3.4   Discussion

With three different kinds of input models, better control on the test case generation is achieved, assuming the models reflect the behavior of the SUT in an accurate manner. If a model is too restrictive, code coverage is decreased for the test case generator and also less reduction can be achieved by the delta debugger. If the model is too lax, i. e., not precise enough, (external) contracts of API functions might be violated and invalid traces are generated.

In order to obtain good code coverage and increase flexibility for delta debugging, but also for reducing modeling effort, the testing framework is able to deal with *under-approximative models* by relying on a callback feature to give certain feedback from the SUT back to the testing framework. Then the testing framework can react immediately when contract violating traces occur. To use this feature, the SUT also has to be equipped with *API contract assertions* similar to assertions used in specification-based testing (cf. for example [15]).

4   Case Study: Model-Based Testing for Lingeling

In this section, we show how the presented testing framework is used for testing the SAT solver Lingeling. Therefore, the three different models have to be specified as well as the different components presented in the previous section. The framework is available at `http://fmv.jku.at/lglmbt`. Before we discuss the details of the testing framework, we shortly review the features of Lingeling.

4.1   Lingeling at a Glance

Lingeling [5] is a SAT solver that interleaves searching with very powerful preprocessing techniques. Preprocessing techniques are effective, but computationally expensive techniques which are traditionally applied only at at beginning of the solving process. In Lingeling, such techniques are integrated within the search process by binding their applications to a given extent. These bindings can be controlled both by command line and programmatically, which cause Lingeling to have more than 140 options with many of them requiring an integer value to be selected. For this purpose, fuzzing the options is extremely valuable for testing combinations of different features. In the implementation of Lingeling, much emphasis is spent on a compact representation of clauses for processing very large input formulas as they occur in practice. The implementation is done in C and consists of more than 20,000 lines of code. Without dedicated tool support for testing as proposed in this paper, finding and eliminating defects would hardly be possible.

Actually, the work presented in this paper can be seen as a crucial technique for enabling the integration of an incremental SAT solving API into Lingeling, which in turn made it possible to use a state-of-the-art SAT solver back-end in our SMT solver Boolector. A substantial part of the success of Boolector in the SMT 2012 competition is attributed to this fact.

Besides explicitly running Lingeling from the command line, the solver can also be included as a library. The API includes more than 80 functions. Additionally to the sequential version of Lingeling, there is also a multi-threaded variant which builds on top of the sequential version. The testing framework discussed in the following has only been used for testing the core library and the sequential solver. The API functions used by the multi-threaded front-end are hard to test with, since they mainly define call-backs. We leave it to future work to extend the framework to the multi-threaded case.

4.2   Test Case Generation

The goal of the test case generator is to produce traces which are valid sequences of calls to Lingeling's API. For our prototype we encoded the models necessary to

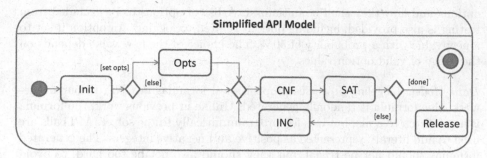

Fig. 3. Simplified API Model of Lingeling

describe valid traces, input data, and options directly in C, which allows direct communication with the solver. For test case generation, no intermediate layer is necessary. By sacrificing generality, the prototypical implementation is tailored towards testing Lingeling and allows to gain a first understanding of the power of the suggested approach for testing a state-of-the-art SAT solver. A sample trace is shown in Fig. 4.

API Model. The API model (see Fig. 3) documents some contracts which have to be fulfilled when using the API. The omitted features deal with additional optimization techniques which have to be called at certain positions within the model. After initialization (state Init), options (state Opts) may be set. The path to be taken is decided by random. By empirical evaluation it turned out that setting options with a probability of 0.5 is a good choice. If the path to Opts is taken, then options are set according to the option model. In the next step, the formula to be solved has to be generated. Here, knowledge of the data model is necessary.

After having created the formula, optimizations are performed with a certain probability. The formula is then handed to the solver. After completing the solving process, the incremental feature of the solver may be tested by changing to the state Inc (this is only possible if the for-

```
init
option actstdmax 80
option bias 2
option ccereleff 3
option cgrmineff 200000
add -58
add 1
add 2
add 0
add -1
add -2
add 0
assume 1
setphase -2
sat
release
```

Fig. 4. Example of a Trace

mula is SAT), to extend the formula with additional constraints, and to start the solving again. Alternatively, the solving process could be stopped. If this is done according to the API contract, some functions to free memory have to be called.

Option Model. The description of the options to be generated uses an introspective API function of Lingeling which allows to query the solver for its available options and how they shall be initialized. A list of options to be excluded from testing is also provided, including options related to logging. An option is set to a new value with a probability of 50 %. The choice of the new value depends on the range of valid option values.

Data Model. Lingeling processes propositional formulas in CNF. In our framework, this formula is randomly generated. Unlike in previous work, the formula is not written to a file, but it is fed programmatically to the solver. API calls are used to add literals, represented as positive and negative integers. The generated formulas should not be trivial, but they should also not be too hard, to avoid that the solver does not terminate. It also has to be ensured that no tautological clauses are generated, i. e., clauses which contain a literal in both polarities.

Experiences showed that formulas with between 10 and 200 variables give the best results. If n is the number of variables, the number of clauses is given by $(n * x)/100$ where x is a number between 390 and 450. Again, the values are based on many years of solver development experience, but related to the phase transition threshold of SAT solving.

The length of individual clauses is decided as follows. Clauses of length one, two or three are special and are handled differently than other clauses. For example, in unary clauses (clauses of length one), the truth value of its literal can be decided immediately and therefore be propagated to all other occurrences of the respective variable. The generation of these three kinds of clauses is fostered by giving them a higher probability to be generated than other clauses. The length of a clause is naturally constrained by the number of variables occurring in a formula. A variable in a clause is negated with the probability of 50 %.

For testing incremental SAT solving, additional clauses have to be generated which are added to the current formulas between calls to the solving routine. These clauses are generated in the same way as just described, over already existing and a certain small number of new variables.

4.3   Delta Debugging and Trace Execution

We developed a delta debugger which reduces a given trace as follows. First, the file containing the trace is parsed and a list of all commands is built. At the moment, about 30 different commands are supported, having either one or no argument. Then the original trace is replayed in order to obtain the *golden* exit status of the execution, which should also be returned by the execution of the reduced trace. Then the rewriting of the trace is initiated.

In principle, only sub-traces are extracted, but it has to be ensured that the API model discussed in the previous subsection is not violated, i. e., certain parts like the initialization and the release commands may not be removed. Also the values of the solver options are changed during the trace reduction process, with the hope that another configuration of the solver triggers the failure earlier.

For replaying the traces, a simple interpreter is provided. This interpreter executes not only the traces produced by the fuzzer and delta debugger, but also traces produced during all runs of the solver. The solver is equipped with a logging functionality implemented by the means of a macro calling a certain API function of Lingeling, which outputs every API call in the required format. Logging can be enabled through an API call or by setting an environment variable (LGLAPITRACE) to point to the trace file.

For dealing with inadequate API models and for realizing the previously described call back functionality, Lingeling internally executes a state machine. If an invalid state transition would be caused by an API call not possible in the current state, a special assertion fails. This gives the feedback to the caller of the API function that the invocation was incorrect. With this information the caller could adopt its behavior accordingly, i.e., in the case of the delta debugger a different kind of reduction is performed.

5   Experimental Evaluation

Our experience in using the presented framework when developing Lingeling is extremely positive. This section describes experiments to corroborate this, measuring efficiency in terms of throughput, code coverage and detect defection capability.

5.1   Experiment 1: Code Coverage

We measured the code coverage with the tool gcov of the GNU compiler collection. The evolution of the code coverage for 10,000 runs is shown in Fig. 5. CNF Fuzzing achieves code coverage of about 75 % after 10,000 runs which could be improved by 5 % by MBT without option fuzzing, and by additional 5 % by MBT with option fuzzing. The difference between CNF Fuzzing and the MBT approaches might be explained by the fact that CNF Fuzzing does not test the incremental feature of the solver. Coverage of 100 % is not possible due to the fact that only correct formulas and traces are generated, so the error handling code is never called. We observed that even for more runs, the values do not change anymore. Creating corrupted input for testing error handling is not within the scope of this work, but might be interesting in the future.

5.2   Experiment 2: Throughput

The effectiveness of random resp. fuzz testing depends not only on the quality of the generated tests, but also on the number of test cases executed per second, which we define as *throughput*. For our MBT approach we achieved a throughput in the order of 251 test cases per second: 919,058 test cases were executed during one hour (3660 seconds) of running the model-based tester on an Intel Xeon E5645 2.40 GHz CPU.

Note, that roughly 10 % of these test cases are actually terminated early due to contract violations. This occurs because the model is not precise enough to entirely exclude invalid API call sequences. Those are executed until the point where the contract violation is detected (by API contract assertions in

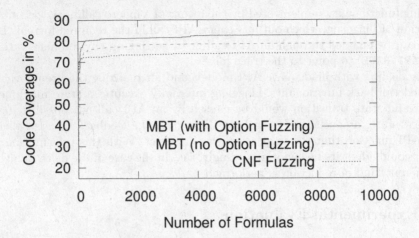

Fig. 5. Comparison of Code Coverage

the library) and thus can still be considered valid test cases. This feature of our approach allows a trade-off between the effort needed to capture API contracts precisely in the model and the effectiveness of testing.

To measure the throughput of file-based fuzzing we piped the output of the fuzzer to Lingeling to avoid disk I/O. Still the throughput did not reach more than 25 runs per second, measured for batches of 100 runs, on the same machine. This is an order of magnitude slower than for MBT. In both cases we used a binary compiled with -O3 but assertion checking enabled (so no -DNDEBUG). By this huge difference in the throughput, the benefits of accessing the solver via the API become directly visible. No time is wasted with I/O and parsing.

Note that fuzz testing is "embarrassingly parallel" and we have successfully used the combination of fuzz testing and delta debugging on a cluster with 128 cores, with the goal to produce smaller failure traces than an existing but large and impossible to delta debug trace obtained from an external user or from failing runs on huge benchmarks.

5.3 Experiment 3: Fault Seeding

In a third experiment we randomly inserted defects by either adding an abort statement or deleting a line in the code of Lingeling. These "mutations" were restricted to the core component of Lingeling in the file lglib.c consisting of 19,141 lines of C code (computed by the Unix wc utility). A mutation is considered as invalid (counted as "not compilable") if the line it affects contains the use of a macro for initializing an option or tracing the API.

This experiment was run on two identical computers (Intel Xeon CPU E5645 2.40 GHz, the same hardware as for Exp. 2) for roughly one week and produced the results presented in Tab. 1. The table is split vertically into three parts: *model-based* fuzzing / delta debugging (Δ dbg) as presented in this paper,

Table 1. Mutation Experiments: 963 mutations, 681 compilable, 404 defective

name	variant	number of successful runs (out of 404)	average time in seconds	average		relative	
				trace size	#lines covered	trace size	#lines covered
model-based, no option fuzzing	actual	398	98.51 %	1.67	2172.94	3796.49	100.00 %	100.00 %
	Δ dbg	398	98.51 %	81.43	291.66	2873.58	13.42 %	75.69 %
model-based, with option fuzzing	actual	397	98.27 %	1.69	2228.53	3951.01	100.00 %	100.00 %
	Δ dbg 1	396	98.02 %	72.30	290.54	2916.24	13.05 %	73.99 %
	Δ dbg 2	390	96.53 %	158.25	51.23	1318.45	2.26 %	32.79 %
file-based, no option fuzzing	actual	357	88.37 %	1.64	2908.97	4356.41	100.00 %	100.00 %
	Δ dbg	347	85.89 %	154.25	1141.55	4084.62	39.53 %	95.24 %
file-based, with option fuzzing	actual	324	80.20 %	1.21	2666.28	3573.27	100.00 %	100.00 %
	Δ dbg	314	77.72 %	179.78	31.19	1325.90	1.18 %	38.05 %
regression, no option Δ dbg	actual	354	87.62 %	0.85	1056.34	4267.77	100.00 %	100.00 %
	Δ dbg	346	85.64 %	37.32	360.15	4207.34	49.11 %	100.00 %
regression, with option Δ dbg	actual	354	87.62 %	0.87	1056.33	4271.84	100.00 %	100.00 %
	Δ dbg	349	86.39 %	160.96	82.83	1641.41	9.51 %	38.83 %

file-based fuzzing / delta debugging as in [4], and *regression* runs over 93 collected and hand-crafted CNF files used for many years in the development of various SAT solvers. The regression testing is of course deterministic and the base-line regression suite (before introducing mutations) takes 10 seconds to complete.

We include runs with and without fuzzing options resp. with and without delta debugging of options. In the experiments for model-based testing with option fuzzing, we distinguish two variants of delta debugging. The first variant "Δ dbg 1" only reduces options explicitly set in the failing test, while default options are not changed. The second variant "Δ dbg 2" considers all options for delta debugging. Note, running regressions only allows to delta-debug options but does not really allow to fuzz them.

The 3rd and 4th columns show the success rate of fuzzing resp. delta debugging with respect to all 404 mutations, for which at least one method was able to produce a failure: an assertion violation, segmentation fault, etc. As in Exp. 2 the executable is optimized (-O3) but does include assertion checking code (no -DNDEBUG). Mutation and compilation time are not taken into account.

Both model-based approaches (with and without option fuzzing) have the highest success rate. Actually, for 31 mutations only these two were successful in producing a failure within a time limit of 100 seconds. The file-based fuzzers did not produce any failure that was not found by model-based testing as well. The regression suite was slightly more successful and detected three failures that no other method could detect. The 5th column contains the average time needed to produce a failure (not including time-outs).

For each compilable mutation, testing resp. fuzzing continued until the first failure or the time limit of 100 seconds was reached. Each failing test case was then subjected to delta debugging with a time limit of one hour. The algorithm for delta debugging depends on the type of testing: trace shrinking for MBT, and CNF reduction for file-based fuzzing and regression testing. Even with a time limit of one hour per test case, some delta debugging runs timed out and thus the success rate dropped slightly (except for model-based testing without option fuzzing, the first row below the header in Table 1).

In order to be able to compare the effectiveness of trace based and CNF based techniques, we show in the remaining columns the size of failing test cases as well as the number of lines executed. The *size* of a failing test is measured in terms of the size of the API trace produced either directly by the model-based tester or obtained implicitly after tracing the API calls when reading and solving the CNF file. Commands to set options are not counted. This size metric allows to compare sizes of test cases across different testers (with and without fuzzing options).

We consider the number of lines executed during one test case as an important metric for the *quality* of the test case. To obtain the number of executed resp. covered lines, the binary was recompiled with debugging support (-g). The compiler was also instructed to include code for producing coverage information. After running the test case the number of executed lines was determined with the help of gcov. For each tester resp. delta debugger the average numbers are calculated over all successful runs, while the relative numbers give the same information, but are normalized w. r. t. the tester.

The experiments showed that our MBT approach is substantially more effective in finding defects than previously used techniques. Taking the time-outs into account, it is also faster and even without option fuzzing produces much smaller test cases. Fuzzing and in particular delta debugging of options is particularly effective in reducing the size of traces. We see a reduction of almost two orders of magnitude by delta debugging options, while delta debugging without touching options gives a reduction of slightly less than one order of magnitude.

6   Related Work

Only few publications about testing and debugging verification back-ends exist. Grammar-based black-box fuzzing and delta debugging for SAT and its extension QSAT have been presented in [4] where the authors showed state-of-art solvers contain defects, not revealed by running the standard benchmark sets as used in competitions. Several works deal with the generation of random formulas (e. g., [10,12,11]), but these focus on theoretical properties of formulas and not on their suitability for supporting the solver development process. Similar approaches are available for SMT [7] and ASP [8].

Model-based testing for verification back-ends as proposed in this work has—to the best of our knowledge—never been applied specifically to verification back-ends, but only to arbitrary software systems. Since the literature on model-based testing is too vast to be discussed in detail, we refer to [16] for a survey. Fuzzing options has been realized in the ConFu approach [17], which randomly tests different configurations of a tool during runtime. To this end, the tester has to annotate the parameters of the function to be tested with constraints. For *model-based option testing*, research on model-based testing software product lines are probably the most related (see for example [18]). A software product line is a family of software systems derived from shared assets. By the means of variability models, the possible configurations (the options) are described which are applicable. However, the variability found in software product lines is more complex than the configuration facilities found in SAT solvers in terms of combination constraints, therefore, for a SAT solver a more focused realization of option fuzzing is possible.

Model-based API testing is for example realized in the tool Modbat [14], which is a Scala-based tool providing an embedded domain-specific language (DSL) for specifying the model. Modbat supports only the testing of Java bytecode, but provides a more sophisticated event handling than necessary for our purposes. In the .NET framework, the Abstract State Machine Language (AsmL) can be used for the automatic generation of method parameters and the automatic derivation of test sequences [19]. In this context, also work has to be mentioned which uses contracts as provided by the API for the generation of test data [20].

Delta debugging for SAT solvers has been described in [7], where the size of a formula is reduced. There, the input data (the formula) is reduced such that a failure still occurs. Shrinking techniques for reducing the size of execution traces are for example described in [21]. Delta debugging traces in the context of SAT solving has—to the best of our knowledge—never been presented before.

7   Conclusion

We propose to apply model-based testing for verification back-ends, like SAT solvers. In this approach, not only the input data is randomly generated, but also sequences of valid API calls. This makes it possible to test, for example, the incremental features of SAT solvers. These incremental features play an important role in verification applications. Besides that, we additionally included option fuzzing in our testing framework, which randomly selects different configurations of the SUT.

We combined the presented model-based testing approach with delta debugging, to reduce failure triggering traces. This combination of model-based testing and delta debugging is a powerful tool for testing verification back-ends. As proof of concept we implemented the proposed testing framework for the SAT solver Lingeling and performed an extensive empirical evaluation. Different kinds of experiments confirmed the effectiveness of model-based testing in combination with delta debugging. Based on these experiments and on our long-time experiences in solver development, we believe that the techniques described in this paper are effective in general, and are particularly useful when applied to other formal reasoning engines like SMT solvers, theorem provers, or model checkers.

In future work, we plan to compare our dedicated mutation tool to more general approaches like Milu [22] and extend the presented testing framework to multi-threaded and reentrant engines. Testing our SMT solver Boolector through its API is another target. Furthermore, we plan to investigate how the design of the input models is correlated with the quality of the generated test cases. Today many developers of SMT and SAT solvers rely on fuzzing and delta debugging from our previous work. Our new approach described in this paper is much more effective and efficient, and is hoped to have a similar impact.

Acknowledgements. We would like to thank Jürgen Holzleitner for sharing his idea of using option fuzzing to increase coverage, as described in his Master Thesis [23]. It increased the efficiency and productivity of our development process considerably, and particularly allowed us to produce much more complex code. Later it was confirmed by John Hughes, through private communication, that techniques for fuzzing parameters of implementations have been used extensively in applications of QuickCheck [15] too.

References

1. D'Silva, V., Kroening, D., Weissenbacher, G.: A survey of automated techniques for formal software verification. TCAD 27(7), 1165–1178 (2008)
2. Biere, A., Heule, M., van Maaren, H., Walsh, T. (eds.): Handbook of Satisfiability. IOS Press (2009)
3. Prasad, M.R., Biere, A., Gupta, A.: A survey of recent advances in SAT-based formal verification. STTT 7(2), 156–173 (2005)
4. Brummayer, R., Lonsing, F., Biere, A.: Automated Testing and Debugging of SAT and QBF Solvers. In: Strichman, O., Szeider, S. (eds.) SAT 2010. LNCS, vol. 6175, pp. 44–57. Springer, Heidelberg (2010)
5. Biere, A.: Lingeling and Friends at the SAT Competition 2011. FMV Report Series Technical Report 11(1) (2011)
6. Davis, M., Logemann, G., Loveland, D.: A machine program for theorem-proving. Communications of the ACM 5(7), 394–397 (1962)
7. Brummayer, R., Biere, A.: Fuzzing and delta-debugging SMT solvers. In: Proc. of the Workshop on Satisfiability Modulo Theories, pp. 1–5. ACM (2009)
8. Brummayer, R., Järvisalo, M.: Testing and debugging techniques for answer set solver development. TPLP 10(4-6), 741–758 (2010)
9. Cuoq, P., Monate, B., Pacalet, A., Prevosto, V., Regehr, J., Yakobowski, B., Yang, X.: Testing static analyzers with randomly generated programs. In: Goodloe, A.E., Person, S. (eds.) NFM 2012. LNCS, vol. 7226, pp. 120–125. Springer, Heidelberg (2012)
10. Creignou, N., Egly, U., Seidl, M.: A Framework for the Specification of Random SAT and QSAT Formulas. In: Brucker, A.D., Julliand, J. (eds.) TAP 2012. LNCS, vol. 7305, pp. 163–168. Springer, Heidelberg (2012)
11. Nudelman, E., Leyton-Brown, K., Hoos, H.H., Devkar, A., Shoham, Y.: Understanding Random SAT: Beyond the Clauses-to-Variables Ratio. In: Wallace, M. (ed.) CP 2004. LNCS, vol. 3258, pp. 438–452. Springer, Heidelberg (2004)
12. Pérez, J.A.N., Voronkov, A.: Generation of Hard Non-Clausal Random Satisfiability Problems. In: Proc. of AAAI/IAAA, AAAI, pp. 436–442. The MIT Press (2005)
13. Misherghi, G., Su, Z.: HDD: hierarchical Delta Debugging. In: Proc. of ICSE, pp. 142–151. ACM (2006)

14. Artho, C., Biere, A., Hagiya, M., Potter, R., Ramler, R., Tanabe, Y., Yamamoto, F.: Modbat: A model-based API tester for event-driven systems. In: Dependable Systems Workshop (2012)
15. Claessen, K., Hughes, J.: Quickcheck: a lightweight tool for random testing of haskell programs. ACM Sigplan Notices 35(9), 268–279 (2000)
16. Utting, M., Pretschner, A., Legeard, B.: A taxonomy of model-based testing approaches. Softw. Test., Verif. Reliab. 22(5), 297–312 (2012)
17. Dai, H., Murphy, C., Kaiser, G.E.: Confu: Configuration fuzzing testing framework for software vulnerability detection. IJSSE 1(3), 41–55 (2010)
18. Cichos, H., Oster, S., Lochau, M., Schürr, A.: Model-Based Coverage-Driven Test Suite Generation for Software Product Lines. In: Whittle, J., Clark, T., Kühne, T. (eds.) MODELS 2011. LNCS, vol. 6981, pp. 425–439. Springer, Heidelberg (2011)
19. Barnett, M., Grieskamp, W., Nachmanson, L., Schulte, W., Tillmann, N., Veanes, M.: Towards a Tool Environment for Model-Based Testing with AsmL. In: Petrenko, A., Ulrich, A. (eds.) FATES 2003. LNCS, vol. 2931, pp. 252–266. Springer, Heidelberg (2004)
20. Liu, L(L.), Meyer, B., Schoeller, B.: Using Contracts and Boolean Queries to Improve the Quality of Automatic Test Generation. In: Gurevich, Y., Meyer, B. (eds.) TAP 2007. LNCS, vol. 4454, pp. 114–130. Springer, Heidelberg (2007)
21. Jalbert, N., Sen, K.: A trace simplification technique for effective debugging of concurrent programs. In: Proc. of FSE, pp. 57–66. ACM (2010)
22. Jia, Y.: Milu (2012), http://www0.cs.ucl.ac.uk/staff/Y.Jia/Milu/
23. Holzleitner, J.: Using feedback to improve black box fuzz testing of SAT solvers. Master's thesis, Johannes Kepler University Linz (2009)

A Metric for Testing
Program Verification Systems*

Bernhard Beckert[1], Thorsten Bormer[1], and Markus Wagner[2]

[1] Department of Informatics, Karlsruhe Institute of Technology
{beckert,bormer}@kit.edu
[2] School of Computer Science, The University of Adelaide
markus.wagner@adelaide.edu.au

Abstract. The correctness of program verification systems is of great importance, and it needs to be checked and demonstrated to users and certification agencies. One of the contributing factors to the correctness of the whole verification system is the correctness of the background axiomatization, respectively the correctness of calculus rules. In this paper, we examine how testing verification systems is able to provide evidence for the correctness of the rule base or the axiomatization. For this, we present a new coverage criterion called axiomatization coverage, which allows us to judge the quality of existing test suites for verification systems. We evaluate this coverage criterion at two verification tools using the test suites provided by each tool.

1 Introduction

Motivation. Correctness of program verification systems is imperative if they are to be used in practice. One may employ formal methods to prove a system or its calculus to be correct. But—as for any other type of software system—testing is of great importance.

In this paper, we bring together proofs and tests not as a combination of both used on a program to be validated, but rather to increase software quality by improving conclusiveness of the verification tool itself. Traditional testing techniques alone are insufficient for this purpose—the typical properties and particularities of program verification systems have to be taken into consideration when designing test suites. It is relevant, for example, that verification systems usually do not just consist of an implementation in an imperative programming language but also include axioms and rules written in a declarative language.

The testing process employed must be systematic and the quality of test suites has to be evaluated. Objective criteria, such as coverage measures, are needed to demonstrate the dependability of verification systems to users and certification agencies.

* Work partially funded by the German Federal Ministry of Education and Research (BMBF) in the framework of the Verisoft XT project under grant 01 IS 07 008. The responsibility for this article lies with the authors.

M. Veanes and L. Viganò (Eds.): TAP 2013, LNCS 7942, pp. 56–75, 2013.

Topic and Structure of this Paper. In this paper, we present a new coverage criterion for testing program verification systems, called axiomatization coverage. We conducted experiments on two verification tools that measure axiomatization coverage of existing test suites, in order to assess the significance of the proposed coverage metric. Our focus is on system tests (as opposed to testing components of the tools); and we test for functional correctness (not usability etc.). Moreover, we only consider tests that can be executed automatically.

The structure of this paper is as follows: First, in Section 2, we clarify what verification systems we consider and discuss their relevant properties. Section 3 is concerned with the test cases we use and the general set-up for testing. In Section 4, we examine the different correctness properties for which we test and explain which kinds of tests relate to what properties. In Section 5, we define a new notion of test coverage for the declarative (axiomatic) part of verification systems. We report on two case studies in Section 6, in which we have evaluated the new test coverage criterion using test suites for two verification systems. Then, in Section 7, we put our work into the context of related work. Finally, in Section 8, we draw conclusions and discuss future work.

2 Target of Evaluation: Program Verification Systems

Modern Program Verification Tools. Every program verification system has to perform (at least) two rather separate tasks: (a) handling the program-language-specific and specification-language-specific constructs, and reducing or transforming them to logical expressions, (b) theory reasoning and reasoning in logics, for handling the resulting expressions and statements over data types. One can either handle these tasks in one monolithic logic/system, or one can use a combination of subsystems.

In this paper, we concentrate on a paradigm of user interaction with the verification tool termed *auto-active verification*, which is used by tools such as VCC [9], or the Jessie plug-in of Frama-C [16] (if automatic provers are used as backend). In auto-active verification, the requirement specification, together with all relevant information to find a proof (e.g., loop invariants) is given to the verification tool right from the start of the verification process—interaction hereafter is not possible.

Both tools mentioned above use several subsystems. A more monolithic approach is taken by the Java Card verification tool KeY [6]; in addition, in KeY, user interaction is possible also during the proof construction stage. In many cases however, KeY can be used in an auto-active manner without relying on user input during proof construction. For the rest of the paper, we restrict all test cases to be provable without interaction. This allows us to treat VCC and KeY in the same way.

Imperative Versus Declarative System Components. Program verification tools have to capture the program language semantics of the programs to be verified. In some tools this information is mostly stored as one huge axiomatization (as, e.g., with logical frameworks like Isabelle/HOL) and the implementation part can be kept relatively small. Other tools (e.g., some static checkers) implicitly contain most of the programming language semantics in their implementation.

To assure the correctness of program verification tools, it is necessary to validate both parts: the implementation, as well as the axiomatization. Only testing the implementation is not sufficient, even if a high code coverage is achieved.

3   Test Cases for Program Verification Systems

As said above, the tests we consider in this paper are system tests, i.e., the verification tool is tested as a whole. Though the correctness of a tool, of course, depends on the correctness of its components and it makes sense to also test these components independently, such unit tests cannot replace testing the integrated verification system. Moreover, not all components are easy to test individually. For example, it is possible (and useful) to unit-test an SMT solver that is used as part of a verification system. But the verification condition generator is hard to test separately as it is very difficult to specify its correct behavior—more difficult, in fact, than specifying the correct behavior of the verification system as a whole. Also, we concentrate on functional tests that can be executed automatically, i.e., usability tests and user-interface properties are not considered.

As is typical for verification tools following the auto-active verification paradigm, we assume that a verification problem consists of a program to be verified and a requirement specification that is added in form of annotations to the program. Which annotations are *compatible* with a program, i.e., which annotation types exist and in which program contexts a particular annotation is allowed, depends on the given annotation language.

If P is a program and A is a set of annotations compatible with P, then we call the pair $P+A$.

Definition 1 (Annotation satisfaction). *We assume that there is a definition of when a program P satisfies a set SPEC of annotations, denoted by* $\models P+SPEC$.

Besides the requirement specification, a verification problem usually contains additional auxiliary annotations that help the system in finding a proof. We assume that all other auxiliary input (e.g., loop invariants) are made part of the testing input, such that the test can be executed automatically.

The possible outcomes of running a verification system on some test case $P+(REQ \cup AUX)$, i.e., a verification problem consisting of a program P, a requirement specification REQ, and auxiliary annotations AUX, are:

proved: The system finds a proof, showing that P satisfies $REQ \cup AUX$.
not provable: The system is able to show that there is no proof (either P does not satisfy REQ or AUX is not sufficient); the system may provide additional information on why no proof exists, e.g., by a counterexample or by showing the current proof state.

timeout: No proof could be found given the allotted resources (time and space).

In order to evaluate the obtained results of a test run, we require for the case studies presented in Sect. 6 that the expected outcome of each test case is provided by the author of the test case.

4   Testing Different Properties

Testing a verification system can exhibit various kinds of failures related to different correctness properties. A verification system can be unsound, i.e., verify an incorrect program to be correct. There can be completeness failures, where the system fails to find a proof for the correctness of a program. There also can be performance failures, where the system's performance is too low either in terms of resource consumption or in terms of the amount and complexity of auxiliary input the user has to provide to be able to prove a program correct. And, of course, the system may crash. While abnormal termination of software is usually a serious concern, a bug that makes the verification system crash is in general less serious than a completeness failure because it cannot be confused with bugs in the program to be verified (the verification target).

How one can test for different kinds of failures, and thus, correctness properties, is discussed in the following subsections. Table 1 summarizes the different test results and the failures they indicate.[1]

Table 1. The different test results and the failures they indicate

Observed	Intended		
	proved	not provable	timeout
proved	—	unsoundness	unsoundness or positive performance anomaly
not provable	incompleteness or performance failure w.r.t. required annotations	—	incompleteness or positive performance anomaly
timeout	incompleteness or performance failure w.r.t. required annotations or resources	unsoundness or performance failure w.r.t. resources	—

---

[1] The possibility of abnormal termination exists in all cases and is not included in the table.

4.1   Testing Soundness

The most important property of verification tools is soundness. This means that whenever the output for a verification problem $P+SPEC$ is "proved", then the program P indeed satisfies the specification $SPEC$.

To reveal a soundness bug, a test case must consist of a program P and a specification $SPEC$ such that P does *not* satisfy $SPEC$. The correct answer for such a verification problem is "not provable" or "timeout", while "provable" indicates a soundness failure.

Programs that satisfy their specification cannot reveal soundness bugs—at least not directly. The exception are cases where the expected answer is "time-out" but the system answers "proved". Such an anomaly—that needs to be investigated by the developer—can either stem from an unexpected good performance or from a short but incorrect proof (i.e., a soundness problem).

4.2   Testing Completeness

As all sound verification systems must be incomplete (Rice's theorem), sound and complete software verification tools cannot exist. Instead the notion of *relative completeness* is used, i.e., completeness in the sense that the system (respectively its calculus) would be complete if it had an oracle for the validity of formulas over arithmetics [10].

In practice, however, all of today's program verification systems are not even relatively complete. This is not only due to resource limitations. Verification systems presuppose auxiliary annotations or other user input. Auto-active verification tools do not attempt to generate all missing auxiliary annotations. Such an "annotation generator" would give auto-active verification systems the (theoretical) property of being relatively complete but would be useless in practice (although in theory it can be built). Thus, it is neither given nor expected that a program verification system is relatively complete. In practice, completeness of verification tool means that if the program is correct w.r.t. its *given* requirement specification REQ, then some auxiliary specification AUX or other required user input *exists* allowing to prove this [5].

Definition 2 (Annotation completeness). *A verification system S is* annotation complete *if for each program P and specification REQ with*

$$\models P+REQ \ ,$$

there is a set AUX of annotations such that

$$\vdash_S P+(REQ \cup AUX) \ ,$$

i.e., S finds a proof for $\models P+(REQ \cup AUX)$.

To reveal a completeness problem, a test case must consist of a program P with annotations $REQ \cup AUX$ such that (a) P satisfies $REQ \cup AUX$ and (b) the annotations are strong enough to prove this, i.e., the expected output is "proved".

If the observed output is "not provable", then a completeness failure is revealed. In that case, a proof may exist using a different (stronger) set AUX' of auxiliary annotations. That is, the system may or may not be annotation complete. The failed test only shows that the expectation that a proof can be found using the annotation set AUX does not hold. The situation is similar with an observed output "timeout". In that case, the system may just be slower than expected or, worse, there may be no proof using AUX or, worst of all, there may be no proof at all for any annotation set AUX'. For both kinds of incorrect output ("not provable" and "timeout") the developer has to further investigate what kind of failure occurred.

One may consider incompleteness of a verification tool to be harmless in the sense that it is noticeable: the user does not achieve the desired goal of constructing a proof and thus knows that something is wrong. In practice, however, completeness bugs can be very annoying, difficult to detect, and time-consuming. A user may look for errors in the program to be verified or blame the annotation AUX when no proof is found for a correct program and try to improve AUX, while in fact nothing is wrong with it. It is therefore very important to systematically test for completeness bugs.

5   A New Coverage Criterion: Axiomatization Coverage

Measuring code coverage is an important method in software testing to judge the quality of a test suite. This is also true for testing verification tools. However, code coverage is not an indicator for how well the declarative logical axioms and definitions are tested that define the semantics of programs and specifications and make up an important part of the system.

To solve this problem, we define the notion of axiomatization coverage. It measures to which extent a test suite exercises the axioms used in a verification system. The idea is to compute the percentage of axioms that are actually used in the proofs or proof attempts for the verification problems that make up a test suite. We distinguish two versions: (a) the percentage of axioms needed to successfully verify correct programs (completeness coverage), and (b) the percentage of axioms used in failed proof attempts for programs not satisfying their specification (soundness coverage).

An erroneous axiom may lead to unsoundness or incompleteness or both. The latter effect, where something incorrect can be derived and something correct cannot, is actually quite frequent. Because of that, completeness tests can reveal soundness bugs and vice versa. Nevertheless, one should use both kinds of tests (soundness and completeness) and, thus, both kinds of coverage.

For the remainder of this paper, especially in the two case studies, we concentrate on the completeness version of axiomatization coverage. If not explicitly stated otherwise, "coverage" will stand for "completeness coverage" in the following.

5.1   Completeness Coverage

For the completeness version of axiomatization coverage, we define an axiom to be *needed* to verify a program, if it is an element of a minimal axiom subset using which the verification system is able to find a proof. That is, if the axiom is removed from the subset, the verifier is not able anymore to prove the correctness of the program.

Definition 3. *A test case* $P+(REQ \cup AUX)$ *covers the axioms in a set Th if* $Th \vdash P+(REQ \cup AUX)$ *but* $Th' \nvdash P+(REQ \cup AUX)$ *for all* $Th' \subsetneq Th$.

According to this definition, not all axioms used in a successful proof for a test case are covered by that test. Some axioms may be redundant, i.e., they (a) can be replaced by (a combination of) other axioms used in the same proof, or (b) do not contribute to the proof because they were applied in "dead ends" of the proof search. For case (b), we argue that it is unlikely that the test case makes a relevant statement about the correctness of the axiom (other than that the axiom does not lead to inconsistencies in this proof). For case (a), we expect that there are different use cases in which to apply one or the other set of axioms and thus there should be test cases able to cover one specific set.

   If we consider particular verification systems with a fixed axiomatization, we can define an axiom to be *strongly* covered, if it is needed in all proofs of the test case that the verification system is able to find using the given axiomatization.

Definition 4. *A test case* $P+(REQ \cup AUX)$ *strongly* covers the axioms in a set Th w.r.t. an axiomatization Ax, if $Th \subseteq Th'$ for all sets $Th' \subseteq Ax$ such that $P+(REQ \cup AUX)$ covers Th'.

Our notion of completeness coverage is rather coarse in that it does not take the structure of the covered axioms (resp. the inference rules in case of the KeY system) into account. One obvious improvement would be to examine in the coverage analysis which part of an axiom is actually needed in a proof—e.g., in case of an implication $A_1 \vee \ldots \vee A_n \to B_1 \wedge \ldots \wedge B_m$, which A_k establishes the premiss and which of the B_k of the conclusion are actually needed further in the proof. Precise definitions of more fine-grained coverage metrics and their evaluation is part of future work.

   Ideally, the coverage definitions would use logical entailment instead of inference. However, as we want to quantify axiom coverage in practice and verification tools are inherently incomplete, the coverage metric is based on the inference relation.

   As a consequence, the axiom coverage of a test suite w.r.t. a system depends on resource constraints (e.g., number of proof steps allowed, timeout or memory limitations) and the implementation of the verification system, most notably the proof search strategy. This implies that when calculating axiom coverage, to get reproducible results, performance of the computer that the verification tool runs on has to be taken into account. In addition, axiom coverage of a test suite has to be recomputed not only when the axiomatization or test suite changes but also whenever parts of the implementation of the verification tool relevant for proof search are modified.

In general, the minimal set of axioms covered by a given verification problem is not unique. So, the question arises of what to do if a test case covers several different axiom sets.

We chose to follow the more conservative approach to consider only one (non-deterministically chosen) axiom set to be covered by any given test case. A pragmatic reason for that choice is that it is very costly to compute all minimal axiom sets covered by a test case. But our conservative choice has another important advantage: If, for example, there is a logically redundant axiom A' that is an instance of some other axiom A, and there are verification problems that can be solved either using the more general axiom A or the more special A', then there are test cases that cover A and A' separately but not at the same time. We will count only one of A and A' to be covered by such a single test case. Now there are two situations to consider: (1) A' is included in the axiom set for good reason as it leads to better performance (shorter proofs) for a certain class of problems. Then there should be a test case in the test suite that can only be proved using A'. This test should have sufficiently low resource bounds so that it cannot be verified using A, and thus demonstrates the usefulness of A'. And there should be a different test case that does not fall in the special class to which A' applies and that can only be solved using A. Then, with the two test cases, both A and A' are covered. (2) A' is really redundant, i.e., it is not possible to construct a test case that can be verified with A' but not with A. Then A' is indeed akin to dead code (which also cannot be covered by test cases) and should be removed.

The way in which we compute the axioms covered by a test case ensures that the non-deterministic choice of the covered axioms is done in a useful way in case there is more than one possibility (see Sect. 6).

5.2   Soundness Coverage

For the soundness version of axiomatization coverage, the above definition of *needed axioms* based on minimal axiom sets is not useful. Instead, an axiom is *used* in a failed proof attempt, if it occurs in the proof search, i.e., the verification system actively used the axiom for proof construction. What "used" means depends on the particular verification system and its calculus.

6   Case Studies

To evaluate the usefulness of our notion of the completeness version of axiomatization coverage, we conducted two case studies. As verification systems to be tested, we chose the VCC tool, as well as the KeY system. For both tools, we chose to evaluate the test suite that is part of the corresponding distribution. In addition, for the KeY tool, we examined a third-party test suite.

Computing Axiomatization Coverage in Practice. We have implemented a framework for the automated execution and evaluation of tests for both tools that computes the completeness version of axiomatization coverage.

To compute an approximation of the axiomatization coverage for a completeness test case $P+SPEC$, the procedure is as follows: in a first step, $P+SPEC$ is verified with the verification tool using the complete axiom base available. Besides gathering information on resource consumption of this proof attempt (e.g., number of proof steps resp. time needed), information on which axioms are actually used in the proof are recorded as set T (e.g., by leveraging Z3's option to generate unsatisfiability cores in case of VCC[2], resp. parsing KeY's explicit proof object). This set T is a first approximation of the completeness coverage of the test case but has to be narrowed down in a subsequent step to yield the actual axiomatization coverage.

For this, in a reduction step, we start from the empty set C of covered axioms. For each axiom t in the set of axioms T used in the first proof run, an attempt to prove $P+SPEC$ using axioms $C \cup (T \setminus \{t\})$ is made. If the proof does not succeed, t is added to set C. Axiom t is removed from T and the next proof iteration starts until $T = \varnothing$.

In all these subsequent proof runs, resource constraints are set to twice the amount of resources needed for the first proof run recorded initially. This allows us to calculate axiom coverage in reasonable time and ensures comparability of coverage measures between computers of different processing power.

The resulting set of axioms C is only an approximation of the coverage of $P+SPEC$. For precise results the above procedure would have to be repeated with C as input as long as the result is different from the input. For practical reasons we compute axiomatization coverage using only one iteration for the following case studies.

Note that it currently takes several minutes to compute the minimal axiom set for an average test case. This is acceptable if the coverage is not computed too often, but a considerable speed-up should be possible using heuristics for choosing the axioms to remove from the set. Divide and conquer algorithms, e.g., akin to binary search, seem to be suited to reduce computation times at first glance. However, they do not help in practice: as the reduction step does not start from the whole axiomatization but rather from the subset T of axioms actually used in a proof, only relatively few axioms remain that are *not* covered and can be discarded in the iterative proof runs. For divide and conquer algorithms to be successful, large sets of axioms which could be discarded at once are needed.

6.1 Testing the Axiomatization of VCC

The Architecture and Workflow of VCC. In the following we give a short overview of the verification workflow and give a description of the architecture of the VCC tool. For a thorough introduction to the VCC methodology, see [9].

---

[2] The coverage experiments in this paper have been produced by an older version of our framework without this feature—however, this only impacts performance of the framework.

Table 2. Coverage measures for the first experiment

earlier version of axiomatization	total	covered	percentage
axioms for C language features	212	84	40%
axioms for specification language features	166	102	61%
all axioms	378	186	49%
later version of axiomatization			
all axioms	384	139	36%

The VCC tool chain allows for modular verification of C programs using method contracts and invariants over data structures. Method contracts are specified by pre- and postconditions. These contracts and invariants are stored as annotations within the source code in a way that is transparent to the regular C compiler. The tool chain translates the annotated C code into first-order logic. Subsequently, the formulas are given to the SMT solver Z3 [17] together with the prelude (the axiomatization) capturing the semantics of C's built-in operators, etc. Z3 checks whether the verification conditions are entailed by the axiomatization. Entailment implies that the original program is correct w.r.t. its specification.

Axiomatization Coverage Results. Using our testing framework, we automatically executed the completeness test cases contained in VCC's test suite and measured both the axiomatization and the code coverage achieved with these tests.

First Experiment. First, we used the test suite shipped with the binary package of VCC version 2.1.20731.0. It consists of 400 test cases, 202 of which are completeness tests. For comparison, we measured axiomatization coverage for two versions of VCC: version 2.1.20731.0, from which the test suite was taken, and version 2.1.20908.0, which is a version about six weeks further into development. The earlier version of the axiomatization contains 378 axioms out of which 186 were covered (49%). A classification of these axioms and the different degrees of coverage for different types of axioms is shown in Table 2.

The later version of the axiomatization contains 384 axioms, of which only 139 were covered (36%), i.e., axiomatization coverage decreased. Investigations revealed that the reason for this decrease is that axioms were modified, e.g., by removing requirements or by adding predicates. Therefore, the old test suite was less adequate to the newer version of VCC.

Second Experiment. In a second experiment, we used VCC version 2.1.30820.1 (one year after the VCC version used in the first experiment), and the accompanying test suite. The examined part of the new test suite that corresponds to the test suite used in the first experiment had been updated and now contains a total of 698 test cases, 417 of which are completeness tests (the rest are soundness tests and tests checking for parser errors). The axiomatization now consists of 439 axioms. Of these 211 were covered by the completeness tests (48%), i.e., axiomatization coverage has increased again to the level of VCC version 2.1.20731.0, due to the updated test suite.

Further, this new version of the test suite contains an additional directory of test cases we did not consider here to be able to compare coverage results with the first experiment. We thus expect even better coverage when taking all tests into consideration.

For this second experiment, we additionally computed the code coverage[3] for the part of VCC that is related to the semantics of the programming and the specification language, i.e., the verification condition generator. Using the same test suite of 417 completeness tests, the resulting code coverage turned out to be 70%. This is an interesting result as it shows that axiomatization coverage (48%) can be quite a bit lower than code coverage (70%). And it is evidence that axiomatization coverage is independent of code coverage. Therefore, axiomatization coverage should indeed be considered in addition to code coverage to judge the quality of a test suite.

Other Insights. Additional investigations showed a further difference between code coverage and axiomatization coverage: The code coverage of *individual* test cases is higher than their axiomatization coverage. Axiomatization coverage can be as low as 1% for some tests, while code coverage is never less than 25%. That is, there is a certain amount of "core code" exercised by all tests, while there are no "core axioms" used by all tests (this may, of course, be different for other verification systems).

Also, the coverage for other elements of the prelude besides axioms, e.g., type declarations, turned out to be much higher than the axiomatization coverage. It was 81% for the first experiment and 72% for the second experiment. It decreased as the new version of the prelude contains declarations related to information-flow analysis, for which no tests have been added to the test suite (yet).

Errors Found in VCC. The main goal of our case study was not to find bugs in VCC but to evaluate the quality of the tests. And it was to be expected that no errors could be detected using VCC's own test suite as those tests, of course, had already been used by the VCC developers for testing.

Using tests from other sources (which had a rather low coverage), we found (only) one completeness failure and no soundness failure. The completeness bug in the axiomatization, which has been fixed in the current version of VCC, related to the ownership model. In some situations it was not possible to prove that some part of the state had not changed after an assignment to a memory location outside that part of the state.

---

[3] Code coverage was computed using the code coverage feature available in Microsoft Visual Studio 2010 Premium.

6.2   Testing the Calculus Rules of KeY

The KeY System. As second target for our case studies we have chosen the KeY[4] tool [6], a verification system for sequential Java Card programs. Similar to VCC, programs can be specified using annotations in the source code. In KeY, the Java Modeling Language (JML) is used to specify properties about Java programs with the common specification constructs like pre- and postconditions for methods and object invariants. Like in other deductive verification tools, the verification task is modularized by proving one Java method at a time.

In the following, we will briefly describe the workflow of the KeY system—in our case, we assume the user has chosen one method to be verified against a single pre-/postcondition pair. First, the relevant parts of the Java program, together with its JML annotations are translated into a sequent in Java Dynamic Logic, a multi-modal predicate logic. Validity of this sequent implies that the program is correct w.r.t. its specification. Proving the validity is done using automatic proof strategies within KeY which apply sequent calculus rules implemented as so-called *taclets*.

The set of taclets provided with KeY plays a similar role as the prelude in case of VCC, as it captures the semantics of Java, built-in abstract data types like sequences etc. In comparison to the prelude of VCC, however, KeY also contains taclets that deal with first order logic formulas, whereas first-order reasoning in VCC is handled by the SMT component Z3.

The development version of KeY as of August 2012, contains about 1500 taclets. However, not all of them are available at a time when performing a proof, as some of the taclets exist in several versions, depending on proof options chosen (e.g., handling integer arithmetic depends on whether integer overflows are to be checked or not).

Automatic proof search is combined with interactive steps of the user, in case a proof is not found automatically. For our purposes, the interactive part of KeY is irrelevant, as we restrict test cases to those that can be proven automatically—otherwise, finding a minimal set of taclets needed to prove a program correct is infeasible.

Results of a verification attempt in KeY are also similar to those in VCC: either the generated Java Card DL formula is valid and KeY is able to prove it; or the generated formula is not valid and the proof cannot be closed; or KeY runs out of resources.

Axiomatization Coverage Results. Using a modified version of our testing framework, we automatically executed the test cases contained in KeY's test suite, as well as parts of a custom Java compiler test suite and measured the taclet completeness coverage.

The procedure used here is similar to reducing VCC's axiomatization. However, the set of taclets to start from is directly taken from the explicit proof object that KeY maintains and that is used to save and load (partial) proofs.

---

[4] See http://www.key-project.org

This object stores sufficient information about each taclet application in the sequent calculus proof, such that the proof can be reconstructed by KeY without performing proof search. These taclet applications recorded normally contain a lot more taclets than are actually relevant for finding the proof. Thus, we reduce the set of taclets used in the proof construction one by one in a second step in the same manner as for VCC.

Third Experiment. In this experiment we used the development version of the KeY tool[5] as of August 16, 2012. As part of the KeY source distribution, a test suite is provided containing 335 test cases of which 327 are completeness and 8 are soundness tests. The complexity of the proof obligations ranges from simple arithmetic problems to small Java programs testing single features of Java, up to more complex programs and properties taken from recent software verification competitions.

From the 327 completeness tests of the KeY test suite, we computed the taclet completeness coverage of 319 test cases testing verification of functional properties—another eight test cases are concerned with the verification of information-flow properties and were omitted due to resource constraints. The test runs were distributed on multiple computers using Amazon's Elastic Compute Cloud service, taking approx. 135 EC2 Compute Unit[6] hours to complete in total.

The overall taclet coverage we computed for the 319 completeness tests was 38% (with 585 out of 1527 taclets covered). Figure 2 shows a histogram of the number of test cases each taclet is covered by. The overall coverage seems to be comparable to the coverage results gained from the VCC test suite. However, in contrast to VCC, KeY also performs first-order reasoning with the help of taclets instead of using an SMT solver—for better comparison with VCC, all such taclets would have to be excluded from coverage computation.

While some features of Java or JML are not covered at all by the current test suite of KeY, for other taclets, low coverage might result from:

(a) the fact that some taclets have been introduced just recently, for a particular use case (e.g., taclets enabling automatic induction proofs in certain cases) and no test cases have been written yet,

(b) redundant taclets that are used to shorten the proof (e.g., the KeY taclet replacing "$F \rightarrow$ true" by "true" for any FOL formula F is made redundant by the taclet replacing implication by its definition, together with the taclet rewriting the result "$\neg F \vee$ true" to "true". This is one example for a taclet used but *not* covered in a proof.) and

(c) obsolete taclets that are still contained in the rule base.

Measures to handle cases (b) and (c) have already been discussed in Sect. 5.1. For case (a), a review and testing process has to ensure that the axiomatization coverage for newly introduced taclets is increased by writing specific test cases.

---

[5] Available at http://i12www.ira.uka.de/~bubel/nightly/

[6] According to Amazon's EC2 documentation, "One EC2 Compute Unit provides the equivalent CPU capacity of a 1.0-1.2 GHz 2007 Opteron or 2007 Xeon processor."

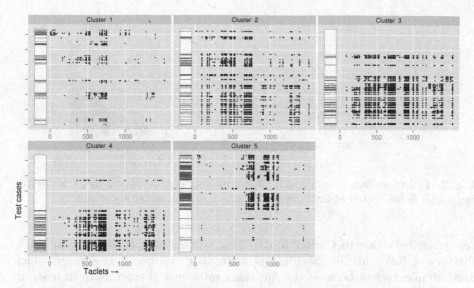

Fig. 1. Groups of similar KeY test cases in terms of taclet coverage. Each point in the diagram indicates a taclet covered by a test case. Clusters are computed by hierarchical clustering using Ward's method and Jaccard distance as measure for dissimilarity between taclet coverage of two test cases. The x-axis shows taclets sorted by group, the y-axis shows test cases sorted by directory. If a test case is contained in a cluster, this is indicated by a red line in the box on the left.

In order to perform a more detailed analysis, coverage results were examined by groups of taclets respectively test cases. For grouping taclets, we used the already existing structure given by the organization of taclets in different files in the KeY distribution—similar taclets (e.g., taclets handling Java language features or taclets for propositional logic) are contained together in one file.

Histograms of the number of test cases a taclet is covered by, split by taclet group, already allowed us to compare the quality of the test suite w.r.t. the different groups: not surprisingly, taclets handling propositional logic or Java heap properties are covered quite often (in both groups over 60% of taclets are covered at least in one test case). On the other end of the spectrum, we were able to locate underrepresented taclet groups, e.g., relevant for Java assertions or the bigint primitive type of JML (with coverage of each group below 10%). This coarse classification already allows us to focus the effort of writing new test cases on constructing specific tests for rarely covered taclet groups.

In order to group similar test cases together to identify commonalities, we used the R environment for statistical computing [19] to cluster test cases. The result of this clustering is shown in Fig. 1.

Two of these test case clusters are notably representative for different types of test cases: while the tests in Cluster 5 mostly encompass a small set of related taclets, tests in Cluster 3 span almost the entire taclet base of KeY. Indeed,

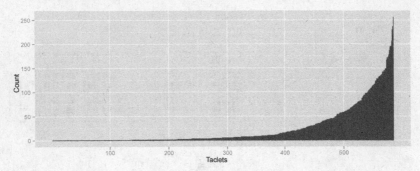

Fig. 2. Taclet coverage counts (y-axis shows number of test cases a taclet is covered by; x-axis shows taclets at least covered by one test case, sorted by y values)

test cases belonging to Cluster 5 have been written as specific tests for single features of KeY—in this case, integer arithmetic and handling strings (which need similar taclets because the functions retrieving characters from a string or getting substrings use integers; the small group of taclets in the upper left corner of Cluster 5 are the taclets handling strings). Test cases corresponding to Cluster 3 are mostly taken from verification competitions dealing with data structures on the heap like linked lists.

We believe that a good test suite for a verification system needs both of these types of test cases *for each taclet*. The need for broader test cases, covering several combinations of taclets, is supported by studies (e.g. [14]) which show that software failures in a variety of domains are often caused by combinations of several conditions. Specialized test cases, in comparison, might simplify testing different aspects of one taclet by being able to better control the context in the proof a taclet will presumably be applied in. As a measure for this, we define the *selectivity* of a test case as the number of taclets covered by the test.

The current state of the KeY test suite w.r.t. this selectivity criterion is shown in Fig. 3. For each taclet, the average selectivity of all test cases covering this taclet is shown, together with the population standard deviation from the average. The leftmost taclets in this diagram are good candidates for which additional test cases might be needed, as they are only covered by specialized test cases. Also taclets with a high selectivity average of the corresponding test cases but low deviation indicate need for improvements, as only broad test cases cover the taclets.

Fourth Experiment. The last experiment we conducted used parts of the test suite of the Java2Jinja[7] compiler [15] in order to increase taclet coverage compared to KeY's own test suite.

The part of Java2Jinja's test suite we considered here is hand-written and consists mostly of small Java programs testing few Java features at a time, often dealing with corner cases of the Java semantics. All tests are run by providing

---

[7] See http://pp.info.uni-karlsruhe.de/projects/quis-custodiet/Java2Jinja

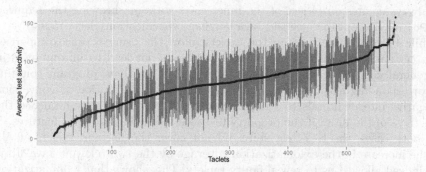

Fig. 3. Average test case selectivity by taclet. Black points: average selectivity (see Sec. 6.2) of all test cases covering a taclet. Population standard deviation of this value from the average is shown as red bars.

concrete, fixed input parameters to the test's main method. The result of the execution of a test is an output to the console—the expected outcome of the test case is given as annotation in the test file. This annotation can easily be converted into a postcondition suitable to be proven with KeY.

From a total of 43 annotated test cases, 21 were applicable to KeY—most of the other tests included features not yet supported by KeY (e.g., Java generics). Of the 21 suitable tests, 12 were directly provable (two thereof using user interaction), the rest of the proofs exceeded allocated time or memory resources.

One result of the test runs was that the Java2Jinja test suite covered 195 of 1527 taclets, corresponding to 13% taclet coverage. Even this small set of additional test cases covered nine taclets that were not covered by KeY's own test suite.

Errors Found in KeY. As already argued in Sect. 6.1, we could not expect to find soundness bugs using KeY's own test suite. Therefore, we performed the last experiment using Java2Jinja's test cases—resulting in two bugs found in the rule base of KeY.

The first bug we discovered is related to implicit conversion of integer literals to strings in Java: in case a negative integer literal is converted to its string representation, the minus sign is placed at the last instead of first position in the resulting string. The Java2Jinja test case that revealed this bug has not been written to test exactly this conversion feature but rather the correct handling of precedences in integer arithmetic. To write an additional test case for this exact feature that increases axiomatization coverage is easy, as exactly one taclet is involved in the bug and the condition under which this taclet is applicable is clearly visible to the user.

The second bug found in the taclets of KeY deals with the creation of inner member classes, using a qualified class instance creation expression. However, the corresponding taclet in KeY that symbolically executes this instance creation expression does not check whether the qualifying expression is null and always creates an object of the inner class without throwing the required `NullPointerException` (see the Java language specification, Sect. 15.9.4).

While both of these bugs in the taclets allow the user to prove properties about certain programs that do not hold, they do not lead to unsoundness in the general case: both bugs are only triggered if the Java program contains the corresponding features (i.e., qualified class instance creation or conversion of negative integer literals to string). In addition, the bugs only influence the correctness of the proof if the property to be verified relies on those features.

In both cases, the KeY test suite did not cover the relevant taclets at all, and the increase in the axiomatization coverage by the two relevant Java2Jinja tests indeed allowed us to reveal faulty taclets. This shows that axiomatization coverage is a useful metric to get a first hint to parts of the axiomatization that may be target for further inspection and validation measures.

7   Related Work

In principle, instead of or in addition to testing, parts of verification tools (in particular the axiomatization and the calculus) can be formally verified. For example, the Bali project [18], the LOOP project [12], and the Mobius project [4], all aimed at the development of fully verified verification systems. Calculus rules of the KeY verification system [6] for Java were verified using the Maude tool [2].

Verifying a verification system is useful, but it cannot fully replace testing; this is further discussed in [7]. The authors claim that verifying a verification tool involves a huge effort that is, to some extent, better directed to improve other qualities of verification systems relevant in practice (e.g., efficiency of the tool). Also some sort of cross-validation between tools is needed, amongst other reasons, as there is no single, authoritative formal language specification for Java. For this, one option mentioned explicitly in [7] is to use "cross-validation with test programs written by different people."

For the theorem provers and SMT solvers that are components of verification systems, there are established problem libraries that can be used as test suites, such as the SMT-LIB library [3]. Alternatively, the results of SMT solvers can be validated using proof checkers. For example, Z3 proofs can be checked using Isabelle [8]. Another example is the Formally Verified Proof Checker that was implemented in ML and formally verified using HOL88 [20].

An interesting application of conformance testing is the official validation test suite for FIPS C (a dialect of C) [13]. To determine how well this test suite covers all features of the C language, a reference implementation of a C compiler was built such that the implementation modules of the compiler could be associated to parts of the C standard. This allowed to relate code coverage of the reference compiler to coverage of the language standard when compiling the programs of the test suite.

In the case studies presented in this paper, the test cases used for coverage analysis were written by hand—coming up with meaningful test cases in this way is a time consuming process and complementing alternatives are worthwhile.

One option to obtain test cases is to use randomly generated programs with known behavior as a basis for comparing the outcome of the tool under test with the expected behavior of the generated program [11]. In order to test parts of Frama-C, the tool Csmith [21] was used to generate random C programs. These C programs output a checksum of their global variables, allowing to compare execution of the program compiled with a reference compiler to analysis results obtained with Frama-C.

Another approach to identify erroneous axioms in an axiomatization is to use model-based testing [1]. In order to test a first-order logic axiom, the user provides an interpretation of the functions and predicates used in the axiom by giving for each a Haskell implementation. The axiom to be tested is then translated into an executable Haskell function (using the user-provided interpretation of functions and predicates). This function is then tested to be true for a set of generated test inputs with the help of a standard Haskell testing framework.

8 Conclusions and Future Work

In this paper, we introduced axiomatization coverage as a new coverage criterion in testing verification systems. We conducted case studies at two verification systems to evaluate the completeness version of the axiomatization coverage of test suites supplied with the corresponding tools—in both cases (not surprisingly) showing a rather low axiomatization coverage.

Already this coarse coverage criterion can be used as a first measure to judge and improve the quality of these existing test suites. Further coverage statistics, like the test case selectivity, may be used additionally to identify axioms that are underrepresented in the test suite. Also clustering test cases similar in their axiomatization coverage may hint at which kind of additional test cases are still missing (e.g., large and complex programs using many program language and specification language features at once; or rather small, specific test cases covering few and similar axioms).

To evaluate the usefulness of our completeness version of axiomatization coverage, in a first step, we tried to increase coverage by additional test cases to uncover erroneous axioms. For this, we used parts of the Java2Jinja test suite to test the KeY verification tool, which revealed two bugs in KeY's rule base.

For the future, we plan to conduct additional case studies to further evaluate our coverage criteria and, in particular, to investigate which kind of tests uncover what kind and what number of errors. Additional test suites not written by tool developers themselves are required though to get useful statistics about bug occurrences.

We plan to investigate the reasons why some axioms are not covered, amongst others, using the help of developers of the verification systems. Afterwards, an experiment is planned to be conducted where we systematically write specific test cases aimed to increase the axiomatization coverage for relevant axioms of the existing test suites. If our assumption that axiomatization coverage is a useful measure is right, we should be able to find further bugs with these tests.

Further, we plan to use combinatorial testing, where combinations of language features and axioms are used in test cases, as well as more fine-grained axiomatization coverage criteria, in contrast to the notion of entire axioms as smallest coverage unit presented in this paper.

Acknowledgements. We thank Andreas Lochbihler, Jonas Thedering and Antonio Zea for providing the Java2Jinja test cases.

References

1. Ahn, K.Y., Denney, E.: Testing first-order logic axioms in program verification. In: Fraser, G., Gargantini, A. (eds.) TAP 2010. LNCS, vol. 6143, pp. 22–37. Springer, Heidelberg (2010)
2. Ahrendt, W., Roth, A., Sasse, R.: Automatic validation of transformation rules for Java verification against a rewriting semantics. In: Sutcliffe, G., Voronkov, A. (eds.) LPAR 2005. LNCS (LNAI), vol. 3835, pp. 412–426. Springer, Heidelberg (2005)
3. Barrett, C., Ranise, S., Stump, A., Tinelli, C.: The satisfiability modulo theories library (SMT-LIB), http://www.smt-lib.org/
4. Barthe, G., et al.: MOBIUS: Mobility, Ubiquity, Security. In: Montanari, U., Sannella, D., Bruni, R. (eds.) TGC 2006. LNCS, vol. 4661, pp. 10–29. Springer, Heidelberg (2007), http://dx.doi.org/10.1007/978-3-540-75336-0_2
5. Beckert, B., Bormer, T., Klebanov, V.: Improving the usability of specification languages and methods for annotation-based verification. In: Aichernig, B.K., de Boer, F.S., Bonsangue, M.M. (eds.) FMCO 2010. LNCS, vol. 6957, pp. 61–79. Springer, Heidelberg (2011)
6. Beckert, B., Hähnle, R., Schmitt, P.H. (eds.): Verification of Object-Oriented Software. LNCS (LNAI), vol. 4334. Springer, Heidelberg (2007)
7. Beckert, B., Klebanov, V.: Must program verification systems and calculi be verified? In: 3rd International Verification Workshop (VERIFY), Workshop at Federated Logic Conferences (FLoC), pp. 34–41 (2006)
8. Böhme, S.: Proof reconstruction for Z3 in Isabelle/HOL. In: 7th International Workshop on Satisfiability Modulo Theories, SMT 2009 (2009)
9. Cohen, E., Dahlweid, M., Hillebrand, M., Leinenbach, D., Moskal, M., Santen, T., Schulte, W., Tobies, S.: VCC: A practical system for verifying concurrent C. In: Berghofer, S., Nipkow, T., Urban, C., Wenzel, M. (eds.) TPHOLs 2009. LNCS, vol. 5674, pp. 23–42. Springer, Heidelberg (2009)
10. Cook, S.A.: Soundness and completeness of an axiom system for program verification. SIAM Journal of Computing 7(1), 70–90 (1978)
11. Cuoq, P., Monate, B., Pacalet, A., Prevosto, V., Regehr, J., Yakobowski, B., Yang, X.: Testing static analyzers with randomly generated programs. In: Goodloe, A.E., Person, S. (eds.) NFM 2012. LNCS, vol. 7226, pp. 120–125. Springer, Heidelberg (2012), http://dx.doi.org/10.1007/978-3-642-28891-3_12
12. Jacobs, B., Poll, E.: Java program verification at Nijmegen: Developments and perspective. In: Futatsugi, K., Mizoguchi, F., Yonezaki, N. (eds.) ISSS 2003. LNCS, vol. 3233, pp. 134–153. Springer, Heidelberg (2004)
13. Jones, D.: Who guards the guardians? (February 1997), http://www.knosof.co.uk/whoguard.html

14. Kuhn, D.R., Wallace, D.R., Gallo, A.M.: Software fault interactions and impli-
    cations for software testing. IEEE Transactions on Software Engineering 30(6),
    418–421 (2004)
15. Lochbihler, A.: A Machine-Checked, Type-Safe Model of Java Concurrency: Lan-
    guage, Virtual Machine, Memory Model, and Verified Compiler. Ph.D. thesis, Karl-
    sruher Institut für Technologie, Fakultät für Informatik (July 2012),
    http://digbib.ubka.uni-karlsruhe.de/volltexte/1000028867
16. Marché, C., Moy, Y.: The Jessie plugin for Deductive Verification in Frama-C—
    Tutorial and Reference Manual (2013), http://krakatoa.lri.fr/jessie.pdf
17. de Moura, L., Bjørner, N.: Z3: An efficient SMT solver. In: Ramakrishnan, C.R.,
    Rehof, J. (eds.) TACAS 2008. LNCS, vol. 4963, pp. 337–340. Springer, Heidelberg
    (2008)
18. von Oheimb, D.: Hoare logic for Java in Isabelle/HOL. Concurrency and Compu-
    tation Practice and Experience 13(13), 1173–1214 (2001)
19. R Core Team: R: A Language and Environment for Statistical Computing. R Foun-
    dation for Statistical Computing, Vienna, Austria (2012),
    http://www.R-project.org
20. von Wright, J.: The formal verification of a proof checker, SRI internal report
    (1994)
21. Yang, X., Chen, Y., Eide, E., Regehr, J.: Finding and understanding bugs in C
    compilers. In: Hall, M.W., Padua, D.A. (eds.) PLDI, pp. 283–294. ACM (2011)

Test Program Generation for a Microprocessor
A Case-Study

Achim D. Brucker[1], Abderrahmane Feliachi[2], Yakoub Nemouchi[2],
and Burkhart Wolff[2]

[1] SAP AG, Vincenz-Priessnitz-Str. 1, 76131 Karlsruhe, Germany
achim.brucker@sap.com
[2] Univ. Paris-Sud, Laboratoire LRI, UMR8623, Orsay, F-91405, France
CNRS, Orsay, F-91405, France
{feliachi,nemouchi,wolff}@lri.fr

Abstract. Certifications of critical security or safety system properties
are becoming increasingly important for a wide range of products. Certi-
fying large systems like operating systems up to Common Criteria EAL
4 is common practice today, and higher certification levels are at the
brink of becoming reality.

To reach EAL 7 one has to formally verify properties on the specification as well as test the implementation thoroughly. This includes tests
of the used hardware platform underlying a proof architecture to be cer-
tified. In this paper, we address the latter problem: we present a case
study that uses a formal model of a microprocessor and generate test
programs from it. These test programs validate that a microprocessor
implements the specified instruction set correctly.

We built our case study on an existing model that was, together with an
operating system, developed in Isabelle/HOL. We use HOL-TESTGEN, a
model-based testing environment which is an extension of Isabelle/HOL.
We develop several conformance test scenarios, where processor models
were used to synthesize test programs that were run against real hardware
in the loop. Our test case generation approach directly benefits from the
existing models and formal proofs in Isabelle/HOL.

Keywords: test program generation, symbolic test case generations,
black box testing, white box testing, theorem proving, interactive testing.

1 Introduction

Certifications demonstrating that certain security or safety requirements are met
by a system are becoming increasingly important for a wide range of products.
Certifications play an increasing role in industrial applications including operating systems and embedded systems. While the certifications of large systems,
including fully functional operating systems up to Common Criteria EAL 4 are
common practice today, higher-levels involve the use of formal methods and
combined test and proof activities, covering various layers of a system including
soft and hardware-components. To reach EAL7 [8] one has to formally verify
properties on the specification as well as test the implementation thoroughly.

M. Veanes and L. Viganò (Eds.): TAP 2013, LNCS 7942, pp. 76–95, 2013.
© Springer-Verlag Berlin Heidelberg 2013

The certification of systems combining software and hardware, such as modern avionics systems, requires to test microprocessors in the context of the developed system. Thus, an isolated verification (and certification) by the chip manufacturer is not enough. *Test program generation*, i.e., generating test cases in terms of low level programs for the microprocessor under test, is a well-established technique for validating processor designs. As it allows to validate processors on the instruction set or assembly level, it is well suitable for validating commercial off-the-shelf (COTS) processors for which, usually, implementation details are not available. Microprocessor vendors that want to support their customers in certification processes can provide them with the necessary test programs. Such a set of test cases is called a *certification kit* and selling usually manually developed certification kits is a profitable business, as is the case for, e.g., avionics certifications according to DO-178 and DO-245 [16].

We present a case study for the model-based generation of test programs (i.e, the basis for a certification kit) for a realistic model of a RISC processor called VAMP. VAMP is inspired by IBM's G5 architecture. In the Verisoft project (see http://www.verisoft.de), a formal model for both the processor and a small operating system has been developed in Isabelle/HOL. We will adapt and reuse the processor model to generate test cases that can be used to check if a given hardware conforms to the model of the VAMP processor. The presented test scenario is of particular interest for the higher levels of certification processes as imposed by Common Criteria EAL 7. Even if the transition from C programs to the processor models has been completely covered by deductive verification methods as in CompCert [18], certification bodies will require test sets checking the conformance of the underlying processor model to real hardware.

At present, specification-level verification and the development of test sets are usually two distinguished tasks. Moreover, test sets for certification kits are usually developed manually. In contrast, our model-based test case generation approach uses the design model that was already used for the verification task. In particular, we are using HOL-TESTGEN to generate test sequences generated from the VAMP model. As HOL-TESTGEN is built on top of Isabelle/HOL, i.e., test specification are expressed in terms of higher-order logic (HOL), we can directly benefit from the already existing verification models. In fact, the tight integration of a verification and a test environment is a distinguishing feature of HOL-TESTGEN.

2   Background

2.1   The Verified Architecture Microprocessor (VAMP)

The Verified Architecture Microprocessor (VAMP) as well as the micro-kernel VAMOS [10] has been developed and verified in the context of the German research projects Verisoft (http://www.verisoft.de) and VerisoftXT (http://www.verisoftxt.de). The goal in particular of the former project was the pervasive formal verification of computer systems from the application level down to the silicon, i.e., the hardware design.

On the *Application Software Layer*, this includes foundational proofs justifying a verification approach for system-level concurrent programs that are running as user processes on the micro-kernel VAMOS [10]. On the *System Software Layer*, VAMOS provides an infrastructure for memory virtualization, for communication with hardware devices, for process (represented as a sequence of assembly instructions), and for inter-process communication (IPC) via synchronous message passing that need to be verified. On the *Tools Layer*, the correctness of the compiler needs to be verified and, finally, on the *Hardware Layer*, the functional correctness of the hardware design is formally verified.

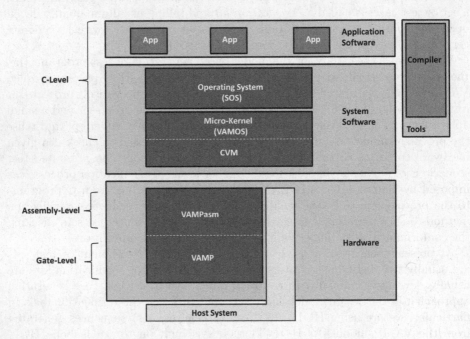

Fig. 1. The Verisoft System Layers

These four layers comprise the Verisoft Architecture (see Figure 1); each of the layers is in itself structured in several sub-layers.

Our work focuses on the hardware layer, more precisely the assembly-level (VAMPasm), i.e., the instruction set of the Verified Architecture MicroProcessor (VAMP) [3]. VAMP is a pipelined reduced instruction set (RISC) processor based on the out-of-order execution principle (see Hennessy and Patterson [15] for details). The VAMPasm (Section 3 presents the formal model we are using in our work) includes 56 instructions: 8 instructions for memory data transfer, 2 instructions for constant data transfer, 2 instructions for register data transfer, 14 instructions for arithmetic and logical operations, 16 instructions for test operations, 6 instructions for shift operations, 6 instructions for control operations as well as 2 instructions for interrupt handling.

In our unit and sequence test scenarios, we generate tests from a formal model of the instruction set, i. e., we test the conformance of the gate level (which corespondents to the implementation in traditional model-based testing) to assembly-level (which corespondents to the model in traditional model-based testing).

2.2   Isabelle/HOL and the HOL-TestGen Framework

Isabelle [20] is a proof assistant based on a kernel ensuring logical correctness. It is highly customizable to a variety of logics, among them first order logic (FOL), Zermelo-Fraenkel set-theory (ZF) and most notably higher-order logic (HOL). The HOL instance is well equipped with a number of components that support for specific specification constructs such as type definitions, (recursive) function definitions involving termination proofs and inductive set definitions. Isabelle is an interactive development environment providing immediate feedback in formal proof attempts and symbolic computations, as well as tools for automatic reasoning such as an term rewriting engine and various decision procedures. Beyond a verification environment, Isabelle can also be understood as a framework for building formal methods tools [24].

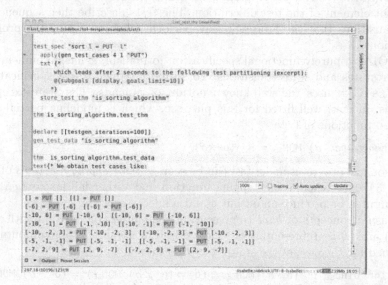

Fig. 2. A HOL-TestGen Session Using the Isabelle/jEdit Front-End

HOL-TestGen [5–7] is such a formal tool built on top of Isabelle/HOL. While Isabelle/HOL is usually seen as "proof assistant," HOL-TestGen (see Figure 2) is used as a document centric modeling environment for the domain specific background theory of a test (the *test theory*), for stating and logically transforming test goals (the *test specifications*), as-well as for the test generation method implemented using Isabelle's tactic procedures. In a nutshell, the test generation method consists of:

1. a *test case generation* phase, which is essentially a process intertwining bounded case-splitting on variables (i.e., applying rules of the form: $x ::$ αlist $= x = [] \wedge \exists al'. x = a \# l'$), simplification with respect to the underlying theory (using, e.g., $|a \# l'| = |l'| + 1$, etc.) and in a CNF-like normal form that leads to partitioning of the input/output relation.
2. a *test data selection* phase, which essentially uses a combination of constraint solvers using random test generation and the integrated SMT-solver Z3 [9] to construct an instance for each partition,
3. a *test execution* phase converts the instantiated test cases ("test oracles") to test driver code that is run against the system under test (SUT).

A detailed account on the symbolic computation performed by the test case generation and test selection procedures is described by Brucker and Wolff [6].

Several approaches for the generation of test cases are possible: while unit-test oriented test generation methods essentially use pre-conditions and post-conditions of system operation specifications, sequence-test oriented approaches essentially use temporal specifications or automata-based specifications of system behavior. In the case of test program generation, the state of the processor is an important element of the test description. The tests describe then sequences of state transitions that the processor may perform when executing the program instructions.

As HOL is a purely functional specification formalism, it has no built-in concepts for states and state transitions. To support sequence test specifications, HOL-TESTGEN uses the well-known notion of monads. The state-exception monad is, in fact, well fitted for this purpose, which is modeling partial state transition functions of type

```
type_synonym (o, σ) MONSE = σ⇀(o ×σ)
```

Using monads, programs under test can be seen as *i/o stepping functions* of type $\iota \Rightarrow (o, \sigma)MON_{SE}$, where each stepping function may either fail for a given state σ and input ι, or produce an output o and a successor state.

The usual concepts of *bind* (representing sequential composition with value passing) and *unit* (representing the embedding of a value into a computation) are defined for the case of the state-exception monad as follows:

```
definition bindSE :: (o, σ) MONSE ⇒(o ⇒(o', σ) MONSE) ⇒(o', σ) MONSE
where bindSE f g = λσ. case f σ of None ⇒ None
                     | Some(out, σ') ⇒g out σ'
```

```
definition unitSE :: o ⇒(o, σ) MONSE
where unitSE e = λσ. Some(e, σ)
```

x ←f; g is written for $\mathrm{bind}_{SE} f(\lambda x.\ g)$ and return for unit_{SE}. On this basis, the concept of a *valid test sequence* (no exception, P yields true for observed output) can be specified as follows:

$$\sigma \models o_1 \leftarrow \mathrm{SUT}\ i_1;\ \ldots;\ o_n \leftarrow \mathrm{SUT}\ i_n;\ \mathrm{return}\ (P\ o_1 \cdots o_n)$$

where $\sigma \models m$ is defined as $(m\ \sigma \neq \mathrm{None} \wedge \mathrm{fst}(m\ \sigma))$. For iterations of i/o stepping functions, an mbind operator can be used, which takes a list of inputs $\iota s = [i_1,\ \ldots,\ i_n]$, feeds it subsequently into SUT and stops when an error occurs. Using mbind, valid test sequences for a program under test SUT satisfying a post-condition P can be reformulated by:

$$\sigma \models os \leftarrow \mathrm{mbind}\ \iota s\ \mathrm{SUT};\ \mathrm{return}(P\ os)$$

which is the HOL-TESTGEN's standard way to represent sequence test specifications. For cases, where a post-condition depends explicitly on the underlying state, we use the state-exception primitive:

definition assert_{SE} :: $(\sigma \Rightarrow \mathrm{bool}) \Rightarrow (o, \sigma)\ \mathrm{MON}_{SE}$
where $\mathrm{assert}_{SE}\ P = (\lambda\sigma.\ \mathrm{if}\ P\ \sigma \mathrm{then}\ \mathrm{Some}(\mathrm{True},\sigma)\ \mathrm{else}\ \mathrm{None})$

instead of return(P).

3   The VAMP Model

The Verified Architecture MicroProcessor (VAMP) [3] is a 32-bit RISC CPU with a DLX-instruction set including floating point instructions, delayed program counter, address translation, and support for maskable nested precise interrupts. The VAMP hardware contains five execution units: the Fixed Point Unit, the Memory Unit, and three Floating Point Units. Instructions have up to six 32-bit source operands and produce up to four 32-bit results. The memory interface [2] of the VAMP consists of two Memory Management Units that access instruction and data caches, which in turn access a physical memory via a bus protocol.

In the context of the Verisoft project, an Isabelle/HOL specification (programmer's model) of the VAMP processor was introduced. The processor consists of a set of transitions defined over the Instruction Set Architecture (ISA) configurations. A configuration is composed of five elements:

1. *Program counter (pcp):* a 30 bit register containing the address of next instruction to be executed, this register is used to fetch an instruction without altering the execution of the current one. This pipelining mechanism is called *delayed pc*.
2. *Delayed program counter (dcp):* a 30 bit register for delayed program counter, containing the currently executed instruction. While the fetch of the next instruction is performed in the *pcp* register, the *dcp* is kept unchanged until the end of the execution of the current instruction.
3. *General purpose registers (gprs):* a register file consisting of 32 registers of 32 bits each. These registers are used in different operations, and can be addressed by their index (0–31). The first register is always set to 0.

4. *Special purpose registers (sprs):* a register file consisting of 32 registers of 32 bits each, used for particular tasks. The first register for instance is the *status* register, containing the interrupts masks. Some registers are used as flags registers or as condition registers. Each special purpose register is addressed directly by its name.
5. *Memory model (mm):* a 2^{32} bytes addressable memory. Different caching and virtual memory infrastructures are implemented in the VAMP system.

The transition relation is defined by the execution of the program instructions defined in the initial configuration. The VAMP implements the full DLX instruction set from Hennessy and Patterson [15]. This set includes load and store operations for double words, words, half words and bytes. It includes also different shift operations, jump-and-link operations and various arithmetic and logical operations.

To avoid the complex and inconvenient bit vector representation of data and instructions, an assembly language was introduced abstracting the VAMP ISA. In this case addresses are represented by natural numbers and registers and memory contents by integers. Our test specifications and experiments are based on this instruction set (assembler) model.

The Isabelle theory of the assembler model is an abstraction of the instruction set architecture. In addition to the representation of addresses as naturals and values as integers, some other ISA features are abstracted. The instructions are represented in an abstract datatype with *readable* names. The address translation is not visible at this level, assembler computations live in linear (virtual) memory space. Interrupts are not visible at this level as well. The assembler configuration is an abstraction of the ISA configuration, defined as a record type with the following fields:

- *pcp:* a natural number representing the program counter,
- *dcp:* a natural number representing the delayed program counter,
- *gprs:* a list of integers representing the general purpose register file,
- *sprs:* a list of integers representing the special purpose register file,
- *mm:* a memory model represented by a mapping from naturals to integers.

The HOL definition of the configuration is given by the ASMcore$_t$ record type. The register file type is defined as a list of integers representing the different registers.

```
type_synonym regcont = int          -- {* contents of register *}
type_synonym registers = regcont list -- {* register file *}

record ASMcoreₜ = dpc  :: nat
                  pcp  :: nat
                  gprs :: registers
                  sprs :: registers
                  mm   :: memₜ
```

Since the assembler representation of addresses and values is less restrictive than the bit vector representation, some conversion functions and restriction predicates were defined to reduce the domain of addresses and values to only meaningful values. This was the case also for the configurations, since the number of registers is not mentioned in the definition of the registers type. The *well-fomedness* of assembler configurations is given by the is_ASMcore predicate. This predicate ensures that register files contain exactly 32 registers each. It also checks that all register and memory cells contain valid values.

```
definition is_ASMcore :: ASMcore_t ⇒bool where
  is_ASMcore st ≡asm_nat (dpc st) ∧
                  asm_nat (pcp st) ∧
                  length (gprs st) = 32 ∧
                  length (sprs st) = 32 ∧
                  (∀ ind < 32. asm_int (reg (gprs st) ind)) ∧
                  (∀ ind < 32. asm_int (sreg (sprs st) ind)) ∧
                  (∀ ad. asm_int (data_mem_read (mm st) ad))
```

The instruction set of the assembler is defined as an abstract datatype instr in Isabelle. All operations mnemonics are used as datatype constructors, associated to their corresponding operands. Different types of instructions can be distinguished: data transfer commands, arithmetic and logical operations, test operations, shift operations, control operations and some basic interrupts.

```
datatype instr =
  -- {* data transfer (memory) *}
   Ilb regname regname immed
 |...
 -- {* data transfer (constant) *}
 | Ilhgi regname immed
 | ...
 -- {* data transfer (registers) *}
 | Imovs2i regname regname
 | ...
 -- {* arithmetic / logical operations *}
 | Iaddio regname regname immed
 | ...
 -- {* test operations *}
 | Iclri regname
 | ...
 -- {* shift operations *}
 | Islli regname regname shift_amount
 | ...
 -- {* control operations *}
 | Ibeqz regname immed
 | ...
 -- {* interrupt *}
 | Itrap immed
 | ...
```

An inductive function is defined over the assembler instructions to provide the semantics of each operation. This function returns for each configuration and instruction, the configuration resulting from executing the instruction in the initial configuration.

```
fun exec_instr :: [ASMcore_t, instr] ⇒ASMcore_t
where
  -- {* Arithmetic Instructions *}
  exec_instr st (Iaddo RD RS1 RS2) =
    arith_exec st int_add (reg (gprs st) RS1)
                (reg (gprs st) RS2) RD
| ...
  -- {* Logical Instructions *}
| exec_instr st (Iand RD RS1 RS2) =
    arith_exec st s_and (reg (gprs st) RS1)
                (reg (gprs st) RS2) RD
| ...
  -- {* Shift Instructions *}
| exec_instr st (Isll RD RS1 RS2) =
    arith_exec st sllog (reg (gprs st) RS1)
                (reg (gprs st) RS2) RD
| ...
```

The transition relation is defined as a function that takes a configuration and returns is successor. The transitions are defined by the execution of the current program instruction given in the delayed program counter.

```
definition Step :: ASMcore_t ⇒ASMcore_t
where    Step st ≡ exec_instr st (current_instr st)
```

These transition relations are used in our study as the basis of test specifications. The assembler model is more abstract than the processor model, consequently, different complex details are made transparent. Examples are interrupts handling and virtual memory and caching, pipelining and instruction reordering. In a black-box testing scenario, an abstract description of the system under test is used as a basis for test generation. This will be the case in our study, where the processor model is used to extract abstract test cases for the processor. The aim of this testing scenario is to check that the processor behaves as described in the assembler model, independently of the internal implementation details.

4   Testing VAMP Processor Conformance

As motivated earlier, we will apply essentially two testing scenarios: model-based *unit testing* and *sequence testing*. In a unit testing scenario, the test specification is described by pre- and post-conditions on the inputs and results produced by the system under test. This scenario assumes control over the initial state and the access to the internal states of the SUT after the test. In sequence testing scenario, only the control of the internal state initialization is necessary, and in some cases the reference to the final state. In principle, the test result is inferred from a sequence system inputs and observed outputs. For any given inputs and state, the system—defined as an i/o stepping function—may either fail or produce outputs and a successor state. The unit testing scenario can be seen as a special form of (one step) sequence testing, where the output state is more or less completely accessible for the test.

In our case study, both testing scenarios are useful. The unit testing scenario will be used to test individually each operation or instruction with different data. Sequence testing will be used to test any sequence of instructions up to a given length. We will address subsets of related instructions separately, a combination of different instruction types is possible but not explored here. We studied four types of instructions: 1. memory related load and store operations, 2. arithmetic operations, 3. logic operations and 4. control-flow related operations.

4.1 Generalities on Model-Based Tests

A general test specification for unit instruction testing would be the following:

test_spec pre $\sigma\,\iota \implies$ SUT $\sigma\,\iota =_k$ exec_instr $\sigma\,\iota$

where $\_ =_{k}\_$ is a specially defined executable equality that compares the content of the registers and just the top k memory cells (instead of infinite memory). $\_ =_k \_$ is our standard conformance relation comparing the state controlled according to the model and the state controlled by the SUT; here, we make the testability assumption that we can trust our test environment that reads the external state and converts it to its abstraction. Note that SUT is a free variable that is replaced during the test execution with the system under test.

Each test case is composed of an instruction, an initial configuration and the resulting configuration after the execution of the instruction. From this test specification, HOL-TESTGEN will produce tests for all possible instructions.Subsets of instructions are isolated by adding a pre-condition in the test specification, specifying the type of the instruction.

For instruction sequence testing, based on the combinators from the state-exception monad (see Section 2.2) mbind, bind $\_ \leftarrow\_; \_$ and the assertion assert$_{SE}$ a test specification can be given specifications of *valid test sequences* from initial state σ_0. In general, there are two kinds of sequence test scenarios: those who involve just observations of the executions of the local steps and those who involve a test over the final state. The former class is irrelevant in our application domain since the local steps are just actions not reporting a computation result. However, the latter scenario may just involve a conformance on the entire state:

test_spec pre ιs::instr list $\implies$
    $(\sigma_0 \models (\_ \leftarrow$mbind ιs exec$_{VAMP}$; assert$_{SE}$ $(\lambda\sigma.\ \sigma =_k$ SUT $\sigma_0\iota$s$)))$

or just a bit of it, e.g., where a computation is finally loaded into register 0 which is finally compared:

test_spec pre ιs::instr list $\implies$
    $(\sigma_0 \models (\_ \leftarrow$mbind $(\iota$s@[load x 0]) exec$_{VAMP}$;
        assert$_{SE}$ $(\lambda\sigma.$ (gprs σ)!0 = (gprs (SUT $\sigma_0\iota$s))! 0)))$

which requires that the last load action(s) are tested before, but makes less assumptions over the execution environment (i. e., a trustworthy implementation of $\_=_{k}\_$). In both schemes σ_0 is the initial state and ιs is the sequence of instructions that will be generated and $\mathsf{exec_{VAMP}}$ is a lifting of $\mathsf{exec\_instr}$ into the state exception monad:

definition $\mathsf{exec_{VAMP}}$ **where** $\mathsf{exec_{VAMP}} \equiv (\lambda \; i \; \sigma. \; \mathsf{Some} \; ((), \; \mathsf{exec\_instr} \; \sigma i))$

The pre-conditions **pre** of our test specifications—also called test purposes—are added to the test specifications to reduce the generated instruction sequences to any given subset.

The initial configuration can also be generated as an input of the test cases. This may produce ill-formed configurations due to their abstract representation in the assembler model. We choose for our study to define and use an empty initial configuration σ_0 that is proved to be well-formed.

4.2 Testing Methodology

Common analysis techniques such as stuck-at-faults [14] are based on the idea that a given circuit design—thus, an implementation—is modified by mutators capturing a particular fabrication fault model, e.g.: one or n wires connecting gates in the circuit are broken. This can be seen conceptually as a white-box mutation technique and has, consequently, all advantages and all draw-backs of an implementation-based testing method compared to all draw-backs and all advantages to its specification-based counterparts. Stack-at-faults are very effective for medium-size circuits and use the structure of the given design to construct equivalence classes tests incorporating directly a fault model. This type of testing technique, however, will not reveal design flaws such as a write-read error under the influence of byte-alignments in the memory.

While we have a VAMP gate-level model in our hands and could have opted for testing technique on this layer, for this paper, we opted to stay on the design level of the VAMP machine. This does not mean that we can not refine with little effort the equivalence classes underlying our tests further: instead of assuming in our test hypothesis that "one write-read of a memory cell successful, thus all write-reads in this cell successful," one could force HOL-TESTGEN to generate finer test classes, by exploring the byte-or the bit-level representations of registers and memory cells.

4.3 Testing Load-Store Operations

To formalize a test purpose restricting our first test scenario to load and store operations, the test purpose $\mathsf{is\_load\_store}$ is used. This predicate returns for each instruction, if it is a load/store operation or not. It is defined just as a constraint over the syntax of the VAMP assembly language:

abbreviation $\mathsf{is\_load\_store\_byte}'$ :: $\mathsf{instr} \Rightarrow \mathsf{bool}$
where $\mathsf{is\_load\_store\_byte}' \; iw \equiv$
$\quad (\exists \; rd \; rs \; imm. \; (\mathsf{is\_register} \; rd \; \wedge \mathsf{is\_register} \; rs \; \wedge \mathsf{is\_immediate} \; imm) \; \wedge$
$\quad\quad\quad\quad iw \in \{\mathsf{Ilb} \; rd \; rs \; imm, \; \mathsf{Ilbu} \; rd \; rs \; imm, \; \mathsf{Isb} \; rd \; rs \; imm\})$

```
definition is_load_store :: instr ⇒bool
where    is_load_store iw ≡is_load_store_word' iw
                          ∨is_load_store_hword' iw
                          ∨is_load_store_byte' iw
```

(the analogous test cases for is_load_store_word' and is_load_store_hword' iw are ommited here for space reasons).

Introducing this predicate in the pre-condition of the test specification reduces the domain of the generated tests to load/store operations. The resulting test specification formally stating the test goal for unit test scenario is given by the following:

```
test_spec is_load_store ι ⟹ SUT σ₀ ι =ₖ exec_instr σ₀ ι
apply (gen_test_cases 0 1 SUT)
store_test_thm load_store_instr
```

The test case generation procedure defined in HOL-TESTGEN is used to preform an exhaustive case splitting on the instructions datatype. Symbolic operands are generated for each instruction to give a set of symbolic test cases. The test generation produced 8 symbolic test cases, corresponding to the different load and store operations. A uniformity hypothesis is stated on each symbolic test case, which will allow us to select one concrete *witness* for each symbolic test case. The final generation state contains 8 *schematic* test cases, associated to 8 uniformity hypotheses. The conjunction of the test cases and the uniformity hypotheses is called a test theorem.

An example of a generated test case and its associated uniformity hypothesis is given in the following. The variables starting with ??X (e. g., ??X4,??X5,) are schematic variables representing one possible witness value.

```
1. SUT σ₀(Ilb ??X7 ??X6 ??X5)
   (...)
2. THYP ((∃x xa xb. SUT σ₀(Ilb xb xa x) (...)) ⟶
        (∀x xa xb. SUT σ₀(Ilb xb xa x) (...)))
```

The second phase of test generation is the test data instantiation. This is done using the gen_test_data command of HOL-TESTGEN. One possible resulting test case is given by the following:

```
SUT σ₀(Ilb 1 0 1) σ₁
```

where σ_1 is the expected final state after executing the given operation. With this kind of test cases, each operation is tested individually, in a unit test style. This kind of test will reveal design faults i. e.if the result of the operation is not correct. It also detects any undesired state modification, like changing some flags or registers.

In a similar way, load and store instruction sequences are characterized using the same predicate is_load_store which is generalized to entire input sequences to the combinator list_all from the HOL-library. Rather than using a fairly difficult to execute characterization in form of an automaton or an extended finite state-machine that introduce some form of symbolic trace, we use monadic combinators of the state-exception monad directly to define valid test sequences constrained by suitable test purposes.

```
test_spec list_all is_load_store (ιs::instr list) ⟹
            (σ₀ ⊨(s ←mbind ιs execVAMP; assertSE (λσ. σ=ₖ SUT σ₀ιs)))
apply (gen_test_cases SUT)
store_test_thm load_stre_instr_seq
```

Note that step two is just the call to the automatic test case generation method (declaring the free variable SUT as the system under test of this test case), and while the third command binds the results of this step to a data-structure called *test environment* with the name load_store_instr_seq. The experimental evaluation of this scenario is discussed in the next section.

One possible generated test case of length 3 is given by the following subgoal:

1. σ_0 ⊨(s ←mbind [Isw ??X597 ??X586 ??X575, Ilbu ??X557 ??X546 ??X535,
            Ilbu ??X517 ??X506 ??X595] execVAMP;
       assertSE (λσ. σ=ₖ SUT σ₀[Isw ??X597 ??X586 ??X575,
                                Ilbu ??X557 ??X546 ??X535,
                                Ilbu ??X517 ??X506 ??X595]))
2. THYP ((∃x1 x2 x3 x4 x5 x6 x7 x8 x9. σ₀⊨(s ←mbind [Isw x1 x2 x3,
       Ilbu x4 x5 x6, Ilbu x7 x8 x9] execVAMP; (...))) ⟶
         (∀x1 x2 x3 x4 x5 x6 x7 x8 x9. σ₀⊨(s ←mbind [Isw x1 x2 x3,
       Ilbu x4 x5 x6, Ilbu x7 x8 x9] execVAMP; (...))))

where the first subgoal gives the schematic test case, and the second subgoal states the uniformity hypothesis for this case.

The generation of test data is done similarly using the gen_test_data command, which instantiate the schematic variables with concrete values.

σ₀ ⊨(s ←mbind [Isw 0 1 8, Ilbu 1 0 -3, Ilbu 3 2 8] execVAMP;
       assertSE (λσ. σ=ₖ SUT σ₀[Isw 0 1 8, Ilbu 1 0 -3, Ilbu 3 2 8]))

this corresponds to the following assembly code sequence:

ISW	0	1	8
LLBU	1	0	-3
LLBU	3	2	8

This test programs will eventually reveal errors related to read and write sequences. Even if each operation is realized in a correct way, the sequencing may contain errors, like errors due to byte alignment or information loss due to pipelining.

In this testing scenario, we consider test post-conditions expressed on the final state of the automaton. This post-condition is expressed using the state-exception primitive assertSE. This scenario is not very realistic in hardware processors, because the final state, in particular the internal processor registers, will not be directly observable. An alternative scenario would be to consider the state-exception primitive return that introduces a step by step checking of the output values. This output value might be, e. g., retrieved from the updated memory cell. Test specification for this kind of scenarios is as follows:

```
test_spec list_all is_load_store ιs ⟹
        (σ₀ ⊨(s ←mbind ι execᵥₐₘₚ'; return (SUT ι s)))
```

which require a modified VAMP where individual steps were wrapped into trusted code that makes, e. g., internal register content explicit.

4.4 Testing Arithmetic Operations

Similarly, we set up a unit test scenario, where we constrain by the test purpose is_arith the operations to be tested to arithmetic ones:

```
test_spec σ= exec_instr σ₀i ⟹is_arith i ⟹SUT σ₀i σ
apply (gen_test_cases 0 1 SUT)
store_test_thm arith_instr
```

At this stage, each arithmetic operation is covered by one generated test case, an example is given in the following:

```
1. SUT σ₀(Iaddi ??X277 ??X266 ??X255) (...)
```

which contains a test case for he addition operation.

A note on the test granularity is at place here: as such, the granularity that HOL-TESTGEN applies to test arithmetic operations is fairly coarse: just one value satisfying all constraints over a variable of type integer is selected. This is a consequence of our model (registers were represented as integers and not as bitvectors of type: 32 word which would be (nowadays) a valuable alternative) as well as the HOL-TESTGEN heuristics to select for each variable just one candidate. The standard workaround would be to introduce in the test purpose definitions more case distinctions, e. g., by x ∈{MinInt} ∪{-50 .. -100} ∪{0} ∪{50 .. -100} which result in finer constraints for each of which a solution in the test selection must be found.

The sequence scenario is analogously:

```
test_spec list_all is_arith (ι::instr list) ⟹
        (σ₀ ⊨(s ←mbind ιs execᵥₐₘₚ; assertₛₑ (λσ. σ=ₖ SUT σ₀ι)))
apply (gen_test_cases SUT)
store_test_thm arith_instr_seq
```

A possible generated sequence is given in the following, resulting from the gen_test_data command.

```
σ₀ ⊨(s ←mbind [Isub 2 1 0, Iadd 1 5 2, Iadd 1 0 4] execᵥₐₘₚ;
        assertₛₑ (λσ. σ=ₖ SUT σ₀[Isub 2 1 0, Iadd 1 5 2, Iadd 1 0 4]))
```

which corresponds to the following assembly code sequence:

```
ISUB 2 1 0
IADD 1 5 2
IADD 1 0 4
```

This sequence corresponds to a subtraction followed by two addition operations.

4.5   Testing Control-Flow Related Operations

Also with branching operations we are following the same theme:

```
test_spec is_branch i ⟹SUT σ₀i =_k exec_instr σ₀i
apply (gen_test_cases 0 1 SUT)
store_test_thm branch_instr
```

This generates unit test cases for branching operations starting from the initial sate σ_0. One example of the generated schematic test cases is given by:

```
1. SUT σ₀(Ijalr ??X27X7) (...)
```

The problem with this scenario is that the initial state is fixed, while the branching operations behavior depends essentially on the flag values. A more interesting scenario would be to consider different initial states, where the flags values are changed for each test case.

In the test sequence generation, the test specification is given as follows:

```
test_spec list_all is_branch (ιs::instr list) ⟹
           (σ₀ ⊨(s ←mbind ιs exec_VAMP; assert_SE (λσ. σ=_k SUT σ₀ιs)))
apply (gen_test_cases SUT)
store_test_thm branch_instr_seq
```

The test sequence and test data generation returns, e.g., this concrete test sequence:

$$\sigma_0 \models (\text{s} \leftarrow\text{mbind [Ij 1, Ijalr 0] exec}_{\text{VAMP}};$$
$$\text{assert}_{\text{SE}}\ (\lambda\sigma.\ \sigma=_k\ \text{SUT}\ \sigma_0[\text{Ij 1, Ijalr 0}]))$$

which corresponds to the following assembly code sequence:

IJ	1
IJALR	0

The test data generation in all the considered scenarios is performed by constraint solving and random instantiation. This leads to test sequences with coarsely grained memory access. As such, an underlying fault-model is somewhat arcane (i.e., interferences of operations in distant memory areas). If one is interested in such faults, a more dense test method should be chosen.

Rather, one would adding additional constraints to reduce the uniformity domain again. One could simply bound the range of addresses to be used in test sequences, or define a used-predicate over input sequences that computes the set of addresses that store-operations write to, and constrain the load-operations to this set, or the like. This kind of constraints can also be used to improve the coverage of our selected data, by dividing the uniformity domain into different interesting sub-domains.

5   Experiences and First Experimental Data

Methodologically, we deliberately refrained in this paper to modify the model—we took it "as is," and added derived rules to make it executable in test scenarios where we assume a reference implementation running against the SUT. For example, the model describes padding functions for bytes, words, and long-words treating the most significant bit differently in certain load and store operations; in the semantic machine model as it was developed in the Verisoft Project, there are comparisons on these padding *functions* themselves—this is possible in HOL, but in no functional executable language, had therefore to be replaced by equivalent formulations exploiting the fact there are only three variants of padding functions, thus a finite number, were actually *used* in the VAMP machine. Another issue is the linear memory in the machine (a total, infinite function from natural numbers to memory cells, i. e., long words); comparisons on memory, as arising in tests where the real state has to be compared against the specified state, had to be weakened to finitized conformance relations.

While as a whole, our approach is done in a pretty generic model-based testing framework, a few adaptions had to be made due to some specialties of this model. For example, since the assembly language has 56 variants, case-splitting over the language explodes fast over the length of test sequences. While sequence tests are methodologically and pragmatically more desirable (less control over the state is assumed), they are therefore more vulnerable to state-space explosion: sequences of length 3 generate at some point of the process $56 + 56^2 + 56^3 = 178808$ cases. In this situation, a few heuristic adaptions (represented on the tactic level) and more significantly, constraints on the level of the test purposes had to be imposed with respect to state-space explosion, test purposes like `list_all is_logic` ι helps to reduce the test sequences to $7 + 7^2 + 7^3$, i. e., a perfectly manageable size (see discussion in the next section).

5.1 Test Generation

As mentioned earlier, we opted for a combination of unit and sequence test scenarios. Unit tests have the drawback of imposing stronger assumptions on testability: it is assumed that the test driver has actually access to registers and memory (which essentially boils down to the fact that we trust code in the test driver that consists of store-operations of registers into the memory). Sequence tests rely on the observed behavior of tests and make weaker assumptions on testability, for the price of being more vulnerable to state-space explosion.

The sequence scenarios on load-and store operations in Section 4.3 uses 39 seconds in the test partitioning phase and 42 seconds in the test data selection phase (measurements were made on a Powerbook with a 2.8 Ghz Intel Core 2 Duo). 1170 subgoals were generated, where one third are explicit test hypothesis and two third are actual test cases. The other scenarios in Section 4.5, Section 4.4 and the more basic Section 4.1 use considerably less time (between two and twenty seconds for the entire process).

5.2 Test Execution

Nevertheless, compile time for the model (as part of the test drivers) was less than a second; compilation of the entire test driver in SML depends, of course, drastically on the size of finally generated tests. Since we restrained via test purposes the test cases in each individual scenario to about 1000, the compile time for a test remained below 3 seconds. Scaling up our test plan is essentially playing with a number of control parameters; however this is usually done only at the end of the test plan development for reasons of convenience.

Our study focuses for the moment on *test generations*; we did not do any experiments against hardware so far. However, there is a hardware-simulator in the sources of the Verisoft-project; in the future, we plan to generate mutants of this simulator and get thus experimental data on the bug-detection capabilities on the generated test sets.

To give an idea on how the test cases will be executed, we did some experiments using the generated executable model. Starting from the abstract model, an executable translation of it in SML is performed using the Isabelle's code-generation facilities. This generated code contains all the type and constant definitions that are needed to execute the different assembler operations on an executable state. A sketch of the generated SML code for the VAMP processor is given in the following:

```
structure VAMP : sig
  datatype num = One | Bit0 of num | Bit1 of num
  datatype 'a set = Set of 'a list | Coset of 'a list
  datatype instr = Ilb of IntInf.int * IntInf.int * IntInf.int |
    ...
    Ijr of IntInf.int | Itrap of IntInf.int | Irfe
  val int_add : IntInf.int -> IntInf.int -> IntInf.int
  val int_sub : IntInf.int -> IntInf.int -> IntInf.int
  val cell2data : IntInf.int -> IntInf.int
  val exec_instr : unit aSMcore_t_ext -> instr -> unit aSMcore_t_ext
  val sigma_0 : unit aSMcore_t_ext
  val execInstrs : unit aSMcore_t_ext -> instr list
                                      -> unit aSMcore_t_ext
  ...
```

where the datatype definition `instr` is generated from the instruction type definition introduced in Section 3. the functions definitions are generated from their corresponding constants and functions defined in the model.

Our fist experiment was the application of the generated test cases on this executable model. Using the HOL-TESTGEN test script generation, two test scripts were generated for load/store and arithmetic operations sequence. For both cases, 585 test cases were generated and then transformed to executable testers. Running all these tests did, obviously, not reveal any error, since the same model was used for test generation and execution.

To evaluate the quality our generated test cases, we introduced some changes to the executable model, producing a mutant model. Three changes were introduced in the `int_add`, `int_sub` and `cell2data` operations of the generated SML code. In this case, a majority of tests detected the errors. For testing the arithmetic operations, we obtained:

```
Number of successful test cases: 303 of 585 (ca. 51%)
Number of warning:                 0 of 585 (ca.  0%)
Number of errors:                  0 of 585 (ca.  0%)
Number of failures:              282 of 585 (ca. 49%)
Number of fatal errors:            0 of 585 (ca.  0%)
```

For testing the load/store operations, we obtained:

```
Number of successful test cases:  54 of 585 (ca.  9%)
Number of warning:                 0 of 585 (ca.  0%)
Number of errors:                  0 of 585 (ca.  0%)
Number of failures:              531 of 585 (ca. 91%)
Number of fatal errors:            0 of 585 (ca.  0%)
```

6   Conclusion and Related Work

6.1   Related Work

Formal verification is widely used in the hardware industry since at least ten years (e.g., [4, 12, 13, 21, 23]). Nevertheless, formal models of complete processors as well as verification approaches that provide an end-to-end verification from the application layer to the hardware design layer are rare. Besides VAMP [10], notably, exceptions are Fox [12] and Appenzeller and Kuehlmann [1]. The closest related work with respect to the processor model is Fox [12] to which our approach should be directly applicable.

Similarly, test program generation approaches for microprocessor instruction sets have been known for a long time (e.g., [11, 17, 19, 22]). Among them manual approaches based on informal descriptions of the instruction set such as Fallah and Takayama [11] or random testing approaches such as Shen et al. [22]. Only a few works suggest to use model-based or specification-based test program generation algorithms, e.g., Kamkin et al. [17] and Mishra and Dutt [19]. These works have in common that they are based on dedicated test models that are independently developed from the verification models. Mishra and Dutt [19] is the most closely related work; the authors are using the explicit state model checker SMV to generate test programs from a dedicated test model for SMV that concentrates on pipelining faults. In contrast, our approach seamlessly integrates the test program generation into an existing verification tool chain, re-using existing verification models.

6.2   Conclusion and Future Work

We presented an approach for testing the conformance of a processor with respect to an abstract model that captures the instruction set (i.e., the assembly-level) of the processor. This abstraction level is particular important as, first, it is the level of detail that is usually available for commercial off-the-shelf (COTS) processors and, second, it is the target level of high-level compilers.

Thus, our approach can, on the one hand, support the certification of the COTS processors for which the manufacturer is neither willing to certify the processor itself or to disclose the necessary internal details. Moreover, our approach helps to bridge the gap between the software layer (e. g., in avionics requiring certification according to DO-178 [16]) and the hardware layer (e. g., in avionics requiring certification according to DO-254 [16]).

As (embedded) systems combining hardware and software components for providing core functionality in safety critical systems (e. g., "fly-by-wire") are used more and more often, we see an increasing need for validation techniques that seamlessly bridge the gap between hardware and software. Consequently, we see this area as the utterly important one for future work: providing a test case generation methodology that can be applied end-to-end in the development process and allows for validating each development step. These test cases, called *certification kits*, are required even if compilers and processors are formally verified: The system builders require them for proving, as part of their certification process, that their are applying the tools correctly (i. e., according to their specification).

Acknowledgement. This work was partially supported by the Euro-MILS project funded by the European Union's Programme [FP7/2007-2013] under grant agreement number ICT-318353.

References

[1] Appenzeller, D.P., Kuehlmann, A.: Formal verification of a powerpc microprocessor. In: Proceedings of the 1995 IEEE International Conference on Computer Design: VLSI in Computers and Processors, ICCD 1995, pp. 79–84 (October 1995), doi:10.1109/ICCD.1995.528794

[2] Beyer, S.: Putting it all together - Formal Verification of the VAMP. PhD thesis, Saarland University, Saarbrücken, Germany (2005)

[3] Beyer, S., Jacobi, C., Kröning, D., Leinenbach, D., Paul, W.J.: Putting it all together – formal verification of the vamp. Int. J. Softw. Tools Technol. Transf. 8(4), 411–430 (2006) ISSN 1433-2779

[4] Biswas, P., Freeman, A., Yamada, K., Nakagawa, N., Uchiyama, K.: Functional verification of the superscalar sh-4 microprocessor. In: Proceeding of the IEEE Compcon 1997, pp. 115–120 (February 1997), doi:10.1109/CMPCON.1997.584682

[5] Brucker, A.D., Wolff, B.: HOL TestGen: An interactive test-case generation framework. In: Chechik, M., Wirsing, M. (eds.) FASE 2009. LNCS, vol. 5503, pp. 417–420. Springer, Heidelberg (2009)

[6] Brucker, A.D., Wolff, B.: On theorem prover-based testing. Formal Aspects of Computing, FAC (2012), doi:10.1007/s00165-012-0222-y, ISSN 0934-5043

[7] Brucker, A.D., Brügger, L., Krieger, M.P., Wolff, B.: HOL-TestGen 1.7.0 user guide. Technical Report 1551, Laboratoire en Recherche en Informatique (LRI), Université Paris-Sud 11, France (April 2012)

[8] Common Criteria. Common criteria for information technology security evaluation (version 3.1), Part 3: Security assurance components (September 2006) Available as document CCMB-2006-09-003

[9] de Moura, L., Bjørner, N.: Z3: An efficient smt solver. In: Ramakrishnan, C.R., Rehof, J. (eds.) TACAS 2008. LNCS, vol. 4963, pp. 337–340. Springer, Heidelberg (2008)

[10] Dorrenbacher, J.: Formal Specification and Verification of Microkernel. PhD thesis, Saarland University, Saarbrücken, Germany (2010)

[11] Fallah, F., Takayama, K.: A new functional test program generation methodology. In: Proceedings of the 2001 International Conference on Computer Design, ICCD 2001, pp. 76–81 (2001), doi:10.1109/ICCD.2001.955006

[12] Fox, A.: Formal specification and verification of arm6. In: Basin, D., Wolff, B. (eds.) TPHOLs 2003. LNCS, vol. 2758, pp. 25–40. Springer, Heidelberg (2003)

[13] Harrison, J.: Formal verification at intel. In: LICS, pp. 45–54. IEEE Computer Society (2003), doi:10.1109/LICS.2003.1210044, ISBN 0-7695-1884-2

[14] Hayes, J.P.: Fault modeling for digital mos integrated circuits. IEEE Transactions on Computer-Aided Design of Integrated Circuits and Systems 3(3), 200–208 (1984), doi:10.1109/TCAD.1984.1270076, ISSN 0278-0070

[15] Hennessy, J.L., Patterson, D.A.: Computer Architecture: A Quantitative Approach, 4th edn. Morgan Kaufmann Publishers Inc., San Francisco (2006) ISBN 0123704901

[16] Hilderman, V., Baghai, T.: Avionics Certification: A Complete Guide to DO-178 (Software), DO-254 (Hardware). Avionics Communications Inc. (2007) ISBN 978-1-885544-25-4

[17] Kamkin, A., Kornykhin, E., Vorobyev, D.: Reconfigurable model-based test program generator for microprocessors. In: IEEE International Conference on Software Testing Verification and Validation Workshop, pp. 47–54 (2011), doi:10.1109/ICSTW.2011.35

[18] Leroy, X.: Formal verification of a realistic compiler. Communications of the ACM 52(7), 107–115 (2009), doi:10.1145/1538788.1538814, ISSN 0001-0782

[19] Mishra, P., Dutt, N.: Specification-driven directed test generation for validation of pipelined processors. ACM Trans. Design Autom. Electr. Syst. 13(3) (2008)

[20] Nipkow, T., Paulson, L.C., Wenzel, M.T.: Isabelle/HOL. LNCS, vol. 2283. Springer, Heidelberg (2002)

[21] Russinoff, D.M.: A mechanically checked proof of correctness of the amd k5 floating point square root microcode. Formal Methods in System Design 14(1), 75–125 (1999)

[22] Shen, H., Ma, L., Zhang, H.: Crpg: a configurable random test-program generator for microprocessors. In: IEEE International Symposium on Circuits and Systems, ISCAS 2005, vol. 4, pp. 4171–4174 (May 2005), doi:10.1109/ISCAS.2005.1465550

[23] Srinivasan, S.K., Velev, M.N.: Formal verification of an intel xscale processor model with scoreboarding, specialized execution pipelines, and impress data-memory exceptions. In: MEMOCODE, vol. 7, pp. 65–74. IEEE Computer Society (2003), doi:10.1109/MEMCOD.2003.1210090, ISBN 0-7695-1923-7

[24] Wenzel, M., Wolff, B.: Building formal method tools in the Isabelle/Isar framework. In: Schneider, K., Brandt, J. (eds.) TPHOLs 2007. LNCS, vol. 4732, pp. 352–367. Springer, Heidelberg (2007)

A Declarative Debugger for Sequential Erlang Programs*

Rafael Caballero[1], Enrique Martin-Martin[1], Adrián Riesco[1],
and Salvador Tamarit[2]

[1] Universidad Complutense de Madrid, Madrid, Spain
rafa@sip.ucm.es, {emartinm,ariesco}@fdi.ucm.es
[2] Universitat Politècnica de València, València, Spain
stamarit@dsic.upv.es

Abstract. Declarative debuggers are semi-automatic debugging tools
that abstract the execution details to focus on the program semantics.
Erroneous computations are represented by suitable trees, which are tra-
versed by asking questions to the user until a bug is found. This paper
applies declarative debugging to the sequential subset of the language
Erlang. The debugger takes the intermediate representation generated
by Erlang systems, known as Core Erlang, and an initial error detected
by the user, and locates an erroneous program function responsible for
the error. In order to represent the erroneous computation, a semantic
calculus for sequential Core Erlang programs is proposed. The debugger
uses an abbreviation of the proof trees of this calculus as debugging trees,
which allows us to prove the soundness of the approach. The technique
has been implemented in a debugger tool publicly available.

Keywords: Declarative debugging, Erlang, Semantics.

1 Introduction

Erlang is a programming language that combines the elegance and expressiveness of functional languages (higher-order functions, lambda abstractions, single
assignments), with features required in the development of scalable commercial
applications (garbage collection, built-in concurrency, and even hot-swapping).
The language is used as the base of many fault-tolerant, reliable software systems. The development of this kind of systems is a complicated process where
tools such as discrepancy analyzers [21], test-case generators [27], or debuggers play an important rôle. In the case of debuggers, Erlang includes a useful
trace-debugger including different types of breakpoints, stack tracing, and other
features. However, debugging a program is still a difficult, time-consuming task,

* Research supported by MICINN Spanish projects *StrongSoft* (TIN2012-39391-
C04-04), *FAST-STAMP* (TIN2008-06622-C03-01) and *LEVITY* (TIN2008-06622-
C03-02), Comunidad de Madrid program *PROMETIDOS* (S2009/TIC-1465), and
Generalitat Valenciana program *PROMETEO* (2011/052). Salvador Tamarit was
partially supported by MICINN Spanish *FPI* grant (BES-2009-015019).

M. Veanes and L. Viganò (Eds.): TAP 2013, LNCS 7942, pp. 96–114, 2013.

and for this reason we think that alternative or complementary debugging tools are convenient. In this paper we take advantage of the declarative nature of the sequential subset of Erlang in order to propose a new debugger based on the general technique known as *declarative debugging* [32]. Also known as declarative diagnosis or algorithmic debugging, this technique abstracts the execution details, which may be difficult to follow in declarative languages, to focus on the results. This approach has been widely employed in the logic [23,36], functional [25,29], multi-paradigm [5,22], and object-oriented [6,20] programming languages.

Declarative debugging is a two-step scheme: it first computes a debugging tree representing a wrong computation, usually using a formal calculus that allows to prove the soundness and completeness of the approach, and then traverses this tree by asking questions to the user until the bug is identified.

The first contribution of the paper is the formalization of a semantic calculus for sequential Core Erlang programs, the intermediate language that Erlang uses to codify all the programs in a uniform representation. An interesting feature of this calculus is that it handles exceptions as usual values, which allows the user to debug expressions giving rise to exceptions in a natural way. The second and main contribution is the development of a framework for the declarative debugging of sequential Erlang programs based on an abbreviation of the proof trees obtained in this calculus as debugging trees. The process starts when the user observes that the evaluation of some expression produces an unexpected result. Therefore, the technique is restricted to terminating computations, a standard constraint in the declarative debugging approach. First, a debugging tree representing the computation is internally built. Each node in the tree corresponds to a function call occurred during the computation, and it is considered *valid* if the function call produced the expected result, and *invalid* otherwise. Then, the debugger asks questions to the user about the validity of some nodes until a buggy node—an invalid node with only valid children—is found and its associated function is pointed out as the cause of the error. The relation between the debugging trees and the proof trees in the semantic calculus allows us to prove the soundness and completeness of the technique. The formal ideas have been put into practice in the development of an Erlang system supporting the declarative debugging of sequential Erlang programs. The tool provides features such as different navigation strategies [33,34], trusting, higher-order functions, support for built-ins, and "don't know" answers.

The rest of the paper is organized as follows: Section 2 describes the related work and the similarities with our approach. Section 3 introduces Erlang and presents an example used throughout the rest of the paper. Section 4 presents the calculus we have tailored for sequential Core Erlang programs, while Section 5 shows how to use the proof trees obtained from this calculus to use declarative debugging. Section 6 outlines the main features of our tool, including a debugging session. Finally, Section 7 concludes and presents the future work.

2   Related Work

The semantics of Erlang is informally described in [2], but there is no *official* formalized semantics. However, several authors have proposed and used different formalizations in their works, most of them aiming to cover the concurrent behavior of the language. In [18], Huch proposes an operational *small step* semantics for a subset of Erlang based on *evaluation contexts* to only perform reductions in certain points of the expression. It covers single-node concurrency (spawning and communication by messages between processes in the same node) and reductions that can yield runtime errors. However, it does not cover other sequential features of the language like lambda abstractions or higher-order functions. Another important small-step semantics for Erlang is proposed in Fredlund's PhD thesis [16]. This semantics is similar to [18] and also uses evaluation contexts but covers a broader subset of the language including single-node concurrency, runtime errors, and lambda abstractions. However, it also lacks support for higher-order features. To overcome the limitations of Fredlund's single-node semantics when dealing with distributed systems, [13] proposes a semantics based on Fredlund's but adding another top-level layer describing nodes. This distributed multi-node semantics for Erlang was further refined and corrected in [35]. Besides standard operational semantics, other approaches have been proposed to formalize Erlang semantics like the one based on congruence in [12], which works with partial evaluation of Erlang programs.

Regarding Core Erlang [8,9],[1] there is no formalized semantics in the literature. However, the language specification [9] contains a detailed but informal explanation of the expected behavior for the evaluation of expressions. The semantics proposed for Core Erlang in this paper—inspired in the semantics previously presented for Erlang, mainly [18,16]—formalizes the behavior explained in [9] and covers all the Core Erlang syntax except concurrency-related expressions (message sending and reception) and *bit string* notation.

Tools for testing and debugging programs are very popular in the Erlang community since long ago. The OTP/Erlang system comes with a classical trace-debugger with both graphical and command line interfaces. This official debugger supports the whole Erlang language—including concurrency—, allowing programmers to establish conditional breakpoints in their code, watch the stack trace of function calls, and inspect variables and other processes, among other features. Another tool included in the OTP/Erlang system is the *DIscrepancy AnaLYZer for ERlang programs* (Dialyzer) [21], a completely automatic tool that performs static analysis to identify software discrepancies and bugs such as definite type errors [31], race conditions [11], unreachable code, redundant tests, unsatisfiable conditions, and more. Model checking tools have also received much attention in the Erlang community [18,3], being *McErlang* [4] one of the most powerful nowadays due to its support for a very substantial part of the Erlang language. Regarding testing tools, the most important ones

---

[1] The official Core Erlang [8,9] should not be confused with the subsets of Erlang that the previous papers covered, although they usually refer them as *some* core Erlang.

are *EUnit* [10] and *Quviq QuickCheck* [19]. The EUnit tool is included in the OTP/Erlang system, and allows users to write their own unit tests to check that functions return the expected values. On the other hand, Quiviq QuickCheck is a commercial software that automatically generates and checks thousands of unit tests from properties stated by programmers.

Declarative debugging is a well-known debugging technique. In [30] a comparison between different debuggers is presented. From this comparison we can see that our debugger has most of the features in state-of-the-art tools, although we still lack some elements such as a graphical user interface, or more navigation strategies. An interesting contribution of our debugger is the debugging of exceptions. Declarative debugging of programs throwing exceptions has already been studied from an operational point of view for the Mercury debugger [22], for Haskell in its declarative debugger Buddha [28], and for Java programs [20]. However, these approaches are operational and do not provide a calculus to reason about exceptions: in Mercury exceptions are considered another potential value and thus functions throwing exceptions are included as standard nodes in the debugging tree; Buddha uses a program transformation to build the debugging tree while executing the program; finally, the approaches for Java return and propagate exceptions without defining the inference rules. Similarly, several calculi handling exceptions, like the ones in [15,14], have been proposed for functional languages. In this paper we present, for the best of our knowledge, the first tool that uses a calculus to perform declarative debugging, allowing us to reason about exceptions as standard values.

Finally, other non-conventional approaches to debugging have been studied in the literature, like abstract diagnosis [1] or symbolic execution [17], but these techniques are not closely related to declarative debugging, so we do not provide a detailed comparison.

3   Erlang

Erlang [2] is a concurrent language with a sequential subset that is a functional language with dynamic typing and strict evaluation. It allows to model programs where different processes communicate through asynchronous messages and gives support to fault-tolerant and soft real-time applications, and also to non-stop applications thanks to the so-called *hot swapping*.

Example 1. Figure 1 presents an example of an Erlang program (for the time being ignore the boxes). The program exports function mergesort/2 that, given a list L and a comparison function Comp, orders the elements of L according to Comp. Function comp/2 is also exported in order to provide an atom comparison function. The rest of functions are used internally. Function merge/3 merges two lists according to a given comparison function. Finally, take/2 and last/2 extract the N first (respectively last) elements of a list. Observe that the code contains calls to built-ins and standard library functions, e.g. is_atom/1 in line 16 or reverse/1 of module lists in line 21. Now the user can write the next expression to sort the list [b,a] using the comparison function comp/2:

```
 1 mergesort([], _Comp) -> [];
 2 mergesort([X], _Comp) -> [X];
 3 mergesort(L, Comp) ->
 4    Half = length(L) div 2,
 5    LOrd1 = mergesort(take(Half, L), Comp),
 6    LOrd2 = mergesort(last(length(L) - Half, L), Comp),
 7    merge(LOrd1, LOrd2, Comp).

 8 merge([], [], _Comp) -> [];
 9 merge([], S2, _Comp) -> S2;
10 merge(S1, [], _Comp) -> S1;
11 merge([H1 | T1], [H2 | T2], Comp)  ->
12    case Comp(H1,H2) of
13       false -> [ H1  | merge([ H2  | T1], T2, Comp)];
14       true ->  [H1 | merge(T1, [H2 | T2], Comp)]
15    end.

16 comp(X,Y) when is_atom(X) and is_atom(Y) -> X < Y.

17 take(0, _List) -> [];
18 take(1, [H|_T]) -> [H];
19 take(_, []) -> [];
20 take(N, [H|T]) -> [ N  | take(N-1, T)].

21 last(N, List) -> lists:reverse(take(N, lists:reverse(List))).
```

Fig. 1. Erlang code implementing mergesort algorithm

merge:mergesort([b,a], fun merge:comp/2). The system evaluates this expression and displays [b,a]. This is an unexpected result, an initial symptom indicating that there is some erroneous function in the program. In the next sections we show how the debugger helps in the task of finding the bug.

The intermediate language Core Erlang [8,9] can be considered as a simplified version of Erlang, where the syntactic constructs have been reduced by removing syntactic sugar. It is used by the compiler to create the final bytecode and it is very useful in our context, because it simplifies the analysis required by the tool. Figure 2 presents its syntax after removing the parts corresponding to concurrent operations, i.e. receive, and also the bit syntax support. The most significant element in the syntax is the expression (*expr*). Besides variables, function names, lambda abstractions, lists, and tuples, expressions can be:

- let: its value is the one resulting from evaluating $exprs_2$ where *vars* are bound to the value of $exprs_1$.
- letrec: similar to the previous expression but a sequence of function declarations (*fname* = *fun*) is defined.
- apply: applies *exprs* (defined in the current module) to a number of arguments.
- call: similar to the previous expression but the function applied is the one defined by $exprs_{n+2}$ in the module defined by $exprs_{n+1}$. Both expressions should be evaluated to an atom.
- primop: application of built-in functions mainly used to report errors.

```
fname  ::= Atom / Integer
lit    ::= Atom | Integer | Float | Char | String | [ ]
fun    ::= fun(var₁ , ... , varₙ) -> exprs
clause ::= pats when exprs₁ -> exprs₂
pat    ::= var | lit | [ pats | pats ] | { pats₁ , ... , patsₙ } | var = pats
pats   ::= pat | < pat, ... , pat >
exprs  ::= expr | < expr, ... , expr >
expr   ::= var | fname | fun | [ exprs | exprs ] | { exprs₁ , ... , exprsₙ }
           | let vars = exprs₁ in exprs₂
           | letrec fname₁ = fun₁ ...fnameₙ = funₙ in exprs
           | apply exprs ( exprs₁ , ... , exprsₙ )
           | call exprsₙ₊₁:exprsₙ₊₂ ( exprs₁ , ... , exprsₙ )
           | primop Atom ( exprs₁ , ... , exprsₙ )
           | try exprs₁ of <var₁ , ... , varₙ> -> exprs₂ catch <var'₁ , ... , var'ₘ> -> exprs₃
           | case exprs of clause₁ ...clauseₙ end | do exprs₁ exprs₂ | catch exprs
ξ      ::= Exception(valₘ)
val    ::= lit | fname | fun | [ vals | vals ] | {vals₁ , ... , valsₙ} | ξ
vals   ::= val | < val, ... , val >
vars   ::= var | < var, ... , var >
```

Fig. 2. Core Erlang's Syntax

- **try-catch**: the expression $exprs_1$ is evaluated. If the evaluation does not report any error, then $exprs_2$ is evaluated. Otherwise, the evaluated expression is $exprs_3$. In both cases the appropriate variables are bound to the value of $cxprs_1$.
- **case**: a pattern-matching expression. Its value corresponds to the one in the body of the first clause whose pattern matches the value of $exprs$ and whose guard evaluates to true. There is always at least one clause fulfilling these conditions, as we explain below.

It is important to know some basis of how the translation from Erlang to Core Erlang is done. One of the most relevant is that the body of a Core Erlang function is always a case-expression representing the different clauses of the original Erlang function. case-expressions as shown below always contain an extra clause whose pattern matches with every value of the case argument and whose body evaluates to an error (reported by a primop). This clause is introduced by the compiler and placed last. Consider, for instance, the function take/2 in Figure 1. The translation to Core Erlang produces the following code:

```
'take'/2 = fun (_cor1,_cor0) ->
      case <_cor1,_cor0> of
         <0,_cor6> when 'true' -> []
         <1,[H|_cor7]> when 'true' -> [H|[]]
         <_cor8,[]> when 'true' -> []
         <N,[H|T]> when 'true' -> ...
         <_cor5,_cor4> when 'true' ->
                 primop 'match_fail' ('function_clause',_cor5,_cor4)
      end
```

Note that the compiler has introduced new variables in the translation with the form _cor followed by an integer. Another important point is the introduction of `let`-expressions. These expressions are not present in Erlang, and in Core are introduced for different reasons. One usage of `let`-expressions in the translation is to ensure that function applications always receive simple expressions (values or variables) as arguments. For instance, the call to `take/2` at line 20 in Figure 1 (`take(N-1, T)`) is translated to Core as:

```
let <_cor2> = call 'erlang':'-'(N, 1) in  apply 'take'/2(_cor2, T)
```

`let`-expressions are also used to translate sequences of Erlang expressions. For instance, the sequence of expressions going from line 4 to line 7 in Figure 1 is translated to the following Core Erlang code:

```
let <_cor2> = call 'erlang':'length'(L)
in let <Half> = call 'erlang':'div'(_cor2, 2)
   in let <L1> = apply 'take'/2(Half, L)
      in let <_cor5> =  call 'erlang':'length'(L)
         in let <_cor6> = call 'erlang':'-'(_cor5, Half)
            in let <L2> = apply 'last'/2(_cor6, L)
               in let <LOrd1> = apply 'mergesort'/2(L1, Comp)
                  in let <LOrd2> = apply 'mergesort'/2(L2, Comp)
                     in  apply 'merge'/3(LOrd1, LOrd2, Comp)
```

It can be observed that the translation from plain Erlang to Core enforces the function applications to receive values or variables as arguments. In principle, we could simplify our language and semantics taking into account these particularities, but our tool allows the more general grammar of Core Erlang for two reasons. First, Core Erlang could be used as intermediate language produced by other languages. Second, the Core Erlang structure could be modified by optimization tools, and thus a particular structure cannot be assumed.

4   A Calculus for Sequential Erlang

This section presents the main rules of our calculus for Core Erlang Sequential Programs (*CESC* in the following). The complete set of rules is presented in [7]. The calculus uses evaluations of the form $\langle exprs, \theta \rangle \rightarrow vals$, where *exprs* is the expression being evaluated, θ is a substitution, and *vals* is the value obtained for the expression. Moreover, we use the notation $\langle exprs, \theta \rangle \rightarrow^i vals$ in some cases to indicate that the ith clause of a function was used to obtain a value. We assume that all the variables for *exprs* are in the domain of θ, and the existence of a global environment ρ which is initially empty and is extended by adding the functions defined by the `letrec` operator. *References to functions*, denoted as r_f, are unique identifiers pointing to the function in the source code (this can be described in general with the tuple *(mod, line, column)* with *line* and *column* the starting position of the function in *mod*). We extend the idea of reference to reserved words, denoted by r, to obtain the module where they are defined, which is denoted by $r.mod$. These references are used to unify the handling of function calls with the inference rule (BFUN), which is explained below. The notation $CESC \models_{(P,T)} \mathcal{E}$, where $\mathcal{E}$ is an evaluation, is employed to indicate that $\mathcal{E}$ can be proven w.r.t. the program P with the proof tree T in *CESC*, while

$CESC \nvDash_P \mathcal{E}$ indicates that $\mathcal{E}$ cannot be proven in $CESC$ with respect to the program P.

The basic rule in our calculus is (VAL), which states that values are evaluated to themselves:

$$(\text{VAL}) \frac{}{\langle vals, \theta \rangle \to vals}$$

The (CASE) rule is in charge of evaluating case-expressions. It first evaluates the expression used to select the branch. Then, it checks that the values thus obtained match the pattern on the ith branch and verify the when guard, while the side condition indicates that this is the first branch where this happens. The evaluation continues by applying the substitution to the body of the ith branch.

$$(\text{CASE}) \frac{\langle exprs'', \theta \rangle \to vals'' \quad \langle exprs'_i \theta', \theta' \rangle \to \text{'true'} \quad \langle exprs_i \theta', \theta' \rangle \to vals}{\langle \text{case } exprs'' \text{ of } \overline{pats_n \text{ when } exprs'_n \text{ -> } exprs_n} \text{ end}, \theta \rangle \to^i vals}$$

where $\theta' \equiv \theta \uplus matchs(pats_i, vals'')$; $\forall j < i.\nexists \theta_j.matchs(pats_j, vals'') = \theta_j \wedge \langle exprs'_j \theta_j, \theta_j \rangle \to \text{'true'}$; and $matchs$ a function that computes the substitution binding the variables to the corresponding values using syntactic matching as follows:

$$matchs(< pat_1, \ldots, pat_n >, < val_1, \ldots, val_n >) = \theta_1 \uplus \ldots \uplus \theta_n,$$

with $\theta_i = match(pat_i, val_i)$ where $match$ is an auxiliary function defined as:

$$match(var, val) = [var \mapsto val]$$
$$match(lit_1, lit_2) = id, \text{ if } lit_1 \equiv lit_2$$
$$match([pat_1 | pat_2], [val_1 | val_2]) = \theta_1 \uplus \theta_2, \text{ where } \theta_i = match(pat_i, val_i)$$
$$match(\{pat_1, \ldots, pat_n\}, \{val_1, \ldots, val_n\}) = \theta_1 \uplus \ldots \uplus \theta_n,$$
$$\text{where } \theta_i = match(pat_i, val_i)$$
$$match(var = pat, val) = \theta[var \mapsto val], \text{where } \theta = match(pat, val)$$

Similarly, the (LET) rule evaluates $exprs_1$ and binds it to the variables. The computation continues by applying the substitution to the body:

$$(\text{LET}) \frac{\langle exprs_1, \theta \rangle \to vals_1 \quad \langle exprs_2 \theta', \theta' \rangle \to vals}{\langle \text{let } vars = exprs_1 \text{ in } exprs_2, \theta \rangle \to vals}$$

where $\theta' \equiv \theta \uplus matchs(vars, vals_1)$.

The (BFUN) rule evaluates a reference to a function, given a substitution binding all its arguments. This is accomplished by applying the substitution to the body of the function (with notation $exprs\theta$) and then evaluating it. This rule takes advantage of the fact that, as explained in Section 3, all Erlang functions are translated to Core Erlang as a case-expression distinguishing the different clauses. The particular branch of the case-expression employed during the computation t (i.e. the i labeling the evaluation) corresponds to the clause used to evaluate the function:

$$(\text{BFUN}) \frac{\langle \text{case } exprs\theta \text{ of } clause_1\theta \ldots clause_m\theta \text{ end}, \theta \rangle \to^i vals}{\langle r_f, \theta \rangle \to^i vals}$$

where $1 \leq i \leq m$ and r_f references to a function f defined as $f/n = \text{fun } (var_1, \ldots, var_n) \text{ -> case } exprs \text{ of } clause_1 \ldots clause_m \text{ end}.$

The rule (CALL) evaluates a function defined in another module:

$$\langle exprs_{n+1}, \theta \rangle \rightarrow Atom_1 \quad \langle exprs_{n+2}, \theta \rangle \rightarrow Atom_2$$

(CALL) $\dfrac{\langle exprs_1, \theta \rangle \rightarrow val_1 \quad \dots \quad \langle exprs_n, \theta \rangle \rightarrow val_n \quad\quad \langle r_f, \theta' \rangle \rightarrow^i vals}{\langle \texttt{call } exprs_{n+1} : exprs_{n+2}(exprs_1, \dots, exprs_n), \theta \rangle \rightarrow vals}$

where $Atom_2/n$ is a function defined in the $Atom_1$ module as $Atom_2/n$ = fun (var_1 , $\dots$, var_n) -> case $exprs$ of $clause_1 \dots clause_m$ end; r_f its reference; $1 \le i \le m$; and $\theta' \equiv \{var_1 \mapsto val_1, \dots, var_n \mapsto val_n\}$.

Analogously, the (CALL_EVAL) rule is in charge of evaluating built-in functions:

$$\langle exprs_{n+1}, \theta \rangle \rightarrow \texttt{'erlang'} \quad \langle exprs_{n+2}, \theta \rangle \rightarrow Atom_2$$

(CALL_EVAL) $\dfrac{\langle exprs_1, \theta \rangle \rightarrow val_1 \quad \dots \quad \langle exprs_n, \theta \rangle \rightarrow val_n \quad\quad eval(Atom_2, val_1, \dots, val_n) = vals}{\langle \texttt{call } exprs_{n+1} : exprs_{n+2}(exprs_1, \dots, exprs_n), \theta \rangle \rightarrow vals}$

where $Atom_2/n$ is a built-in function included in the erlang module.

Finally, the rule (APPLY$_3$)[2] indicates that first we need to obtain the name of the function, which must be defined in the current module (extracted from the reference to the reserved word apply) and then compute the arguments of the function. Finally the function, described by its reference, is evaluated using the substitution obtained by binding the variables in the function definition to the values for the arguments:

$$\langle exprs, \theta \rangle \rightarrow Atom/n$$

(APPLY$_3$) $\dfrac{\langle exprs_1, \theta \rangle \rightarrow val_1 \quad \dots \quad \langle exprs_n, \theta \rangle \rightarrow val_n \quad\quad \langle r_f, \theta' \rangle \rightarrow^i vals}{\langle \texttt{apply}^r \, exprs(exprs_1, \dots, exprs_n), \theta \rangle \rightarrow vals}$

where $Atom/n \notin dom(\rho)$ (i.e., it was not defined in a letrec expression); r is the reference to apply; $Atom/n$ is a function defined in the current module $r.mod$ as $Atom/n$ = fun (var_1 , $\dots$, var_n) -> case $exprs$ of $clause_1 \dots clause_m$ end; r_f its reference; $1 \le i \le m$; and $\theta' \equiv \overline{[var_n \mapsto val_n]}$.

We can use this calculus to build the proof tree for any evaluation. For example, Figure 3(top) shows the proof tree for $\langle \texttt{mergesort/2([b,a]}, \texttt{comp/2)}, id \rangle \rightarrow$ [b,a], where ms stands for mergesort/2 and c for the comparison function comp/2. Note that the root of the tree contains the identity substitution and that all the arguments are evaluated (in this case by using the rule (VAL)) before really reducing the function in $\bigtriangledown_1$.

The proof tree $\bigtriangledown_1$ is partially shown in Figure 3(middle), where $r_{\texttt{ms}}$ is the reference to mergesort and θ_1 is {_cor1 $\mapsto$ [b,a]; _cor0 $\mapsto$ c}. The root of this tree presents some of the features described in Section 3: the function has been translated as a case-expression and Core Erlang variables (_cor1 and _cor0) have been introduced to check whether they match any clause. This matching is

---

[2] The rule (APPLY$_1$) executes a function previously defined in a letrec, while (APPLY$_2$) executes functions defined as lambda abstractions. See [7] for details.

accomplished by evaluating the values to themselves in the premises of (CASE), and then checking that the condition holds trivially by evaluating 'true' to itself. The computation continues by evaluating the body of this branch, which is represented in ∇_2.

The tree in Figure 3(bottom) shows ∇_2, where θ_2 extends θ_1 with {Comp $\mapsto$ c; L $\mapsto$ [b,a]}, l stands for the built-in function length/2, and m for merge/3. It first computes the length of the list, that is kept in a new variable _cor2, and then used to split the list, as explained in the translation to Core Erlang at the end of Section 3. Note that length/2 is evaluated with (CALL_EVAL), an inference rule for applying built-in functions. Finally, the subtree ∇_3 stands for several inferences using the (LET) rule that bind all the variables until we reach the function merge/3([b], [a], comp), which is executed using the (APPLY$_3$) as shown for the proof tree on the top of the figure. Note that this node indicates that the 4th clause of the function merge/3 has been used. The rest of the ∇ and the substitutions θ, θ', and θ'' are not relevant and are not described.

5   Debugging with Abbreviated Proof Trees

Our debugger detects functions incorrectly defined by asking questions to the user about the *intended interpretation* of the program, which is represented as a set of the form $\mathcal{I} = \{\ldots,\ m.f(val_1,\ \ldots, val_n) \to vals,\ \ldots\}$ where m is a module name (omitted for simplicity in the rest of the section), f is a user-defined function in module m, and $val_1, \ldots, val_n, vals$ are values such that the user expects $f(val_1, \ldots, val_n) \to vals$ to hold. The validity of the nodes in a proof tree is obtained defining an *intended interpretation calculus*, $ICESC$, which contains the same inference rules as $CESC$, except by the (BFUN) rule, which is replaced by the following:

$$(\mathsf{BFUN}_{\mathcal{I}})\frac{}{\langle r_f, \theta \rangle \to vals}$$

where r_f references a program function f/n = fun(var_1 , $\ldots$, var_n) -> B, (B represents the body of the function), and $f(var_1\theta, \ldots, var_n\theta)$ -> $vals) \in \mathcal{I}$.

Analogously to the case of $CESC$, the notation $ICESC \models_{(P,\mathcal{I},T)} \mathcal{E}$ indicates that the evaluation $\mathcal{E}$ can be proven w.r.t. the program P and the intended interpretation $\mathcal{I}$ with proof tree T in $ICESC$, while $ICESC \nvDash_{(P,\mathcal{I})} \mathcal{E}$ indicates that $\mathcal{E}$ cannot be proven in $ICESC$. The tree T, the program P, and the intended interpretation $\mathcal{I}$ are omitted when they are not needed. The rôle of the two calculi is further clarified by the next two assumptions:

1. If an evaluation $e\theta \to vals$ is computed by some Erlang system with respect to P then $CESC \models_P \langle |e|, \theta \rangle \to |vals|$, with $|\cdot|$ the transformation that converts an Erlang expression into a Core expression.
2. If a reduction $e\theta \to vals$ computed by some Erlang system is considered unexpected by the user then $ICESC \nvDash_{P,\mathcal{I}} \langle |e|, \theta \rangle \to |vals|$.

Thus, $CESC$ represents the actual computations, while $ICESC$ represents the 'ideal' computations expected by the user. Next we define some key concepts:

Definition 1. *Let P be a program with intended interpretation $\mathcal{I}$. Let $\mathcal{E} \equiv \langle e, \theta \rangle \to vals$ be an evaluation such that $CESC \models_P \mathcal{E}$. Then we say that:*

1. *$\mathcal{E}$ is* valid *when $ICESC \models_{(P,\mathcal{I})} \mathcal{E}$, and* invalid *when $ICESC \not\models_{(P,\mathcal{I})} \mathcal{E}$.*
2. *A node is* buggy *if it is invalid with valid premises.*
3. *Let r_f be a reference to a function $f/n = \mathtt{fun(}\ var_1, \ldots, var_n\ \mathtt{)} \mathtt{->} B$, and θ a substitution. Then $\langle r_f, \theta \rangle$ is a* wrong function instance *iff there exists a value v such that $ICESC \not\models_{(P,\mathcal{I})} \langle r_f, \theta \rangle \to v$ and $ICESC \models_{(P,\mathcal{I})} \langle B\theta, \theta \rangle \to v$.*
4. *$P_{\langle e, \theta \rangle}$ denotes the (Core Erlang) program $P \cup \{\ \mathtt{main/0} = \mathtt{fun()} \mathtt{->} \mathtt{case\ <>}$ $\mathtt{of\ <>\ when\ 'true'\ ->}\ |e\theta|\ \mathtt{end}\ \}$, with $|\cdot|$ the operator converting Erlang code into Core Erlang code, and $\mathtt{main}$ a new identifier in P.*

The first two items do not need further explanations. In order to understand the third point observe that we cannot say that a function is wrong simply because it computes an unexpected result, since this can be due to the presence of wrong functions in its body. Instead, a wrong function instance corresponds to a function that produces an erroneous result assuming that all the functions in its body are correct. Finally, the purpose of definition of $P_{\langle e, \theta \rangle}$ is to introduce the expression producing the initial symptom as part of the program. The two following auxiliary results are a straightforward consequence of the coincidence of $CESC$ and $ICESC$ in all the rules excepting (BFUN):

Lemma 1. *Let T be a $CESC$-proof tree and let N be a node in T conclusion of an inference rule different from* (BFUN) *with all the premises valid. Then N is valid.*

Lemma 2. *Let T be a $CESC$-proof tree which does not use the* (BFUN) *inference. Then all the nodes in T are valid.*

The next theorem uses the two lemmas to establish that $CESC$ proof trees are suitable for debugging.

Theorem 1. *Let P be a Core Erlang program, $\mathcal{I}$ its intended interpretation, and $e\theta \to vals$ an unexpected evaluation computed by an Erlang system. Then:*

1. *There is a proof tree T such that $CESC \models_{(P_{\langle e, \theta \rangle}, T)} \langle r_{\mathtt{main}}, id \rangle \to |vals|$.*
2. *T contains at least one buggy node N verifying:*
   (a) *N is the conclusion of a* (BFUN) *inference rule of the form $\langle r_f, \theta \rangle \to vals$ with $f \neq \mathtt{main}$.*
   (b) *$\langle r_f, \theta \rangle$ is a wrong function instance.*

$$\text{(APPLY}_3)\ \dfrac{\text{(VAL)}\ \overline{\langle ms, id\rangle \to ms}\quad \langle [b,a], id\rangle \to [b,a]\quad \text{(VAL)}\ \overline{\langle c, id\rangle \to c}\quad \nabla_1}{\langle \text{apply ms}([b,a],c), id\rangle \to [b,a]}$$

where Proof tree ∇_1 is defined as:

$$\text{(BFUN)}\ \dfrac{\text{(CASE)}\ \dfrac{\text{(VAL)}\ \overline{\langle [b,a],c\rangle \to \langle [b,a],c\rangle}\quad \text{(VAL)}\ \overline{'true' \to^3 'true'}\quad \nabla_2}{\langle \text{case } \langle [b,a],c\rangle \text{ of } \dots \langle L,Comp\rangle \text{ when } 'true' \text{ -> } exp, \theta_1\rangle \to^3 [b,a]}}{\langle rms, \theta_1\rangle \to^3 [b,a]}$$

and Proof tree ∇_2 is defined as:

$$\text{(LET)}\ \dfrac{\text{(CALL.EVAL)}\ \dfrac{\langle \text{call 'erlang':'1'}([b,a]), \theta_2\rangle \to 2\quad \nabla\quad \nabla\quad \nabla}{\langle \text{let _cor2 = call 'erlang':'1'}([b,a]) \text{ in } \dots \text{ in apply 'm'}(L0rd1, L0rd2, c), \theta_2\rangle \to [b,a]}}{\nabla_3}$$

$$\text{(LET)}\ \dfrac{\text{(APPLY}_3)\ \dfrac{\nabla\quad \nabla\quad \text{(BFUN)}\ \dfrac{\langle rm, \theta''\rangle \to^4 [b,a]}{}\quad \nabla}{\langle \text{apply 'm'}([b],[a],c), \theta'\rangle \to [b,a]}}{\langle \text{apply 'm'}(L0rd1, L0rd2, c), \theta_2\rangle \to [b,a]}$$

Fig. 3. Proof tree for mergesort$([b,a],c) \to [b,a]$

Proof Sketch

1. By assumption 1, there is a proof tree T' such that $CESC \models_{P,T'} \langle |e|, \theta \rangle \to |vals|$. From T' it is easy to construct a proof tree T'' for $\langle |e|\theta, id \rangle \to |vals|$. Then, the tree T such that $CESC \models_{(P_{\langle e, \theta \rangle}, T)} \langle r_{\text{main}}, id \rangle \to |vals|$ starting by an application of the (BFUN) inference rule for main/0 at the root, followed by a (CASE) inference with the body of main/0 (see Definition 1, item 4) and then followed by T''.

2. Every proof tree with an invalid root contains a buggy node [24].

    (a) $\langle e, \theta \rangle \to vals$ is unexpected, by assumption 2, $ICESC \nvDash_{P,\mathcal{I}} \langle |e|, \theta \rangle \to |vals|$, and it is easy to check that then $ICESC \nvDash \langle |e|\theta, id \rangle \to |vals|$. Hence, the root of T'' is invalid and T'' contains a buggy node N. Since T'' is a subtree of T which does not contain main/0 then the node is not related to this function. Moreover, since all the inference rules except for (BFUN) are both in $CESC$ and in $ICESC$, and the buggy node has all its premises valid, by Lemma 1 N is the conclusion of a (BFUN) inference. Thus, N is of the form $\langle r_f, \theta \rangle \to vals$, $f \neq \text{main}$.

    (b) By Definition 1.2 the buggy node N in T'' (and therefore in T) verifies:
        i. N is invalid, and thus by Definition 1.1: $ICESC \nvDash_{(P,\mathcal{I})} \langle r_f, \theta \rangle \to vals$.
        ii. The premises of N in T are valid. N is the conclusion of a (BFUN) rule, and then the only premise corresponds to the proof in $CESC$ of the function body B. Since it is valid, by Definition 1.1 the proof in $CESC$ implies the proof in $ICESC$.

        By 2(b)i and 2(b)ii and according to Definition 1.3, $\langle r_f, \theta \rangle$ is a wrong function instance.   □

Although the previous result shows that the proof trees obtained by using $CESC$ might be used as debugging trees, they contain many questions difficult to answer for the user, including the results of nested applications, or even new statements introduced in the Core representation of the program. In order to overcome these difficulties we abbreviate the proof tree keeping only the relevant information for detecting buggy nodes.

Definition 2. *Let P be a program and $\langle e, \theta \rangle \to vals$ an evaluation. A tree T is an Abbreviated Proof Tree (APT in short) for the evaluation with respect to P, iff there is a proof tree T' such that $CESC \models_{(P_{\langle e, \theta \rangle}, T')} \langle r_{main}, id \rangle \to vals$, and $T = APT(T')$ with the transformation APT defined as follows:*

$$APT \left(\text{(BFUN)} \frac{T}{\mathcal{E}} \right) = \frac{APT(T)}{\mathcal{E}}$$
$$APT \left(\text{(R)} \frac{T_1 \dots T_n}{\mathcal{E}} \right) = APT(T_1) \dots APT(T_n), \text{ with (R)} \neq \text{(BFUN)}$$

The transformation keeps the conclusion of (BFUN) inferences, removing the rest of the nodes. Observe that the result is a single tree because the root of T' always corresponds to the application of (BFUN) to an evaluation over main/0.

$$\frac{\triangledown_1 \quad \texttt{t(1,[b,a])} \to \texttt{[b]} \quad \texttt{ms([a],c)} \to \texttt{[a]} \quad \triangledown_2 \quad \texttt{ms([b],c)} \to \texttt{[b]}}{(\circ) \ \texttt{ms([b,a],c)} \to \texttt{[b,a]}}$$

$$\texttt{main()} \to \texttt{[b,a]}$$

where:

$$\triangledown_1 = \frac{\texttt{m([a],[],c)} \to \texttt{[a]} \quad \texttt{c(b,a)} \to \texttt{false}}{(\circ, \bullet) \ \texttt{m([b],[a],c)} \to \texttt{[b,a]}} \qquad \triangledown_2 = \frac{\texttt{t(1,[a,b])} \to \texttt{[a]}}{\texttt{l(1,[b,a])} \to \texttt{[a]}}$$

Fig. 4. Abbreviated Proof tree for `mergesort([b,a],comp)` → `[b,a]`

The structure of the APTs is similar to the *evaluation dependence tree* employed in functional languages [26]. The main difference, apart from the particularities of each language, is that in our case the APTs are obtained from a semantic calculus, which allows us to prove their adequacy as debugging trees:

Theorem 2. *Let P be a Core Erlang program, $\mathcal{I}$ its intended interpretation, and $e\theta \to vals$ an unexpected evaluation. Let T' be such that $CESC \models_{(P_{(e,\theta)},T')} \langle r_{main}, id \rangle \to vals$, and $T = APT(T')$. Then T contains at least one buggy node N including a wrong instance of a user function different from `main/0`.*

Proof Sketch

As observed in the sketch of Theorem 1, there is a tree T'', subtree of T', which contains a buggy node N not associated to `main`. By construction (Definition 2) N is in T, and thus N is the invalid root of a subtree of T which does not contain `main/0`. Hence T contains a buggy node N not associated to `main/0`.

Let $N_1, \ldots, N_k$ be the direct descendants of N in T' which correspond to conclusions of (BFUN) inferences. By Definition 2 these nodes are the premises of N in T, and since N is buggy then $N_1, \ldots, N_k$ must be valid. Applying Lemma 1 it is easy to check that all the intermediate nodes between N and $N_1, \ldots, N_k$ are valid. This proves that all the premises of N in T' which are ancestors of (BFUN) inferences are valid. The rest of the premises of N in T' are roots of proof trees without (BFUN) inferences, and by Lemma 2 are valid as well. Thus N is buggy in T', and by Theorem 1 it contains a wrong function instance. □

Therefore, during the debugging process the user only needs to answer questions about the validity of nodes in the APT, which corresponds exactly to the evaluations in the intended interpretation. Figure 4 shows the APT for our running example. The calls to `reverse/1` have been removed because predefined functions are automatically trusted. The evaluations $\langle r_f, \theta \rangle \to vals$ are shown with the more user-friendly form $f(var_1\theta, \ldots, var_n\theta) \to vals$, which is also the form employed by the debugger. For the sake of space we use c for `comp/2`, t for `take/2`, l for `last/2`, ms for `mergesort/2`, and m for `merge/3`. The invalid nodes are preceded by ∘ and the only buggy node is preceded also by •.

6 System Description

The technique described in the previous sections has been implemented in Erlang. The tool is called `edd` and it has approximately 1000 lines of code. It is publicly available at `https://github.com/tamarit/edd`.

When a user detects an unexpected result, edd asks questions of the form call = value, where the user has the option to answer either *yes* (y) or *no* (n). In addition to these two responses, the user can answer *don't know* (d), when the answer is unknown; *inadmissible* (i), when the question does not apply; or *trusted* (t), when the user knows that the function is correct and further questions are not necessary. Before starting the debugger, the user can also define a number of functions to be trusted. The user can also *undo* (u), which reverts to the previous question, and *abort* (a), which closes the debugging session. Moreover, the tool includes a memoization feature that stores the answers *yes*, *no*, *trusted*, and *inadmissible*, preventing the system from asking the same question twice. Finally, it is worth noting that the answer *don't know* is used to ease the interaction with the debugger but it may introduce incompleteness, so we did not consider it in our proofs; if the debugger reaches a deadlock due to these answers it will inform the user about this fact.

The system can internally utilize two different navigation strategies [33,34], *Divide & Query* and *Heaviest First*, in order to choose the next node and therefore the next question presented to the user.

Both strategies help the system to minimize the number of questions and they can be switched during the session with option s. The rest of the section shows how the tool is used through a debugging session. Assume the user has decided to use edd to debug the error shown in Section 3. The debugging session with the default *Divide & Query* navigation strategy is:

```
> edd:dd("merge:mergesort([b,a], fun merge:comp/2)").
Please, insert a list of trusted functions [m1:f1/a1, m2:f2/a2 ...]:
merge:merge([b], [a], fun merge:comp/2) = [b, a]?: n
```

The strategy selects the subtree marked with (○, ●) in Figure 4, because the whole tree (without the dummy node for main and the node for the initial call, that we know is wrong because the user is using the debugger) has 8 nodes and this subtree, with 3 nodes, is the closest one to half the size of the whole tree. The question associated to the node, shown above, asks the user whether she expects to obtain the list [b,a] when evaluating merge([b], [a], fun merge:comp/2). She answers no because this is obviously an unexpected result. Thus, the subtree rooted by this node becomes the current debugging tree.

```
merge:comp(b, a) = false?: t
```

The next question corresponds to one of the children of the previous node. In this case the tool asks to the user whether the result for comp(b, a) is false. The answer is t, which removes all the nodes related to the function comp (in this case the answer only affects this node, but trusting a function may remove several nodes in general). The next question is:

```
merge:merge([a], [], fun merge3:comp/2) = [a]?: y
```

In this case the function merge produces the expected result, so the user says yes. Since the first answer marked a node as invalid node and the next two answers indicated that all its children are correct, the tool infers that the node (o, •) in Figure 4 is buggy:[3]

```
Call to a function that contains an error:
merge:merge([b], [a], fun merge:comp/2) = [b, a]
Please, revise the fourth clause:
merge([H1 | T1], [H2 | T2], Comp) ->  case Comp(H1, H2) of
      false -> [H1 | merge([H2 | T1], T2, Comp)];
      true -> [H1 | merge(T1, [H2 | T2], Comp)]
   end.
```

This information is enough to find the error, marked by boxes in the definition of merge in Section 3. It is corrected by using [H2 | merge([H1 | T1], T2, Comp)].

Although this change fixes the error for the list [b,a], when mergesort is executed with a larger list, like [o,h,i,o], a new problem arises:

```
> merge:mergesort([o,h,i,o], fun merge:comp/2).
** exception error: no function clause matching
merge:comp(2,h) (merge.erl, line 16)
      in function  merge:merge/3 (merge.erl, line 12)
      in call from merge:mergesort/2 (merge.erl, line 7)
```

Note that the information given by the system is not useful to find the error, since merge and mergesort seem correct. Moreover, the user is sure that the error is not in comp/2, even though it receives a erroneous argument, and hence she has marked it as trusted. The user decides to follow a *Top Down* strategy in this session. The debugging session runs as follows:

```
> edd:dd("merge:mergesort([o,h,i,o], fun merge:comp/2)",top_down).
Please, insert a list of trusted functions [m1:f1/a1, m2:f2/a2 ...]:
merge:comp/2
merge:mergesort([2, h], fun merge:comp/2) = {error, match_fail}?: i
merge:last(2, [o, h, i, o]) = [i, 2]?: n
merge:take(2, [o, i, h, o]) = [2, i]?: n
merge:take(1, [i, h, o]) = [i]?: y
Call to a function that contains an error:
merge:take(2, [o, i, h, o]) = [2, i]
Please, revise the fourth clause:
take(N, [H | T]) -> [N | take(N - 1, T)].
```

The answer to the first question is *inadmissible*, because the user considers that the function mergesort/2 is intended to sort lists of atoms, and the list contains an integer. In this case the debugger shows that the problem is in the function take/2. In fact, if we inspect the code in Section 3 (the box in the definition of take) we realize that it contains an error. It should be [H | take(N - 1, T)].

After these changes all the errors have been solved. Note that only seven questions were required to locate two errors, one of them involving exceptions.

---

[3] Note that we have used here the debugging tree to explain the main ideas of the technique, although it is not needed during a standard debugging session.

7 Concluding Remarks and Ongoing Work

Debugging is usually the most time-consuming phase of the software life cycle, yet it remains a basically unformalized task. This is unfortunate, because formalizing a task introduces the possibility of improving it. With this idea in mind we propose a formal debugging technique that analyzes proof trees of erroneous computations in order to find bugs in sequential Erlang programs. A straightforward benefit is that it allows to prove the soundness and completeness of the scheme. Another benefit is that, since the debugger only requires knowing the intended meaning of the program functions, the team in charge of the debugging phase do not need to include the actual programmers of the code. This separation of rôles is an advantage during the development of any software project.

Although most of the applications based on Erlang employ the concurrent features of the language the concurrency is usually located in specific modules, and thus specific tools for debugging the sequential part are also interesting. Our debugger locates the error based only on the intended meaning of the user functions, and thus abstracts away the implementation details. It can be viewed as complementary to the trace debugger already included in Erlang: first the declarative debugger is used for singling out an erroneous program function and then the standard tracer is employed for inspecting the function body. The declarative debugger is particularly useful for detecting wrong functions that produce unexpected exceptions, as shown in the running example included in the paper. The main limitation of the proposal is that an initial unexpected result must be detected by the user, which implies in particular that it cannot be used to debug non-terminating computations.

We have used these ideas to implement a tool that supports different navigation strategies, trusting, and built-in functions, among other features. It has been used to debug several buggy medium-size programs, presenting an encouraging performance. More information can be found at `https://github.com/tamarit/edd`.

As future work we plan to improve the location of the bug inside a wrong function, which implies an extended setting taking into account the code defining the functions. Another interesting line of future work consists on extending the current framework to debug concurrent Core Erlang programs. This extension will require new rules in the calculus to deal with functions for creating new processes and sending and receiving messages, as well as the identification of new kinds of errors that the debugger can detect.

References

1. Alpuente, M., Ballis, D., Correa, F., Falaschi, M.: An integrated framework for the diagnosis and correction of rule-based programs. Theoretical Computer Science 411(47), 4055–4101 (2010)
2. Armstrong, J., Williams, M., Wikstrom, C., Virding, R.: Concurrent Programming in Erlang, 2nd edn. Prentice-Hall, Englewood Cliffs (1996)

3. Arts, T., Benac Earle, C., Sánchez Penas, J.J.: Translating Erlang to muCRL. In: Proceedings of the International Conference on Application of Concurrency to System Design, ACSD 2004, pp. 135–144. IEEE Computer Society Press (June 2004)
4. Benac Earle, C., Fredlund, L.A.: Recent improvements to the McErlang model checker. In: Proceedings of the 8th ACM SIGPLAN Workshop on ERLANG, ERLANG 2009, pp. 93–100. ACM, New York (2009)
5. Caballero, R.: A declarative debugger of incorrect answers for constraint functional-logic programs. In: Antoy, S., Hanus, M. (eds.) Proceedings of the 2005 ACM SIGPLAN Workshop on Curry and Functional Logic Programming, WCFLP 2005, Tallinn, Estonia, pp. 8–13. ACM Press (2005)
6. Caballero, R., Hermanns, C., Kuchen, H.: Algorithmic debugging of Java programs. In: López-Fraguas, F. (ed.) Proceedings of the 15th Workshop on Functional and (Constraint) Logic Programming, WFLP 2006, Madrid, Spain. Electronic Notes in Theoretical Computer Science, vol. 177, pp. 75–89. Elsevier (2007)
7. Caballero, R., Martin-Martin, E., Riesco, A., Tamarit, S.: A calculus for sequential erlang programs. Technical Report 03/13, Departamento de Sistemas Informáticos y Computación (April 2013)
8. Carlsson, R.: An introduction to Core Erlang. In: Proceedings of the Erlang Workshop 2001, In Connection with PLI (2001)
9. Carlsson, R., Gustavsson, B., Johansson, E., Lindgren, T., Nyström, S.-O., Pettersson, M., Virding, R.: Core Erlang 1.0.3 language specification (November 2004), http://www.it.uu.se/research/group/hipe/cerl/doc/core_erlang-1.0.3.pdf
10. Carlsson, R., Rémond, M.: EUnit: a lightweight unit testing framework for Erlang. In: Proceedings of the 2006 ACM SIGPLAN Workshop on Erlang, ERLANG 2006, p. 1. ACM, New York (2006)
11. Christakis, M., Sagonas, K.: Static detection of race conditions in Erlang. In: Carro, M., Peña, R. (eds.) PADL 2010. LNCS, vol. 5937, pp. 119–133. Springer, Heidelberg (2010)
12. Christensen, N.H.: Domain-specific languages in software development - and the relation to partial evaluation. PhD thesis, DIKU, Dept. of Computer Science, University of Copenhagen, Denmark (July 2003)
13. Claessen, K., Svensson, H.: A semantics for distributed Erlang. In: Proceedings of the 2005 ACM SIGPLAN Workshop on Erlang, ERLANG 2005, pp. 78–87. ACM, New York (2005)
14. David, R., Mounier, G.: An intuitionistic lambda-calculus with exceptions. Journal of Functional Programming 15(1), 33–52 (2005)
15. de Groote, P.: A simple calculus of exception handling. In: Dezani-Ciancaglini, M., Plotkin, G.D. (eds.) TLCA 1995. LNCS, vol. 902, pp. 201–215. Springer, Heidelberg (1995)
16. Fredlund, L.-A.: A Framework for Reasoning about Erlang Code. PhD thesis, The Royal Institute of Technology, Sweden (August. 2001)
17. Hähnle, R., Baum, M., Bubel, R., Rothe, M.: A visual interactive debugger based on symbolic execution. In: Pecheur, C., Andrews, J., Nitto, E.D. (eds.) 25th IEEE/ACM International Conference on Automated Software Engineering, ASE 2010, pp. 143–146. ACM (2010)
18. Huch, F.: Verification of erlang programs using abstract interpretation and model checking. SIGPLAN Not. 34(9), 261–272 (1999)
19. Hughes, J.: QuickCheck testing for fun and profit. In: Hanus, M. (ed.) PADL 2007. LNCS, vol. 4354, pp. 1–32. Springer, Heidelberg (2007)

20. Insa, D., Silva, J.: An algorithmic debugger for Java. In: Lanza, M., Marcus, A. (eds.) Proceedings of the 26th IEEE International Conference on Software Maintenance, ICSM 2010, pp. 1–6. IEEE Computer Society (2010)
21. Lindahl, T., Sagonas, K.: Detecting software defects in telecom applications through lightweight static analysis: A war story. In: Chin, W.-N. (ed.) APLAS 2004. LNCS, vol. 3302, pp. 91–106. Springer, Heidelberg (2004)
22. MacLarty, I.: Practical declarative debugging of Mercury programs. Master's thesis, University of Melbourne (2005)
23. Naish, L.: Declarative diagnosis of missing answers. New Generation Computing 10(3), 255–286 (1992)
24. Naish, L.: A declarative debugging scheme. Journal of Functional and Logic Programming 1997(3) (1997)
25. Nilsson, H.: How to look busy while being as lazy as ever: the implementation of a lazy functional debugger. Journal of Functional Programming 11(6), 629–671 (2001)
26. Nilsson, H., Sparud, J.: The evaluation dependence tree as a basis for lazy functional debugging. Automated Software Engineering 4, 121–150 (1997)
27. Papadakis, M., Sagonas, K.: A PropEr integration of types and function specifications with property-based testing. In: Proceedings of the 2011 ACM SIGPLAN Erlang Workshop, pp. 39–50. ACM Press (2011)
28. Pope, B.: Declarative debugging with Buddha. In: Vene, V., Uustalu, T. (eds.) AFP 2004. LNCS, vol. 3622, pp. 273–308. Springer, Heidelberg (2005)
29. Pope, B.: A Declarative Debugger for Haskell. PhD thesis, The University of Melbourne, Australia (2006)
30. Riesco, A., Verdejo, A., Martí-Oliet, N., Caballero, R.: Declarative debugging of rewriting logic specifications. Journal of Logic and Algebraic Programming 81(7-8), 851–897 (2012)
31. Sagonas, K., Silva, J., Tamarit, S.: Precise explanation of success typing errors. In: Proceedings of the ACM SIGPLAN 2013 Workshop on Partial Evaluation and Program Manipulation, PEPM 2013, pp. 33–42. ACM, New York (2013)
32. Shapiro, E.Y.: Algorithmic Program Debugging. ACM Distinguished Dissertation. MIT Press (1983)
33. Silva, J.: A comparative study of algorithmic debugging strategies. In: Puebla, G. (ed.) LOPSTR 2006. LNCS, vol. 4407, pp. 143–159. Springer, Heidelberg (2007)
34. Silva, J.: A survey on algorithmic debugging strategies. Advances in Engineering Software 42(11), 976–991 (2011)
35. Svensson, H., Fredlund, L.-A.: A more accurate semantics for distributed Erlang. In: Proceedings of the 2007 SIGPLAN Workshop on ERLANG Workshop, ERLANG 2007, pp. 43–54. ACM, New York (2007)
36. Tessier, A., Ferrand, G.: Declarative diagnosis in the CLP scheme. In: Deransart, P., Hermenegildo, M.V., Maluszynski, J. (eds.) DiSCiPl 1999. LNCS, vol. 1870, pp. 151–174. Springer, Heidelberg (2000)

Initiating a Benchmark
for UML and OCL Analysis Tools

Martin Gogolla[1], Fabian Büttner[2,*], and Jordi Cabot[2]

[1] University of Bremen, Germany
[2] AtlanMod, École des Mines de Nantes - INRIA, LINA, France

Abstract. The Object Constraint Language (OCL) is becoming more
and more popular for model-based engineering, in particular for the development of models and model transformations. OCL is supported by
a variety of analysis tools having different scopes, aims and technologi-
cal corner stones. The spectrum ranges from treating issues concerning
formal proof techniques to testing approaches, from validation to verification, and from logic programming and rewriting to SAT-based technologies. This paper is a first step towards a well-founded benchmark
for assessing validation and verification techniques on UML and OCL
models. The paper puts forward a set of UML and OCL models together
with particular questions for these models roughly characterized by the
notions consistency, independence, consequences, and reachability. The
paper sketches how these questions are handled by two OCL tools, USE
and EMFtoCSP. The claim of the paper is not to present a complete
benchmark right now. The paper is intended to initiate the development
of further UML and OCL models and accompanying questions within
the UML and OCL community. The OCL community is invited to check
the presented UML and OCL models with their approaches and tools
and to contribute further models and questions which emphasize the
possibilities offered by their own tools.

1   Introduction

Model-driven engineering (MDE) as a paradigm for software development is gain-
ing more and more importance. Models and model transformations are central
notions in modeling languages like UML, SysML, or EMF and transformation
languages like QVT or ATL. In these approaches, the Object Constraint Language (OCL) can be employed for expressing constraints and operations, thus
OCL plays a central role in MDE. A variety of OCL tools is currently available,
but it is an open issue how to compare these tools and how to support developers in choosing the OCL tool appropriate for their project. This paper puts
forward a set of UML and OCL models together with particular questions for
these models. This set of models is intended to be a first version of an OCL
analysis tool benchmark to be developed within the OCL and UML community.

---

* This research was partially funded by the Nouvelles Équipes program of the Pays
  de la Loire region (France).

M. Veanes and L. Viganò (Eds.): TAP 2013, LNCS 7942, pp. 115–132, 2013.

The current benchmark consists of four UML and OCL models: CivilStatus (CS), WritesReviews (WR), DisjointSubclasses (DS), and ObjectsAsIntegers (OAI). These models employ and emphasize different UML and OCL language features and pose different computational challenges for the analysis tools and their underlying technologies like provers, solvers, or finders: Plain invariants and enumerations in CS, association multiplicities in WR, classifier generalization in DS, and recursive operation definitions with inherited association ends and constraints in OAI. The accompanying questions can be roughly characterized by the partly overlapping notions consistency, independence, consequences, and reachability: under the label 'consistency' we discuss whether there exist object diagrams for the model at all, 'independence' concentrates on whether the invariants are nonredundant, 'consequences' studies how to formally deduce new properties from the explicitly stated ones, and 'reachability' focuses on how to characterize all object diagrams of a model and how to construct an object diagram with stated properties. The benchmark does not expect that all questions can be fully answered by a considered tool, but it expects that it is discussed to what extent and in which direction an approach or tool can help to answer the question.

The structure of the rest of this paper is as follows. The next section gives a short introduction to OCL. Section 3 introduces the first version of our benchmark. Four example models with accompanying questions are introduced. As a proof of concept for the applicability of the models, Sect. 4 and Sect. 5 show how these models and questions are handled by two concrete tools and how the models must be fine-tuned to become processable by the respective tool, if needed. These two tools have been selected to illustrate how the models can be used to evaluate tools. Section 6 puts forward a list of topics that could be addressed in future work. Section 7 discusses related work and some (not all) approaches suitable to be subject to an OCL analysis tool benchmark. The paper is finished in Sect. 8 with concluding remarks. Furthermore, the paper is extended by an additional document [14] in which all models are detailed in the formats .use and .ecore and all details of the benchmark examples for the tools USE and EMFtoCSP are made available.

2   OCL in 5 Minutes

The Object Constrains Language (OCL) is a textual, descriptive expression language. OCL is side effect free and is mainly used for phrasing constraints and queries in object-oriented models. Most OCL expressions rely on a class model which is expressed in a graphical modeling language like UML, MOF or EMF. The central concepts in OCL are objects, object navigation, collections, collection operations and boolean-valued expressions, i.e., formulas. Let us consider these concepts in connection with the object diagram in Fig. 1 which belongs to the class diagram in Fig. 3. This class diagram captures part of the submission and reviewing process of conference papers. A more detailed description of the class diagram and the corresponding constraints is given later in Section 2.2. The class diagram defines classes with attributes (and operations, not used in

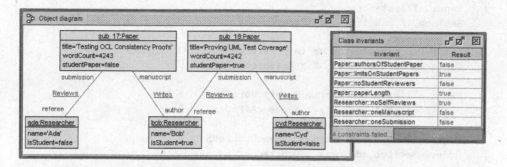

Fig. 1. Object Diagram for WR

this example) and associations with roles and multiplicities which restrict the number of possible connected objects.

Objects: An OCL expression will often begin with an object literal or an object variable. For the system state represented in the object diagram, one can use the objects `ada,bob,cyd` of type `Researcher` and `sub_17,sub_18` of type `Paper`. Furthermore variables like `p:Paper` and `r:Researcher` can be employed.

Object Navigation: Object navigation is realized by using role names from associations (or object-valued attributes, not occurring in this example) which are applied to objects or object collections. In the example, the following navigation expressions can be stated. The first line shows the OCL expression and the second line the evaluation result and the type of the expression and the result.

```
bob.manuscript
sub_17 : Paper

bob.manuscript.referee
Set{ada} : Set(Researcher)

cyd.manuscript.referee.manuscript.referee
Bag{ada} : Bag(Researcher)

sub_17.author->union(sub_17.referee)
Set{ada,bob} : Set(Researcher)
```

Collections: Collections can be employed in OCL to merge different elements into a single structure containing the elements. There are four collection kinds: sets, bags, sequences and ordered sets. Sets and ordered sets can contain an elements at most once, whereas bags and sequences may contain an element more than once. In sets and bags the element order is insignificant, whereas sequences and ordered sets are sensitive to the element order. For a given class, the operation allInstances yields the set of current objects in the class.

```
Paper.allInstances
Set{sub_17,sub_18} : Set(Paper)

let P=Paper.allInstances in P.referee->union(P.author)
Bag{ada,bob,bob,cyd} : Bag(Researcher)

Paper.allInstances->sortedBy(p|p.wordCount)
Sequence{sub_18,sub_17} : Sequence(Paper)

Sequence{bob,ada,bob,cyd,ada}->asOrderedSet
OrderedSet{bob,ada,cyd} : OrderedSet(Researcher)
```

Collection Operations: There is a number of collection operations which contribute essentially to the expressibility of OCL and which are applied with the arrow operator. Among further operations, collections can be tested on emptiness (isEmpty, notEmpty), the number of elements can be determined (size), the elements can be filtered (select, reject), elements can be mapped to a different item (collect) or can be sorted(sortedBy), set-theoretic operations may be employed (union, intersection), and collections can be converted into other collection kinds (asSet, asBag, asSequence, asOrderdSet). Above, we have already used the collection operations union, sortedBy, and asOrderedSet.

```
Paper.allInstances->isEmpty
false : Boolean

Researcher.allInstances->size
3 : Integer

Researcher.allInstances->select(r | not r.isStudent)
Set{ada,cyd} : Set(Researcher)

Paper.allInstances->reject(p | p.studentPaper)
Set{sub_17} : Set(Paper)

Paper.allInstances->collect(p | p.author.name)
Bag{'Bob','cyd'} : Bag(String)
```

Boolean-Valued Expressions: Because OCL is a constraint language, boolean expressions which formalize model properties play a central role. Apart from typical boolean connectives (and, or, not, =, implies, xor), universal and existential quantification are available (forAll, exists).

```
Researcher.allInstances->forAll(r,s | r<>s implies r.name<>s.name)
true : Boolean

Paper.allInstances->exists(p | p.studentPaper and p.wordCount>4242)
false : Boolean
```

Boolean expressions are frequently used to describe class invariants and operation pre- and postconditions.

3   Benchmark for UML and OCL Models (V-2013-04-05)

This section introduces the current benchmark models. We believe these four models offer a representative set of challenges and modeling language features.

3.1   CivilStatus (CS)

The simple class model in Fig. 2 with one class, one association, one operation defined with OCL, and two enumerations describes the civil status of persons. The six invariants require that (1) all attributes take defined values only, (2) the name attribute values follow a particular format, (3) the name attribute is unique among all persons, (4) a female person does not possess a wife, (5) a male person does not possess a husband,[1] and (6) a person has a spouse, if and only if the civil status attribute holds the value married.

Questions: (Questions are given names in order to reference them)

ConsistentInvariants: Is the model consistent? Is there at least one object diagram satisfying the UML class model and the explicit OCL invariants?

Independence: Are the invariants independent? Is there an invariant which is a consequence of the conditions imposed by the UML class model and the other invariants?

Consequences: Is it possible to show that a stated new property is a consequence of the given model? As a concrete question in terms of the model, one may ask: Is the model bigamy-free? Is it possible to have a person possessing both a wife and a husband?

LargeState: Is it possible to automatically build valid object diagrams in a parameterized way with a medium-sized number of objects, e.g. 10 to 30 objects and appropriate links, where all attributes take meaningful values and all links are established in a meaningful way? For example, a female person named Ada could be married in role wife to a male person named Bob occupying the husband role. These larger object diagrams are intended to explain the used model elements (like classes, attributes and associations) and the constraints upon them by non-trivial, meaningful examples to domain experts not necessarily familiar with formal modeling techniques.

3.2   WritesReviews (WR)

The class model in Fig. 3 has the classes Paper and Researcher and two associations in between. The first two invariants (1) oneManuscript and (2) oneSubmission basically sharpen the 0..1 multiplicities to 1..1 multiplicities. In order to discuss alternative models, these two invariants will later be switched off for the construction of object diagrams. The next five invariants require that (3) a paper cannot be refereed by one of its authors, (4) the paper

---

[1] We are aware of the fact that we are only dealing with 'traditional marriages' with traditional roles, and not with more modern concepts like 'common law marriages'.

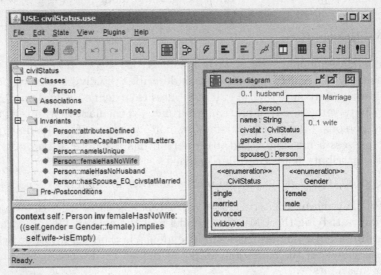

```
context Person
  inv attributesDefined: name<>null and civstat<>null and
      gender<>null
  inv nameCapitalThenSmallLetters:
    let small:Set(String)=
      Set{'a','b','c','d','e','f','g','h','i','j','k','l','m',
          'n','o','p','q','r','s','t','u','v','w','x','y','z'} in
    let capital:Set(String)=
      Set{'A','B','C','D','E','F','G','H','I','J','K','L','M',
          'N','O','P','Q','R','S','T','U','V','W','X','Y','Z'} in
    capital->includes(name.substring(1,1)) and
    Set{2..name.size}->forAll(i |
      small->includes(name.substring(i,i)))
  inv nameIsUnique: Person.allInstances->forAll(self2|
      self<>self2 implies self.name<>self2.name)
  inv femaleHasNoWife: gender=#female implies wife->isEmpty
  inv maleHasNoHusband: gender=#male implies husband->isEmpty
  inv hasSpouse_EQ_civstatMarried: (spouse()<>null)=(civstat=#married)
```

Fig. 2. Class Diagram and Invariants for CS

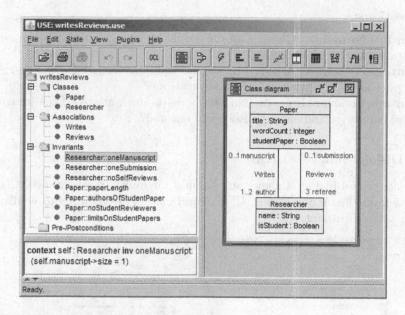

```
context Researcher inv oneManuscript:
  self.manuscript->size=1
context Researcher inv oneSubmission:
  self.submission->size=1
context Researcher inv noSelfReviews:
  self.submission->excludes(self.manuscript)
context Paper inv paperLength:
  self.wordCount < 10000
context Paper inv authorsOfStudentPaper:
  self.studentPaper=self.author->exists(x | x.isStudent)
context Paper inv noStudentReviewers:
  self.referee->forAll(r | not r.isStudent)
context Paper inv limitsOnStudentPapers:
  Paper.allInstances->exists(p | p.studentPaper) and
  Paper.allInstances->select(p | p.studentPaper)->size < 5
```

Fig. 3. Class Diagram and Invariants for WR

must obey a given length by restricting the attribute wordCount, (5) one of the authors of a studentPaper must be a student, (6) students are not allowed to review papers, and (7) there must be at least one student paper, but no more than 4 student papers are allowed (assumed that there are Paper objects at all).

Questions:

InstantiateNonemptyClass: Can the model be instantiated with non-empty populations for all classes?

InstantiateNonemptyAssoc: Can the model be instantiated with non-empty populations for all classes and all associations?

InstantiateInvariantIgnore: Can the model be instantiated if the invariants oneManuscript and oneSubmission are ignored?

3.3   DisjointSubclasses (DS)

The class model in Fig. 4 shows an example for multiple inheritance. Class D inherits from class B and class C. Class B and class C are required to be disjoint by the stated invariant.

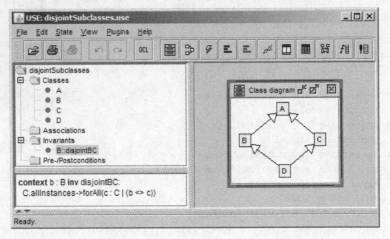

```
context b:B inv disjointBC: C.allInstances->forAll(c|b<>c)
```

Fig. 4. Class Diagram and Invariants for WR

Questions:

InstantiateDisjointInheritance: Can all classes be populated? Is it possible to build objects for class D?

InstantiateMultipleInheritance: Can class D be populated if the constraint disjointBC is ignored?

A light extension of this benchmark model might add attributes a, b, c, and d to all classes having the type Integer. A hypothetical example constraint for class D might then require self.d=2*self.a. It would be interesting to see whether a tool syntactically allows to reference the attribute a from class D.

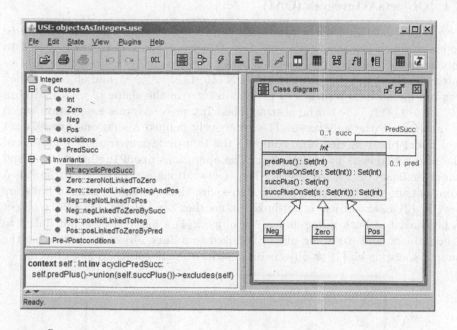

```
context Int
  inv acyclicPredSucc:
    predPlus()->union(succPlus())->excludes(self)
context Zero
  inv zeroNotLinkedToZero:
    not predPlus()->union(succPlus())->exists(i|
      i.oclIsTypeOf(Zero))
  inv zeroNotLinkedToNegAndPos:
    not predPlus()->union(succPlus())->exists(n,p|
      n.oclIsTypeOf(Neg) and p.oclIsTypeOf(Pos))
context Neg
  inv negNotLinkedToPos:
    not predPlus()->union(succPlus())->exists(p|
      p.oclIsTypeOf(Pos))
  inv negLinkedToZeroBySucc:
    succPlus()->exists(z|z.oclIsTypeOf(Zero))
context Pos
  inv posNotLinkedToNeg:
    not predPlus()->union(succPlus())->exists(n|
      n.oclIsTypeOf(Neg))
  inv posLinkedToZeroByPred:
    predPlus()->exists(z|z.oclIsTypeOf(Zero))
```

Fig. 5. Class Diagram and Invariants for WR

3.4   ObjectsAsIntegers (OAI)

The class model in Fig. 5 introduces one abstract superclass `Int` and three concrete subclasses `Neg`, `Zero`, and `Pos`. Objects of class `Zero` are intended to represent the integer 0, objects of class `Neg` are intended to represent a negative integer in the shape of a normal form `(...((0-1)-1)...)-1`, and objects of class `Pos` are intended to represent a positive integer in the shape of a normal form `(...((0+1)+1)...)+1`. The abstract class `Int` possesses one association which is inherited to the subclasses. The recursively defined operations `predPlus()` and `succPlus()` in class `Int` compute the (non-reflexive) transitive closure of the association ends `pred` and `succ`. The operations `predPlusOnSet(...)` and `succPlusOnSet(...)` are internal helper operations not intended to be called from outside the class. The invariants require that (1) the `PredSucc` links are acyclic, (2) a `Zero` object is not linked to another `Zero` object, (3) a `Zero` object is not linked to both a `Neg` and a `Pos` object, (4) a `Neg` object is not linked to a `Pos` object, and (5) a `Neg` object is linked to a `Zero` object by employing the `succ` association end. `Pos` objects are restricted analogously to `Neg` objects.

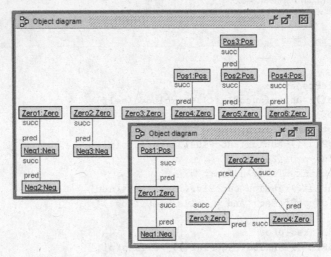

Fig. 6. Example Object Diagrams for OAI

The upper object diagram in Fig. 6 shows a valid system state for OAI, the lower one an invalid system state with some invariants violated. For example, invariant zeroNotLinkedToNegAndPos is violated in the left connected component of the lower object diagram. The upper object diagram displays the object representation of the integer sequence $-2, -1, 0, +1, +2, +1$. Every connected component of the object diagram corresponds to an integer. The lower object diagram has two connected components, where both components taken in isolation already violate the model invariants, but obey the class diagram multiplicities.

Questions:

ObjectRepresentsInteger: Is it true that any connected component of a valid object diagram for the model either corresponds to the term *zero* or to a term of the form $succ^n(zero)$ with $n > 0$ or to a term of the form $pred^n(zero)$?

IntegerRepresentsObject: Is it true that any term of the form *zero* or of the form $succ^n(zero)$ or of the form $pred^n(zero)$ corresponds to a valid object diagram for the model?

A slight extension of the current benchmark might ask a tool to find a minimal constraint subset (or all constraint subsets) such that the same invariants are implied as above.

4 Handling the Benchmark in USE

USE is a tool that allows modelers to check and test UML and OCL models. It allows model validation and verification based of enumeration and SAT-based techniques. USE allows the developer to construct object diagrams with a specialized language called ASSL (A Snapshot Sequence Language). All details can be traced from the provided additional material [14].

4.1 CivilStatus (CS)

For the CS example, there are three procedures which aim to construct object diagrams: (1) `generateWorld(numFemale:Integer, numMale:Integer, numMarriage:Integer)` can build object diagrams satisfying all constraints and object diagrams violating particular constraints, (2) `largerWorld(num-Female:Integer, numMale:Integer, numMarriage:Integer)` can build larger object diagrams (up to 26 female persons and 26 male persons with at most 26 marriages) satisfying all constraints, and (3) `attemptBigamy()` tries to construct an object diagram including bigamy.

ConsistentInvariants: The consistency of the invariants in combination with the class diagram model inherent constraints is shown by a calling `generateWorld(1,1,1)` with all invariants activated.

Independence: The independence of the six invariants is shown by six calls to `generateWorld(1,1,1)` where before each single call exactly one invariant is negated and the other invariants are activated.

Consequences: The fact that the model is bigamy-free is demonstrated by a call to `attemptBigamy()`. In that procedure a large number of possible object diagrams with three persons and all possible assignments of roles and attribute values is considered and checked. No object diagram showing bigamy is found.

LargeState: A larger object diagram is constructed by the call `largerWorld(5,7,4)` which constructs a system state with five female persons, seven male persons, and four marriages.

4.2   WritesReviews (WR)

For the WR example, one ASSL procedure is provided: `generateWorld(num-Pap:Integer, numRes:Integer, fillAttr:Boolean)`. The parameters determine the number of papers, the number of researchers, and whether the object attributes should be filled with actual values.

InstantiateNonemptyClass,InstantiateNonemptyAssoc: A call to `generateWorld(4,4,false)` yields the answer that no valid object diagram can be constructed. The attribute values are not taken into account. This shows that the multiplicities cannot be satisfied in the considered search space.

InstantiateInvariantIgnore: If the two invariants `oneManuscript` and `oneSubmission` are deactivated, a valid object diagram can be constructed by calling `generateWorld(1,4,true)`. The attributes take meaningful values in the constructed object diagram.

4.3   DisjointSubclasses (DS)

For the model DS the ASSL procedure `generateWorld(noA:Integer, noB:Integer, noC:Integer, noD:Integer)` is employed.

InstantiateDisjointInheritance: A call to `generateWorld(1,1,1,1)` with invariant `disjointBC` activated does not yield a valid object diagram.

InstantiateMultipleInheritance: Calling `generateWorld(1,1,1,1)` with invariant `disjointBC` deactivated does return a valid object diagram, naturally with all objects of class D being also objects in class B and class C.

4.4   ObjectsAsIntegers (OAI)

For the model OAI, the ASSL procedure `generateWorld(intNum:Integer, predSuccNum:Integer)` constructs an object diagram with `intNum` objects for class `Int` and `predSuccNum` links between these `Int` objects. The constructed object diagram does not necessarily obey the invariants, but the results can be looked at being test cases for human inspection.

ObjectRepresentsInteger: We have generated various test cases with the above ASSL procedure and found no counter examples for the stated question resp. claim. However, we do not have solid formal arguments that the claim is valid.

IntegerRepresentsObject: One can formulate an ASSL procedure `generate-Int(i:Integer)` that constructs the appropriate object diagram of class `Int`: Exactly one `Zero` object will be created; if $i < 0$, the respective number of `Neg` objects will be created and linked to the single `Zero` object in a correct way; if $i > 0$, the procedure will create `Pos` objects, analogously.

5   Handling the Benchmark in EMFtoCSP

Consistency checking and model instantiation are performed transparently in EMFtoCSP by internally creating a constraint satisfaction problem (CSP) that is satisfiable iff the model plus the OCL constraints satisfy the given correctness property. The user has to specify ranges for the class and association extents and for the attribute domains. All details are provided in the additional material [14].

5.1   CivilStatus (CS)

For running the CivilStatus checks, the range 0..5 was used for the Person class and the range 0..25 for the Marriage association. The string length of the name attribute was set to 0..10 (EMFtoCSP supports the String datatype and its operations [6]). We omitted the invariants attributesDefined and nameCapitalThenSmallLetters. The first holds implicitly because of the search space configuration, the second currently cannot be parsed by the EMFtoCSP front-end.

ConsistentInvariants: The consistency of the invariants in combination with the class diagram inherent constraints is shown by running EMFtoCSP with the described search bounds, selecting 'weak satisfiability' as the verification property, yielding a valid object diagram as proof.

Independence: The independence of the four considered invariants is shown by verifying four modified versions of CivilStatus, where one of the invariants is negated in each run. Using the described search bounds, each run yields an instance that is valid w.r.t. the modified version.

Consequences: The fact that the model is bigamy-free is demonstrated by amending CivilStatus with a constraint notIsBigamyFree that requires an instance with bigamy and then showing the unsatisfiability of that model using the described search bounds.

LargeState: Adding an invariant niceInstance to CivilStatus restricts the names to a meaningful set and the gender to be consistent with the name (e.g., name = 'Ada' implies gender = 1). We set the search bounds to 7 persons and 3 marriages and EMFtoCSP yields a valid instance.

5.2   WritesReviews (WR)

For running the WritesReviews checks, 0..5 was used for both classes and 0..25 for both associations, the string lengths were set to 0..10 and the range of wordCount to 0..10000.

InstantiateNonemptyClass: Checking 'weak consistency' shows that the model and the constraints are unsatisfiable within the above search bounds.

InstantiateNonemptyAssoc: Checking 'strong consistency' shows that the model and the constraints are unsatisfiable within the above search bounds.

InstantiateInvariantIgnore: Checking 'weak consistency' on a modified version of WritesReviews, in which both oneManuscript and oneSubmission are commented out, yields a satisfying instance.

5.3 DisjointSubclasses (DS)

The front-end of EMFtoCSP does currently not support multiple inheritance, although the UML/OCL constraint library that is used in the background provides all necessary predicates.

5.4 ObjectsAsIntegers (OAI)

EMFtoCSP does currently not solve models with recursive operations.

6 Discussion

The benchmark as presented in this paper is a first step in the definition of a complete set of UML and OCL models that the modeling community could accept as valid. More importantly, the community could start to compare and to improve current MDE approaches and tools, similar to what other communities in Software Engineering are already doing.

The models that we have discussed give a taste of the difficulties that anybody working on a new OCL analysis technique should consider. Nevertheless, our long term goal is the complete specification of a full benchmark model suite covering all known challenging verification and validation scenarios. The need for such a benchmark was one of the outcomes of the last OCL Workshop. However, the notion 'challenging scenario' is not universal and debatable, in the sense that depending on the formalism used by a given tool a scenario may be easy or extremely demanding. With proposing this benchmark and its hopefully coming evolution, we want developers to evaluate the existing approaches, realize which are the strengths and drawbacks of each one, and choose a tool or an approach according to their specific needs. Speaking generally, for an OCL analysis tool benchmark there are challenges in two dimensions: (a) challenges related to the complexity of OCL (i.e., the complete and accurate handling of OCL) and (b) challenges related to the computational complexity of the underlying problem. Both should be treated in the benchmark.

Based on our own experience we believe that at least the following scenarios should be covered by models in the benchmark:

1. Mostly local constraints: models with many constraints but where all constraints are local, i.e., they only involve a single class or a cluster of closely related classes.
2. Mostly global constraints: models with many constraints but where all constraints are global, i.e., they usually involve a large percentage of the classes in the model, e.g. a constraint forcing all classes in the model to have the same number of instances.
3. Models with tractable constraints, i.e., constraints that can be solved 'trivially' by simple propagation steps.
4. Models with hard, non-tractable constraints, e.g., representations of NP-hard problems.

5. Highly symmetric problems, i.e., that require symmetry breaking to efficiently detect unsatisfiability.
6. Intensive use of Integer arithmetic allowing large ranges for integer values and employing heavily arithmetic and operation like inequality.
7. Intensive use of Real arithmetic.
8. Intensive use of String values and operations on strings. So far, String attributes are mostly ignored [6] or simply regarded as integers which prohibits the verification of OCL expressions including String operations other than equality and inequality.
9. Many redundant constraints: is the approach able to detect the redundancies and benefit from them to speed up the evaluation?
10. Sparse models: instances with comparably few links offer optimization opportunities that could be exploited by tools.
11. Support for recursive operations, e.g. in form of fixpoint detection or static unfolding.
12. Intensive use of the 'full' semantic of OCL (like the undefined value or collection semantics); this poses a challenge for the lifting to two-valued logics.
13. Problems that have large instances (with many objects).

Alternative models for each of these scenarios should be part of the benchmark to cover different goals in the evaluation. For instance, when evaluating the correctness of the results provided by a given tool we should execute satisfiable and unsatisfiable versions of each model and when evaluating its performance and scalability we should feed the tool increasingly larger versions of the same model.

We hope that as soon as these benchmarks become available the interested community (from developers of tools to tool users) will start applying them on a variety of tools and approaches, which will allow us to clarify and better understand the differences among the plethora of approaches and tools for OCL solving that are now available. However, we have to keep in mind that as discussed in the previous section, the results of the benchmark have to be interpreted with care. A bad score of a tool for a given model can be attributed to different reasons, from a simple syntax problem (maybe the tool does not support one of the OCL operations used in an expression even if this operation is not a key part of the benchmark) to a limitation of the tool or a limitation of the underlying tool formalism. This difference is important too. In a further step, we want to able not only to compare the tools themselves but to use the benchmark to study the limits of frequently used provers, solvers or finders when applied to the OCL realm.

7   Potential Tools to Be Considered and Related Work

We have conducted the benchmark with the tools USE [15] and UMLtoCSP resp. EMFtoCSP [7,16]. Other validation and verification tools for OCL which are possible candidates to be examined under the benchmark are UML2Alloy [2], the planned USE extension arising from [19], the ITP/OCL tool [12], mOdCL [21] and MOMENT-OCL[4]. Furthermore, the OCL tools OCLE, ROCLET, and OCTOPUS would be benchmark candidates, but the projects seem to be inactive since years (http://lci.cs.ubbcluj.ro/ocle/, http://www.roclet.org [dead link], http://octopus.sourceforge.net/).

There is variety of other validation approaches for OCL based on SMT [13,25] or SAT [23]. Description logics has been used as a basis for OCL expressions and constraints [20,8] and for querying UML class diagram models [9].

On the prover side HOL-OCL combines Isabelle with UML and OCL [5], the Key project attempted theorem proving in connection with the commercial UML tool Together [3], and encoding of OCL into PVS was studied in [18]. We would expect that completeness problems as appearing in OAI ('Does the set of all object diagrams of the model correspond to the integers?') could be handled more adequately in proof-oriented approaches. An application of a combination of proof and test techniques in connection with OCL was described in a case study [22]. Elements from that work might be considered for future versions of the benchmark.

Testing approaches aiming at tool support were put forward in [10,1]. The benchmark might also be applicable for code generation as in Dresden OCL [17] or MDT/OCL [24]. Last, the feature model for model development environments [11] could be connected to the benchmark.

8   Conclusion

The approach proposed here is only first step towards a more complete benchmark. We concentrated on four models with eleven questions and claims. We already have a sufficient coverage of OCL and questions, but more models and items are needed. We would be happy if other groups would contribute. We think more elaboration on complexity questions should be done in order to answer, for example, questions attacking the extent to which a tool can produce and deal with larger states or assert properties in larger states. A classification of questions and items suitable for proof techniques or for test techniques seems to be needed as well.

Acknowledgments. The comments of the referees have helped to improve the paper. Many thanks to the other developers of USE and EMFtoCSP. Without their work this contribution would not have been possible.

References

1. Bernhard, K.: Aichernig and Percy Antonio Pari Salas. Test Case Generation by OCL Mutation and Constraint Solving. In: QSIC, pp. 64–71. IEEE Computer Society (2005)
2. Anastasakis, K., Bordbar, B., Georg, G., Ray, I.: On Challenges of Model Transformation from UML to Alloy. Software and System Modeling 9(1), 69–86 (2010)

3. Beckert, B., Giese, M., Hähnle, R., Klebanov, V., Rümmer, P., Schlager, S., Schmitt, P.H.: The KeY system 1.0 (Deduction Component). In: Pfenning, F. (ed.) CADE 2007. LNCS (LNAI), vol. 4603, pp. 379–384. Springer, Heidelberg (2007)
4. Boronat, A., Meseguer, J.: Algebraic Semantics of OCL-Constrained Metamodel Specifications. In: Oriol, M., Meyer, B. (eds.) TOOLS EUROPE 2009. LNBIP, vol. 33, pp. 96–115. Springer, Heidelberg (2009)
5. Brucker, A.D., Wolff, B.: HOL-OCL: A Formal Proof Environment for UML/OCL. In: Fiadeiro, J.L., Inverardi, P. (eds.) FASE 2008. LNCS, vol. 4961, pp. 97–100. Springer, Heidelberg (2008)
6. Büttner, F., Cabot, J.: Lightweight String Reasoning for OCL. In: Vallecillo, A., Tolvanen, J.-P., Kindler, E., Störrle, H., Kolovos, D. (eds.) ECMFA 2012. LNCS, vol. 7349, pp. 244–258. Springer, Heidelberg (2012)
7. Cabot, J., Clarisó, R., Riera, D.: UMLtoCSP: A Tool for the Formal Verification of UML/OCL Models using Constraint Programming. In: Stirewalt, R.E.K., Egyed, A., Fischer, B. (eds.) ASE, pp. 547–548. ACM (2007)
8. Cadoli, M., Calvanese, D., De Giacomo, G., Mancini, T.: Finite Model Reasoning on UML Class Diagrams Via Constraint Programming. In: Basili, R., Pazienza, M.T. (eds.) AI*IA 2007. LNCS (LNAI), vol. 4733, pp. 36–47. Springer, Heidelberg (2007)
9. Calì, A., Gottlob, G., Orsi, G., Pieris, A.: Querying UML Class Diagrams. In: Birkedal, L. (ed.) FOSSACS 2012. LNCS, vol. 7213, pp. 1–25. Springer, Heidelberg (2012)
10. Cabrera Castillos, K., Dadeau, F., Julliand, J., Taha, S.: Measuring Test Properties Coverage for Evaluating UML/OCL Model-Based Tests. In: Wolff, B., Zaïdi, F. (eds.) ICTSS 2011. LNCS, vol. 7019, pp. 32–47. Springer, Heidelberg (2011)
11. Chimiak-Opoka, J.D., Demuth, B.: A Feature Model for an IDE4OCL. ECE-ASST 36 (2010)
12. Clavel, M., Egea, M.: ITP/OCL: A Rewriting-Based Validation Tool for UML+OCL Static Class Diagrams. In: Johnson, M., Vene, V. (eds.) AMAST 2006. LNCS, vol. 4019, pp. 368–373. Springer, Heidelberg (2006)
13. Clavel, M., Egea, M., de Dios, M.A.G.: Checking Unsatisfiability for OCL Constraints. Electronic Communications of the EASST 24, 1–13 (2009)
14. Gogolla, M., Büttner, F., Cabot, J.: Initiating a Benchmark for UML and OCL Analysis Tools: Additional Material. Technical report, University of Bremen (2013), http://www.db.informatik.uni-bremen.de/publications/intern/GBC2013addon.pdf
15. Gogolla, M., Büttner, F., Richters, M.: USE: A UML-Based Specification Environment for Validating UML and OCL. Science of Computer Programming 69, 27–34 (2007)
16. Gonzalez, C.A., Büttner, F., Clariso, R., Cabot, J.: EMFtoCSP: A Tool for the Lightweight Verification of EMF Models. In: Gnesi, S., Gruner, S., Plat, N., Rumpe, B. (eds.) Proc. ICSE 2012 Workshop Formal Methods in Software Engineering: Rigorous and Agile Approaches, FormSERA (2012)
17. Hußmann, H., Demuth, B., Finger, F.: Modular Architecture for a Toolset Supporting OCL. Sci. Comput. Program. 44(1), 51–69 (2002)
18. Kyas, M., Fecher, H., de Boer, F.S., Jacob, J., Hooman, J., van der Zwaag, M., Arons, T., Kugler, H.: Formalizing UML Models and OCL Constraints in PVS. Electr. Notes Theor. Comput. Sci. 115, 39–47 (2005)

19. Maraee, A., Balaban, M.: Efficient Reasoning About Finite Satisfiability of UML Class Diagrams with Constrained Generalization Sets. In: Akehurst, D.H., Vogel, R., Paige, R.F. (eds.) ECMDA-FA. LNCS, vol. 4530, pp. 17–31. Springer, Heidelberg (2007)
20. Queralt, A., Artale, A., Calvanese, D., Teniente, E.: OCL-Lite: Finite Reasoning on UML/OCL Conceptual Schemas. Data Knowl. Eng. 73, 1–22 (2012)
21. Roldán, M., Durán, F.: Dynamic Validation of OCL Constraints with mOdCL. ECEASST 44 (2011)
22. Schleipen, M.: A Concept for Conformance Testing of AutomationML Models by Means of Formal Proof using OCL. In: ETFA, pp. 1–5. IEEE (2010)
23. Wille, R., Soeken, M., Drechsler, R.: Debugging of Inconsistent UML/OCL Models. In: Rosenstiel, W., Thiele, L. (eds.) DATE, pp. 1078–1083. IEEE (2012)
24. Willink, E.D.: Re-Engineering Eclipse MDT/OCL for Xtext. ECEASST 36 (2010)
25. Yatake, K., Aoki, T.: SMT-Based Enumeration of Object Graphs from UML Class Diagrams. ACM SIGSOFT Software Engineering Notes 37(4), 1–8 (2012)

Speeding Up Algorithmic Debugging
Using Balanced Execution Trees*

David Insa[1], Josep Silva[1], and Adrián Riesco[2]

[1] Departamento de Sistemas Informáticos y Computación,
Universitat Politècnica de València, Valencia, Spain
{dinsa,jsilva}@dsic.upv.es
[2] Departamento de Sistemas Informáticos y Computación,
Universidad Complutense de Madrid, Madrid, Spain
ariesco@fdi.ucm.es

Abstract. Algorithmic debugging is a debugging technique that uses a data structure representing all computations performed during the execution of a program. This data structure is the so-called *Execution Tree* and it strongly influences the performance of the technique. In this work we present a transformation that automatically improves the structure of the execution trees by collapsing and projecting some strategic nodes. This improvement in the structure implies a better behavior and performance of the standard algorithms that traverse it. We prove that the transformation is sound in the sense that all the bugs found after the transformation are real bugs; and if at least one bug is detectable before the transformation, then at least one bug will also be detectable after the transformation. We have implemented the technique and performed several experiments with real applications. The experimental results confirm the usefulness of the technique.

1 Introduction

Debugging is one of the most difficult and less automated tasks in object-oriented programming. The most extended technique is still based on the use of breakpoints. Breakpoints allow the programmer to manually inspect a computation. She must decide where to place the breakpoints and use them to inspect the values of strategic variables. Between the point where the effect of a bug is observed, and the point where the bug is located, there can be hundreds or thousands of lines of code, thus, the programmer must navigate the computation in order to find the bug. Ideally, breakpoints should be placed in a way that the amount of code inspected is reduced as much as possible.

There exists a debugging technique called *algorithmic debugging* (AD) [15] that tries to automate the problem of inspecting a computation in order to find

* This work has been partially supported by the Spanish *Ministerio de Ciencia e Innovación* under grants TIN2008-06622-C03-02 and TIN2012-39391-C04-04, by the *Generalitat Valenciana* under grant ACOMP/2009/017, and by the *Comunidad de Madrid* under grant S2009/TIC–1465. David Insa has been partially supported by the Spanish *Ministerio de Educación* under grant AP2010-4415.

M. Veanes and L. Viganò (Eds.): TAP 2013, LNCS 7942, pp. 133–151, 2013.
© Springer-Verlag Berlin Heidelberg 2013

a bug. AD is a semi-automatic debugging technique that produces a dialogue between the debugger and the programmer to locate bugs. This technique relies on the programmer having an *intended interpretation* of the program. In other words, some computations of the program are correct and others are wrong with respect to the semantics intended by the programmer. Therefore, algorithmic debuggers compare the actual results of subcomputations with those expected by the programmer. By asking questions to the programmer or using a formal specification the system can identify precisely the location of a bug.

The idea behind AD is that the own debugger selects automatically the places that should be inspected. The advantage is that the debugger knows a priori the length of the computation, and thus it can perform a dichotomic search inspecting the subcomputation located in the middle of the remaining suspicious area. This allows the debugger to efficiently explore the computation. Moreover, the places inspected are always method invocations and thus, it is easy for the programmer to decide if the result produced by an invocation with given arguments is correct or not.

Conceptually, AD is a two-phase process: During the first phase, a data structure that represents the execution of the program, the *Execution Tree* (ET), is built; while in the second phase a *navigation strategy* is used to iteratively select nodes in the ET. The debugger asks a question related to each selected node to an external oracle (typically the user). With every answer the debugger prunes a part of the ET until a single node remains. The bug is located in the method associated with this node.

In this work we introduce a technique that changes the structure of the ET in such a way that the navigation strategies present an almost optimal behavior. The objective of the technique is to balance[1] the ET in such a way that navigation strategies prune half of the ET at every step, because they can always find a node that divides the search area in half. Our experiments with real programs show that the technique reduces (as an average) the number of questions to the oracle by around 30%.

In order to show the general idea of the technique with an example, we need to explain first how the ET is constructed. The ET contains nodes that represent subcomputations of the program. Therefore, the information of the ET's nodes refer to method executions. Without loss of generality, we will base our examples on programs implemented using the Java language, although our ET transformations and the balancing technique are conceptually applicable to any ET, independently of the language it represents.

Our technique is particularly useful for object-oriented programs because (i) it allows the programmer to ignore the operational details of the code to concentrate on the validity of the effects produced by method executions. In general, the programmer does not need to look at the source code to interact with the debugger: she only has to answer questions related to the effects of the computations. (ii) The technique is very powerful in presence of iterative loops which are inexistent in other paradigms (e.g., functional).

---

[1] Note that throughout this paper we use *balanced* to indicate that the tree becomes *binomial*.

Initial position

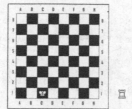
Final position

Expected position

```
public class Chess {
  public static void main(String[] args) {
    Chess p = new Chess();
    Position tower = new Position();
    Position king = new Position();
    king.locate(5,1);
    tower.locate(8,1);
    p.castling(tower,king);
  }
  void castling(Position t,Position k) {
    if (t.x!=8){
        for(int i=1; i<=2; i++) {t.left();}
        for(int i=1; i<=2; i++) {k.right();}
    } else{
        for(int i=1; i<=3; i++) {t.right();}
        for(int i=1; i<=2; i++) {k.left();}
    }
  }
}
public class Position {
    int x, y;
    void locate(int a, int b) {x=a; y=b;}
    void up() {y=y+1;}
    void down() {y=y-1;}
    void right() {x=x+1;}
    void left() {x=x-1;}
}
```

Fig. 1. Example program

In the object-oriented paradigm, an ET is constructed as follows: Each node of the ET is associated with a method execution. It contains all the information needed to decide whether the method execution produced a correct result. This information includes the call to the method with its arguments and the result, and the values of all the attributes that are in the scope of this method, at the beginning and at the end of the execution (observe, e.g., that exception objects are also in the scope). This information allows the programmer to know whether all the effects of the method execution correspond to her intended semantics. The root node of the ET is the initial method execution of the program (e.g., *main*).

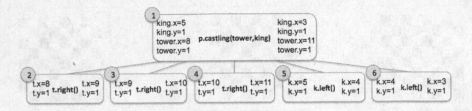

Fig. 2. ET associated with the call `p.castling(tower,king)` of the program in Figure 1

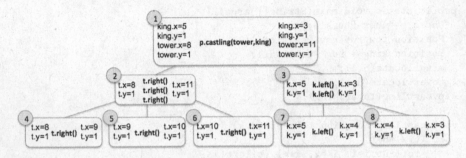

Fig. 3. Balanced ET associated with the call `p.castling(tower,king)` for Figure 1

For each node n with associated method m, and for each method execution m' invoked by m, a new node associated with m' is added to the ET as a child of n.

Example 1. Consider the Java program in Figure 1. It has a bug, and thus it wrongly simulates a movement on a chessboard. The `p.castling(tower,king)` call produces the (wrong) movement shown in the chessboards of the figure. Figure 2 depicts the portion of the ET associated with `p.castling(tower,king)`. With this ET, all current navigation strategies need to ask about the six nodes. In contrast, if we balance this ET with our transformation, the bug is found with at most three questions.

Our technique presents three important advantages that make it useful for AD. First, it can be easily adapted to other programming languages. We have implemented it for Java and it can be directly used in other object-oriented languages, but it could be easily adapted to other languages such as C or Haskell using the analogy between methods and functions. Second, the technique is quite simple to implement and can be integrated into any existing algorithmic debugger with small changes. And third, the technique is conservative. If the questions triggered by the new nodes are difficult to answer, the user can answer "I don't know" and continue the debugging session as in the standard ETs. Moreover, the user can naturally get back to the original ET in case it is needed.

The rest of the paper has been organized as follows. In Section 2 we introduce some preliminary definitions that will be used in the rest of the paper. In Section 3 we explain our technique and its main applications, and we introduce the algorithms used to balance ETs. The correctness of the technique is proved in Section 4. Then, in Section 5, we present our implementation and some experiments carried out with real Java programs. Section 6, discusses the related work. Finally, Section 7 concludes.

2   Algorithmic Debugging

In this section we introduce some notation and formalize the notion of execution tree used in the rest of the paper. For the purpose of this work, we consider ETs as labeled trees. We need to formally define the notions of context and method execution before we provide a definition of ET.

Definition 1 (Context). *Let $\mathcal{P}$ be a program, and X the execution of a method in $\mathcal{P}$. The* context *of X at a particular instant t is $\{(a, v) \mid a$ is an attribute in the scope of X at instant t and v is the value of $a\}$.*

Roughly, the context of a method at a particular instant of its execution is composed of all the variables of the program that are visible at this moment. Clearly, these variables can be other objects that in turn contain other variables. In a realistic program, each node contains several data structures that could change during the execution. All this information (the context at the beginning and at the end of the execution of the method) should be visualized together with the call to the method so that the programmer can decide whether it is correct.[2]

Definition 2 (Method Execution). *Let $\mathcal{P}$ be a program and X an execution of $\mathcal{P}$. Then, each method execution* done in X is represented with a triple $\mathcal{E} = (b, m, e)$ *where m represents the call to the method with its arguments and the returned value, b is the context of the method in m at the beginning of its execution, and e is the context of the method in m at the end of its execution. A* composite method execution *is a nonempty sequence of method executions $\langle (b_1, m_1, e_1), (b_2, m_2, e_2), \ldots, (b_n, m_n, e_n) \rangle$ that we represent as $(b_1, m_1, m_2, \ldots, m_n, e_n)$.*

Thanks to the declarative properties of AD, we can ignore the operational details of an execution. From the point of view of the debugger an execution is a finite tree of method executions. This can be modeled with the following grammar:

$$T = (b, m[L], e) \qquad L = \epsilon \qquad L = TL$$

where the terminal m is a method of the program and b and e represent the context at the beginning and at the end of the execution of the method. For instance, p.castling(tower,king) in Example 1 can be represented with the tree:

$(b_1, \text{p.castling}(\text{tower}, \text{king})$
$\quad [(b_2, \text{t.right}()[], e_1), (e_1, \text{t.right}()[], e_2), (e_2, \text{t.right}()[], e_3),$
$\quad (b_3, \text{k.left}[], e_4), (e_4, \text{k.left}[], e_5)], e_6)$

---

[2] We refer the reader to [8] for a brief explanation about how this information is displayed in our implementation.

With this tree, we can construct the ET in Figure 2. Roughly speaking, an ET is a tree whose nodes represent method executions and the parent-child relation is defined by the tree produced by the grammar. Formally,

Definition 3 (Execution Tree). *Given a program $\mathcal{P}$ and a method execution $\mathcal{E}$, the execution tree (ET) of $\mathcal{P}$ with respect to $\mathcal{E}$ is a tree $t = (V, E)$ where $\forall v \in V$, v is a composite method execution, and*

- *The root of the ET is $\mathcal{E}$.*
- *For each pair of method executions $\mathcal{E}_1$, $\mathcal{E}_2 \in V$, we have that $(\mathcal{E}_1 \to \mathcal{E}_2) \in E$ iff*
  1. *during the execution of the method associated with $\mathcal{E}_1$, the method associated with $\mathcal{E}_2$ is invoked, and*
  2. *from the instant when $\mathcal{E}_1$ starts until the instant when $\mathcal{E}_2$ starts, there does not exist a method execution $\mathcal{E}_3$ such that $\mathcal{E}_3$ has started but not ended.*

Note that we use $(v \to v')$ to denote a directed edge from v to v'. From now on, we will assume that there exists an intended semantics $\mathcal{I}$ of the program being debugged. It corresponds to the model the programmer had in mind while writing the program, and it contains, for each method m and each context b of m at the beginning of its execution, the expected context e at the end of its execution, that is, $(b, m, e) \in \mathcal{I}$. Moreover, given this atomic information, we are able to deduce judgments of the form $(b, m_1; \ldots; m_n, e)$ with the inference rule Tr, that defines the transitivity for the composition of methods

$$\frac{(b, m_1, e') \quad (e', m_2; \ldots; m_n, e)}{(b, m_1; \ldots; m_n, e)} \; \mathsf{Tr} \text{ if } n > 1$$

and we say that $\mathcal{I} \models (b, m_1; \ldots; m_n, e)$. Using this intended semantics we can formally define the correctness of method executions.

Definition 4 (Correctness of Method Executions). *Given a method execution $\mathcal{E}$ and the intended semantics of the program $\mathcal{I}$, we say that $\mathcal{E}$ is correct if $\mathcal{E} \in \mathcal{I}$ or $\mathcal{I} \models \mathcal{E}$ and wrong otherwise.*

Once the ET is built, in the second phase the debugger uses a strategy to traverse the ET asking the oracle about the correctness of the information stored in each node. If the method execution of a node is wrong, it answers NO. Otherwise, it answers YES. Using these answers, the debugger identifies a buggy node that is associated with a buggy source code of the program.

Definition 5 (Buggy Node). *Given an ET $t = (V, E)$, a buggy node of t is a node $v \in V$ such that (i) the method execution of v is wrong and (ii) $\forall v' \in V$, $(v \to v') \in E$, v' is correct.*

According to Definition 5, when all the children of a node with a wrong computation (if any) are correct, the node becomes buggy and the debugger locates a bug in the part of the program associated with this node [13]. A buggy node detects a *buggy method*, which informally stands for methods that return an incorrect context even though all the methods executions performed by them are correct.

Lemma 1 (Buggy Method). *Given an ET* $t = (V, E)$, *and a buggy node* $v \in V$ *in* t *with* $v = (b, m, e)$, *then* m *contains a bug.*

Proofs of all technical results are available in [8].

Due to the fact that questions are asked in a logical order (i.e., consecutive questions refer to related parts of the computation), *top-down search* is the strategy that has been traditionally used (see, e.g., [2,3,9]) to measure the performance of different debugging tools and methods. It basically consists of a top-down (assuming that the root is on top), left-to-right traversal of the ET. When the answer to the question of a node is NO, then the next question is associated with one of its children. When the answer is YES, the next question is associated with one of its siblings. Therefore, the node asked is always a child or a sibling of the previous asked node. Hence, the idea is to follow the path of wrong computations from the root of the tree to the buggy node.

However, selecting always the leftmost child does not take into account the size of the subtrees that can be explored. Binks proposed in [1] a variant of top-down search in order to consider this information when selecting a child. This variant is called *heaviest first* because it always selects the child with the biggest subtree. The objective is to avoid selecting small subtrees that have a lower probability of containing a bug.

Another important strategy is *divide and query* (D&Q) [14], that always selects the node whose subtree's size is the closest one to half the size of the tree. If the answer is YES, this node (and its subtree) is pruned. If the answer is NO the search continues in the subtree rooted at this node. This strategy asks, in general, fewer questions than top-down search because it prunes near half of the tree with every question. However, its performance is strongly dependent on the structure of the ET. If the ET is balanced, this strategy is query-optimal.

There are many other strategies: variants of top-down search [11,5], variants of D&Q [6], and others [10,15]. A comparison of strategies can be found in [15]. In general, all of them are strongly influenced by the structure of the ET.

Example 2. An AD session for the ET in Figure 2 using D&Q follows (YES and NO answers are provided by the programmer):

```
Starting Debugging Session...
(2)  t.x=8,   t.y=1  >>>  t.right()      >>>  t.x=9,   t.y=1        ? YES
(3)  t.x=9,   t.y=1  >>>  t.right()      >>>  t.x=10, t.y=1         ? YES
(4)  t.x=10, t.y=1  >>>  t.right()      >>>  t.x=11, t.y=1         ? YES
(5)  k.x=5,   k.y=1  >>>  k.left()       >>>  k.x=4,   k.y=1        ? YES
(6)  k.x=4,   k.y=1  >>>  k.left()       >>>  k.x=3,   k.y=1        ? YES
(1)  king.x=5,                                        king.x=3,
     king.y=1,  >>>  p.castling(tower,king)  >>>  king.y=1,  ? NO
     tower.x=8,                                     tower.x=11,
     tower.y=1                                      tower.y=1
Bug found in method: castling(Position t, Position k) of class Chess.
```

The debugger points out the buggy method, which contains the bug. In this case, `t.x!=8` should be `t.x==8`. Note that, to debug the program, the programmer only has to answer questions. It is not even necessary to see the code.

3   Collapsing and Projecting Nodes

Even though the strategy heaviest first significantly improves top-down search, its performance strongly depends on the structure of the ET. The more balanced the ET is, the better. Clearly, when the ET is balanced, heaviest first is much more efficient because it prunes more nodes after every question. If the ET is completely balanced, heaviest first is equivalent to divide and query and both are query-optimal.

3.1   Advantages of Collapsing and Projecting Nodes

Our technique is based on a series of transformations that allows us to collapse/project some nodes of the ET. A collapsed node is a new node that replaces some nodes that are then removed from the ET. In contrast, a projected node is a new node that is placed as the parent of a set of nodes that remain in the ET. This section describes the main advantages of collapsing/projecting nodes:

Balancing Execution Trees. If we augment an ET with projected nodes, we can strategically place the new nodes in such a way that the ET becomes balanced. In this way, the debugger speeds up the debugging session by reducing the number of asked questions.

Example 3. Consider again the program in Figure 1. The portion of the ET associated with p.castling(tower,king) is shown in Figure 2. We can add projected nodes to this ET as depicted in Figure 3. Note that now the ET becomes balanced, and hence, many strategies ask fewer questions. For instance, in the worst case, using the ET of Figure 2 the debugger would ask about all the nodes before the bug is found. This is due to the broad nature of this ET that prevents strategies from pruning any nodes. In contrast, using the ET of Figure 3 the debugger prunes almost half of the tree with every question. In this example, with the standard ET of Figure 2, D&Q produces the following debugging session (numbers refer to the codes of the nodes in the figure):

```
Starting Debugging Session...
(2) YES  (3) YES  (4) YES  (5) YES  (6) YES  (1) NO
Bug found in method: castling(Position t, Position k) of class Chess.
```

In contrast, with the ET of Figure 3, D&Q produces this session:

```
Starting Debugging Session...
(2) YES  (3) YES  (1) NO
Bug found in method: castling(Position t, Position k) of class Chess.
```

Skipping Repetitive Questions. Algorithmic debuggers tend to repeat the same (or very similar) question several times when it is associated with a method execution that is inside a loop. In our example, this happens in for (int i=1; i<=3; i++) {t.right();}, which is used to move the tower three positions to the right. Here, the nodes

```
{t.x=8,  t.y=1}  t.right()  {t.x=9,  t.y=1}
{t.x=9,  t.y=1}  t.right()  {t.x=10, t.y=1}
{t.x=10, t.y=1}  t.right()  {t.x=11, t.y=1}
```

could be projected to the node

```
{t.x=8,  t.y=1}  t.right(); t.right(); t.right()  {t.x=11, t.y=1}
```

This kind of projection, where all the projecting nodes refer to the same method, has an interesting property: If the projecting nodes are leaves, then they can be deleted from the ET. The reason is that the new projected node and the projecting nodes refer to the same method. Therefore, it does not matter what computation produced the bug, because the bug will necessarily be in this method. Hence, if the projected node is wrong, then the bug is in the method pointed to by this node. When the children of the projected node are removed, we call it *collapsed node*.

Note that, in this case, the idea is not to add nodes to the ET as in the previous case, but to delete them. Because the input and output of all the questions relate to the same attributes (i.e., x and y), then the user can answer them all together, since they are, in fact, a sequence of operations whose output is the input of the next question (i.e., they are chained). Therefore, this technique allows us to treat a set of questions as a whole. This is particularly interesting because it approximates the real behavior intended by the programmer. For instance, in this example, the intended meaning of the loop was to move the tower three positions to the right. The intermediate positions are not interesting; only the initial and final ones are meaningful for the intended meaning.

Example 4. Consider the ET of Figure 3. Observe that, if the projected nodes are wrong, then the bug must be in the unique method appearing in the projected node. Thus, we could collapse the node instead of projecting it. Hence, nodes 4, 5, 6, 7, and 8 could be removed; and thus, with only three questions we could discover any bug in any node.

Enhancing the Search of Algorithmic Debugging. One important problem of AD strategies is that they must use a given ET without any possibility of changing it. This often prevents strategies from selecting nodes that prune a big part of the ET, or from selecting nodes that concentrate on the regions with a higher probability of containing the bug. Collapsing some subtrees into a single node can help to solve these drawbacks.

The initial idea of this section was to use projected nodes to balance the ET. This idea is very interesting in combination with D&Q, because it can cause the debugging session to be optimal in the worst case (its query complexity is $O(b \cdot log\ n)$, where b is the branching factor and n is the number of nodes in the ET). However, this idea can be further extended in order to force the strategies to ask questions related to parts of the computations with a higher probability

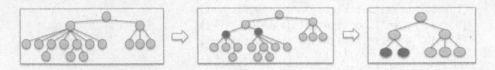

Fig. 4. Transformation of ETs

of containing the bug. Concretely, we can replace parts of the ET with a collapsed node in order to avoid questions related to this part. If the debugging session determines that the collapsed node is wrong, we can expand it again to continue the debugging session inside this node. Therefore, with this idea, the original ET is transformed into a tree of ETs that can be explored when it is required. Let us illustrate this idea with an example.

Example 5. Consider the leftmost ET in Figure 4. This ET has a root that started two subcomputations. The computation on the left performed ten method executions, while the computation on the right performed only three. Hence, in this ET, all the existing strategies would explore first the left subtree.[3] If we balance the left branch by inserting projected nodes we get the new ET shown on the right of the previous one. This balanced ET requires (on average) fewer questions than the previous one; but the strategies will still explore the left branch of the root first.

Now, let us assume that the debugger identified the right branch as more likely to be buggy (e.g., because it contains recursive calls, because it is non-deterministic, because it contains calls with more arguments involved or with complex data structures...). We can change the structure of the ET in order to make AD strategies start by exploring the desired branch. In this example we can remove from the ET the nodes that were projected. The new ET is shown on the right of Figure 4. With this ET the tool explores first the right branch of the root. Observe that it is not necessary that the nodes that were projected refer to the same method. They can be completely different and independent computations. However, if the debugger determines that they are probably correct, they can be omitted to direct the search to other parts of the ET. Of course, they can be expanded again if required by the strategy (e.g., if the debugger cannot find the bug in the other nodes).

Disadvantages. Given these benefits, we must talk of a potential drawback: the difficulty of the questions related to the new nodes. The new questions may be more difficult to answer than the previous ones, but the user can avoid these difficult questions as we will discuss later. However, the nodes encapsulated in the new projected/collapsed are intimately related, as we explain in the next section, and thus in many situations the question is more related to the behavior the user had in mind when writing the code than the original questions (i.e., the behavior of the whole loop vs. the behavior of each single call inside the loop).

---

[3] Current strategies assume that all nodes have the same probability of being buggy, therefore, heavy branches are explored first.

3.2   Collapsing and Projecting Algorithms

In this section we define a technique that allows us to balance an ET while keeping the soundness and completeness of AD. The technique is based on two basic transformations for ETs (namely *collapse leaf chain* and *project chain*, described respectively by Algorithms 1 and 2), and on a new data structure called an *Execution Forest* (EF) that is a generalization of an ET.

Definition 6 (Execution Forest). *An* execution forest *is a tree* $t = (V, E)$ *whose internal vertices* V *are method executions and whose leaves are either method executions or execution forests.*

Roughly speaking, an EF is an ET where some subtrees have been replaced (i.e., collapsed) by a single node. Note that this recursive definition of EF is more general than the one for ET because an ET is an instance of an EF where no collapsed nodes exist. We can now define the two basic transformations of our technique. Both transformations are based on the notion of *chain*. Informally, a chain is formed by an ordered set of sibling nodes in which the final context produced by a node of the chain is the initial context of the next node. Chains often represent a sequence of method executions performed one after the other during an execution. Formally,

Definition 7 (Chain). *Given an EF* $t = (V, E)$ *and a set* $C \subset V$ *of n nodes with associated method executions* $\mathcal{E}_1, \mathcal{E}_2, \ldots, \mathcal{E}_n$ *we say that C is a* chain *iff*

- $\exists v \in V$ *such that* $\forall c \in C \; . \; (v \to c) \in E$,
- $\forall i, j, 1 \le i < j \le n$, *the method associated with* $\mathcal{E}_i$ *is executed before the method associated with* $\mathcal{E}_j$, *and*
- $\forall j, 1 \le j \le n - 1$, *if* $\mathcal{E}_j == (e_j, m_j, e_{j+1})$
    then $\mathcal{E}_{j+1} = (e_{j+1}, m_{j+1}, e_{j+2})$

The first condition ensures that all the elements in the chain are siblings. The second condition ensures that the elements are executed one after the other. The third condition ensures that for all nodes in the chain the final context of a node is the initial context of the next chained node. Note that, by the definition of context, only those attributes that can be affected by the execution of the methods are taken into account. It is common to find chains when one or more methods are executed inside a loop.

The basic transformations of chains are described by Algorithms 1 and 2. Algorithm 1 is in charge of collapsing chains, that consists in creating a new node *colnode* with initial context the context at the beginning of the first node of the chain, final context the context at the end of the last node of the chain, and with the composition of the methods in the chain as associated method. Then, the nodes in the chain (and thus their edges) are removed from the tree and the new node is linked to the parent of the nodes in C, thus reducing the size of the EF. Algorithm 2 is in charge of projecting chains, and works in a similar way to the previous algorithm. Given a tree t and a chain C in the tree, it removes from t the edges between each $c \in C$ and its parent *parent*, and then introduces a new node *prjnode* built as explained before, that is linked to each c as their new parent, and to *parent* as its new child.

Algorithm 1. Collapse Leaf Chain

Input: An EF $t = (V, E)$ and a set of nodes $C \subset V$
Output: An EF $t' = (V', E')$
Preconditions: C is a chain with nodes $(a_1, m_1, a_2), (a_2, m_2, a_3), \ldots, (a_n, m_n, a_{n+1})$ and $\nexists v \in V . (c \to v) \in E$, with $c \in C$
begin
1) $parent = u \in V$ such that $\forall c \in C, (u \to c) \in E$
2) $colnode = (a_1, m, a_{n+1})$ with $m = m_1; m_2; \ldots; m_n$
3) $V' = (V \setminus C) \cup \{colnode\}$
4) $E' = ((E \setminus \{(parent \to v) \in E \mid v \in C\}) \cup \{(parent \to colnode)\}$
end
return $t' = (V', E')$

Algorithm 2. Project Chain

Input: An EF $t = (V, E)$ and a set of nodes $C \subset V$
Output: An EF $t' = (V', E')$
Preconditions: C is a chain with nodes $(a_1, m_1, a_2), (a_2, m_2, a_3), \ldots, (a_n, m_n, a_{n+1})$
begin
1) $parent = u \in V$ such that $\forall c \in C, (u \to c) \in E$
2) $prjnode = (a_1, m, a_{n+1})$ with $m = m_1; m_2; \ldots; m_n$
3) $V' = V \cup \{prjnode\}$
4) $E' = ((E \setminus \{(parent \to v) \in E \mid v \in C\}) \cup \{(parent \to prjnode)\} \cup \{(prjnode \to c) \mid c \in C\}$
end
return $t' = (V', E')$

Algorithm 3 is in charge of removing the chains of leaves that can be collapsed. It first computes in the initialization all the maximal chains (i.e., chains that are not subchains of other chains) of nodes that are leaves and are related to the same methods. Then, for each of these chains, it applies Algorithm 1 to collapse them by removing the chain from the tree and adding the corresponding collapsed node.[4]

Our method for balancing EFs is implemented by Algorithm 4. This algorithm first uses Algorithm 3 to shrink the EF (line 1) by collapsing as many nodes as possible; and then it balances this shrunken EF by projecting some nodes. The objective is to divide the tree into two parts with the same weight (i.e., number of nodes). Therefore, we first compute the half of the size of the EF (lines 4 and 5). If a child of the root is already heavier than half the size of the tree, then, the weight of this node is not taken into account in the balancing process because the question associated to this node will be the first question asked (lines 9-15). Otherwise, it projects the part of a chain whose weight is as close as possible

---

[4] Note that, since these chains are usually found when a loop or a recursive call is used, our approach generates nodes whose questions are very close to the intended meaning the programmer had in mind while developing the program and thus, although the new questions comprise a bigger context, they may be even easier to answer than the "atomic" ones.

Algorithm 3. Shrink EF

Input: An EF $t = (V, E)$
Output: An EF $t' = (V', E')$
Preconditions: Given a node v, $v.method$ is the name of the method in v
Initialization: $t' = t$, set $\mathcal{S}$ contains all the maximal chains of t such that for each chain $s = \{c_1, \ldots, c_n\}$ of $\mathcal{S}$, $\forall x$, $1 \le x \le n - 1$, $c_x.method == c_{x+1}.method$, and $\nexists v \in V$. $(c \to v) \in E$, with $c \in s$
begin
1)   **while** $(\mathcal{S} \ne \emptyset)$
2)   take a chain $s \in \mathcal{S}$
3) $\mathcal{S} = \mathcal{S} \backslash \{s\}$
4) $t' = collapseChain(t', s)$
   end while
end
return t'

---

to half the weight of the root (lines 16-24). This allows us to prune half of the subtree when asking a question associated with a projected node. In the case that the heavier node (lines 13-15) or the projected chain (lines 18-19) belongs to a bigger chain, it must be cut with function *cutChain* producing new (smaller) chains that are also processed. Of course, the size of the chains already processed is not taken into account when dividing the successive (sub)chains (because they will be already pruned during a debugging session).

If a chain is very long, it can be cut in several subchains to be projected and thus better balance the EF. In order to cut chains we use the function *cutChain*:

function $cutChain(\text{chain } \{c_1, \ldots, c_n\}, \text{ int } i, \text{ int } j)$
   if $i > 2$ **then** $s_{ini} = \{c_1, \ldots, c_{i-1}\}$ **else** $s_{ini} = \emptyset$ **end if**
   if $n - j > 1$ **then** $s_{end} = \{c_{j+1}, \ldots, c_n\}$ **else** $s_{end} = \emptyset$ **end if**
return (s_{ini}, s_{end})

This function removes from a chain a subchain delimited by indices i and j. As a result, depending on the indices, it can produce two subchains that are located before and after the subchain. Note that when the initial index i is 2, there is only one node remaining before the subchain, and thus, because it is not a chain, $\emptyset$ is returned. The same happens on the right.

The algorithm finishes when no more chains can be projected. Trivially, because the number of chains and their length are finite, termination is ensured. In addition, Algorithm 4 is able to balance the EF while it is being computed. Concretely, the algorithm should be executed for each node of the EF that is completed (i.e., the final context of the method execution is already calculated, thus all the children of this node are also completed). Note that this means that the algorithm is applied bottom-up to the nodes of the EF. Hence, when balancing a node, all the descendants of the node have been already balanced. This also means that modern debuggers that are able to debug programs with uncompleted ETs [7] can also use the technique, because the ET can be balanced while being computed.

Algorithm 4. Shrink & Balance EF

Input: An EF $t = (V, E)$ whose root is $root \in V$
Output: An EF $t' = (V', E')$
Preconditions: Given a node v, $v.weight$ is the size of the subtree rooted at v
begin
1) $t' = shrink(t)$
2) $children = \{v \in V' \mid (root \to v) \in E'\}$
3) $\mathcal{S} = \{s \mid s \text{ is a maximal chain in } children\}$
4) $rootweight = root.weight$
5) $weight = rootweight/2$
6) **while** $(\mathcal{S} \neq \emptyset)$
7) $child = c \in children$ such that $\nexists c' \in children, c \neq c' \wedge c'.weight > c.weight$
8) $distance = |weight - child.weight|$
9)   **if** $(child.weight \geq weight$ or $\nexists s, i, j$ s.t. $s = \{c_1, \ldots, c_n\} \in \mathcal{S}$ and $(|W - weight| <$ $distance)$ with $W = \sum_{x=i}^{j} c_x.weight)$
10)   **then** $children = children \backslash \{child\}$
11) $rootweight = rootweight - child.weight$
12) $weight = rootweight/2$
13)   **if** $(\exists s \in \mathcal{S}$ such that $s = \{c_1, \ldots, c_n\}$ and $child = c_i, 1 \leq i \leq n)$
14)   **then** $(s_{ini}, s_{end}) = cutChain(s, i, i)$
15) $\mathcal{S} = (\mathcal{S} \backslash \{s\}) \cup s_{ini} \cup s_{end}$
          end if
      else
16)   find an s, i, j such that $s = \{c_1, \ldots, c_n\} \in \mathcal{S}$ and $\sum_{x=i}^{j} c_x.weight$ is as close as possible to $weight$
17) $s' = \{c_i, \ldots, c_j\}$
18) $(s_{ini}, s_{end}) = cutChain(s, i, j)$
19) $\mathcal{S} = (\mathcal{S} \backslash \{s\}) \cup s_{ini} \cup s_{end}$
20) $t' = projectChain(t', s')$
21)   **for each** $c \in s'$
22) $rootweight = rootweight - c.weight$
          end for each
23) $children = (children \backslash s')$
24) $weight = rootweight/2$
      end if
    end while
end
return $t' = (V', E')$

---

4   Correctness

Our technique for balancing EFs is based on the transformations presented in the previous section. We present in this section the theoretical results about soundness and completeness, whose proofs are available in [8].

Theorem 1 (Completeness and soundness of EFs). *Given an EF with a wrong root, it contains a buggy node which is associated with a buggy method.*

Completeness and soundness are kept after our transformations. In particular, an EF with a buggy node still has a buggy node after any number of collapses or projections.

Theorem 2 (Chain Collapse Correctness). *Let* $t = (V, E)$ *and* $t' = (V', E')$ *be two EFs, being the root of* t *wrong, and let* $C \subset V$ *be a chain such that all nodes in the chain are leaves and they have the same associated method. Given* $t' = $ `collapseChain(t,C)`,

1. t' *contains a buggy node.*
2. *Every buggy node in* t' *is associated with a buggy method.*

Theorem 3 (Chain Projection Correctness). *Let* $t = (V, E)$ *and* $t' = (V', E')$ *be two EFs, and let* $C \subset V$ *be a chain such that* $t' = $ `projectChain(t,C)`.

1. *All buggy nodes in* t *are also buggy nodes in* t'.
2. *Every buggy node in* t' *is associated with a buggy method.*

We also provide in this section an interesting result related to the projection of chains. This result is related to the incompleteness of the technique when it is used intra-session (i.e., in a single debugging session trying to find one particular bug). Concretely, the following result does not hold: *A buggy node can be found in an EF if and only if it can be found in its balanced version.*

In general, our technique ensures that all the bugs that caused the wrong behavior of the root node (i.e., the wrong final context of the whole program) can be found in the balanced EF. This means that all those buggy nodes that are responsible of the wrong behavior are present in the balanced EF.

However, AD can find bugs by a fluke. Those nodes that are buggy nodes in the EF but did not cause the wrong behavior of the root node can be undetectable with some strategies in the balanced version of the EF. The opposite is also true: It is possible to find bugs in the balanced EF that were undetectable in the original EF. Let us explain it with an example.

Example 6. Consider the EFs in Figure 5. The EF on the right is the same as the one on the left but a new projected node has been added. If we assume the following intended semantics (expressed with triples of the form: initial context, method, final context) then grey nodes are wrong and white nodes are right:

$$x = 1 \; g() \; x = 4 \qquad x = 4 \; g() \; x = 4 \qquad x = 1 \; f() \; x = 2$$
$$x = 3 \; h() \; x = 3 \qquad x = 4 \; h() \; x = 4$$

Note that in the EF on the left, only nodes 2 and 3 are buggy. Therefore, all the strategies will report these nodes as buggy, but never node 1. However, node 1 contains a bug but it is undetectable by the debugger until nodes 2 and 3 have been corrected. Nevertheless, observe that nodes 2 and 3 did not produce the wrong behavior of node 1. They simply produced two errors that, in combination, produced by a fluke a global correct behavior.

Now, observe in the EF on the right that node 1 is buggy and thus detectable by the strategies. In contrast, nodes 2 and 3 are now undetectable by top-down search (they could be detected by D&Q). Thanks to the balancing process, it has been made explicit that three different bugs are in the EF.

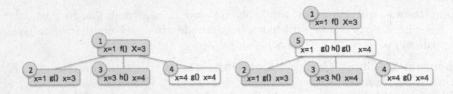

Fig. 5. New buggy nodes revealed

5   Implementation

We have implemented the technique presented in this paper and integrated it into an algorithmic debugger for Java. The implementation allows the programmer to activate the transformations of the technique and to parameterize them in order to adjust the size of the projected/collapsed chains. It has been tested with a collection of small to large programs including real applications (e.g., an interpreter, a compiler, an XSLT processor, etc.) producing good results, as summarized in Table 1. All the information related to the experiments, the source code of the tool, the benchmarks, and other materials can be found at http://www.dsic.upv.es/~jsilva/DDJ/examples/.

Each benchmark has been evaluated assuming that the bug could be in any node. This means that each row of the table is the average of a number of experiments. For instance, cglib was tested 1.216 times (i.e., the experiment was repeated choosing a different node as buggy, and all nodes were tried). For each benchmark, column ET nodes shows the size of the ET evaluated; column Pr./Co. shows the number of projected/collapsed nodes inserted into the EF; column Pr./Co. nodes shows the number of nodes that were projected and collapsed by the debugger; column Bal. time shows the time needed by the debugger to balance the whole EF; column Quest. shows the average number of questions done by the debugger before finding the bug in the original ET; column Q. bal. shows the average number of questions done by the debugger before finding the bug in the balanced ET; finally, column (%) shows the improvement achieved with the balancing technique. Clearly, the balancing technique has an important impact in the reduction of questions with a mean reduction of 30% using top-down.

Essentially, our debugger produces the EF associated with any method execution specified by the user (by default main) and transforms it by collapsing and projecting nodes using Algorithm 4. Finally, it is explored with standard strategies to find a bug. If we observe again Algorithms 1, 2, and 3, a moment of thought should convince the reader that their cost is linear with the branching factor of the EF. In contrast, the cost of Algorithm 4 is quadratic with the branching factor of the EF. On the practical side, our experiments reveal that the average cost of a single collapse (considering the 1.675 collapses) is 0,77 msec, and the average cost of a single projection (considering the 1.235 projections) is 17,32 msec. Finally, the average cost for balancing an EF is 2.818,25 msec.

Our algorithm is very conservative because it only collapses or projects nodes that belong to a chain. Our first experiments showed that if we do not apply

Table 1. Benchmark results

Benchmark	ET nodes	Pr./Co.	Pr./Co. nodes	Bal. time	Quest.	Q. bal.	%
NumReader	12 nodes	0/0	0/0 nodes	0 msec	6,46	6,46	0,00 %
Orderings	72 nodes	2/14	5/45 nodes	0 msec	11,47	8,89	22,46 %
Factoricer	62 nodes	7/0	17/0 nodes	0 msec	13,89	7,90	43,09 %
Sedgewick	41 nodes	3/8	7/24 nodes	0 msec	18,79	7,52	59,95 %
Clasifier	30 nodes	4/7	10/20 nodes	0 msec	15,52	6,48	58,21 %
LegendGame	93 nodes	12/20	28/40 nodes	0 msec	16,00	9,70	39,36 %
Cues	19 nodes	3/1	8/2 nodes	0 msec	10,40	8,20	21,15 %
Romanic	123 nodes	20/0	40/0 nodes	0 msec	25,06	16,63	33,66 %
FibRecursive	6724 nodes	19/1290	70/2593 nodes	344 msec	38,29	21,47	43,92 %
Risk	70 nodes	7/8	19/43 nodes	0 msec	30,69	10,28	66,50 %
FactTrans	198 nodes	5/0	12/0 nodes	0 msec	18,96	14,25	24,88 %
RndQuicksort	88 nodes	3/3	9/0 nodes	0 msec	12,88	10,40	19,20 %
BinaryArrays	132 nodes	7/0	18/0 nodes	0 msec	15,56	10,58	32,03 %
FibFactAna	380 nodes	3/29	9/58 nodes	0 msec	30,13	29,15	3,27 %
NewtonPol	46 nodes	1/3	2/40 nodes	0 msec	23,09	4,77	79,35 %
RegresionTest	18 nodes	1/0	3/0 nodes	0 msec	6,84	6,26	8,46 %
BoubleFibArrays	214 nodes	0/40	0/83 nodes	0 msec	12,42	12,01	3,33 %
ComplexNumbers	68 nodes	17/9	37/18 nodes	16 msec	20,62	10,20	50,53 %
StatsMeanFib	104 nodes	3/20	6/56 nodes	0 msec	12,33	11,00	10,81 %
Integral	25 nodes	0/2	0/22 nodes	0 msec	8,38	3,38	59,63 %
TestMath	51 nodes	1/2	2/5 nodes	0 msec	12,77	11,65	8,73 %
TestMath2	267 nodes	7/13	16/52 nodes	31 msec	66,47	58,33	12,24 %
Figures	116 nodes	8/3	16/6 nodes	0 msec	13,78	12,17	11,66 %
FactCalc	105 nodes	3/11	8/32 nodes	0 msec	19,81	12,64	36,19 %
SpaceLimits	127 nodes	38/0	76/0 nodes	0 msec	40,85	29,16	28,61 %
Argparser	129 nodes	31/9	70/37 nodes	16 msec	20,78	12,71	38,85 %
Cglib	1216 nodes	67/39	166/84 nodes	620 msec	80,41	65,01	19,15 %
Javassist	1357 nodes	10/8	28/24 nodes	4.745 msec	79,52	77,50	2,54 %
Kxml2	1172 nodes	260/21	695/42 nodes	452 msec	79,61	28,21	64,56 %
HTMLcleaner	6047 nodes	394/90	1001/223 nodes	8.266 msec	169.49	138,85	18,08 %
Jtestcase	4151 nodes	299/27	776/54 nodes	1.328 msec	85,05	80,52	5,32 %

any restriction in the use of chains, the technique produces EFs that are much more balanced. Repeating the experiments in this way (considering all 23.257 experiments) produced a query reduction of 42%. However, this reduction comes with a cost: the complexity of the questions may be increased. Therefore, we only apply the transformations when the question produced is not complicated (i.e., when it is generated by a chain). This has produced good results. In the case that the question of a collapsed/projected node was still hard to answer, our tool gives the possibility of answering "I don't know", thus skipping the current question and continuing the debugging process with the other questions (e.g., with the children). This means that, if the programmer is able to find the bug with the standard ET, she will also be able with the balanced EF. That is, the introduction of projected nodes is conservative and cannot cause the debugging session to stop.

6 Related Work

We are not aware of other approaches for balancing the structure of the ET. However, besides our approach, there exist other transformations devoted to reducing the size of the ET, and thus the number of questions performed. Our implementation allows us to balance an already generated ET, and it also allows us to automatically generate the balanced ET. This can be done by collapsing or projecting nodes during their generation. However, conceptually, our technique is a post-ET generation transformation.

The most similar approach is the tree compression technique introduced by Dave and Chitil [5]. This approach is also a conservative approach that transforms an ET into an equivalent (smaller) ET where the same bugs can be detected. The objective of this technique is essentially different: it tries to reduce the size of the ET by removing redundant nodes, and it is only applicable to recursive calls. A similar approach to tree compression is declarative source debugging [4], that instead of modifying the tree implements an algorithm to prevent the debugger from selecting questions related to nodes generated by recursive calls.

Another approach which is related to ours was presented in [12], where a transformation for list comprehensions of functional programs was introduced. In this case, it is a source code (rather than an ET) transformation to translate list comprehensions into equivalent functions that implement the iteration. The ET produced can be further transformed to remove the internal nodes of the ET reducing the size of the final ET as in the tree compression technique. Both techniques are orthogonal to the balancing of the ET, thus they both can be applied before balancing.

7   Conclusions

This work presents a new technique that allows us to automatically balance standard ETs. This technique has been implemented, and experiments with real applications confirm that it has a positive impact on the performance of AD.

From a theoretical point of view, two important results have been proved. The projection and the collapse of nodes do not prevent finding bugs, and the bugs found after the transformations are always real bugs. Another interesting and surprising result is the fact that balancing ETs can discover bugs undetectable with the original ET and can also change the order in which bugs are found.

In our current experiments, we are now taking advantage of the Execution Forests. This data structure allows us to apply more drastic balancing transformations. For instance, it allows us to collapse a whole subtree of the EF. This permits to avoid questions related to some parts of the EF and direct the search in other direction. In this respect, we do not plan to apply this transformation to chains, but to subtrees; based on approximations of the probability of a subtree to be buggy.

Execution forests provide a new dimension in the search that allows the debugger to go into a collapsed region and explore it ignoring the rest of the EF; and also to collapse regions so that search strategies can ignore them.

References

1. Binks, D.: Declarative Debugging in Gödel. PhD thesis, University of Bristol (1995)
2. Caballero, R.: A Declarative Debugger of Incorrect Answers for Constraint Functional-Logic Programs. In: Proc. of the 2005 ACM SIGPLAN Workshop on Curry and Functional Logic Programming, WCFLP 2005, pp. 8–13. ACM Press (2005)

3. Caballero, R., Hermanns, C., Kuchen, H.: Algorithmic debugging of Java programs. In: López-Fraguas, F.J. (ed.) Proc. of the 15th Workshop on Functional and (Constraint) Logic Programming, WFLP 2006, Madrid, Spain. ENTCS, vol. 177, pp. 75–89. Elsevier (2007)
4. Calejo, M.: A Framework for Declarative Prolog Debugging. PhD thesis, New University of Lisbon (1992)
5. Davie, T., Chitil, O.: Hat-delta: One Right Does Make a Wrong. In: Seventh Symposium on Trends in Functional Programming, TFP 2006 (April 2006)
6. Hirunkitti, V., Hogger, C.J.: A Generalised Query Minimisation for Program Debugging. In: Fritzson, P.A. (ed.) AADEBUG 1993. LNCS, vol. 749, pp. 153–170. Springer, Heidelberg (1993)
7. Insa, D., Silva, J.: Scaling up algorithmic debugging with virtual execution trees. In: Alpuente, M. (ed.) LOPSTR 2010. LNCS, vol. 6564, pp. 149–163. Springer, Heidelberg (2011)
8. Insa, D., Silva, J., Riesco, A.: Speeding up algorithmic debugging using balanced execution trees—detailed results. Technical Report 04/13, Departamento de Sistemas Informáticos y Computación (April 2013)
9. Kokai, G., Nilson, J., Niss, C.: GIDTS: A Graphical Programming Environment for Prolog. In: Workshop on Program Analysis For Software Tools and Engineering, PASTE 1999, pp. 95–104. ACM Press (1999)
10. MacLarty, I.: Practical Declarative Debugging of Mercury Programs. PhD thesis, Department of Computer Science and Software Engineering, University of Melbourne (2005)
11. Maeji, M., Kanamori, T.: Top-Down Zooming Diagnosis of Logic Programs. Technical Report TR-290, Japan (1987)
12. Nilsson, H.: Declarative Debugging for Lazy Functional Languages. PhD thesis, Linköping, Sweden (May 1998)
13. Nilsson, H., Fritzson, P.: Algorithmic Debugging for Lazy Functional Languages. Journal of Functional Programming 4(3), 337–370 (1994)
14. Shapiro, E.Y.: Algorithmic Program Debugging. MIT Press (1982)
15. Silva, J.: A Survey on Algorithmic Debugging Strategies. Advances in Engineering Software 42(11), 976–991 (2011)

Generating Test Suites with Augmented Dynamic Symbolic Execution*

Konrad Jamrozik[1], Gordon Fraser[2],
Nikolai Tillman[3], and Jonathan de Halleux[3]

[1] Saarland University, Saarbruecken-66123, Germany
jamrozik@cs.uni-saarland.de
[2] University of Sheffield, UK
gordon.fraser@sheffield.ac.uk
[3] Microsoft Research, WA, USA
{nikolait,jhalleux}@microsoft.com

Abstract. Unit test generation tools typically aim at one of two objectives: to explore the program behavior in order to exercise automated oracles, or to produce a representative test set that can be used to manually add oracles or to use as a regression test set. Dynamic symbolic execution (DSE) can efficiently explore all simple paths through a program, exercising automated oracles such as assertions or code contracts. However, its original intention was not to produce representative test sets. Although DSE tools like Pex can retain subsets of the tests seen during the exploration, customer feedback revealed that users expect *different* values than those produced by Pex, and sometimes also *more* than one value for a given condition or program path. This threatens the applicability of DSE in a scenario without automated oracles. Indeed, even though all paths might be covered by DSE, the resulting tests are usually not sensitive enough to make a good regression test suite. In this paper, we present *augmented dynamic symbolic execution*, which aims to produce representative test sets with DSE by augmenting path conditions with additional conditions that enforce target criteria such as boundary or mutation adequacy, or logical coverage criteria. Experiments with our APEX prototype demonstrate that the resulting test cases can detect up to 30% more seeded defects than those produced with Pex.

1 Introduction

Automated tools for structural testing are typically applied in one of two possible scenarios: 1) to exercise automated oracles, for example provided in terms of partial specifications, code contracts, assertions, or generic properties such as program crashes; or 2) to produce a representative test suite that needs to be enhanced with test oracles by a developer. Dynamic symbolic execution (DSE) [5] is one of the most successful approaches to exercising automated oracles,

---

* A preliminary version of this paper was published as a short paper discussing the idea for mutation and boundary analysis without evaluation in [15].

M. Veanes and L. Viganò (Eds.): TAP 2013, LNCS 7942, pp. 152–167, 2013.
© Springer-Verlag Berlin Heidelberg 2013

and there are many successful applications ranging from parametrized unit testing [23] to white-box fuzzing [12].

However, the application of DSE in the alternative scenario where representative test suites are desired is less explored. Tools like Microsoft's Pex [23] use simple heuristics to filter the test cases explored during DSE to retain subsets achieving branch coverage. However, there is no systematic way to produce *several* values for an individual branch or path, so it becomes difficult to implement other criteria such as boundary value analysis. This is problematic for regression testing: After changing a program a new DSE exploration would again just exercise the current behavior with respect to automated oracles, yet to find regression faults we need to execute the tests produced from an earlier version. However, as the DSE exploration might miss important values, this may lead to inferior regression test suites, potentially missing regression faults. Developer feedback has shown that these additional values are also missed during "Pex exploration", where Pex summarizes what a function does. For example, Pex always first tries to use 0 or `null`, and then uses values obtained from an SMT solver, but developers would prefer to see values that they can relate to the code, such as boundary values, and not `null`.

To overcome these issues, in this paper we present *augmented dynamic symbolic execution* (ADSE): This approach takes the path conditions generated from a program during regular DSE and augments them with additional conditions to make sure that the constraint solver returns interesting values, resulting in a test suite satisfying a criterion underlying the augmentation. To determine what constitutes an interesting value we consider *boundary values, mutation testing, logical coverage criteria,* and *error conditions.* In detail, the contributions of this paper are as follows:

Augmented DSE: We describe a generic approach to influence the test data produced with DSE by transforming path conditions.

Instantiations of ADSE: We describe several instantiations of augmented DSE; note that most of the underlying transformations have already been used in the past, yet always in a problem-specific context. In particular, we formulate the following transformations in terms of ADSE:

Boundary Value DSE: We instantiate augmented DSE such that boundary value inputs are generated with dynamic symbolic execution.

Mutation Testing DSE: We instantiate augmented DSE such that test cases that are good at killing mutants are derived with DSE.

Logical Coverage DSE: We instantiate augmented DSE such that test cases that satisfy logical coverage criteria are derived with DSE.

Error Condition DSE: We instantiate augmented DSE such that error conditions such as division by zero or overflows are triggered together with regular values.

Evaluation: We have implemented the approach in our APEX prototype as an extension to the popular Pex test generation tool, and present the results of an evaluation on a set of path conditions extracted with Pex.

2 Background

The availability of efficient constraint solvers has made it feasible to apply them to the task of generating test data. This is usually done by solving path conditions generated with symbolic execution. Symbolic execution maps a program path to a set of conditions on the inputs of the program. Branching conditions (e.g., if, while) represent the individual conditions in these sets, and the conditions are based on expressions on the input variables. Any input satisfying the conditions will follow this path through the control flow graph.

Unfortunately, constraint solvers cannot reason about a program's environment and run into scalability issues as programs become nontrivial in size. *Dynamic symbolic execution* (DSE) addresses these problems by using concrete executions to derive path conditions for feasible paths, which are systematically explored by negating individual conditions and deriving new inputs. Various tools implement DSE (e.g., DART [10], CUTE [21], Symbolic JPF [2], Pex [23], and others).

APEX is built on top of the Pex [23] tool, which performs DSE on the .NET platform. The main intended application of Pex and other DSE-based tools is to explore program paths with respect to automatically verifiable specifications such as assertions. Whenever Pex finds a new branch during DSE that was not covered before, a test case for this branch is added to the final test suite.

Many systematic test generation approaches are focused on branch conditions and branch coverage. To apply existing tools to different target criteria, a common approach is to transform these criteria to branch coverage problems. This for example has been done for division by zero errors [4], null pointer exceptions [19], mutation testing [26], or boundary value analysis and logical coverage criteria [18]. Here, additional test objectives are explicitly included in the program code as new branch instructions, allowing for reuse of tools maximizing branch coverage. There are several drawbacks to such an approach:

- A substantial, platform-dependent code manipulation architecture needs to be implemented, considerably increasing the complexity.
- Applied transformations have to conform to underlying language syntax, making them less flexible, harder to combine and cumbersome for dynamical adaptation of exploration targets.
- The code with transformations incorporated is still a subject to optimizations done by the underlying DSE engine, which can reverse or alter the applied modifications in an unexpected way, possibly causing path explosion.

For sure there would be ways to work around these drawbacks. However, in sum these are severe shortcomings threatening the practical applicability of source-transformation based approaches in the context of DSE. In contrast, ADSE performs all its transformations directly on the path conditions, avoiding these issues.

```
1 void methodUnderTest(int x, int y) {
2    if (x >= 3 && x <= 7) {
3      if (y - x >= 0 || y >= 4) {
4        // block_A
5      } else {
6        // block_B
7      };
8    } else {
9      // block_C
10   };
11 }
```

Fig. 1. Code example to illustrate DSE

3 Augmented Dynamic Symbolic Execution

3.1 Generating Test Suites with DSE

Dynamic symbolic execution first executes a program using concrete values, which are usually randomly chosen, or default values. Along the execution path chosen, conditions are collected, such that the resulting path condition represents the control flow path – any solution to the path condition will follow the same path. For example, assume that the example in Figure 1 is first executed with the concrete values $(0, 0)$. The first `if` statement evaluates to false, which means the condition $\neg(x \geq 3 \wedge x \leq 7)$ is added to the conditions for this path, and block C is reached. Now this condition is negated to derive a new path condition, $x \geq 3 \wedge x \leq 7$, for which a constraint solver produces a solution such as $(5, 0)$. This new input is executed, covering block B, and the conditions along the new path are collected: $(x \geq 3 \wedge x \leq 7) \wedge \neg(y - x \geq 0 \vee y \geq 4)$. Here, again a condition not yet explored is chosen, negated, and the resulting path condition is solved, producing for example $(5, 5)$, which finally also reaches block A.

During the DSE exploration done by Pex a separate test suite T is generated. Whenever an input S generated by DSE executes a branch that is not yet covered by T, then a test with this input is added to T; furthermore in Pex all tests that trigger exceptions are added to T.

3.2 Augmenting Path Conditions

Augmentation may only increase the quality of the test suite, but needs to preserve the branch coverage of the test suite produced without augmentation. A basic prerequisite of our approach is therefore that the augmentation of a path condition does not change the execution path the path condition represents, or if it does, the inputs fulfilling the original path conditions are retained in the resulting augmented test suite.

Definition 1 (Control Flow Graph). *The **control flow graph** of a program is a directed graph $CFG = (B, E)$, where B is the set of basic blocks and E is the set of transitions. There is one dedicated entry node $s \in B$, and one dedicated exit node $e \in B$.*

The function $R(B)$ maps each $b \in B$ to its immediate control dependent branch condition c, where $R(s) = true$, and function $N(c)$ maps each condition c to its node $b \in B$. A path from the start node of the control flow graph is a control flow path:

Definition 2 (Control Flow Path). *A **control flow path** is a sequence of transitions $\langle t_1, \ldots t_n \rangle$, where $t_1 = s$ and $(t_i, t_{i+1}) \in E$. If $t_n = e$ the path is complete.*

Each control flow path can be represented as a path condition:

Definition 3 (Path Condition). *A **path condition** is a conjunction of branch conditions $P = \bigwedge_{i \in \{1..n\}} c_i$, such that every input m satisfying P (denoted $m \models P$) allows to execute the control flow path $\langle s, N(c_1), \ldots, N(c_n) \rangle$, assuming there are no jumps. If $N(c_n) = e$ then the path condition is complete.*

We use $C \in P$ as a shorthand when referring to the individual branch conditions in a path condition.

When applying ADSE in a scenario where we require additional values for one particular program path it is important to make sure that the original control flow path is not changed. We call this type of augmentation *strict*:

Definition 4 (Strictly Augmented Path Condition). *A **strictly augmented path condition** P' for path condition P is a transformation of P such that $\forall (I \in inputs)(I \models P' \Rightarrow I \models P)$.*

If we would replace test cases obtained from original path conditions with those obtained from strictly augmented path conditions, we run into the risk of losing branch coverage due to possibility of augmented path conditions infeasibility. In the worst case, no strictly augmented path condition is feasible, thus resulting in no tests generated. Furthermore, each condition will be augmented at least twice, as it will usually be explored in both true and false valuation. This may lead to an unnecessary overhead for verbose augmentations (e.g., mutation testing). Therefore, we define *weak* augmentation such that resulting augmented conditions only need to share a prefix path:

Definition 5 (Weakly Augmented Path Condition). *A **weakly augmented path condition** P' for path condition P at branch condition c_i is a transformation of P such that $\forall j < i : P_j = P'_j$.*

When applying weak augmentation it is important to include the original path conditions for test generation in order to guarantee the branch coverage does not decrease.

A transformation criterion is a function that takes as input a path condition, and produces a set of augmented path conditions as a result.

Definition 6 (Transformation Criterion). *A transformation criterion is a function $\mathcal{T}(P)$ that creates a set of augmented path conditions $\mathcal{P}'$ based on P.*

Algorithm 1. Test suite generation using weak augmentation.

Require: Program M
Require: Transformation Criterion $\mathcal{T}$
Ensure: Test Suite T

```
 1: procedure GENERATESUITEAUGMENTED(M)
 2:     T ← {}
 3:     while none of the exploration bounds were reached do
 4:         P ← get next path condition
 5:         S ← solve P
 6:         if S is satisfiable and covers new branch then
 7:             t ← test with S as input
 8:             T ← T ∪ {t}
 9:             for P' ∈ AUGMENTCONDITION(T,P) do
10:                 S' ← solve P'
11:                 if S' is satisfiable then
12:                     t' ← test with S' as input
13:                     T ← T ∪ {t'}
14:     end while
15:     return T;
16: end procedure
```

Given a transformation criterion $\mathcal{T}(P)$, we can now use DSE to produce a test suite using Algorithm 1. Each time a path condition is selected for test generation (Line 4), and it covers a new branch, we add a test based on it (to retain the code coverage) and apply the transformation function, to try to solve all augmented path conditions. The solution (concrete input values) to each such augmented path condition is added to the resulting test suite after discarding redundant solutions (see Section 3.3). The process ends if any of the exploration bounds is reached, for example in terms of a time limit or limit in the number of path conditions to explore.

The path condition is a conjunction of branch and loop conditions encountered during program execution. The AUGMENTCONDITION($\mathcal{T}$,P) call from line 9 weakly augments each of these conditions, one at a time, and discarding all conditions following the augmented condition. For example, assume that in path condition $C_1 \wedge C_2 \wedge C_3 \wedge C_4$ the condition C_1 has already been augmented. When augmenting C_2 the resulting condition would be $C_1 \wedge C_2'$.

3.3 Handling Redundancy

In normal DSE, the constraint solver is only queried for path conditions which lead to execution of a new control flow path. In contrast, the augmentation may lead to a set of path conditions that all follow the same control flow path. Thus, there is the possibility that the solution to one augmented path condition satisfies some of other augmented conditions for the same path condition. This is a typical problem in coverage-oriented test generation, and is often countered by applying minimization as a post-processing step (e.g., [20]).

Algorithm 1 first solves all augmented path conditions. In principle, a further optimization can be added to check if previous test cases already satisfy a new augmented condition. In practice, however, we achieved a higher speedup by simply parallelizing Algorithm 1, because many augmented path conditions turn out to be unsatisfiable. The satisfiable solutions are then minimized using a simple heuristic: Solutions are sorted descending by the length of the path conditions from which they were obtained. Next, sequentially, each of these solutions is evaluated against the other augmented path conditions. If it turns out that a given augmented path condition is satisfiable with a previous solution, the solution obtained directly from this path condition is discarded. As a result, we obtain a minimized set of solutions satisfying the same augmented path conditions; this set is represents the test suite returned to the user.

When dealing with path conditions, each condition in the source code may occur several times in one path condition. In particular, loop guards may be repeated many times. For example, consider the following loop:

```
while ( x != 0 ) {
  list.add( x % 10 );
  x = x / 10;
}
```

Assuming the loop unrolled exactly 3 times the pc will be a conjunction of conditions as follows:

$$x \neq 0, \; list[0] = x \bmod 10,$$
$$x/10 \neq 0, \; list[1] = x/10 \bmod 10,$$
$$x/10/10 \neq 0, \; list[2] = x/10/10 \bmod 10,$$
$$x/10/10/10 = 0$$

Here, one division operator occurred in conditions 9 times (3^2) after 3 unrollings and all these occurrences may be targets for augmentation, which could lead to scalability problems. In principle, one can avoid augmenting duplicate occurrences of the same code location by incorporating ADSE directly into the underlying DSE engine, such that it has the required mapping of path conditions to source code statements. Based on this information, one can avoid to augment more than one condition corresponding to the same source code statement, if desired.

4   Augmentation Criteria

We now instantiate the transformation criterion for different common testing objectives, such as boundary value analysis, mutation testing, or general logical coverage criteria.

4.1   Boundary Value Testing

For a given path condition, any input values satisfying this condition will follow the represented path and will thus exhibit the same behavior. DSE therefore assumes that it is sufficient to test each path only once, and it does not matter which value out of the domain for this path is chosen. However, this only holds under the assumption that there is a complete specification that can decide correctness for every path. From the test suite point of view, a single representative per path is sufficient to test for *functional* faults, but not to test for *domain* faults [25].

For example, if the condition in Line 2 of Figure 1 is wrongly implemented and x should range from 2 to 7 instead of 3 to 7, then a test suite derived with DSE might not be able to detect this fault. Similarly, if such a test suite is used for regression testing, then changes in the value domains would not be detected.

An idea that was proposed early on [25] and has been focus of research over the years (e.g., [17,18]) is that testing should focus on values around the boundaries of domains. Using boundary values instead of whatever the underlying constraint solver suggests has the potential to increase the regression fault sensitivity of a test suite produced with DSE, and it also has the potential to make test cases easier to understand, as in many cases values obtained would have an obvious relation to conditions in source code.

There are several different ways to derive boundary values using ADSE. A simple method to derive values at the boundaries of relational comparisons is to augment relational conditions as follows (e.g., [18]):

$$
\begin{aligned}
A = B &\to A = B & A \leq B &\to A = B & A < B &\to A = B - 1 \\
A \neq B &\to A = B - 1 & A \geq B &\to A = B & A > B &\to A = B + 1
\end{aligned}
\tag{1}
$$

Boundary value analysis typically requires not only a value at the boundary, but also representative values from somewhere within the domain. This can be achieved by either selecting different values instead of 1 in the above transformation, or by additional conditions as follows:

$$
\begin{aligned}
A \leq B &\to A < B & A < B &\to A < B - 1 \\
A \geq B &\to A > B & A > B &\to A > B + 1
\end{aligned}
\tag{2}
$$

Boundary analysis usually also requires to use values on the other side of a boundary, i.e., values outside the target domain. Boundary value analysis thus leads to weakly augmented path conditions, such that we include the original path conditions to ensure there are representative values for all branch conditions.

4.2 Mutation Testing

Mutation testing [7] is a technique where simple syntactic changes (mutations) are applied to the code in order to simulate faults. The main application of this is to quantify the sensitivity of a test suite with respect to changes in the code, and thus to estimate its effectiveness at detecting real faults. However, mutants can also be used to drive test generation. In particular, by mutating constraints we can create inputs that weakly kill mutants [14]; i.e., the state is changed locally after the mutated statement. Mutants are based on actual fault models and thus should be representative of real faults, and experiments have confirmed that generated mutants are indeed similar to real faults for the purpose of evaluating testing techniques [3]. The estimation of effectiveness is quantified in the mutation score, which is the ratio of detected (killed) mutants to mutants in total. Mutants that survive the test cases offer guidance in where the test suite needs improvement.

Different types of mutations can be defined in terms of mutation operators, where each mutation operator typically can be applied to several different locations in a program, each time resulting in a new mutant; usually, only mutants that differ by a single change from the original program are considered.

In APEX, we have implemented the following mutation operators:

ROR, LOR, AOR: *Relational/Logical/Arithmetic operator replacement* (3 different mutation operators) replace respectively a relational, logical and arithmetic operator with all its other variants.

UOI: *Unary operator insertion* inserts increment, decrement, negation, and bitwise complement operators to variables and constants.

CRO: *Constant replacement operator* replaces variables and arbitrary constants with constants 0, 1 and -1.

For example, Line 2 consists of a conjunction of two comparisons; the LOR operator would replace the && with ||, xor and ROR would replace x <= 7 with x < 7, x == 7, x >= 7, etc. UOI would result in (x+1) <= 7 and all other variations. Given a mutation operator M, the augmentation should ensure that for a given condition C there is a value for each of the mutants $C' \in M(C)$ that distinguishes between C and C'. Therefore, a weak augmentation function for condition C simply is to join mutant and original condition with an xor, such that a resulting test input evaluates different for C and C':

$$\mathcal{T}(C) = \{C \oplus \neg C' \mid \forall C' \in M(C)\} \qquad (3)$$

4.3   Logical Coverage

The third instantiation of ADSE we consider in this paper is on coverage criteria for logical predicates, as common in source code. Note that DSE tools operating on the byte-code such as Symbolic JPF [2] or Pex do not need to treat complex logical predicates, as usually complex predicates in source code are compiled to nested atomic predicates in byte-code. However, if the instrumentation for DSE is done on the source code (e.g., [21]) or it is done on a model level (e.g., [16]) then complex predicates can exist and need to be covered.

The transformation of logical predicates to conditions that enforce test generation for different coverage criteria is well studied in other domains, e.g., when representing coverage criteria as temporal logic predicates for model checking [8]. To apply this to our context, we adopt the notation used in [1]: A logical *predicate* (branch condition) consists of *clauses* conjoined with logical operators. Without augmentation, the result of DSE is thus a test suite satisfying predicate coverage.

We consider general active clause coverage (GACC), which is a version of MCDC [6]. It requires that for each clause in a logical predicate there exists a state such that the clause determines the value of the predicate, and the clause has to evaluate to true and to false. For example, the branch in Line 3 in Figure 1 consists of two clauses, $y - x \leq 0$ and $y \geq 4$. Each of the two clauses determine either the true or false outcome of the predicate only if the other one evaluates to false. In general, a clause C determines a predicate P if the following xor-expression is true, where $P_{C,x}$ denotes P with C replaced with x: $P_{C,True} \oplus P_{C,False}$.

Consequently, the transformation of a predicate P requires that for every clause $C \in P$ we add a condition such that P is true and C determines the outcome of P:

$$\mathcal{T}(P) = \{P \wedge (P_{C,True} \oplus P_{C,False}) \mid C \in P\} \qquad (4)$$

Note that GACC tests always come in pairs, as the MCDC definition requires that the clause C has to be shown to make P evaluate to true and to false. We assume that the DSE exploration will lead to application of the transformation to both P and $\neg P$. In practice, this means that the above transformation will usually achieve that C evaluates to true and to false. Theoretically, however, simply using determination to augment the condition might also lead to a pair of tests where a clause evaluates to the same value in both cases, yet the determined outcome of the condition differs. This can be overcome by considering the values of individual clauses across transformations as will be described below.

In contrast to GACC, General Inactive Clause Coverage (GICC) requires a clause to *not* determine the outcome of the predicate, i.e., changing the value of the clause does not change the value of the predicate. For example, GICC requires that each of the two clauses in the predicate in Line 3 in Figure 1 has to evaluate to true and to false without changing the outcome of the predicate. If the outcome of the predicate is true, then that means the other clause has to be true; if the predicate is false, then in this example there is no way a clause can not determine this outcome. GICC is also known as Reinforced Condition/Decision Coverage [24]. The following transformation creates a pair of augmented conditions for every clause in a predicate:

$$\mathcal{T}(P) = \{P \wedge C \wedge \neg(P_{C,True} \oplus P_{C,False}) \mid C \in P\} \cup$$
$$\{P \wedge \neg C \wedge \neg(P_{C,True} \oplus P_{C,False}) \mid C \in P\}$$

This transformation again uses the determination function to require the predicate P to evaluate to true with clause C evaluating to true, and also with C evaluating to false, such that C does not determine P. Again, GICC also requires that the same is also shown for $\neg P$, and we assume that $\neg P$ is also augmented as part of the DSE exploration.

There are stronger versions of GACC and GICC, which require that the other clauses in the predicates do not change their values for any given pair of tests for a clause C. This can be achieved by keeping track of values across transformations. For example, if we know that clause C evaluated to true in the first of a pair of GACC tests, then in the second we can add the condition $C = false$. In fact, when adding this requirement the resulting test set will satisfy the stricter CACC (Correlated Active Clause Coverage) criterion, which requires that the considered clause determines the outcome of a predicate, and both the predicate and the clause evaluate to true and false.

4.4   Error Conditions

The fourth instance of ADSE we consider in this paper is that of error conditions: While many expressions can be efficiently tested in terms of the explicitly listed conditions on the value ranges, there are often implicit conditions that can lead to erroneous behavior. For example, if the expression x/y is part of a condition, then if $y = 0$ the outcome of the expression is division by zero fault, while for any other value the expression is valid. There have been attempts to make such implicit error conditions explicit to allow test generation tools to cover these cases (e.g., [4, 19]), Pex makes these branches explicit [23], and SAGE includes such conditions in the properties it checks for [11].

If the underlying symbolic execution engine does not make such branches explicit (e.g., Pex or SAGE make them explicit, but other tools might not), then error conditions can be explicitly enforced using ADSE. For example,

$$\mathcal{T}(P) = \begin{cases} \{P\} & \text{if there are no divisions in } P \\ \{P \wedge x = 0 \mid \forall x : \text{divisors in } P\} \cup & \\ \{P \wedge x \neq 0 \mid \forall x : \text{divisors in } P\} & \text{otherwise.} \end{cases} \qquad (5)$$

In a similar way, other error conditions can be used to augment path conditions. For example, every arithmetic condition can be augmented to a version where there is an overflow and one where there is none; every array access with a non-constant value can be augmented to one version where the index is within the range, and one where it is out of range; every pointer access can be augmented to a version where the pointer is `null` and one where it is not.

5   Evaluation

Our APEX prototype implements the described approach as an extension to the Pex tool, and we applied it to a set of example functions to evaluate the effects of the condition augmentation on the resulting test suite size as well as fault detection ability. Pex operates on .NET byte-code (CIL), and all complex predicates in the source code are translated to atomic conditions in the byte-code. Furthermore, the symbolic execution engine in Pex already makes error conditions explicit as branches. Consequently, our evaluation focuses on boundary value and mutation analysis. In our evaluation we aim to determine how augmentation with boundary value and mutation analysis affects the fault detection ability, test suite size, the number of conditions that need to be solved, and time required for computation.

Table 1. Mutants killed using DSE and augmented with boundary value and mutation analysis

Averages: DSE: 59.22%, Boundary Augmentation: 67.90%, Mutation Augmentation: 75.29%

Function	DSE	Bounds	Mutation	Function	DSE	Bounds	Mutation
Factorial	87.10%	92.86%	93.88%	FindMiddle	58.65%	64.69%	74.60%
Power	61.35%	85.66%	90.91%	WrapInc	76.32%	87.50%	95.00%
MaxValue	68.33%	88.28%	89.37%	Remainder	58.87%	74.97%	82.92%
Fibonacci	84.76%	87.80%	89.02%	ToOctal	28.71%	33.16%	40.77%
GCD	41.74%	41.04%	58.07%	ToHex	51.97%	61.03%	70.11%
WBS	27.76%	26.28%	28.27%	Roops avg.	65.08%	71.52%	90.56%

5.1   Experimental Setup

APEX is based on of Pex, but needs to access path conditions and change the test generation strategy that is applied, which is not possible through the public Pex extension interface. Without modifying Pex itself, we implemented APEX in terms of a Pex extension that collects the path conditions Pex uses to generate tests, and external tool processing them in order to derive tests. The resulting APEX prototype can automatically generate unit test suites using ADSE, requiring nothing but the byte-code of the unit under test. APEX leverages PexWizard, custom Pex-extensions and external tools written in C# to fulfill its tasks.

We ran experiments on 11 standalone methods and one class with multiple methods; Factorial, Power, MaxValue, Fibonacci, GCD (GreatestCommonDenominator), Remainder, ToOctal and ToHex are taken from DSA[1], WBS is taken from [22], and FindMiddle and WrapRoundCounter are examples used in [9]; Roops avg.[2] denotes results averaged over a set of 44 methods of integer examples contained in the Roops test generation benchmark. In our experiments, we consider the boundary value and mutation transformations in detail. We do not consider logical coverage as there are only few complex branch conditions in the byte-code-based symbolic execution performed by Pex, and we also do not consider error conditions as Pex already makes these explicit.

To determine the effectiveness of ADSE we applied the boundary value and mutation testing transformations to all our examples, and measured the resulting mutation scores in both cases, as well as the resulting number of test cases, path conditions solved and time elapsed. For boundary value analysis, we generated conditions to derive values directly at the boundaries and using a representative value.

5.2   Results

Table 1 lists the mutation scores achieved with ADSE against mutants of path conditions, as described in Section 4.2; in almost all cases there is a clear improvement over the mutation scores of the branch-coverage test set produced by Pex. Boundary value testing leads to lower mutation scores for GCD and WBS;

---

[1] http://dsa.codeplex.com/
[2] http://code.google.com/p/roops/

Table 2. # of tests of augmented test suite / # of path conditions solved using boundary value and mutation analysis, and time

| Function | Tests/Conditions | | | Time | | |
	DSE	Boundary	Mutation	DSE	Boundary	Mutation
Factorial	4/4	6/11	8/98	<1s	<1s	<1s
Power	4/4	10/31	15/286	<1s	<1s	1s
MaxValue	5/5	11/38	15/367	<1s	<1s	1s
Fibonacci	6/6	7/15	9/164	<1s	<1s	<1s
GCD	4/4	4/17	27/1,004	<1s	<1s	2m54s
WBS	18/18	101/174	365/2,508	<1s	2s	1m48s
FindMiddle	11/11	25/180	71/2,240	<1s	<1s	19s
WrapInc	2/2	4/6	6/40	<1s	<1s	<1s
Remainder	11/11	33/139	64/1,838	<1s	1s	58s
ToOctal	6/6	18/301	71/14,524	<1s	16s	35m59s
ToHex	14/14	24/382	101/11,395	<1s	9s	12m27s
Roops avg.	2.05/2.05	2.36/4.68	5.50/94.39	<1s	<1s	<1s
Average	7.25/7.25	20.45/108.22	63.13/2,879.87	<1s	2s	4m32s

for these examples there seem to be more mutants that are not related to boundary values, such that the boundary values represent an unlucky choice. There is of course a potential bias in these results as the mutants used for evaluation are the same as used to produce test cases. However, the aim of this experiment is not to evaluate different coverage criteria, but to demonstrate the general feasibility of ADSE, and that APEX can satisfy the augmented path conditions to a high degree.

> *In our experiments, ADSE resulted in up to 30% higher mutation scores.*

Table 2 reveals where the increase in mutation score comes from: The number of tests produced is considerably higher than in Pex's branch-coverage test sets. The table shows the size of test suites produced by augmentation and number of path conditions that were solved.

> *In our experiments, ADSE increased the average number*
> *of tests by up to 9 times over branch coverage.*

Constraint solving can be very expensive, and as the augmentation increases the number of conditions that need to be solved, this can be problematic with respect to the scalability of the approach. Table 2 summarizes the number of conditions that were passed to the constraint solver with and without augmentation (this includes the conditions that are solved as part of the regular DSE exploration), and the right hand side of Table 2 summarizes the time it took to emit the augmented test suites, running on 7 out of 8 logical cores of Intel(R) Core(TM) i7-2675QM CPU @ 2.20GHz processor and 8 GB RAM. The increase is significant, and depends on the actual transformation used. Little surprising, mutation analysis leads to the largest number of augmented path conditions, and thus also significantly increases the effort that goes into test generation.

The fact that mutation testing has scalability issues is well known, and there are ways to improve the performance, primarily by more fine-grained control over path conditions. Other techniques include summarizing loops [13], which directly addresses the scalability problem with loop unrollings (see 3.3), or sampling mutants instead of exhaustively considering all of them. Such techniques can theoretically be applied to ADSE as well. Furthermore, there are techniques to reduce the number of calls to the constraint solver (e.g., [11]).

The ToOctal example has the largest increase in the number of path conditions, and this and ToHex are instances of the loop unrolling problem described in Section 3.3. As our current prototype is not directly integrated into Pex it does not have access to a mapping between path conditions and code, making it impossible to avoid this problem.

> *On average, ADSE lead to a modest increase in computational time,*
> *but the worst case was over 2160 times slower than normal DSE.*

5.3   Threats to Validity

The focus of this evaluation is to demonstrate that ADSE can result in better test suites, where the meaning of "better" can be defined by any transformation criterion. There are several threats to the validity of these experiments:

Threats to *construct validity* are on how the performance of a testing technique is defined. We measured the quality of the resulting test sets in terms of their mutation score on path conditions, not the source code. However, in practice developers might have different preferences such as whether the chosen values are similar to values a human tester might have chosen. Furthermore, an increase in mutation score might not be desirable if it comes with a significant increase of the test suite size. The mutation score in our experiments was computed by the same tool used to generate mutation augmented test suites, so the results may be biased. As we used a standard set of mutation operators it is likely that other mutation analysis tools would result in similar scores; however, in general quantifying the relation between different coverage criteria is not the objective of this paper.

Threats to *internal validity* might come from how the empirical study was carried out. To reduce the probability of having faults in our APEX prototype, it has sizable unit test suite and makes heavy use of Code Contracts. The size of the chosen example functions means that there is a threat to *external validity* regarding the generalization to other types of software. The main limitation enforcing our choice of case study subjects was that our approach is not fully implementable through the public Pex extension API.

6   Conclusions

DSE can efficiently generate inputs to cover all (simple) paths in a program. Yet, the use of DSE to produce test suites with high coverage of established test criteria has not been explored in depth. In this paper we describe a technique that transforms the path conditions that DSE handles such that DSE produces test suites satisfying any chosen coverage criterion. We have instantiated this augmented dynamic symbolic execution for boundary value analysis, mutation analysis, logical coverage criteria, and error conditions, demonstrating that the resulting test suites are superior at detecting faults to the simple branch coverage test suites produced by Pex.

There are several immediate applications of ADSE: First, a common application reported by Pex users is to simply explore the behavior of a function or program. In this case, the programmer simply looks at the test data produced by Pex, and can thus profit from a wider range of interesting cases. For example, if there is a predicate on $5 \times x == y \times z$ then a valid assignment (and the one chosen by Pex) would be to assign 0 to x, y, and z. Mutation analysis or boundary values would lead to different (more interesting) values.

The second application is a traditional scenario in automated testing when there is no automated oracle available. Here, the aim is often to produce test sets that satisfy a given criterion, for example a logical coverage criterion.

A third application scenario is regression testing: When software evolves, one needs a regression test suite to check for regression faults. The stronger the test suite, the more sensitive it is against regression faults, and thus ADSE can offer to improve regression test suites.

ADSE also has the potential to extend DSE in many ways not immediately targeted by the transformations we described in this paper. Augmenting comprehensibility by transforming to human-readable values (e.g., for strings) or performance testing are just two possible augmentations.

Finally, in our evaluation we demonstrated that augmentation can lead to test suites satisfying different criteria. However, we have not yet investigated which criteria are most useful in practice. For example, the mutation testing experiments indicate scalability problems, which might justify the use of sampling techniques to generate stronger test sets without expensive constraint solving on too many individual mutants. Furthermore, our current prototype is implemented as an extension to Pex, whereas a tighter tool integration would offer further opportunities for optimization. This and other improvements will be the focus of our future work.

Acknowledgments. Thanks to Florian Gross for comments on earlier versions of this paper. This project has been funded by DFG grant Ze509/5-1.

References

1. Ammann, P., Offutt, J.: Introduction to Software Testing, 1st edn. Cambridge University Press (2008)
2. Anand, S., Păsăreanu, C.S., Visser, W.: JPF-SE: a symbolic execution extension to Java PathFinder. In: Grumberg, O., Huth, M. (eds.) TACAS 2007. LNCS, vol. 4424, pp. 134–138. Springer, Heidelberg (2007)
3. Andrews, J.H., Briand, L.C., Labiche, Y.: Is mutation an appropriate tool for testing experiments? In: Proc. ICSE 2005, pp. 402–411. ACM (2005)
4. Bhattacharya, N., Sakti, A., Antoniol, G., Guéhéneuc, Y.-G., Pesant, G.: Divide-by-zero exception raising via branch coverage. In: Cohen, M.B., Ó Cinnéide, M. (eds.) SSBSE 2011. LNCS, vol. 6956, pp. 204–218. Springer, Heidelberg (2011)

5. Cadar, C., Sen, K.: Symbolic execution for software testing: three decades later. Commun. ACM 56(2), 82–90 (2013)
6. Chilenski, J.J., Miller, S.P.: Applicability of modified condition/decision coverage to software testing. Software Engineering Journal, 193–200 (1994)
7. DeMillo, R.A., Lipton, R.J., Sayward, F.: Hints on test data selection: Help for the practicing programmer. Computer 11(4), 34–41 (1978)
8. Fraser, G., Wotawa, F., Ammann, P.E.: Testing with model checkers: a survey. Softw. Test. Verif. Reliab. 19, 215–261 (2009)
9. Ghani, K., Clark, J.A.: Strengthening inferred specifications using search based testing. In: Proc. SBST, pp. 187–194. IEEE Computer Society Press (2008)
10. Godefroid, P., Klarlund, N., Sen, K.: Dart: directed automated random testing. In: Proc. PLDI, pp. 213–223 (2005)
11. Godefroid, P., Levin, M.Y., Molnar, D.A.: Active property checking. In: Proc. EMSOFT 2008, pp. 207–216. ACM (2008)
12. Godefroid, P., Levin, M.Y., Molnar, D.A.: Sage: Whitebox fuzzing for security testing. ACM Queue 10(1), 20 (2012)
13. Godefroid, P., Luchaup, D.: Automatic partial loop summarization in dynamic test generation. In: Proc. ISSTA 2011, pp. 23–33. ACM (2011)
14. Howden, W.E.: Weak mutation testing and completeness of test sets. IEEE TSE 8(4), 371–379 (1982)
15. Jamrozik, K., Fraser, G., Tillmann, N., De Halleux, J.: Augmented dynamic symbolic execution. In: Proc. ASE 2012, pp. 254–257. ACM (2012)
16. Joebstl, E., Weiglhofer, M., Aichernig, B.K., Wotawa, F.: When bdds fail: Conformance testing with symbolic execution and smt solving. In: Proc. ICST 2010, pp. 479–488. IEEE Computer Society (2010)
17. Kosmatov, N., Legeard, B., Peureux, F., Utting, M.: Boundary coverage criteria for test generation from formal models. In: Proc. ISSRE, pp. 139–150. IEEE Computer Society (2004)
18. Pandita, R., Xie, T., Tillmann, N., de Halleux, J.: Guided test generation for coverage criteria. In: Proc. ICSM 2010, pp. 1–10. IEEE Computer Society (2010)
19. Romano, D., Di Penta, M., Antoniol, G.: An approach for search based testing of null pointer exceptions. In: Proc. ICST 2011, pp. 160–169. IEEE (2011)
20. Rothermel, G., Harrold, M.J., Ostrin, J., Hong, C.: An empirical study of the effects of minimization on the fault detection capabilities of test suites. In: Proc. ICSM 1998, pp. 34–43. IEEE Computer Society Press (1998)
21. Sen, K., Marinov, D., Agha, G.: CUTE: a concolic unit testing engine for C. In: Proc. ESEC/FSE-13, pp. 263–272. ACM (2005)
22. Staats, M., Păsăreanu, C.: Parallel symbolic execution for structural test generation. In: Proc. ISSTA 2010, pp. 183–194. ACM (2010)
23. Tillmann, N., de Halleux, J.: Pex–white box test generation for.NET. In: Beckert, B., Hähnle, R. (eds.) TAP 2008. LNCS, vol. 4966, pp. 134–153. Springer, Heidelberg (2008)
24. Vilkomir, S.A., Bowen, J.P.: Reinforced condition/decision coverage (rc/dc): A new criterion for software testing. In: Bert, D., Bowen, J.P., Henson, M.C., Robinson, K. (eds.) ZB 2002. LNCS, vol. 2272, pp. 291–308. Springer, Heidelberg (2002)
25. White, L.J., Cohen, E.I.: A domain strategy for computer program testing. IEEE Trans. Softw. Eng. 6, 247–257 (1980)
26. Zhang, L., Xie, T., Zhang, L., Tillmann, N., de Halleux, J., Mei, H.: Test generation via dynamic symbolic execution for mutation testing. In: Proc. ICSM 2010, pp. 1–10. IEEE Computer Society (2010)

A Lesson on Proof of Programs
with Frama-C. Invited Tutorial Paper

Nikolai Kosmatov, Virgile Prevosto, and Julien Signoles

CEA, LIST, Software Reliability Laboratory, PC 174, 91191 Gif-sur-Yvette France
`firstname.lastname@cea.fr`

Abstract. To help formal verification tools to make their way into industry, they ought to be more widely used in software engineering classes. This tutorial paper serves this purpose and provides a lesson on formal specification and proof of programs with FRAMA-C, an open-source platform dedicated to analysis of C programs, and ACSL, a specification language for C.

Keywords: deductive verification, Frama-C, ACSL, program specification, teaching.

1 Introduction

Recent advances on proof of programs based on deductive methods allow verification tools to be successfully integrated into industrial verification processes [1,2]. However, their usage remains mostly confined to the verification of the most critical software. One of the obstacles to their deeper penetration into industry is the lack of engineers properly trained in formal methods. A wider use of formal verification methods and tools in industrial verification requires their wider teaching and practical training for software engineering students as well as professionals.

This tutorial paper presents a lesson on proof of programs in the form of several exercises followed by their solutions. It is based on our experience in teaching at several French universities over the last four years. This experience shows that, for the majority of students, theoretical courses (like lectures on Hoare logic [3] and weakest precondition calculus [4]) are insufficient to learn proof of programs. We discuss the difficulties of the lesson for a student, necessary background, most frequent mistakes, and emphasize some points that often remain misunderstood. This lesson assumes that students have learned the basics of formal specification such as precondition, postcondition, invariant, variant, assertion.

In our lesson, we use FRAMA-C [5,6], an open-source platform dedicated to the analysis of C programs and developed at CEA LIST. Being open-source is an important advantage for teaching: FRAMA-C is available on all major Linux distributions, and can be easily installed by a local network administrator at any university. FRAMA-C gathers several static analysis techniques in a single collaborative framework. In particular, two different plug-ins are dedicated to proof of programs: JESSIE [7,8] and WP [9]. The latter is newer and aims to be better integrated into the rest of the platform. Up to now, we have used JESSIE in our lessons because it is more stable and its level of integration into the platform is not an issue for teaching.

M. Veanes and L. Viganò (Eds.): TAP 2013, LNCS 7942, pp. 168–177, 2013.

All static analyzers of FRAMA-C, including JESSIE, share a common specification language, called ACSL [10]. This language allows FRAMA-C analyzers to collaborate in an effective way [11]. Before proving programs, the students must learn to formally specify them, so we include ACSL in our lesson which thereby mixes program specification and program verification. ACSL syntax was designed to stay close to C, and students do not have any problem to learn it on-the-fly with a language manual at hand. Thus we do not include a detailed presentation of ACSL in this paper.

The paper is organized as follows. The lesson is presented in three parts: discovery of the JESSIE tool (Section 2), specification of C programs in ACSL (Section 3) and their verification with JESSIE (Section 4). Section 5 presents our teaching experience feedback. Section 6 provides some related work and concludes.

2   Introductory Exercices

2.1   Safety Checks for Arithmetic Overflows

Question 1. Run JESSIE to prove the following program:

```
/*@ ensures x >= 0 && \result == x || x < 0 && \result == -x;
    assigns \nothing; */
int abs(int x) { return ( x >= 0 ) ? x : -x; }
```

Can you explain the unproved safety property? Write a precondition restricting the values of x, for example, to the interval −1000 . . . 1000 and re-run the proof.

Answer. The postcondition for the given program is proved, but JESSIE reports an unproved safety check for an arithmetic overflow risk in -x. Since INT_MIN = - INT_MAX - 1, the expression -x provokes an overflow for x = INT_MIN. Restricting the values of x to −1000 . . . 1000 in the precondition avoids this risk, and the proof succeeds for the complete specified program:

```
/*@ requires -1000 <= x <= 1000;
    ensures x >= 0 && \result == x || x < 0 && \result == -x;
    assigns \nothing; */
int abs(int x) { return ( x >= 0 ) ? x : -x; }
```

Discussion. Arithmetic overflows are responsible for well-known critical software crashes, but most students ignore these issues. JESSIE helps them to understand this point. Notice that the weakest possible precondition avoiding overflows in abs would be x > INT_MIN. Finally, the contract has an assigns clause that specifies that abs is not supposed to modify the global state of the program. We will go back on this clause in the next section.

2.2   Safety Checks for Pointer Validity

Question 2. Consider the following function swapping the values referred by its inputs:

```
int swap(int *p1, int *p2) { int tmp = *p1; *p1 = *p2; *p2 = tmp; }
```

a) Specify the postcondition and run JESSIE to prove the program. Explain the results you observe. Add a precondition and re-run the proof.

b) Explain the role of the `assigns` clause you put in the postcondition. (Did you?) Give an example of a wrong implementation that would be proved by JESSIE without it.

Answer. **a)** We first add the following postcondition:

```
/*@ ensures \old(*p1) == *p2 && \old(*p2) == *p1;
    assigns *p1, *p2; */
```

Here `\old(*p1)` refers to the value of `*p1` before the call. JESSIE proves the postcondition, but indicates a safety alarm at each dereference of the pointers `p1` and `p2`. Indeed, the validity of these pointers is supposed to be guaranteed by the caller, so it should be explicitly specified by the precondition as follows:

```
/*@ requires \valid(p1) && \valid(p2);
    ensures \old(*p1) == *p2 && \old(*p2) == *p1;
    assigns *p1, *p2; */
int swap(int *p1, int *p2) { int tmp = *p1; *p1 = *p2; *p2 = tmp; }
```

After running JESSIE again, we see that the safety properties are now proved as well.

b) The `assigns` clause specifies here which variables can be modified by the function. Without this clause, the following erroneous implementation can be proved:

```
int shared; // a global variable that should not be modified in swap
int swap(int *p1, int *p2) { shared = *p1; *p1 = *p2; *p2 = shared; }
```

Discussion. The students often forget to specify validity of memory accesses. This exercise insists on this point and shows safety checks for pointer validity in JESSIE. Another common error is a missing or incorrect `assigns` clause. Considering counter-examples is an excellent way to make students aware of the problem.

3   Lesson on Program Specification

The goal of this lesson is to formally specify a well-known but non-trivial function that searches an element in a sorted array. This can be split in several steps of increasing difficulty to introduce the most useful ACSL constructs.

3.1   Function Contracts

Question 3. Write the ACSL formal specification corresponding to the following informal specification of function `find_array`. Explain its clauses.

```
/* [find_array(arr, len, query)] returns any index [idx] of the sorted array
   [arr] of length [len] such that arr[idx] == query. If such an index does not
   exist, it returns -1. */
int find_array(int* arr, int len, int query);
```

Answer. Here is a correct answer which provides `requires, ensures` and `assigns` clauses.

```
/*@ requires len >= 0;
    requires \valid(arr+(0..(len-1)));
    requires \forall integer i, j; 0 <= i <= j < len ==> arr[i] <= arr[j];
    ensures (\exists integer i; 0 <= i < len && arr[i] == query) ==>
            0 <= \result < len && arr[\result] == query;
    ensures (\forall integer i; 0 <= i < len ==> arr[i] != query) ==>
            \result == -1;
    assigns \nothing; */
int find_array(int* arr, int len, int query);
```

The three preconditions respectively say that:

- the given array length must be positive or zero,
- the array must contain at least `len` valid memory cells which can be safely read,
- the array must be sorted.

The two `ensures` clauses respectively state that:

- if the array contains `query` at some index between `0` and `len-1`, then the value `\result` returned by the function is between these bounds, and `arr[\result] == query`,
- if all the elements of the array are different of `query`, the returned value is `-1`.

The `assigns` clause specifies here that no memory location may be modified by the function since it must have no observable effect on the memory from the outside.

Discussion. Maybe surprisingly, the main mistake is not related to big clauses like complex quantifications and implications. Students actually tend to forget implicit specifications on the length of the array and the validity of its cells (usually they do not forget the `assigns` clause after previous exercises). At this point, it is important to emphasize this specific weakness of informal specifications which often contain implicit, unwritten parts. Additionally, we can show that writing several `requires` and `ensures` clauses may be clearer than writing a single clause of each type with a big conjunction.

3.2 Behaviors

Question 4. Modify the previous ACSL specification in order to use two distinct behaviors corresponding to whether the element `query` is found or not. Explain your changes.

Answer. Here is a correct answer which defines two behaviors `exists` and `not_exists`.

```
/*@ requires \forall integer i, j; 0 <= i <= j < len ==> arr[i] <= arr[j];
    requires len >= 0;
    requires \valid(arr+(0..(len-1)));

    assigns \nothing;

    behavior exists:
      assumes \exists integer i; 0 <= i < len && arr[i] == query;
      ensures 0 <= \result < len;
      ensures arr[\result] == query;

    behavior not_exists:
      assumes \forall integer i; 0 <= i < len ==> arr[i] != query;
      ensures \result == -1; */
int find_array(int* arr, int len, int query);
```

The `assumes` clauses are the activation conditions of the behaviors: if in some behavior this clause is valid, the `ensures` clause of this behavior must be satisfied.

Discussion. The usual students' question is the difference between an `assumes` clause (which is an assumption) and a `requires` clause (which is also allowed in a behavior and contains a requirement which must be satisfied by the caller, so it needs a proof). It is also important to explain that behaviors correspond to specifying by cases and to show that this new specification is much clearer than the previous one which is equivalent and uses implications instead.

3.3 Logical Predicates

Question 5. Modify the previous specification to define and use two logical predicates:

- `sorted` which states that a given array is sorted,
- `mem` which states that an element belongs to a given array.

Answer. Here is a correct answer.

```
/*@ predicate sorted(int* arr, integer length) =
      \forall integer i, j; 0 <= i <= j < length ==> arr[i] <= arr[j];

    predicate mem(int elt, int* arr, integer length) =
      \exists integer i; 0 <= i < length && arr[i] == elt; */

/*@ requires sorted(arr,len);
    requires len >= 0;
    requires \valid(arr+(0..(len-1)));

    assigns \nothing;

    behavior exists:
      assumes mem(query, arr, len);
      ensures 0 <= \result < len;
      ensures arr[\result] == query;

    behavior not_exists:
      assumes ! mem(query, arr, len);
      ensures \result == -1; */
int find_array(int* arr, int len, int query);
```

The first `requires` clause of the function now uses the predicate `sorted` while the `assumes` clauses of both behaviors use predicate `mem`.

Discussion. Some students have difficulties with this question since they do not remark that the `assumes` clauses of both behaviors are the exact opposite to each other: a minimal logical background is actually required here. After that, we can explain the difference between a predicate (a parameterized logical proposition), a logic function (which *defines* a logical term depending on its parameters), and a programming function (which *computes* a value depending on its parameters). The three notions allow the user to write cleaner code/specification without redundancy.

3.4 Testing the Specification

Students often feel more comfortable when they can interact with the computer to gain confidence in their answer. Unlike in the verification phase of Sec. 4, usual specification process does not allow such interactions, except for type-checking the ACSL contract. It is possible to overcome this issue by providing a test function that calls the specified function on sample cases: the specification written by the students must then imply the assertions of the test function.

Question 6. Check with JESSIE that your specification allows to prove the assertions of the following function (note that the pre-condition of the last call should not be satisfied, as we deliberately give an unsorted array to `find_array`).

```
void main () {
  int array[] = { 0, 4, 5, 5, 7, 9 };
  int idx = find_array(array,6,7);
  /*@ assert idx == 4; */
  idx = find_array(array,6,5);
  /*@ assert idx == 2 || idx == 3; */
  idx = find_array(array,5,9);
  /*@ assert idx == -1; */
  array[0] = 6;
  // pre-condition should be broken
  idx = find_array(array,4,6);
}
```

Answer. The answers to Questions 3, 4 and 5 pass this test.

Discussion. This question allows students to catch some specification errors by them-selves. In particular, the fact that a successful call must return a value between `0` and `len-1` is often overlooked. When missing, the first two assertions of `main` are not prov-able: nothing in ACSL prevents some memory cell `arr[i]` with an index `i` outside of `0..5` from containing `query` as well. Although some guidance may be required to go from noticing that an assertion is not proved up to writing a correct specification of `find_array`, this approach is very helpful for testing the specification and explaining specification problems.

3.5 Modular Verification and Function Calls

Question 7. In the following program, the functions `abs` and `max` are declared but not defined.

```
// returns absolute value of given integer x>INT_MIN
int abs ( int x );

// returns maximum of x and y
int max ( int x, int y );

// returns maximum of absolute values of given integers x>INT_MIN and y>INT_MIN
int max_abs( int x, int y ) {
  x=abs(x);
  y=abs(y);
  return max(x,y);
}
```

a) Specify the three functions and prove the function `max_abs`.
b) Remove the precondition of the function `max_abs` and re-run the proof. Observe and explain the proof failure.
c) Remove the postcondition of the function `max` and re-run the proof. Observe and explain the proof failure.

Answer. **a)** Here is a specified program that is proved by JESSIE. The specifications are pretty much self-explanatory based on the previous examples.

```
#include<limits.h>
/*@ requires x > INT_MIN;
    ensures x >= 0 && \result == x || x < 0 && \result == -x;
    assigns \nothing; */
int abs ( int x );
```

```
/*@ ensures \result >= x && \result >= y;
    ensures \result == x || \result == y;
    assigns \nothing; */
int max ( int x, int y );

/*@ requires x > INT_MIN && y > INT_MIN;
    ensures \result >= x && \result >= -x &&
       \result >= y && \result >= -y;
    ensures \result == x || \result == -x ||
       \result == y || \result == -y;
    assigns \nothing; */
int max_abs( int x, int y ) {
  x=abs(x);
  y=abs(y);
  return max(x,y);
}
```

b) If the precondition of the function `max_abs` is removed, JESSIE does not manage to prove that the precondition of `abs` is satisfied each time it is called. Indeed, in modular verification the precondition must be ensured by the caller, and it cannot be proved if the inputs of `max_abs` can be equal to INT_MIN.

c) If the postconsition of the function `max` is removed, JESSIE cannot prove the postcondition of `max_abs`. Indeed, the proof of the caller relies on the contract of the callee (whose code is not necessarily defined in the same file).

Discussion. This question illustrates specific roles of preconditions and postconditions in modular verification. Note that pre- and postconditions of the caller and of the callee have dual roles in the caller's proof. The precondition of the caller is assumed and the postcondition of the caller must be ensured. On the contrary, the precondition of the callee must be ensured by the caller, while the postcondition of the callee is assumed in the caller's proof.

4   Lesson on Program Verification

Once a correct specification has been written, the next exercises deal with verifying that a given implementation is conforming to this specification. The main difficulty here consists in finding appropriate *loop invariants* for each loop of the program. An invariant is a property that holds when entering the loop the first time and is preserved by one step of the loop. In other words, it must hold after 0 step, and if we assume that it holds after n steps, it must hold after $n + 1$ step. By induction, the invariant thus holds when we exit the loop[1]. Moreover, the invariants are *the only thing* that is known about the state of the program after the loop. They must thus be strong enough to allow us to prove post-conditions, but not too strong, or we won't be able to prove the invariants themselves. Finding the correct balance requires some training as explained below.

4.1   Safety

Question 8. Write loop invariants to prove all safety properties for the following implementation of `find_array`.

---

[1] Loop termination is handled in the next section.

```
int find_array(int* arr, int length, int query) {
  int low = 0;
  int high = length - 1;
  while (low <= high) {
    int mean = low + (high -low) / 2;
    if (arr[mean] == query) return mean;
    if (arr[mean] < query) low = mean + 1;
    else high = mean - 1;
  }
  return -1;
}
```

Answer. The following invariants show that `low` and `high` (thus `mean`) are within `arr`'s bounds:

```
/*@ loop invariant 0 <= low;
    loop invariant high < length; */
```

Discussion. Students usually don't have issue finding these invariants, as they arise quite naturally from the loop structure itself. An important point however is that `low <= high` is *not* an invariant, as it is not preserved by the last step of an unsuccessful search, where we end up with `low == high + 1`.

4.2 Loop Invariants

Question 9. Prove that the invariants written in Question 8 hold (fix them if necessary).

Answer. The invariants above are correct.

Question 10. Write the loop invariants that allow to prove the post-conditions of behaviors `exists` and `not_exists` and prove that they are correct.

Answer. The following invariants are necessary:

```
/*@ loop invariant \forall integer i; 0 <= i < low ==> arr[i] < query;
    loop invariant \forall integer i; high < i < length ==> arr[i] > query; */
```

Discussion. These invariants are much more difficult to write than the ones that ensure safety. Indeed, they do not stem directly from the code itself. Rather, they provide the main correctness argument of the algorithm: because the array is sorted, the array elements to the left of `low` are smaller than `query`, while the array elements to the right of `high` are greater than `query`. Hence, we can restrict the search to the interval `low..high`.

4.3 Loop Variant and Program Termination

Question 11. Provide a `loop variant` that ensures that the loop always terminates.

Answer. We need a positive integer expression decreasing at each step, so we take:

```
/*@ loop variant high - low + 1; */
```

Discussion. A helpful hint to find a loop variant without giving a formal definition is to look for an upper bound for the number of remaining loop iterations. At each step we decrease the diameter of the interval `low..high` where the element `query` can still be found, hence `high-low+1` gives such an upper bound. Program termination is usually left at the end of the lesson as it is mainly orthogonal to the other proof obligations.

5   Teaching Feedback and Discussion

Our experience shows that a deep theoretical course on Floyd-Hoare logic is not mandatory for the practical session on proof of programs. After comparing students having missed the lectures with others who have attended a complete theoretical course, we can say that, for program specification and proof exercises, good programming skills seem even more helpful than good knowledge of the underlying theory. Theoretical courses by themselves are definitely not sufficient to learn proof of programs.

The exercises of this lesson correspond to the difficult points that should be thoroughly exercised in practice. First, it is important to write correct specifications (Section 3). Proving a function f with a wrong specification is a very common error. For instance, a too strong precondition that prevents calling f in legitimate contexts or a too weak postcondition that forgets to state something about the state after the execution of f will not be detected by running JESSIE on f alone. When writing a postcondition, most students focus on the returned values and forget to specify that the function under verification does not modify variables when it is not supposed to do so.

Section 3.4 shows how students can "test" their specification before attempting to verify the implementation. Nevertheless, the instructor should check the specification of each student even if everything is proved at the end.

A major difficulty in program verification is to understand the role of an invariant. Many students need some time to understand that a loop invariant is a summary of the effects of the n first steps of the loop and that this is the only thing that is known on the state of the program after these steps. Thus, writing an invariant strong enough to enable proving the annotations below the loop (including post-conditions) and preserved by a loop step is often a delicate task.

Another important difficulty of proof of programs with automatic tools is analysis of proof failures. Basically, a proof failure can be due to an incorrect implementation (a bug), a wrong specification or the incapability of the automatic prover to prove the the required property. In the first case, it is sufficient to fix the bug. In many cases, test generation can help to find a counter-example. In the second case, the unproved property is not necessarily the erroneous one. Attentive analysis of the proof obligation may help to understand its proof failure. The problem can be due to an earlier incorrect or missing clause (such as a precondition, a loop invariant of the current loop, a loop invariant of a previous, or outer, or inner loop, the contract of a previously called function, etc.). Additional statements (assertions, lemmas, stronger loop invariants, etc.) may help the prover in some cases. They can also help the user to understand which part of a complex property is too difficult for the automated prover. Finally, when nothing else works, an interactive proof assistant (such as Isabelle, Coq and PVS) can be used to finish the proof.

6   Related Work and Conclusion

Usage of tools in formal verification courses is getting some traction [12]. In particular, the KeY tool for Java is used at a couple of universities [13]. Like KeY, FRAMA-C and JESSIE benefit from their open-source nature and the fact that they target existing languages, already known to students. However, they are used for the moment at a very small number of institutions [14], and very limited introductory material with exercices is available [15], [16, Chap. 9]. FRAMA-C is also part of an experiment in online programming training [17].

In this paper, we demonstrated by a small practical session how JESSIE can be used for teaching formal software verification. Our experience shows that JESSIE is perfectly adequate for this purpose since it benefits from an expressive specification language, adequate documentation, ease of use and installation. We hope that this work will be helpful in teaching proof of programs and will contribute to the introduction of formal methods based techniques and tools into industrial software engineering.

References

1. Randimbivololona, F., Souyris, J., Baudin, P., Pacalet, A., Raguideau, J., Schoen, D.: Applying Formal Proof Techniques to Avionics Software: A Pragmatic Approach. In: Wing, J.M., Woodcock, J., Davies, J. (eds.) FM 1999. LNCS, vol. 1709, pp. 1798–1815. Springer, Heidelberg (1999)
2. Delmas, D., Duprat, S., Baudin, P., Monate, B.: Proving temporal properties at code level for basic operators of control/command programs. In: 4th European Congress on Embedded Real Time Software (2008)
3. Hoare, C.A.R.: An axiomatic basis for computer programming. Communications of the ACM 12(10), 576–580, 583 (1969)
4. Dijkstra, E.W.: Guarded commands, nondeterminacy and formal derivation of programs. Communications of the ACM 18(8), 453–457 (1975)
5. Correnson, L., Cuoq, P., Kirchner, F., Prevosto, V., Puccetti, A., Signoles, J., Yakobowski, B.: Frama-C User Manual (October 2011), http://frama-c.com
6. Cuoq, P., Kirchner, F., Kosmatov, N., Prevosto, V., Signoles, J., Yakobowski, B.: Frama-C, a program analysis perspective. In: Eleftherakis, G., Hinchey, M., Holcombe, M. (eds.) SEFM 2012. LNCS, vol. 7504, pp. 233–247. Springer, Heidelberg (2012)
7. Moy, Y.: Automatic Modular Static Safety Checking for C Programs. PhD thesis, University Paris 11 (January 2009)
8. Moy, Y., Marché, C.: Jessie Plugin Tutorial
9. Correnson, L., Dargaye, Z.: WP Plug-in Manual, version 0.5 (January 2012)
10. Baudin, P., Filliâtre, J.C., Hubert, T., Marché, C., Monate, B., Moy, Y., Prevosto, V.: ACSL: ANSI/ISO C Specification Language (February 2011)
11. Correnson, L., Signoles, J.: Combining Analyses for C Program Verification. In: Stoelinga, M., Pinger, R. (eds.) FMICS 2012. LNCS, vol. 7437, pp. 108–130. Springer, Heidelberg (2012)
12. Feinerer, I., Salzer, G.: A comparison of tools for teaching formal software verification. Formal Aspects of Computing 21(3) (2009)
13. KeY Project: Uses of KeY for teaching, http://www.key-project.org/teaching/
14. Frama-C: Uses of Frama-C for teaching, http://bts.frama-c.com/dokuwiki/doku.php?id=mantis:frama-c:teaching
15. Burghardt, J., Gerlach, J., Hartig, K., Pohl, H., Soto, J.: ACSL by Example. A fairly complete tour of ACSL features through various functions inspired from C++ STL. Version 7.1.0 (for Frama-C Nitrogen)
16. Almeida, J.C.B., Frade, M.J., Pinto, J.S., de Sousa, S.M.: Rigorous Software Development, An Introduction to Program Verification. Undergraduate Topics in Computer Science. Springer (2011)
17. Quan, T., Nguyen, P., Bui, T., Le, T., Nguyen, A., Hoang, D., Nguyen, V., Nguyen, B.: iiOSProTrain: An Interactive Intelligent Online System for Programming Training. Journal of Advances in Information Technology 3(1) (2012)

Evaluation of ASLan Mutation Operators*

Johan Oudinet[1], Alberto Calvi[2], and Matthias Büchler[1]

[1] Technische Universität München, Germany
[2] Dipartimento di Informatica, Università di Verona, Italy

Abstract. The AVANTSSAR validation platform is an automated toolset for validating trust and security aspects of Service-Oriented Architectures (SOAs). Models and security properties are specified in low-level AVANTSSAR Specification Language (ASLan) and there are three dedicated model-checkers that can validate if such models satisfy the security properties. However, the implementation may deviate from the specification and may contain some vulnerabilities that an attacker could exploit to violate the defined security properties. We have designed a set of semantic mutation operators to inject such vulnerabilities in an ASLan specification. Here we present the implementation of those mutation operators as Extensible Stylesheet Language Transformation (XSLT) scripts. Then, we evaluate the interest of using semantic mutation operators instead of syntactic ones by comparing the number of mutants that lead to the generation of a test case (i.e., a potential attack) and the resulting test suite for a set of existing ASLan specifications.

1 Introduction

ASLan [Armando et al., 2012] is an input language for model-checkers that are dedicated to verify security properties of SOAs. Such model-checkers consider a Dolev-Yao model for the intruder capabilities [Dolev and Yao, 1983] and can report traces when an intruder, with these capacities, violates the security properties. Therefore, the ASLan model describes only the behavior of honest users of the system, and analyzing them helps in detecting security issues at design time.

Recently, Büchler et al. [2012] have proposed a mutation-based testing approach to check for security issues in Web applications starting from secure specifications. A secure specification only contains traces that satisfy the given security properties. The main idea is to inject well-known vulnerabilities in the model to see if such vulnerabilities could lead to an attack that violates one of the specified security properties. If so, it is possible to try that attack on the real system; moving from verification at design time to testing a corresponding implementation. In this approach, the model-checker is used as a tool to generate test cases for a class of vulnerabilities, with respect to the injected vulnerability.

---

* This work was partially supported by the FP7-ICT-2009-5 Project no. 257876, "SPaCIoS: Secure Provision and Consumption in the Internet of Services".

M. Veanes and L. Viganò (Eds.): TAP 2013, LNCS 7942, pp. 178–196, 2013.
© Springer-Verlag Berlin Heidelberg 2013

To implement this mutation-based approach for ASLan specifications, we propose and have implemented the following steps: (i) the modeler describes (parts of) the semantic of an ASLan model as XML elements, (ii) the Abstract Syntax Tree (AST) of the model is extracted, (iii) a mutation operator, modeled as an XSLT script, injects a specific vulnerability into the ASLan model with regards to its semantic, (iv) the mutated AST is translated back into an ASLan model and the model-checker checks if there is any attack on this mutant.

The mutants generated by such semantic mutation operators could also be generated by syntactic changes. Therefore, the research question behind this work is to empirically evaluate if the selection of mutants produced by a semantic change is pertinent to the generation of potential attacks against a SOA implementation. We compare the results, in terms of number of found attacks, of either applying semantic changes or syntactic changes to a set of existing ASLan specifications.

The main contributions of this paper are: (i) an implementation of the model-based fault injection approach to the ASLan model, (ii) an empirical evaluation of semantic versus syntactic mutation operators that shows that semantic mutations operators can save a lot of time by both generating much less mutants to get the same amount of potential attacks and simplifying the execution of these attacks thanks to knowing which vulnerability is exploited.

Section 2 gives a brief introduction to ASLan for readers that are not familiar to this formal language. Then, Section 3 presents the parametrized syntactic mutation operators that have been implemented. Next, Section 4 describes the list of vulnerabilities that can be injected via semantic mutation operators, which are built on top the syntactic ones. Section 5 explains the tool workflow. Section 6 analyzes the experiment results. Finally, Section 7 summarizes the related work and Section 8 sums up the main results and points out some perspectives.

2   ASLan Modeling Language Description

In this section, we give an overview of the ASLan language and describe the most important features illustrated by simple examples.

A model given in the ASLan specification language defines a transition system, given by a set of states, a set of initial states, and a transition relation. A state is a set of ground facts that are true in that state. In the presence of Horn clauses, the closure of a state could in general be an infinite set of facts. Therefore the closure is carried out only implicitly. An excerpt of an exemplary ASLan specification modeling one of the Role Based Access Control (RBAC) lessons from WebGoat [OWASP, 2011] is reported in Listing 1.1. The transition relation is defined according to the rules in the `rules` section. They define which set of states are reachable from a state. For example, the rule `step_002` can be triggered by any honest agent (i.e., `not(dishonest(Server_Actor))`), which plays the role of the server. Note that `state_Server(Server_Actor, S_IID, 1, User)` bounds the value of the `Server_Actor` variable in `not(dishonest(Server_Actor))` with the state in which the server has to be in order to execute the transition. Since the `iknows` fact is used to model the intruder knowledge and ASLan's semantics assumes the intruder controls the network, the last condition, i.e. `iknows(crypt(ck(Server_Actor),pair(ctag,login(User_1,password(User_1,Server_Actor)))))`, states that a specific message has to be present in the network. When all these conditions composing the Left Hand Side (LHS) of the rule are satisfied, the rule can be applied. Namely, the fact terms on the Right Hand Side (RHS) of the step are introduced in the next state and, therefore, they will identify the new set of facts holding in the reached state, modulo state closure[1].

Section `signature` contains the declaration of subtypes and functions. For example, in Listing 1.1, `cookie` is a sub-type of `message` and `profileOf` is a symbolic function from `agent` to `message`. Then, Section `types` contains the type of all constants and variables. This implies that an identifier cannot be used with two different types even though the scope of each variable is limited to the rule it appears in. In our example, there are four constants of type agent: `root`, `tom`, `jerry`, and `webServer`.

Section `inits` contains the initial states of the transition system. In Listing 1.1, there is a single initial state where the agent `i` is marked as a dishonest agent and the intruder knows the private keys of this agent. Thus, the intruder can decrypt (resp. sign) any message sent to (resp. emitted by) agent `i`. When the first transition, i.e. `step_001`, is applied the intruder learns all `tom`'s keys, because we wanted to model the fact that `tom` is a dishonest agent. This means that the intruder can operate using a different agent name, i.e. `tom` instead of `i`.

Horn clauses are defined in the section `hornClauses` and serve for declaring implicit facts which hold in every state that fulfills some conditions. The fact on the left of the `:-` symbol holds every time the facts on the right of this symbol hold. For example, the Horn clause `public_login` says that the fact `iknows(login(Login_arg_1,Login_arg_2))` is implicitly present in every state in which both `iknows(Login_arg_1)` and `iknows(Login_arg_2)` facts hold. Such a clause states that the intruder can use the symbolic function `login` to build new terms starting from his knowledge, i.e. the function is available to the intruder. Similarly, the Horn clause `inv_login_1` says that the `login` function is partially invertible because the intruder knows the first argument of every corresponding evaluation of this function he knows.

Finally, in section `goals`, a set of attack states and/or LTL goals can be defined. An attack state is a list of facts identifying a set of states which, when reached by the transition system, triggers a violation. An LTL goal is an LTL formula which has to be satisfied by the transition system. The exemplary goal in Listing 1.1 is an attack state which is used to identify all possible states in which the intruder has access to a profile, i.e. `iknows(profileOf(AgentP_goal))`, without having the proper authorization, i.e. `not(isAuthorizedToView(i, AgentP_goal))`.

---

[1] Fact retraction occurs when a fact appears in the LHS of a step but does not appear in its RHS. The only exception is the `iknows` fact, which is persistent and can never be retracted.

Listing 1.1. ASLan excerpt for one of the RBAC lessons from WebGoat

```
section signature:
    cookie < message
    profileOf : agent -> message
    login : agent * symmetric_key -> message
section types:
    root,tom,jerry,webServer : agent
section hornClauses:
    hc public_login(Login_arg_1, Login_arg_2) :=
        iknows(login(Login_arg_1, Login_arg_2)) :-
            iknows(Login_arg_1),iknows(Login_arg_2)
    hc inv_login_1(Login_arg_1, Login_arg_2) :=
        iknows(Login_arg_1) :-
            iknows(login(Login_arg_1, Login_arg_2))
section inits:
    initial_state init :=
    iknows(inv(ak(i))).
    iknows(inv(ck(i))).
    iknows(inv(pk(i))).
    dishonest(i).
    state_Environment(root, 0, 1).
    true.
    [...]
section rules:
    step step_001(Actor, IID, IID_1) :=
        state_Environment(Actor, IID, 1)
        =[exists IID_1]=>
        dishonest(tom).
        iknows(inv(ak(tom))).
        iknows(inv(ck(tom))).
        iknows(inv(pk(tom))).
        iknows(password(tom, webServer)).
        [...]
    step step_002(Server_Actor, S_IID, User, User_1) :=
        iknows(crypt(ck(Server_Actor), pair(ctag, login(User_1, password(
            User_1, Server_Actor))))).
        not(dishonest(Server_Actor)).
        state_Server(Server_Actor, S_IID, 1, User)
        =>
        authenticated(User_1).
        iknows(listStaffOf(User_1)).
        state_Server(Server_Actor, S_IID, 1, User_1)
    step step_003(Agent, Server_Actor, S_IID, User, User_2) :=
        authenticated(User_2).
        isAuthorizedToView(User_2, Agent).
        iknows(sign(inv(ak(User_2)), pair(atag, pair(Server_Actor,
            viewProfileOf(Agent))))).
        not(dishonest(Server_Actor)).
        state_Server(Server_Actor, S_IID, 1, User)
        =>
        iknows(crypt(ck(User_2), sign(inv(ak(Server_Actor)), pair(stag, pair(
            User_2, profileOf(Agent)))))).
        authenticated(User_2).
        state_Server(Server_Actor, S_IID, 1, User_2)
    step step_004(Agent, Server_Actor, S_IID, User, User_3) :=
        iknows(sign(inv(ak(User_3)), pair(atag, pair(Server_Actor,
            viewProfileOf(Agent))))).
        not(isAuthorizedToView(User_3, Agent)).
        not(dishonest(Server_Actor)).
        authenticated(User_3).
        state_Server(Server_Actor, S_IID, 1, User)
        =>
        authenticated(User_3).
        state_Server(Server_Actor, S_IID, 1, User)
section goals:
    attack_state secret_profiles(AgentP_goal) :=
      iknows(profileOf(AgentP_goal)).not(isAuthorizedToView(i,. AgentP_goal))
```

3   Parametrized Syntactic Mutation Operators

In this section, we present Fact Assertion (FA) and Function Remover (FR), the two parametrized syntactic mutation operators we have implemented. The former inserts a fact into the initial state of the transition system, therefore, modifying the set of initial assumptions. The latter changes the conditions to trigger a rule by removing a symbolic function from its LHS. Each operator takes as parameter a regular expression which restricts the application of the syntactic changes only to specific symbols matching the expression.

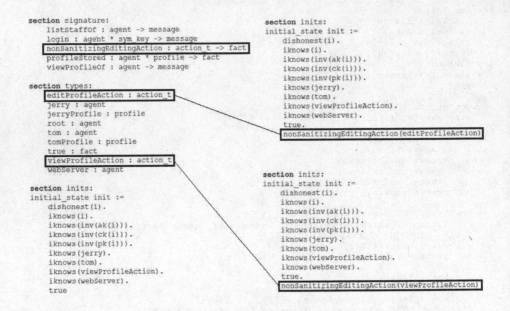

Fig. 1. Example of applying the FA operator with parameter "`nonSanit.*`"

Each mutant generated by the FA operator differs from the original specification in the initial state only. The initial state of the mutant contains one fact more than in the original specification. Thus, the FA operator adds an assumption to the set of initial assumptions. Supposing the regular expression "`nonSanit.*`" is used to parametrize the syntactic operator, Figure 1 (right) shows the mutated initial states which are generated by mutating the original state in Figure 1 (left). In the `section signature` of the original model, only the `nonSanitizingAction` function has an image of type `fact` and matches the regular expression defined by the parameter. Thus, all possible constant symbols of type `action_t`, which can be found in the `section types` of the original specification, are used to build the `fact` terms that are added to the initial state of each resulting mutant.

Each mutant generated by the FR operator, instead, differs from the original specification in one transition step. The mutated step has one term on the LHS

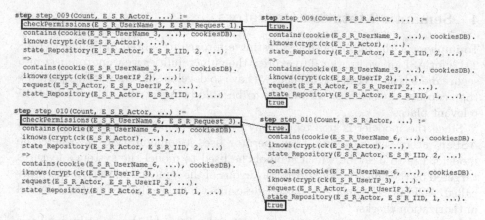

Fig. 2. Example of applying the FR operator with parameter "`check.*`"

replaced by the `true` fact. The replaced term is either `contains` or `iknows`[2], or it is a function symbol that appears in the `signature` section and it has `fact` as return type. Figure 2 shows an example of application of the FR operator to an ASLan specification with "`check.*`" passed as parameter. Each of the modified steps (Figure 2, right) replaces its original counterpart in one of the two resulting mutated specification. As it is shown in Figure 2, the function matching the parameter passed to the syntactic operator is `checkPermissions`, and it is thus replaced by a `true` fact. A `true` fact is added on the RHS of the mutated step as well. This is necessary because, accordingly to ASLan's semantics, when a fact appears only on the LHS of a step, it means that the fact has to hold in the state before the step's execution, but it will not hold in the next one. Since `true` has to hold in every state, the FR operator adds it also to the RHS.

The reported examples show how it is possible to limit the number of generated mutants by restricting the application of a syntactic mutation operator to a specific set of symbols. Actually, applying the FR operator to the ASLan excerpt reported on the left side of Figure 2 without passing any parameter (or, likewise, passing "`.*`") would have result in generating 8 different mutants instead of 2. Indeed, there are 8 function terms appearing on the LHS of the steps which can be replaced by `true` facts in the mutants.

Parametrize syntactic mutation operators not only limits the number of mutants generated but, more important, it allows us to implement semantic changes as it is described in the next section.

Listing 1.2. Configuration for the ACFlaw operator

```
<acflaw>
  <authz>check.*</authz>
</acflaw>
```

---

[2] These symbols are part of the ASLan Prelude file, which contains a set of predefined Horn clauses, constants, and function symbols. Every AVANTSSAR model-checker imports this file in addition to any ASLan specification.

4   Semantic Mutation Operators

To implement the mutation-based testing approach presented in [Büchler et al., 2012] for ASLan, we first need to express the vulnerabilities we want to inject into secure models at ASLan level. Then, we have to develop some mutation operators that capture the semantic of models to be able to inject the vulnerabilities in relevant places.

Since the modeler is free to use any symbolic name to specify a system in ASLan, every semantic mutation operator uses a configuration file where the modeler has to describe which symbols he used to model the system's features targeted by the mutation. For example, in one of the semantic mutation operators called ACFlaw, the modeler has to describe which symbolic functions model authorization checks.

We designed semantic mutation operators for five well-known vulnerabilities affecting SOAs, and in particular Web Applications, according to the MITRE's top 25 [S. Christey, 2011]:

- Improper Neutralization of Special Elements used in an SQL Command
- Improper Neutralization of Input During Web Page Generation
- Missing Authentication for Critical Function
- Missing Authorization
- Missing Encryption of Sensitive Data

One of our goals is to provide a library of semantic mutation operators covering as much as possible all the known vulnerabilities that may affect SOAs. Such a library would allow a security analyst to select the operators accordingly to the vulnerabilities he wants to inject and he would just have to provide the information about the semantics of the ASLan specification he wants to mutate.

So far, we have designed three semantic mutation operators. The ACFlaw operator injects a "Missing Authorization" by removing a symbolic function that models an authorization check from the conditions to trigger a rule. Therefore, it uses the FR syntactic operator, presented in the previous section, and sets its parameter according to the configuration file. Listing 1.2 shows an example where the modeler specified that any symbolic function starting with the prefix check should be considered as an authorization check. Such a configuration file can be used to set the ACFlaw operator to produce the mutated steps showed in Figure 2 (right) starting from the steps in Figure 2 (left).

The Data Sanitization Flaw (DSFlaw) injects either an "Improper Neutralization of Special Elements used in an SQL Command" ("SQL injection", for short) or an "Improper Neutralization of Input During Web Page Generation" ("Cross Site Scripting (XSS)", for short). The DSFlaw operator achieves that by tagging elements either as non correctly sanitizing or inputs as already corrupted. Since it adds a new condition on inputs or elements, the DSFlaw operator is built on top of the FA syntactic operator. For example, Listing 1.3 shows the configuration of the DSFlaw operator for one of the specification in which non correctly sanitizing actions can be tagged by all function symbols matching the "nonSanit.*" expression, and in which function matching the maliciousProfile expression

Listing 1.3. Configuration for the DSFlaw operator

```
<dsflaw>
  <saniz>Sanitizing|maliciousProfile</saniz>
</dsflaw>
```

Listing 1.4. Configuration for the CCFlaw operator

```
<ccflaw>
  <netw>iknows</netw>
</ccflaw>
```

can be used to mark an element as being corrupted. An example of application of the DSFlaw operator with such a configuration is shown in Figure 1, where the original initial state on the left is replaced, in each of the resulting mutants, by one of the mutated states on the right side.

Finally the third semantic operator, the Communication Channel Flaw (CCFlaw), targets vulnerabilities in the communication channels. Thus, it covers both "Missing Authentication for Critical Function" and "Missing Encryption of Sensitive Data". As in the case of the ACFlaw, it is built on top of the FR syntactic operator. Listing 1.4 shows the configuration of this operator where functions responsible for the network communication are specified. Usually, in an ASLan model, the intruder is the network so it uses the `iknows` fact. If we apply the CCFlaw operator to the model in Listing 1.1, we obtain a total of 3 mutants where respectively the steps `step_002`, `step_003` and `step_004` has a `true` fact instead the original `iknows` fact on the LHS (and another `true` fact on the RHS to prevent its retraction). The mutated steps are shown in Listing 1.5.

Since ASLan has few grammar rules, only two syntactic mutation operators are enough for designing semantic operators to inject at least five different vulnerabilities into ASLan specifications. Indeed, removing any of the facts in the LHS of a step can lead to the injection of different vulnerabilities. For example, whenever the FR operator removes a fact modeling a check over the user's credentials, it injects a "Missing Authorization" vulnerability. If the removed fact is an `iknows` fact the operator may inject a "Missing Authentication for Critical Function" vulnerability, because an `iknows` fact on the LHS can model the reception of a signed message.

All the three semantic mutation operators we designed make use of just one syntactic operator at a time and, therefore, generating a subset of all possible mutants that could be obtained with this syntactic operator. However, it may be necessary to apply several changes in an ASLan model to inject a vulnerability and, therefore, to design semantic operators applying more than one syntactic operator. For example, a semantic operator which applies twice the FR operator could be used to inject a "Missing Authorization" vulnerability tailored for more complex authorization mechanisms relying on more than one condition at a time.

Another relevant aspect of our semantic operators is that they inject specific vulnerabilities. Knowing which vulnerability has been injected in a mutant is a fundamental advantage for the instantiation phase occurring after the model-checker

```
step step_002(Server_Actor, S_IID, User, User_1) :=
    true.
    not(dishonest(Server_Actor)).
    state_Server(Server_Actor, S_IID, 1, User)
    =>
    authenticated(User_1).
    iknows(listStaffOf(User_1)).
    state_Server(Server_Actor, S_IID, 1, User_1).

step step_003(Agent, Server_Actor, S_IID, User, User_2) :=
    authenticated(User_2).
    isAuthorizedToView(User_2, Agent).
    true.
    not(dishonest(Server_Actor)).
    state_Server(Server_Actor, S_IID, 1, User)
    =>
    iknows(crypt(ck(User_2), sign(inv(ak(Server_Actor)), pair(stag, pair(
        User_2, profileOf(Agent)))))).
    authenticated(User_2).
    state_Server(Server_Actor, S_IID, 1, User_2).
    true

step step_004(Agent, Server_Actor, S_IID, User, User_3) :=
    true.
    not(isAuthorizedToView(User_3, Agent)).
    not(dishonest(Server_Actor)).
    authenticated(User_3).
    state_Server(Server_Actor, S_IID, 1, User)
    =>
    authenticated(User_3).
    state_Server(Server_Actor, S_IID, 1, User).
    true
```

has generated an attack trace. Indeed, the trace is interpreted as a test case for
the implementation, but has to be instantiated in order to replace all abstract values with concrete ones. This process is straightforward for those values which are
known, e.g. IP address at which the application can be accessed, but it is complex
for those values related to the attack vectors, e.g. malicious scripts. Without knowing which vulnerability has been injected, it would not be possible to instantiate
the trace without the intervention of the security analyst who has to tell to the
test execution engine which class of payloads to use.

5   Tool Description

We provide a tool to mutate an ASLan model using semantic mutation operators
that are based on syntactic ones. In order to use our tool, a user has to provide
both an ASLan model and a description of its semantic as an XML file, which
is necessary for the semantic mutation operators as described in Section 4.

Fortunately, the AVANTSSAR Platform [Armando et al., 2012] comes with
the ASLan++-Connector which contains an XML component which allows one
to translate an ASLan model into an XML file that represents the corresponding
AST and *vice versa*. Therefore we decided to implement the mutation operators

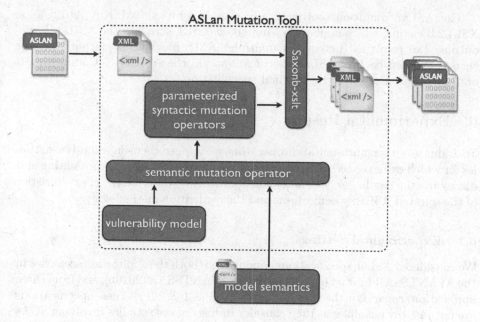

Fig. 3. Workflow and architecture of the ASLan Mutation Tool

at the XML representation level of the AST. In fact, as shown in Figure 3, we mutate the XML file, producing several XML mutants, and we translate them back to ASLan that is the input format for the AVANTSSAR's model-checkers.

By applying mutation at ASLan level via XML we can profit from the wide set of technologies available for managing and manipulating XML-like files, like XSLT. XSLT 2.0 [M. Kay, 2007] is a language designed to be used in conjunction with XPath 2.0 [A. Berglund et al., 2007] which allows one to define transformation rules for XML files to generate other XML file(s). With XPath it is possible to navigate through the structure of an XML file and manage its nodes, its elements (attributes) and basic data types (strings, integers). This allows us to define mutation operators as transformation rules for the input file. For example, we can perform checks on the fact symbols appearing on the LHS of ASLan step transitions using the path `aslan/rules/step/lhs/facts`. Scripts written in XSLT are called XML stylesheets and have the extension `.xsl`. Each script is composed by a set of `xsl:template` elements which contain rules that has to be applied to the matching elements of the input file (e.g., XML nodes, attributes) in order to build the output file(s).

Figure 3 also shows the architecture of the ASLan mutation tool. A semantic mutation operator implements a vulnerability injection at the model level by modifying specific parts of the AST according to the model semantic. It is therefore an XSLT script that calls one or several XSLT scripts, which are syntactic mutation operators, with specific parameters in order to perform the intended semantic changes.

The ASLan mutation tool internally uses saxonb-xslt [M. Kay, 2012] as a XSLT2.0 engine, which applies the configured XSLT script to the XML file and outputs the result as (potentially multiple) XML files. These output files are then translated back to ASLan specifications via the ASLan++-Connector, to obtain ASLan mutants of the original specification.

6 · Experimental Results

To evaluate our semantic mutation operators, we applied them on several case studies for which we have access to a secure ASLan specification. Before presenting and discussing the results for each mutation operator, we describe the characteristics of the selected ASLan specifications and the evaluation methodology.

6.1   Experimental Settings

We considered ASLan specifications coming from both the application scenarios in the AVANTSSAR Library of problem cases [AVANTSSAR, 2010b], and from three application scenarios in the SPaCIoS project [SPaCIoS, 2012]. These specifications are not just toy examples as they consider industrial case studies involving SOAs belonging to different fields such as e-Government, e-Commerce, and e-Health.

Table 1 summarizes the characteristics of each ASLan model and the results of validating it with Constraint Logic based Attack Searcher (CL-AtSe) [Turuani, 2006], which is one of the three model-checkers in the AVANTSSAR platform. We chose CL-AtSe because it better supports the ASLan features employed in the selected case studies (see [AVANTSSAR, 2010a] for the list of supported features of each AVANTSSAR model-checkers). For the model characteristics, the three columns list the number of rules, Horn clauses, and goals in the ASLan file. We

Table 1. Characteristics of each ASLan specification

Specification	Model			CL-AtSe		
	Rules	HCs	Goals	nb	Time (s)	Verdict
CRP.stat	16	21	11	2	4039	safe
ECR	23	45	8	1	17	safe
Google-SAML-SSO_one-wa_expl-pseudo_v2	15	17	2	1	3	inconcl.
Google-SAML-SSO_one-wa_v1	15	17	2	1	1	inconcl.
Google-SAML-SSO_v0	15	17	2	1	4	inconcl.
IDMXScene2_Safe	15	30	7	2	1	inconcl.
Infobase_Scene1	11	13	8	2	54	safe
PTD	18	43	17	1	200	safe
PTD_VisaBank	19	38	14	1	6	safe
SAML_SSO-SP_init-CCM_bil-1SSL	11	31	1	1	198	inconcl.
wg_rbac_1	9	15	1	1	1	safe
wg_rbac_3	9	17	1	1	1	safe
wg_stored_xss_goal2	14	23	1	1	2	safe

recall that the rules represent the possible choices that the model-checker has to consider to go to the next state, that each Horn clause describes how an implicit fact may be deduced from the explicit facts that hold in a state and, finally, that each goal is (usually) an attack state that the model-checker tries to reach. The last three columns give information on the model-checker itself: the value of the --nb option, the elapsed time to validate the model, and the verdict. Since CL-AtSe is a bounded model-checker, the option --nb defines the maximum number of iterations per rule that the model-checker can consider. The default value is 1 but we know that for some specifications, this value must be higher in order to consider relevant scenarios. Basically, increasing this value increases the number of traces that are analyzed by the model-checker. Therefore, this value should be kept as low as possible to speed up the model-checking phase. The elapsed time needed by the model-checker to give a verdict may slightly vary from one execution to another. Thus, we run the analysis 3 times and kept the median value. The Time column is used to set the time limit for the verification of each mutant. The reported verdict for these secure models should be safe. However, CL-AtSe reported an inconclusive verdict for some specifications. It means that it did not find any attack but it left out from the analysis some parts of the specification. In these particular cases, CL-AtSe could not handle some Horn clauses. Nevertheless, we are sure that all these specifications are also safe because we analyzed them using the two other model-checkers (i.e., SATMC [Armando et al., 2009] and OFMC [Mödersheim and Viganò, 2009]). Still, for the sake of getting homogeneous statistics, we only used CL-AtSe to validate all the mutated models, and this fact did not prevent us from finding attacks for mutants derived by mutating those inconclusive specifications.

Since each of the presented semantic mutation operators uses just one syntactic operator to perform the vulnerability injection in an ASLan model, we can compare the number of mutants and abstract attack traces generated by both. Ideally, our semantic mutation operators should generate much less mutants but still find the same abstract attack traces. Note that if a semantic mutation operator applies more than one syntactic change, we could compare it to the corresponding *higher-order* syntactic mutation operator from which the generated mutants would also be a subset.

6.2 Results of Applying Syntactic and Semantic Mutation Operators

Table 2 and Table 3 show the results of applying the two syntactic mutation operators (i.e., without any semantic restriction). They may generate a lot of mutants (e.g., almost 30000 for the FA operator) but the percentage of mutants for which CL-AtSe reports a non-empty[3] abstract attack trace is quite low (0.4%).

---

[3] The FA operator modifies the initial state which may end up in violating a security property right from the beginning. In such cases, CL-AtSe reports an attack with an empty attack trace. We ignore these results in the Attacks column since we aim at turning the abstract attack traces into test cases.

Even worse, most of the abstract attack traces found for each specification are identical. For example, among the 19 attacks found by the FA operator on the `wg_stored_xss_goal2` specification, there are only 3 different traces, which are shown in Listing 1.6. The two first traces can reveal an attack if the viewed profile (i.e., tom's or jerry's profile) contains some malicious code. The last trace is a classical stored XSS attack where a compromised agent, `tom`, edits his own profile to insert some malicious code and an honest agent, `jerry`, views this profile afterward. Thus, as reported in Table 7, the resulting test suites are composed of only 88 and 6 different test cases for the FR and FA operator, respectively.

Table 2. Mutants obtained with the FR operator

Specification	Mutants	model-checker reports			
		Attacks	Safe	Inconclusive	Timeout
CRP.stat	43	8	26	0	9
ECR	66	21	28	0	17
Google-SAML-SSO_one-wa_expl-pseudo_v2	31	6	0	25	0
Google-SAML-SSO_one-wa_v1	31	1	0	30	0
Google-SAML-SSO_v0	31	6	0	25	0
IDMXScene2_Safe	33	4	0	29	0
Infobase_Scene1	34	9	23	0	2
PTD	57	19	33	0	5
PTD_VisaBank	51	19	32	0	0
SAML_SSO-SP_init-CCM_bil-1SSL	23	2	0	20	1
wg_rbac_1	21	2	19	0	0
wg_rbac_3	21	1	20	0	0
wg_stored_xss_goal2	32	0	32	0	0
Total	**474**	**98**	**213**	**129**	**34**

Table 4, Table 5, and Table 6 show the application of each semantic operator presented in Section 4. If no mutant was generated for one specification, then this specification is not listed on the table. Even though such operators generate much less mutants, they are able to find most of the different attacks found with the two syntactic operators. In particular, Table 7 shows that the DSFlaw operator leads to all the 3 different attacks discovered for the `wg_stored_xss_goal2` specification by applying the FA operator. While, out of 88 different attacks found after analyzing the mutants generated by the FR operator, the ACFlaw and the CCFlaw operators find 60 of them.

We analyzed the traces found with the syntactic operators that were not found by any of the semantic operators. It appears that the syntactic mutants responsible of such traces differ from the original models by a missing `disnohest (agent)` fact and, therefore, they allow a honest agent to perform a step normally reserved to a dishonest agents. This most likely ends in a violation of one of the security properties but with a spurious attack. For example, in `Infobase_Scene1`, the reported attack consists in an honest agent sending his encrypted password

Table 3. Mutants obtained with the FA operator

Specification	Mutants	Attacks	model-checker reports		
			Safe	Inconclusive	Timeout
CRP.stat	2734	12[†]	152	0	14
ECR	23873	0[†]	188	0	5
Google-SAML-SSO_one-wa_expl-pseudo_v2	28	0	0	28	0
Google-SAML-SSO_one-wa_v1	28	0	0	28	0
Google-SAML-SSO_v0	28	0	0	28	0
IDMXScene2_Safe	404	0	0	404	0
Infobase_Scene1	39	1	38	0	0
PTD	332	0	268	0	64
PTD_VisaBank	824	0	184	0	640
SAML_SSO-SP_init-CCM_bil-1SSL	9	0	0	9	0
wg_rbac_1	218	7[†]	200	0	0
wg_rbac_3	148	2	146	0	0
wg_stored_xss_goal2	485	19	463	0	3
Total	**29150**	**41**	**1639**	**497**	**726**

[†] empty attack traces are not reported in the Attacks column

Listing 1.6. Three different attacks found on wg_stored_xss_goal2

```
% AAT1: tom profile is malicious
jerry *->* <ws>: login(jerry,password(jerry,ws))
<jerry> *->* ws: login(jerry,password(jerry,ws))
ws *->* <jerry>: listStaffOf(jerry)
<ws> *->* jerry: listStaffOf(jerry)
jerry *->* <ws>: viewProfileOf(tom)
<jerry> *->* ws: viewProfileOf(tom)
ws *->* <jerry>: profileOf(tom)
<ws> *->* jerry: profileOf(tom)
% AAT2: jerry profile is malicious
jerry *->* <ws>: login(jerry,password(jerry,ws))
<jerry> *->* ws: login(jerry,password(jerry,ws))
ws *->* <jerry>: listStaffOf(jerry)
<ws> *->* jerry: listStaffOf(jerry)
jerry *->* <ws>: viewProfileOf(jerry)
<jerry> *->* ws: viewProfileOf(jerry)
ws *->* <jerry>: profileOf(jerry)
<ws> *->* jerry: profileOf(jerry)
% AAT3: tom inserts some malicious data in his profile and jerry accesses it
<tom> *->* ws: login(tom,password(tom,ws))
ws *->* <tom>: listStaffOf(tom)
<tom> *->* ws: viewProfileOf(tom)
ws *->* <tom>: profileOf(tom)
<tom> *->* ws: editProfileOf(tom)
ws *->* <tom>: profileOf(tom)
jerry *->* <ws>: login(jerry,password(jerry,ws))
<jerry> *->* ws: login(jerry,password(jerry,ws))
ws *->* <jerry>: listStaffOf(jerry)
<ws> *->* jerry: listStaffOf(jerry)
jerry *->* <ws>: viewProfileOf(tom)
<jerry> *->* ws: viewProfileOf(tom)
ws *->* <jerry>: profileOf(tom)
<ws> *->* jerry: profileOf(tom)
```

Table 4. Mutants obtained with the ACFlaw operator (based on the FR operator)

		model-checker reports			
Specification	Mutants	Attacks	Safe	Inconclusive	Timeout
IDMXScene2_Safe	6	2	0	4	0
Infobase_Scene1	4	3	1	0	0
wg_rbac_1	2	1	1	0	0
wg_rbac_3	3	1	2	0	0
Total	**15**	**7**	**4**	**4**	**0**

Table 5. Mutants obtained with the CCFlaw operator (based on the FR operator)

		model-checker reports			
Specification	Mutants	Attacks	Safe	Inconclusive	Timeout
CRP.stat	11	6	3	0	2
ECR	12	6	2	0	4
Google-SAML-SSO_one-wa_expl-pseudo_v2	6	6	0	0	0
Google-SAML-SSO_one-wa_v1	6	1	0	5	0
Google-SAML-SSO_v0	6	6	0	0	0
IDMXScene2_Safe	9	2	0	7	0
Infobase_Scene1	6	4	2	0	0
PTD	17	10	2	0	5
PTD_VisaBank	13	12	1	0	0
SAML_SSO-SP_init-CCM_bil-1SSL	6	2	0	1	3
wg_rbac_1	4	0	4	0	0
wg_rbac_3	4	0	4	0	0
wg_stored_xss_goal2	6	0	6	0	0
Total	**106**	**55**	**24**	**13**	**14**

Table 6. Mutants obtained with the DSFlaw operator (based on the FA operator)

		model-checker reports			
Specification	Mutants	Attacks	Safe	Inconclusive	Timeout
wg_stored_xss_goal2	16	5	11	0	0
Total	**16**	**5**	**11**	**0**	**0**

over the network. This does not compromise the secrecy of the password by itself, but the internal rule of the model that gives the password of dishonest users to the intruder has been executed by an honest user, and so, the model-checker concludes it is a violation of the password secrecy.

Mutating the specifications and analyzing all the generated mutants took almost a day for the FR operator and more than a week for the FA operator, on

Table 7. Size of the resulting test suite and time to produce it

Mutation operator	Attacks	Time (m)
FR	88	1352
ACFlaw	7	3
CCFlaw	53	312
semantics based on FR (ACFlaw+CCFlaw)	60	315
FA	6	11710
FA[†]	3	28
DSFlaw[†]	3	1

[†] only for `wg_stored_xss_goal2`

an Intel(R) Xeon(R) CPU 2.60GHz with 4 GB of RAM. However, the same task has been performed in less than 6 hours for the semantic operators based on FR (i.e., CCFlaw and ACFlaw operators). Since the DSFlaw operator could be applied only on `wg_stored_xss_goal2`, we compared the times required to generate and analyze mutants obtained by applying the FA and DSFlaw operators only on that specification. DSFlaw needs only 1 minute to find three different attack traces, while the FA operator runs for 28 minutes and does not find more attacks.

7 Related Work

Our work is closely related to mutation testing [DeMillo et al., 1979, Jia and Harman, 2011]. Even though mutation testing usually aims at assessing the effectiveness of a test suite to detect small syntactic changes introduced into a program, it can also be used to generate and not assess test cases. This idea was successfully applied for specification-based testing from AutoFocus, HLPSL or SMV models in the security context [Ammann et al., 2001, Büchler et al., 2011, Dadeau et al., 2011, Wimmel and Jürjens, 2002]. Our work differs in that we start by real vulnerabilities in Web applications and correlate them with specific mutation operators, called semantic mutation operators. It allows us to automatize the instantiation of the generated test cases since we know which vulnerability is supposed to be exploited.

Recently, Clark et al. [2013] have introduced the notion of semantic mutation testing. Even though they apply it in a different context — identifying developer's misunderstandings due to several possible interpretations of the same programming language —, our model-based fault injection approach also aims at detecting real faults, which implies having a test suite that consider the semantic of the model.

From a technical point of view, we were looking for a generic framework where given a grammar of ASLan, we could design our parametrized syntactic mutation operators. Surprisingly, we found only one framework that could fit our need [Simão and Maldonado, 2002]. Unfortunately, MuDeL is not maintained anymore and we did not manage to use it even though the authors kindly sent us the source code. Since XSLT is widely used for XML transformations and an ASLan specification can be exported to an XML file, we chose to implement our mutation operators as XSLT scripts.

8   Conclusion

In this paper, we presented an implementation of the semantic-based mutation operators for ASLan specifications. Then, we compared the number of mutants and abstract attack traces obtained when applying either semantic or syntactic operators. As expected, the semantic operators produce much less mutants. However, the percentage of mutants that lead to an abstract attack is higher (i.e., 40% instead of 0.4%).

Analyzing the mutants obtained with the semantic operators was much faster and allowed us to generate most of the potential attacks (i.e. test cases) that could be obtained with the corresponding syntactic mutants. Furthermore, an attack that is not found by a semantic operator is usually a spurious attack, in the sense that the modification introduced by the syntactic operator does not correspond to any vulnerability but to the internal logic of the model; hence, the attack trace is not an attack but simply a normal execution where the model-checker reports a security violation because of the modification on how to interpret the step execution.

Another advantage of employing our semantic mutation operators consists in knowing which vulnerability has been injected in a mutant, therefore, if an abstract attack trace is generated from this mutant, we know which vulnerability should be exploited. This knowledge is important when instantiating the abstract attack trace for a real system, because it helps in choosing which payload to use (e.g., an XSS payload to exploit an XSS vulnerability). Thus, even if we could see the additional need for the model semantic as a disadvantage with regards to the syntactic mutation operators, it is balance when the abstract attack trace has to be instantiated.

As ASLan is a language with few grammar rules, creating the syntactic mutation operators was not too difficult. We could even take advantage of XSLT thanks to the XML representation of an ASLan specification provided by the AVANTSSAR platform. However, the relative simplicity of the language makes the semantic more dependent on the naming convention used by the modeler. Indeed, configuring the semantic mutation operators was easier for the models we were familiar with.

We are currently working on implementing similar vulnerability injections for high-level AVANTSSAR Specification Language (ASLan++), which as a language with more complex structure should help us in identifying relevant parts of the model. Another extension we are also working on consists in adding a specific goal and function symbols associated to the injected vulnerabilities. Thus, we could look for generic attacks like SQL injection or XSS attacks even though the modeler did not consider them when writing the security properties guaranteed by his model.

References

Berglund, A., et al.: XML Path Language (XPath) 2.0, 2nd edn. (2007),
http://www.w3.org/TR/xpath20/

Ammann, P., Ding, W., Xu, D.: Using a model checker to test safety properties. In: ICECCS, pp. 212–221 (2001)

Armando, A., Carbone, R., Compagna, L.: LTL Model Checking for Security Protocols. Journal of Applied Non-Classical Logics, Special Issue on Logic and Information Security, 403–429 (2009)

Armando, A., et al.: The AVANTSSAR platform for the automated validation of trust and security of service-oriented architectures. In: Flanagan, C., König, B. (eds.) TACAS 2012. LNCS, vol. 7214, pp. 267–282. Springer, Heidelberg (2012)

AVANTSSAR. Deliverable 4.2: AVANTSSAR Validation Platform V.2. (2010a), www.avantssar.eu

AVANTSSAR. Deliverable 5.4: Assessment of the AVANTSSAR Validation Platform (2010b), www.avantssar.eu

Büchler, M., Oudinet, J., Pretschner, A.: Security mutants for property-based testing. In: Gogolla, M., Wolff, B. (eds.) TAP 2011. LNCS, vol. 6706, pp. 69–77. Springer, Heidelberg (2011)

Büchler, M., Oudinet, J., Pretschner, A.: Semi-automatic security testing of web applications from a secure model. In: SERE, pp. 253–262. IEEE (2012) ISBN 978-0-7695-4742-8

Clark, J.A., Dan, H., Hierons, R.M.: Semantic mutation testing. Science of Computer Programming 78(4), 345–363 (2013),
http://www.sciencedirect.com/science/article/pii/S0167642311000992,
doi:10.1016/j.scico.2011.03.011, ISSN 0167-6423

Dadeau, F., Héam, P.-C., Kheddam, R.: Mutation-based test generation from security protocols in HLPSL. In: Software Testing, Verification and Validation (ICST), pp. 240–248 (2011)

DeMillo, R.A., Lipton, R.J., Sayward, F.G.: Program Mutation: A New Approach to Program Testing. In: Infotech State of the Art Report, Software Testing, pp. 107–126 (1979)

Dolev, D., Yao, A.: On the Security of Public-Key Protocols. IEEE Transactions on Information Theory 2(29) (1983)

Jia, Y., Harman, M.: An analysis and survey of the development of mutation testing. TSE 37(5), 649–678 (2011)

Kay, M.: XSL Transformations (XSLT) Version 2.0. (2007),
http://www.w3.org/TR/xslt20/

Saxonica Limited, Kay, M.: SAXON - The XSLT and XQuery Processor (2012),
http://saxon.sourceforge.net/

Mödersheim, S., Viganò, L.: The Open-source Fixed-point Model Checker for Symbolic Analysis of Security Protocols. In: Aldini, A., Barthe, G., Gorrieri, R. (eds.) FOSAD 2007/2008/2009. LNCS, vol. 5705, pp. 166–194. Springer, Heidelberg (2009)

OWASP. OWASP WebGoat Project (2011),
https://www.owasp.org/index.php/
Category:OWASP_WebGoat_Project

Christey, S.: CWE/SANS Top 25 Most Dangerous Software Errors (2011),
  http://cwe.mitre.org/top25/index.html
da, A., Simão, S., Maldonado, J.C.: MuDeL: a language and a system for describing
  and generating mutants. Journal of the Brazilian Computer Society 8, 73–86 (2002)
SPaCIoS. Deliverable 5.2: Proof of Concept and Tool Assessment V.2. (2012)
Turuani, M.: The cl-atse protocol analyser. In: Pfenning, F. (ed.) RTA 2006. LNCS,
  vol. 4098, pp. 277–286. Springer, Heidelberg (2006),
  http://dx.doi.org/10.1007/11805618_21
Wimmel, G., Jürjens, J.: Specification-based test generation for security-critical systems using mutations. In: George, C.W., Miao, H. (eds.) ICFEM 2002. LNCS,
  vol. 2495, pp. 471–482. Springer, Heidelberg (2002)

Solving Constraints for Generational Search

Daniel Pötzl and Andreas Holzer

Vienna University of Technology (TU Wien)

Abstract. Concolic testing is an automated software testing method that combines concrete and symbolic execution to achieve high code coverage and expose bugs in the program under test. During an execution of the program, constraints over the input variables are collected. Then, by changing these constraints in a systematic manner and solving the thereby derived constraint systems, new inputs can be obtained that force the program to execute along yet undiscovered program paths. The performance of the constraint solving step is crucial for the scalability of such an approach. In this paper, we are specifically concerned with solving the constraint systems obtained when employing the concolic testing search strategy known as Generational Search. We implemented several methods for preprocessing and solving the systems using the SMT solvers MATHSAT, STP, YICES, and Z3, and evaluated the methods and solvers on constraints generated by the concolic execution engine CREST.

1 Introduction

Concolic testing [10,15,16] is a method of software testing that aims at achieving high code coverage while finding bugs such as assertion violations or segmentation faults. The term *concolic*, proposed by Sen et al. [15], is an amalgamation of the terms *concrete* and *symbolic*, which refers to the fact that the program under test is executed both concretely and symbolically. This means that the program is executed both on concrete inputs, and on symbols representing arbitrary input values (we use $\alpha_1, \alpha_2, \ldots$ to denote such input symbols).

During concolic execution, a *path constraint* $PC = \langle \varphi_0, \ldots, \varphi_{n-1} \rangle$ is collected, which is a sequence of *constraints* φ_i. These constraints are formulas over the input symbols. Logically, we define $\langle \varphi_0, \ldots, \varphi_{n-1} \rangle \Leftrightarrow \varphi_0 \wedge \ldots \wedge \varphi_{n-1}$. Each constraint φ_i corresponds to a conditional statement (such as an `if` statement) that was executed. By negating one of these constraints φ_i, for $i < n$, and solving the *child path constraint* $PC_i = \langle \varphi_0, \ldots, \varphi_{i-1}, \neg \varphi_i \rangle$, an input can be obtained that drives the program along a different execution path. By systematically negating the constraints in observed path constraints, one can obtain a procedure that executes a new program path with each new input. This way, coverage can be progressively increased.

Consider the example in Figure 1. We assume that a and b are symbolic input variables. This means that the concolic testing tool assigns symbols to them at the start of the execution (let's say α_1 to a and α_2 to b). Moreover, the concolic testing tool also controls the concrete input values. A concrete input is denoted

M. Veanes and L. Viganò (Eds.): TAP 2013, LNCS 7942, pp. 197–213, 2013.
© Springer-Verlag Berlin Heidelberg 2013

as a mapping from input symbols to concrete values, e. g. $I = \{\alpha_1 \mapsto 3, \alpha_2 \mapsto 0\}$. When the function is called with this input, it takes the **then**-branches of the first two nested **if** statements, and the **else**-branch of the last **if** statement. The path constraint collected is thus $PC = \langle \alpha_1 > 0, \alpha_2 \neq 5, a \not> 3 \rangle$ and input I is a solution to PC. As described in Section 2, this fact can be exploited to speed up the solving of the child path constraints.

```
func(a, b) {
    if a > 0
        if b ≠ 5
            ...
        if a > 3
            ...
}
```

Fig. 1. Example code

The strategy by which different execution paths of the program under test are explored is termed a concolic testing search strategy. Which strategy to choose depends on the coverage goal and types of faults one intends to expose. *Generational search* [11] is a search strategy that aims at achieving high block coverage fast, while retaining the ability to potentially search the whole space of program paths. The basic idea is to solve many child path constraints PC_i of a single path constraint PC, thereby obtaining many new inputs. Then, the program under test is executed *concretely* on all those inputs. After that, based on some fitness criterion (e. g. the number of new basic blocks covered), one of these concrete runs is chosen and executed concolically (by using the same input that was used for the concrete run), thereby obtaining a new path constraint PC'. With this path constraint, the procedure is repeated.

Generational search is used in the concolic testing tool SAGE [11] from Microsoft. There, SAGE has been running perpetually since 2008 on more than 100 servers on average, automatically testing hundreds of applications [5]. In the remainder of the paper, we specifically target at solving constraints obtained during generational search. For a detailed explanation of generational search, we refer the reader to Godefroid et al. [11].

In this paper, we evaluate the performance of different constraint solving strategies for linear integer constraints obtained by concolic execution. We compare the performance of these strategies when using two different logics and different SMT solvers.

Organization. In Section 2, we discuss several methods to speed up the constraint solving step in the generational search. We have implemented a framework (based on the concolic execution engine CREST [2]) to test these methods, and, in Section 3, we provide experimental data showing their performance. In Section 4, we discuss related work and, in Section 5, we conclude and state future directions for research.

2   Solving Constraints

Before discussing several methods to speed up the constraint solving step in the generational search, we define the problem we aim to solve:

```
 1  function BasicSolveAll(PC, b)
 2  begin
 3  │   solutions ← ∅
 4  │   for i ← b to |PC| − 1 do
 5  │   │   PC_i ← ⟨φ_0, ..., φ_{i-1}, ¬φ_i⟩
 6  │   │   if PC_i is satisfiable then
 7  │   │   │   S ← solution of PC_i
 8  │   │   │   solutions ← solutions ∪ {S}
 9  │   │   end
10  │   end
11  │   return solutions
12  end
```

Fig. 2. BasicSolveAll

Problem statement. Given (1) a path constraint $PC = \langle \varphi_0, \ldots, \varphi_{n-1} \rangle$ obtained during concolic execution of the program under test, with the φ_i's being linear integer constraints with integer coefficients and an integer-valued constant part, (2) a bound b, and (3) the previous input[1] I to the program, compute solutions to all satisfiable child path constraints $PC_i = \langle \varphi_0, \ldots, \varphi_{i-1}, \neg\varphi_i \rangle$, $b \leq i < |PC|$.

The bound b is a detail of the generational search [11]. The most straightforward, and least efficient, way to solve the above problem is to solve each PC_i separately. This approach is implemented by the BasicSolveAll() function shown in Figure 2. This function takes the path constraint PC, and the bound b, and returns solutions to all satisfiable child path constraints PC_i, for $b \leq i < |PC|$. As the PC_i's share many constraints, an idea to optimize constraint solving is to reuse information across solving runs.

2.1 Iterative Constraint Strengthening

We describe two methods to solve the child path constraints inspired by the *iterative constraint strengthening* [13] method. The two methods work by encoding all child path constraints PC_i, for $b \leq i < |PC|$, of a path constraint PC into a single formula. For simplicity, we describe the encodings only for the bound $b = 0$.

Encoding 1. We use the formula $\overline{PC} = \neg\varphi_0 \vee (\varphi_0 \wedge (\neg\varphi_1 \vee (\ldots \wedge (\neg\varphi_{n-2} \vee (\varphi_{n-2} \wedge (\neg\varphi_{n-1}))) \ldots)))$ to encode all child path constraints PC_i. A solution to an arbitrary PC_i satisfies $\overline{PC}$ and conversely, every solution of $\overline{PC}$ satisfies exactly one PC_i. We can thus compute solutions to all satisfiable PC_i's by successively computing solutions to $\overline{PC}$ that satisfy different PC_i's. This can be done by at each step adding the formula $\neg PC_i$ to $\overline{PC}$ when the computed solution satisfies

---

[1] Recall that this input is a solution to PC (assuming the collected constraints are precise), and parts of it could thus be reused to solve the PC_i's.

PC_i. Then, in the next step when we solve the now refined formula $\overline{PC}$, we obtain a solution to another PC_j (provided $\overline{PC}$ is still satisfiable). We repeat this procedure until $\overline{PC}$ becomes unsatisfiable. For the approach just described, we exploit the incremental solving capabilities of modern SMT solvers.

Encoding 2. The second approach works by introducing for each constraint φ_i a propositional variable p_i, and using the formula $\widehat{PC} = (\neg\varphi_0 \wedge \neg p_0) \vee ((\varphi_0 \wedge p_0) \wedge ((\neg\varphi_1 \wedge \neg p_1) \vee (\ldots \wedge ((\neg\varphi_{n-2} \wedge p_{n-2}) \vee ((\varphi_{n-2} \wedge p_{n-2}) \wedge ((\neg\varphi_{n-1} \wedge \neg p_{n-1}))))\ldots)))$. Similarly as above, every solution to $\widehat{PC}$ satisfies a PC_i and every solution to a PC_i can be extended with values for the p_i's such that a solution to $\widehat{PC}$ is obtained. The approach is again to compute in each iteration a solution to $\widehat{PC}$ that satisfies a different PC_i. However, this time previous solutions can be excluded by adding the corresponding propositional formula made up of the p_i's. That is, when the previous solution satisfied $PC_i = \langle\varphi_0, \ldots, \varphi_{i-1}, \neg\varphi_i\rangle$, then PC_i is excluded by adding $\neg(p_1 \wedge \ldots \wedge p_{i-1} \wedge \neg p_i)$.

We also implemented several variations of the above two schemes. However, they all performed similar, and therefore, in Section 3, we only give experimental results for the two variants just described.

2.2   Push-Pop Encoding

SMT solvers usually provide functionality to add a formula to a given logical context (we denote this function by SolverAssert()). Later, the satisfiability of this context can be checked (function SolverCheck()), which amounts to checking the satisfiability of the conjunction of the formulas in the logical context. After a call to SolverCheck(), additional formulas can be added to the same logical context. When SolverCheck() is then called again, information gained in previous runs is reused to speed up the check. When the logical context is satisfiable, a solution to the conjunction of the formulas can be retrieved (function SolverGetSolution()). Additionally, SMT solvers commonly provide push and pop operations (we denote them by SolverPush() and SolverPop()). Solver-Push() creates a backtracking point, to which it can be returned by SolverPop(). When SolverPop() is called, then, those formulas that have been added to the logical context after the call to SolverPush() are removed.

This feature is exploited by the PushPopSolveAll() method shown in Figure 3. The algorithm solves all child path constraints PC_i of a path constraint PC, for $b \le i < |PC|$. In lines 4-6, the constraints common to all child path constraints are added to the logical context of the used solver. Then, in each iteration of the main loop, one of the child path constraints PC_i, for $b \le i < |PC|$, is solved. Before adding a negated constraint, a backtracking point is created by calling SolverPush(). After the associated child path constraint has been solved, we backtrack via SolverPop(). Then, the non-negated version of the constraint is added to the logical context. The method proved to be very efficient in practice, as witnessed by the experimental results given in the next section.

```
 1  function PushPopSolveAll(PC, bound)
 2  begin
 3  │   solutions ← ∅
    │   // Constraints below the bound.
 4  │   for i ← 0 to bound − 1 do
 5  │   │   SolverAssert(φ_i)
 6  │   end
    │   // Solve child path constraints.
 7  │   for i ← bound to |PC| − 1 do
 8  │   │   SolverPush()
 9  │   │   SolverAssert(¬φ_i)
10  │   │   sat ← SolverCheck()
11  │   │   if sat then
12  │   │   │   S ← SolverGetSolution()
13  │   │   │   solutions ← solutions ∪ {S}
14  │   │   end
15  │   │   SolverPop()
16  │   │   SolverAssert(φ_i)
17  │   end
18  │   return solutions
19  end
```

Fig. 3. PushPopSolveAll

```
 1  function PreprocessingSolveAll(PC, b, I)
 2  begin
 3  │   newinputs ← ∅
 4  │   PC, b ← RemoveDuplicates(PC, b)
 5  │   set ← SeparateConstraints(PC, b)
 6  │   foreach (PC^(i), b^(i)) ∈ set do
 7  │   │   solutions ← SolveAll(PC^(i), b^(i))
 8  │   │   foreach S ∈ solutions do
 9  │   │   │   newinput ← Merge(S, I)
10  │   │   │   newinputs ← newinputs ∪ {newinput}
11  │   │   end
12  │   end
13  │   return newinputs
14  end
```

Fig. 4. PreprocessingSolveAll

2.3   Preprocessing Steps

The constraint solving efficiency can be increased by first preprocessing the path constraint PC. The skeleton of the algorithm incorporating preprocessing is shown in Figure 4. It takes a path constraint PC, a bound b, and the previous input I. The two preprocessing steps are *duplicate constraint removal* (line 4) and *constraint separation* (line 5). The former simply removes duplicate constraints from PC and adjusts the bound accordingly. The latter decomposes the path constraint PC into shorter *path subconstraints* $PC^{(1)}, \ldots, PC^{(m)}$, with associated bounds $b^{(1)}, \ldots, b^{(m)}$. We say $PC^{(i)}$ is a path subconstraint of a path constraint PC when the constraints in $PC^{(i)}$ are a subset of the constraints in PC, and they occur in the same order as in PC. In lines 6-12 of the algorithm, all *child path subconstraints* $PC_j^{(i)}$, for $0 \le i < n$ and $b^{(i)} \le j < |PC^{(i)}|$, are solved (denoted by the abstract SolveAll() function). The SolveAll() function can be replaced by any of the solving methods discussed in the previous section (e.g. BasicSolveAll() or PushPopSolveAll()). In line 9, the solutions to the child path subconstraints are merged with the previous input. This is done by supplementing the solution with the mappings from the input [15]. Let for instance $S = \{\alpha_1 \mapsto 7\}$ be a solution and $I = \{\alpha_1 \mapsto 4, \alpha_2 \mapsto 1\}$ be an input. Then Merge(S, I) yields $I' = \{\alpha_1 \mapsto 7, \alpha_2 \mapsto 1\}$. Finally, in line 13, the set of new inputs is returned.

Duplicate Removal. As mentioned above, the constraints collected by CREST are linear integer constraints. Such constraints can easily be represented in canonical form[2]. For instance, this can be done by (1) combining like terms, (2) listing the variables and constant part in a prescribed order, (3) on a prescribed side of the relational operator, (4) removing unary $+$ and $-$ operators except for the first term, (5) removing parentheses, and (6) rewriting $<$-constraints in terms of $\le$ (or vice-versa). For example, consider the constraint $-x + (-3y) + 2x < 7$. Then, according to the above rules, its canonical form is $x - 3y - 6 \le 0$. Constraints collected by CREST satisfy rules (1)-(5). We modified CREST such that also (6) is satisfied.

Having constraints in canonical form enables us to remove more constraints during the duplicate removal step. Duplicates are removed by linearly scanning through PC from the beginning and putting the constraints into a hash set. Whenever a constraint is encountered that is already in the set, it is removed from PC. The duplicate removal not only has the effect that the child path constraints become shorter, but also that certain unsatisfiable child path constraints are removed. The reason is that when PC contains several instances of a constraint φ, the child path constraints associated with the negations of all but the first occurrence of φ are unsatisfiable.

Whenever a constraint is removed from PC that is below the bound (i.e. elements φ_i with $i < b$), the bound must be decreased by one. Consider for instance the path constraint $PC = \langle \alpha_1 > 0, \alpha_1 > 0, \alpha_2 \ne 0, \alpha_3 \le 0 \rangle$, and a bound of 2. After the duplicate removal, the path constraint becomes $PC' = \langle \alpha_1 > 0, \alpha_2 \ne 0, \alpha_3 \le 0 \rangle$. For this new path constraint the bound must be set to 1, such that the same inputs are generated from it as from PC. When a constraint φ_i with $i \ge b$ is removed, the bound stays the same. As can be seen in Figure 4, line 4, the RemoveDuplicates() function takes the old bound, and returns an adjusted bound.

---

[2] We say constraints are in canonical form when two constraints are logically equivalent iff they have the same representation.

Constraint Separation. During constraint separation, a path constraint PC is decomposed into shorter path subconstraints $PC^{(1)}, \ldots, PC^{(m)}$, and new bounds $b^{(1)}, \ldots, b^{(m)}$ are associated to them. The decomposition is based on the notion of constraint independence:

Definition 1 (Constraint Independence, [15]). *We say two constraints φ_i and φ_j that are part of a path constraint PC are* dependent *iff either*
1. *φ_i and φ_j have a common symbolic variable, or*
2. *there is a constraint φ_k in PC such that φ_i and φ_k, and φ_j and φ_k are dependent.*

Otherwise, we say the constraints are independent.

In the preprocessing step, path subconstraints $PC^{(1)}, \ldots, PC^{(m)}$ are computed such that all constraints within a $PC^{(i)}$ are dependent, and for $\varphi \in PC^{(i)}, \varphi' \in PC^{(j)}, i \neq j$, φ and φ' are independent. This decomposition allows to solve the child path constraints of PC more efficiently. As mentioned by Cadar et al. [4], the decomposition can be computed efficiently using a disjoint-set data structure [6]. Such a decomposition algorithm is given in [14].

As an example, assume concolic execution with input I yielded the path constraint $PC = \langle \alpha_1 > 0, \alpha_2 \neq 3, \alpha_1 + \alpha_3 = 0, 3 \cdot \alpha_2 \leq 10 \rangle$. Suppose further that the associated bound is 2, i.e. the child path constraints $PC_2 = \langle \alpha_1 > 0, \alpha_2 \neq 3, \alpha_1 + \alpha_3 \neq 0 \rangle$, and $PC_3 = \langle \alpha_1 > 0, \alpha_2 \neq 3, \alpha_1 + \alpha_3 = 0, 3 \cdot \alpha_2 \nleq 10 \rangle$ should be solved. The decomposition of PC into independent path subconstraints yields $PC^{(1)} = \langle \alpha_1 > 0, \alpha_1 + \alpha_3 = 0 \rangle$, and $PC^{(2)} = \langle \alpha_2 \neq 3, 3 \cdot \alpha_2 \leq 10 \rangle$. To both of these path subconstraints, a bound of 1 is associated. Then, instead of solving PC_2 and PC_3 directly, the shorter constraints $PC_1^{(1)} = \langle \alpha_1 > 0, \alpha_1 + \alpha_3 \neq 0 \rangle$ and $PC_1^{(2)} = \langle \alpha_2 \neq 3, 3 \cdot \alpha_2 \nleq 10 \rangle$ are solved. To complete the solutions, they are supplemented with values from the previous input I (line 9). That way, solutions to PC_2 and PC_3 are obtained.

2.4   Simplified Constraints

Up to now, we have implicitly assumed that the path constraint PC collected during concolic execution is precise (i.e. that all expressions were collected exactly as they appear in the source code), and consequently that the input I with which the program was executed is a solution to it. However, usually the path constraint contains just approximations of the operations performed by the program. For example, CREST collects only linear integer constraints. Hence, for instance, non-linear expressions of the form $a \cdot b$, with a and b being symbolic variables, are simplified by replacing a by its concrete value. Additionally, external functions (such as system calls and library functions) may not be executed concolically but only concretely.

One particular consequence of this is that the path constraint obtained during an execution may be unsatisfiable. Consider for instance the code snippet in Figure 5. There, neg() is an external function that is not executed concolically. It multiplies variable a by -1. Assume that a and b are symbolic input variables, to which the symbols α_1 and α_2 are assigned at the beginning. Assume further that concolic execution is started, and a and b receive the concrete value 1. Therefore, all three `if` statements take the **then**-branch, and the path constraint $PC = \langle \alpha_1 > 0, \alpha_1 < 0, \alpha_2 > 0 \rangle$ is obtained. As can be seen, the path constraint is unsatisfiable, as the effect of the `neg()` function is not tracked. As the first two constraints of PC are contradictory, the child path constraint $PC_2 = \langle \alpha_1 > 0, \alpha_1 < 0, \alpha_2 \not> 0 \rangle$ is unsatisfiable, even though the associated path is feasible. Thus, when a path constraint has a (short) prefix that is unsatisfiable, many child path constraints are unsatisfiable as well. In the context of generational search, this means that only a small number of inputs (or none at all in the worst case) can be generated from the path constraint.

```
func(a, b) {
    if a > 0
        neg(&a)
    if a < 0
        ...
    if b > 0
        ...
}
```

Fig. 5. Example code

This problem is somewhat alleviated by the constraint separation preprocessing step. Consider again the path constraint PC from the previous paragraph. The constraint separation step breaks it down into the path subconstraints $PC^{(1)} = \langle \alpha_1 > 0, \alpha_1 < 0 \rangle$ and $PC^{(2)} = \langle \alpha_2 > 0 \rangle$. Then, by solving $PC_0^{(2)} = \langle \alpha_2 \not> 0 \rangle$ to get a value for α_2 and reusing the old assignment for α_1, an input can be obtained that makes the program take the **else**-branch at the last `if` statement. Thus, when using constraint separation, often more inputs can be generated from a path constraint. In the next section, we provide experimental data regarding this issue.

3   Experiments

We evaluate the constraint solving methods previously described for the SMT solvers MATHSAT 5.1.6 [12], STP [9] (revision 1661 from the official SVN repository), YICES 1.0.34 [8], and Z3 4.0 [7]. We implemented the methods using the C APIs of the solvers. To encode the linear integer constraints, we used both the linear arithmetic and bitvector parts of the APIs (except for STP, which only provides bitvector functionality). Later, in Section 3.3, we provide experimental data for both approaches.

3.1   Test Environment

All experiments were run on a 2.10 GHz Intel Core i3-2310M laptop with 4 GB of RAM, and running the 64-bit version of Ubuntu 12.10, with Linux kernel 3.5.0-17-generic. To prevent dynamic CPU frequency adjustment during the testing runs, the CPU governor of the kernel was set to performance mode for all cores. This can be accomplished via the command `sudo cpufreq-set -r -g performance`. It usually ensures that the cores constantly run with the highest clock frequency. Under special circumstances, the CPU may still be downclocked, e. g. to prevent overheating. The tests were run with the lowest niceness value of -20 (highest priority).

3.2   Benchmarks

To evaluate the solving methods and preprocessing steps, we use path constraints generated by CREST when run on two benchmarks provided by its developers (grep 2.2 and vim 5.7), and on two additional benchmarks (avl and sort). We refer to each path constraint as a *test case*. We used CREST to generate 30 test cases from each of the four benchmark programs.

The grep utility was instrumented such that it matches a pattern of 20 symbolic characters against a sequence of 40 symbolic characters. A path constraint obtained by running CREST on this benchmark consequently contains at most 60 different input symbols (denoted by $\alpha_1, \alpha_2, \ldots$ before). In the vim benchmark, the functions safe_vgetc() and vgetc() were replaced by versions returning symbolic characters. The two functions provide inputs to most of the modes of vim. The length of the input was restricted to 20 symbolic characters.

The avl benchmark consists of three AVL tree data structures on which a sequence of insertions, retrievals and deletions is performed. The elements inserted into the trees are $(key, value)$ pairs. The key determines where an element is placed in a tree, and is a string of symbolic characters. The total number of symbolic characters over all $(key, value)$ pairs is 60. The sort benchmark consists of two lists of symbolic characters (each of length 25) that are first sorted using Quicksort, and then merged. Finally, the sortedness of the resulting list is verified.

Choice of Benchmarks. The benchmark programs were chosen such that most operations they perform, apart from array and struct accesses and pointer dereferences, can be represented with sufficient precision as linear integer operations. For avl and sort, this holds for all operations. Moreover, these two benchmarks do not call external, uninstrumented functions. The grep and vim benchmarks contain a small number of operations not representable using just linear integer arithmetic (such as bitwise operations), and also make use of external, uninstrumented functions [14].

Parameters of the Test Cases. Table 1 shows several parameters of the test cases. The first row indicates the average and maximum number of constraints per test case (i. e. path constraint $PC = \langle \varphi_0, \ldots, \varphi_{n-1} \rangle$) over all 30 test cases. The second row gives the number of satisfiable child path constraints $PC_i = \langle \varphi_0, \ldots, \varphi_{i-1}, \neg \varphi_i \rangle$, $0 \leq i < |PC|$. The parameters are thus given for bound $b = 0$. The third row states the number of satisfiable child path subconstraints $PC_j^{(i)}$, $0 \leq j < |PC^{(i)}|$ over all path subconstraints $PC^{(i)}$ into which the path constraint PC is decomposed by the constraint separation preprocessing step. The last row gives the number of duplicate constraints per path constraint.

As can be seen in lines 2 and 3 of the table, for the reasons outlined in Section 2.4, more inputs can be computed from a path constraint for grep and vim when using constraint separation. For avl and sort, the number is just the same as they do not call external, uninstrumented functions and only perform linear integer operations (apart from array and struct accesses). Finally, the

Table 1. Parameters of the test cases used to evaluate the solving methods. The test cases are path constraints PC generated during concolic testing with CREST on grep, vim, avl and sort. For all four programs, 30 test cases were used.

	grep avg.	grep max.	vim avg.	vim max.
Constraints in PC	1,128	1,713	1,546	3,664
Satisfiable PC_i's	173	386	610	2,254
Satisfiable $PC_j^{(i)}$'s (when using CS)	182	386	850	2,254
Duplicate constraints in PC	687	1,058	181	922
	avl avg.	avl max.	sort avg.	sort max.
Constraints in PC	960	1,016	303	320
Satisfiable PC_i's	130	152	254	271
Satisfiable $PC_j^{(i)}$'s (when using CS)	130	152	254	271
Duplicate constraints in PC	809	836	0	0

number of duplicate constraints can be quite high, as witnessed by the entries for the grep and avl benchmarks.

3.3   Results and Observations

The experimental results are shown in Tables 2-5. Results are provided both for the approach where the linear integer constraints were encoded using the linear arithmetic modules of the solvers, and the approach where the linear integer constraints were encoded using bitvectors. For the different solving methods, results are provided for combinations with the preprocessing steps duplicate removal (DR) and constraint separation (CS). The entries in the tables indicate the time (in milliseconds) it took to solve all child path constraints respectively child path subconstraints (when using CS), for bound $b = 0$, averaged over the 30 test cases. For entries with a >, at least one test case timed out (timeout 300s).

For the iterative constraint strengthening methods, when encoding the constraints using bitvectors, the memory consumption was very high for YICES. On the larger grep and vim test cases, the test framework claimed too much memory and was subsequently killed by the kernel. When constraint separation is enabled, the instances to solve become much smaller, and then all test cases could be solved. Hence, results are only given in combination with constraint separation (the other entries contain a $-$).

In the following, we comment on several observations we made when running the experiments and interpret the results.

SMT Solvers are Buggy. We found one bug in each of MATHSAT and YICES, and three bugs in STP. In Z3, we did not encounter a bug. For two of the STP bugs, we extracted minimal examples that exhibit the bugs, and reported them to the developers. At the time of writing, the bugs have not been fixed yet. For the remaining bugs, we yet have to extract examples and report them. In the following, we describe the bugs and our workarounds.

The bug in YICES manifested in both the linear arithmetic and bitvector implementations of the push-pop method. On some test cases, it reported some formulas as satisfiable that were in fact unsatisfiable. To circumvent the problem, we replaced the code portion consisting of a push operation followed by a formula assertion (lines 8-9 in Figure 3) by a retractable assertion (id = yices_assert_retractable(ctx, f)). The function returns an assertion identifier id. Later, when the pop operation is invoked (line 15 in Figure 3), we would retract the assertion (yices_retract(ctx, id)). This alternative implementation is functionally equivalent to an implementation with push and pop operations. However, it performed slightly slower. To highlight that an alternative implementation of PushPopSolveAll() was used for YICES, the respective entries in the result tables are marked with a dagger (†).

With STP, we encountered two problems on the iterative constraint strengthening methods. First, on some test cases the STP library crashed. Second, it yielded wrong results on certain test cases, reporting some satisfiable formulas as unsatisfiable and vice-versa. By trial and error, we found that the two problems can be circumvented by adding the code portion vc_push(vc); vc_pop(vc); after a query to STP, and before the next assertion that excludes the current solution.[3] As these normally unnecessary push and pop operations slow down STP, the entries in the result tables affected by this workaround are marked with a star (∗). Another problem we encountered was that the STP library leaked memory. Normally, it keeps track of all the expressions that are created, and deletes them when vc_Destroy() is called. However, we found that when we ran our test framework for a long time, the memory consumption would continually increase until it was killed by the kernel. Our workaround was to explicitly delete the created expressions via a call to vc_DeleteExpr().

For the bitvector implementation of Encoding1, MathSAT computed wrong solutions on some of the test cases. There, it would compute a wrong solution to the formula $\overline{PC}$ (see Section 2.1). This is the only bug we have not found a workaround for. To highlight that some of the test cases were solved wrongly, the affected entries in the result tables are marked with a double dagger (‡).

The Preprocessing Steps are Effective. The performance of all solving methods increases when they are combined with the duplicate removal and constraint separation preprocessing steps. Even when the case the preprocessing steps optimize for does not occur (e. g. a path constraint contains no duplicates), they do not incur any significant overhead. This is because the runtime is clearly dominated by the actual solving. This can be seen on the sort benchmark. The duplicate removal had no effect since the test cases did not contain duplicate constraints (see Table 1). The constraint separation had no effect since all constraints were dependent. This means that the decomposition of the path constraint PC yields PC itself.

The Linear Integer Arithmetic Modules of the Solvers are Faster at Solving the Linear Integer Constraints than the Bitvector Modules. The discrepancy was

---

[3] Adding only vc_push(vc) would suffice, but by also adding vc_pop(vc), the number of checkpoints STP has to maintain does not increase.

Table 2. Linear integer arithmetic and linear bitvector arithmetic constraint solving results for the 30 vim test cases. For each test case, the time to solve for all child path constraints resp. child path subconstraints (when using CS) was measured (in milliseconds). The entries indicate the average time over the 30 test cases.

| Method | Linear Integer Arithmetic | | | Linear Bitvector Arithmetic | | | |
	Z3	MathSAT	Yices	Z3	MathSAT	Yices	STP
Basic	> 47,726	29,532	> 51,163	43,512	> 49,871	> 159,364	> 75,906
Basic+DR	> 45,418	26,528	> 44,062	38,429	> 45,948	> 139,388	> 72,711
Basic+CS	2,529	2,925	5,069	4,301	4,333	26,155	4,413
Basic+DR+CS	2,162	**2,505**	4,154	3,619	3,734	21,059	4,013
Encoding1	> 42,146	> 46,613	13,459	> 52,041	> 53,272‡	–	> 199,777*
Encoding1+DR	> 41,182	> 44,207	12,225	> 50,392	> 50,107‡	–	> 199,118*
Encoding1+CS	1,892	3,203	1,012	6,784	> 33,511‡	> 300,000	60,110*
Encoding1+DR+CS	1,855	3,031	949	6,576	3,878‡	> 300,000	57,158*
Encoding2	> 104,572	> 51,283	3,328	> 66,497	> 53,820	–	> 209,403*
Encoding2+DR	> 103,625	> 46,887	3,049*	> 56,182	> 50,162	–	> 207,556*
Encoding2+CS	1,356	3,388	381	5,749	4,179	> 217,680	> 83,408*
Encoding2+DR+CS	1,523	3,266	367	5,370	4,022	> 219,878	> 78,642*
PushPop	1,424	> 93,233	252†	1,278	13,791	15,791†	> 72,831
PushPop+DR	1,419	> 93,230	242†	1,253	13,382	14,235†	> 70,587
PushPop+CS	515	4,303	128†	568	2,829	3,198†	3,767
PushPop+DR+CS	**510**	4,307	**123**†	**528**	**2,765**	**2,969**†	**3,504**

Table 3. Linear integer arithmetic and linear bitvector arithmetic constraint solving results for the 30 grep test cases. For each test case, the time to solve for all child path constraints resp. child path subconstraints (when using CS) was measured (in milliseconds). The entries indicate the average time over the 30 test cases.

| Method | Linear Integer Arithmetic | | | Linear Bitvector Arithmetic | | | |
	Z3	MathSAT	Yices	Z3	MathSAT	Yices	STP
Basic	7,987	8,908	19,387	12,479	10,796	94,264	13,226
Basic+DR	2,262	2,463	3,880	3,376	3,206	21,089	5,233
Basic+CS	773	867	759	1,017	919	3,138	727
Basic+DR+CS	340	405	292	441	468	1,338	449
Encoding1	1,370	2,184	820	2,650	3,006‡	–	> 67,023*
Encoding1+DR	1,090	1,746	529	2,167	2,647‡	–	> 52,723*
Encoding1+CS	121	228	71	222	294‡	> 151,451	1,397*
Encoding1+DR+CS	113	217	54	210	279‡	> 151,543	1,307*
Encoding2	3,995	3,443	330	3,569	3,345	–	> 97,004*
Encoding2+DR	1,499	2,131	163	2,109	2,474	–	> 59,829*
Encoding2+CS	118	304	69	182	347	744	1,988*
Encoding2+DR+CS	102	242	45	156	286	673	1,658*
PushPop	148	3,092	68†	203	1,000	10,989†	10,517
PushPop+DR	111	3,075	**32**†	138	553	> 10,626†	4,549
PushPop+CS	134	221	64†	184	260	292†	550
PushPop+DR+CS	**99**	**192**	38†	**113**	**190**	**175**†	**381**

Table 4. Linear integer arithmetic and linear bitvector arithmetic constraint solving results for the 30 `avl` test cases. For each test case, the time to solve for all child path constraints resp. child path subconstraints (when using CS) was measured (in milliseconds). The entries indicate the average time over the 30 test cases.

Method	Linear Integer Arithmetic			Linear Bitvector Arithmetic			
	Z3	MathSAT	Yices	Z3	MathSAT	Yices	STP
Basic	3,083	5,343	10,369	15,000	42,717	118,346	13,832
Basic+DR	601	1,146	603	8,504	31,628	15,058	9,784
Basic+CS	1,550	2,560	4,303	7,687	21,577	55,568	7,309
Basic+DR+CS	296	568	254	3,816	16,741	6,587	5,416
Encoding1	876	952	930	4,996	28,861‡	–	41,853*
Encoding1+DR	324	548	189	3,941	29,701‡	–	27,497*
Encoding1+CS	419	452	407	3,673	26,808‡	> 300,000	18,635*
Encoding1+DR+CS	179	278	113	3,543	26,056‡	> 300,000	14,026*
Encoding2	2,608	1,637	341	13,612	43,433	19,160	95,545*
Encoding2+DR	182	615	70	4,359	28,283	15,097	32,603*
Encoding2+CS	511	739	172	8,712	29,968	7,452	34,673*
Encoding2+DR+CS	115	303	45	2,738	25,956	11,481	15,485*
PushPop	106	430	66†	1,735	12,673	14,091†	11,238
PushPop+DR	69	380	18†	1,575	12,268	8,445†	9,482
PushPop+CS	81	240	52†	1,013	9,489	6,213†	6,025
PushPop+DR+CS	**43**	**192**	**14†**	**974**	**9,268**	**3,683†**	**5,143**

Table 5. Linear integer arithmetic and linear bitvector arithmetic constraint solving results for the 30 `sort` test cases. For each test case, the time to solve for all child path constraints resp. child path subconstraints (when using CS) was measured (in milliseconds). The entries indicate the average time over the 30 test cases.

Method	Linear Integer Arithmetic			Linear Bitvector Arithmetic			
	Z3	MathSAT	Yices	Z3	MathSAT	Yices	STP
Basic	1,701	3,560	1,783	73,646	140,195	89,996	54,168
Basic+DR	1,693	3,540	1,766	72,391	140,334	90,080	52,820
Basic+CS	1,690	3,529	1,769	67,132	140,099	90,473	54,137
Basic+DR+CS	1,688	3,533	1,769	68,091	140,325	90,547	52,053
Encoding1	1,155	2,054	644	49,614	> 285,098‡	> 300,000	164,532*
Encoding1+DR	1,159	2,052	647	49,842	> 284,925‡	> 300,000	167,449*
Encoding1+CS	1,160	2,056	663	49,809	279,801‡	> 300,000	167,873*
Encoding1+DR+CS	1,157	2,057	658	49,775	> 285,171‡	> 300,000	166,301*
Encoding2	682	2,147	293	49,415	> 297,947	14,302	132,042*
Encoding2+DR	684	2,142	283	49,815	> 298,001	14,269	132,248*
Encoding2+CS	682	2,140	307	49,482	> 297,890	14,246	133,696*
Encoding2+DR+CS	686	2,143	287	49,473	> 298,838	14,257	132,132*
PushPop	**132**	953	28†	**21,066**	62,913	13,122†	51,864
PushPop+DR	**132**	953	28†	21,213	61,615	**13,035†**	51,800
PushPop+CS	133	**952**	29†	21,850	**61,594**	13,051†	**51,676**
PushPop+DR+CS	**132**	954	**28†**	21,084	61,656	13,043†	51,739

especially large for the `avl` and `sm` benchmarks. We believe the reason for this is that most of the constraints for these two benchmarks contain two symbolic variables (i.e. are of the form $\alpha_1 - \alpha_2 \leq 0$), while for the `grep` and `vim` benchmarks, the vast majority of constraints contain just one variable (i.e. are of the form $3\alpha_1 = 6$). This could indicate that the more complex linear integer constraints become, the greater the linear arithmetic modules outperform the bitvector modules.

The Push-Pop Method Outperforms the Other Methods. The results clearly show that the push-pop method outperforms the other methods, both when using the linear arithmetic modules and when using the bitvector modules of the solvers. The only exception is the linear arithmetic MATHSAT implementation of the push-pop method. On the `vim` benchmark, it actually performed slowest (see Table 2). Inspection of Table 1 shows that the `vim` test cases contain the greatest number of constraints and the most satisfiable child path constraints per path constraint. The combination of these two facts may be the reason for the bad performance of MATHSAT in this case. The MATHSAT bitvector implementation of the push-pop method performed far better on the `vim` benchmark than the linear arithmetic implementation.

The Iterative Constraint Strengthening Methods Provide No Clear Improvement Over the Basic Method. The two most significant performance differences between the iterative constraint strengthening methods and the basic method occurred for YICES and STP. First, YICES performed better on the linear arithmetic implementations of the iterative constraint strengthening methods than on the linear arithmetic implementation of the basic method. In contrast, STP performed better on the basic method than on the iterative constraint strengthening methods. All solvers performed similar on both iterative constraint strengthening methods. The exception is YICES, which performed better on Encoding2 than on Encoding1 (often by significant margins, as witnessed by the bitvector entries in Table 5).

4   Related Work

Several ways of preprocessing the (child) path constraints have been described in the literature. Sen et al. [15] introduced the notion of constraint independence. They described a preprocessing step that determines the constraints independent of the last, negated constraint of a child path constraint. Then, for the variables in these constraints, the previous input is reused. When attempting to generate several new inputs from a path constraint, it is more efficient to compute a decomposition into several path subconstraints. As mentioned by Cadar et al. [4], this can be done by using a disjoint-set data structure [6]. An algorithm that uses this data structure is given in [14].

A second standard optimization is duplicate constraint removal [15]. As previously mentioned, to maximize the effectiveness of duplicate removal, it is desirable that equivalent constraints have the same representation. Another optimization, termed constraint subsumption, was introduced by Godefroid et al. [11]. There, for the constraints generated at the same conditional statement, a syntactic check is performed if one constraint is definitely implied by another one. The implied constraints are removed before querying the solver.

An optimization introduced by KLEE [3] is the so-called counterexample cache. It stores the results of previous solver queries, along with solutions (variable assignments) obtained from successful queries. Before handing a formula to the solver, the cache is inspected if that formula (or a similar one) has been solved before. If yes, the result is reused. An interesting feature of the cache is that the formulas need not be exact matches. For instance, if an attempt to solve the unsatisfiable formula $\langle \alpha_1 < 3, \alpha_1 = 3 \rangle$ is made and the result is put into the cache, then a query for $\langle \alpha_1 < 3, \alpha_1 = 3, \alpha_2 > 0 \rangle$ will produce a hit in the cache, since the constraints form a superset of the constraints in the first query. Since the first formula is unsatisfiable, the second formula must be unsatisfiable as well.

The method of iterative constraint strengthening by which our encodings were inspired was introduced in [13]. There, iterative constraint strengthening was used for generating test cases from a program and a coverage-specification. A finite unwinding of the whole program is instrumented with a set of test goals and is encoded as a Boolean SAT formula. Then, an incremental SAT solver is used to derive input vectors for each feasible test goal.

Previously, there has not been a comparison of constraint solvers for use in concolic testing. A good place to look for comparisons of SMT solvers is the website of the annual Satisfiability Modulo Theories Competition (SMT-COMP) [1]. There, solvers compete against each other in various theory categories.

In this paper, we have focused on solving the constraints generated by the generational search [11]. However, there are also other search strategies. The depth-first search (DFS) strategy, in which the program paths are explored in a DFS manner, was proposed first [16]. It could be combined with the solving strategies introduced in this paper, by solving all the child path constraints of a path constraint right away, and storing the thereby obtained inputs for later use when the search backtracks. Other search strategies are random branch search [2], in which at each iteration a new input is generated from a randomly chosen child path constraint, and CFG-directed search [2], in which the child path constraints to solve are chosen based on whether they lead closer to currently uncovered branches.

5 Conclusion and Future Work

This paper tackled the problem of solving the child path constraints of a path constraint (which is a sequence of linear integer constraints) obtained by concolic execution of the program under test. Two related methods of encoding the child path constraints into a single formula were presented, and a method based on the push and pop operations of SMT solvers. The methods were evaluated for MATHSAT, STP, YICES and Z3, and in combination with the duplicate removal and constraint separation preprocessing steps. While the performance of the iterative constraint strengthening methods was somewhat disappointing, the push-pop method proved to be very efficient in the experimental evaluation.

For future work, it remains to investigate whether the push-pop method performs equally well on more precise constraints (e.g. including bitwise operations and array expressions). Also, the solving methods could be combined with additional preprocessing steps, such as the constraint subsumption optimization [11].

Acknowledgments. This work received funding in part by the Austrian National Research Network S11403-N23 (RiSE) of the Austrian Science Fund (FWF), and by the Vienna Science and Technology Fund (WWTF) grant PROSEED.

References

1. SMT-COMP (2012), http://smtcomp.sourceforge.net/2012, (accessed January 31, 2013)
2. Burnim, J., Sen, K.: Heuristics for Scalable Dynamic Test Generation. In: Proceedings of the 23rd IEEE/ACM International Conference on Automated Software Engineering (ASE 2008), L'Aquila, Italy, September 15-19, pp. 443–446. IEEE (2008)
3. Cadar, C., Dunbar, D., Engler, D.R.: KLEE: Unassisted and Automatic Generation of High-Coverage Tests for Complex Systems Programs. In: Draves, R., van Renesse, R. (eds.) Proceedings of the 8th USENIX Symposium on Operating Systems Design and Implementation, OSDI 2008, San Diego, California, USA, December 8-10, pp. 209–224. USENIX Association (2008)
4. Cadar, C., Ganesh, V., Pawlowski, P.M., Dill, D.L., Engler, D.R.: EXE: Automatically generating inputs of death. In: Juels, A., Wright, R.N., di Vimercati, S.D.C. (eds.) Proceedings of the 13th ACM Conference on Computer and Communications Security, CCS 2006, Alexandria, VA, USA, October 30-November 3, pp. 322–335. ACM (2006)
5. Cadar, C., Godefroid, P., Khurshid, S., Pasareanu, C.S., Sen, K., Tillmann, N., Visser, W.: Symbolic execution for software testing in practice: preliminary assessment. In: Taylor, R.N., Gall, H., Medvidovic, N. (eds.) Proceedings of the 33rd International Conference on Software Engineering, ICSE 2011, Waikiki, Honolulu, HI, USA, May 21-28, pp. 1066–1071. ACM (2011)
6. Cormen, T.H., Leiserson, C.E., Rivest, R.L., Stein, C.: Introduction to Algorithms, 3rd edn. The MIT Press (2009)
7. de Moura, L., Bjørner, N.: Z3: An Efficient SMT Solver. In: Ramakrishnan, C.R., Rehof, J. (eds.) TACAS 2008. LNCS, vol. 4963, pp. 337–340. Springer, Heidelberg (2008)
8. Dutertre, B., De Moura, L.: The Yices SMT solver 2, 2 (2006), Tool paper at: http://yices.csl.sri.com/tool-paper.pdf
9. Ganesh, V., Dill, D.L.: A Decision Procedure for Bit-Vectors and Arrays. In: Damm, W., Hermanns, H. (eds.) CAV 2007. LNCS, vol. 4590, pp. 519–531. Springer, Heidelberg (2007)

10. Godefroid, P., Klarlund, N., Sen, K.: DART: Directed Automated Random Testing. In: Sarkar, V., Hall, M.W. (eds.) Proceedings of the ACM SIGPLAN 2005 Conference on Programming Language Design and Implementation, Chicago, IL, USA, June 12-15, pp. 213–223. ACM (2005)
11. Godefroid, P., Levin, M.Y., Molnar, D.A.: Automated Whitebox Fuzz Testing. In: Proceedings of the Network and Distributed System Security Symposium, NDSS 2008, San Diego, California, USA, February 10-13. The Internet Society (2008)
12. Griggio, A.: A Practical Approach to Satisability Modulo Linear Integer Arithmetic. JSAT 8(1/2), 1–27 (2012)
13. Holzer, A., Schallhart, C., Tautschnig, M., Veith, H.: Query-Driven Program Testing. In: Jones, N.D., Müller-Olm, M. (eds.) VMCAI 2009. LNCS, vol. 5403, pp. 151–166. Springer, Heidelberg (2009)
14. Pötzl, D.: Achieving High Coverage and Finding Bugs in Sequential and Concurrent Software. Master's thesis, Vienna University of Technology (2012)
15. Sen, K., Marinov, D., Agha, G.: CUTE: A concolic unit testing engine for C. In: Wermelinger, M., Gall, H. (eds.) Proceedings of the 10th European Software Engineering Conference held jointly with 13th ACM SIGSOFT International Symposium on Foundations of Software Engineering, Lisbon, Portugal, September 5-9, pp. 263–272. ACM (2005)
16. Williams, N., Marre, B., Mouy, P., Roger, M.: PathCrawler: Automatic Generation of Path Tests by Combining Static and Dynamic Analysis. In: Dal Cin, M., Kaâniche, M., Pataricza, A. (eds.) EDCC 2005. LNCS, vol. 3463, pp. 281–292. Springer, Heidelberg (2005)

Divergent Quiescent Transition Systems*

Willem G.J. Stokkink, Mark Timmer, and Mariëlle I.A. Stoelinga

Formal Methods and Tools, Faculty of EEMCS
University of Twente, The Netherlands
{w.g.j.stokkink,m.timmer,marielle}@utwente.nl

Abstract. Quiescence is a fundamental concept in modelling system behaviour, as it explicitly represents the fact that no output is produced in certain states. The notion of quiescence is also essential to model-based testing: if a particular implementation under test does not provide any output, then the test evaluation algorithm must decide whether or not to allow this behaviour. To explicitly model quiescence in all its glory, we introduce Divergent Quiescent Transition Systems (DQTSs).

DQTSs model quiescence using explicit δ-labelled transitions, analogous to Suspension Automata (SAs) in the well-known ioco framework. Whereas SAs have only been defined implicitly, DQTSs for the first time provide a fully-formalised framework for quiescence. Also, while SAs are restricted to convergent systems (i.e., without τ-cycles), we show how quiescence can be treated naturally using a notion of fairness, allowing systems exhibiting divergence to be modelled as well. We study compositionality under the familiar automata-theoretical operations of determinisation, parallel composition and action hiding. We provide a non-trivial algorithm for detecting divergent states, and discuss its complexity. Finally, we show how to use DQTSs in the context of model-based testing, for the first time presenting a full-fledged theory that allows ioco to be applied to divergent systems.

1 Introduction

Quiescence is a fundamental concept in modelling system behaviour. It explicitly represents the fact that in certain states no output is provided. The absence of outputs is often essential: an ATM, for instance, should deliver money only once per transaction. This means that its state just after payment should be quiescent: it should not produce any output until further input is given. On the other hand, the state before payment should clearly not be quiescent. Hence, quiescence may or may not be considered erroneous behaviour. Consequently, the notion of quiescence is essential in model-based testing, where it is detected by means of a timeout. If a particular implementation under test does not provide any output, then the test evaluation algorithm must decide whether to produce a pass verdict (allowing quiescence at this point) or a fail verdict (prohibiting quiescence at this point).

---

* This research has been partially funded by NWO under grants 612.063.817 (SYRUP), Dn 63-257 (ROCKS) and 12238 (ArRangeer), and by the EU under grant 318490 (SENSATION).

M. Veanes and L. Viganò (Eds.): TAP 2013, LNCS 7942, pp. 214–231, 2013.
© Springer-Verlag Berlin Heidelberg 2013

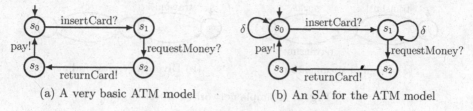

(a) A very basic ATM model   (b) An SA for the ATM model

Fig. 1. Deriving a suspension automaton[1]

Origins. The notion of quiescence was first introduced by Vaandrager [1] to obtain a natural extension of blocking states: if a system is input-enabled (i.e., always ready to receive inputs), then no states are blocking, since each state has outgoing input transitions. Quiescence models the fact that a state would be blocking when considering only the internal and output actions. In the context of model-based testing, Tretmans introduced *repetitive quiescence* [2,3]. This notion emerged from the need to continue testing, even in a quiescent state: in the ATM example above, we may need to test further behaviour arising from the (quiescent) state s_0. To accommodate this, Tretmans introduced the *Suspension Automaton* (SA) as an auxiliary concept [4]. An SA is obtained from an Input-Output Transition System (IOTS) by first adding a self-loop labelled by the quiescence label δ to each quiescent state and subsequently determinising the model. For instance, the ATM automaton in Fig. 1a has quiescent states s_0 and s_1; the corresponding SA is depicted in Fig. 1b.

Limitations of Current Treatments. While previous work [1,2,3,4] convincingly argued the need for quiescence, no comprehensive theory of quiescence existed thus far. A severe restriction is that SAs cannot cope with divergence (cycles consisting of internal actions only), since this may introduce newly quiescent states. The TGV framework [5] handles divergence by adding δ-labelled self-loops to such states. However, this treatment is in our opinion not satisfactory: quiescence due to divergence, expressing that no output will ever be produced, can in [5] be followed by an output action, which is counterintuitive. The current paper shows that an appropriate theory for quiescence that can cope with divergence is far from trivial.

Divergence does often occur in practice, e.g., due to action hiding. Therefore, current model-based testing approaches are not able to adequately handle such systems; in this paper, we fill this gap.

Example 1.1. Consider the simplified network protocol shown in Figure 2a. It is obtained as the parallel composition of a sending node (transmitting a message) and a receiving node (sending positive and negative acknowledgements). If only

---

[1] Since we require systems to be input-enabled, these models are technically not correct. However, this could easily be fixed by adding self-loops to all states for each missing input. We chose to omit these for clarity of presentation.

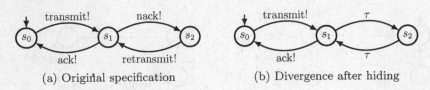

(a) Original specification   (b) Divergence after hiding

Fig. 2. A simple network protocol

the initial transmission and success of this transmission are considered observable behaviour, the other actions (needed for parallel composition, but irrelevant in the final system) can be hidden, and the system shown in Figure 2b appears. Here, divergence may occur in states s_1 and s_2 (for instance, when retransmission was implemented erroneously and never succeeds). So, observation of quiescence is possible from these states, but simply adding δ-loops does not work anymore. After all, quiescence indicates the *indefinite* absence of outputs, and adding δ-loops to these states would allow outputs to occur after the δ-transitions. Hence, more sophisticated constructs are needed.

In addition to the divergence issue, quiescence was never treated as a first-class citizen: SAs cannot be built from scratch, and, even though important conformance relations such as ioco are defined in terms of them, SAs have been defined as an auxiliary construct and have never been studied extensively in isolation. In particular, their closure properties under standard operations like parallel composition and action hiding have not been investigated much.

Our Approach. This paper remediates the shortcomings of previous work by introducing *Divergent Quiescent Transition Systems* (DQTSs). DQTSs represent quiescence explicitly using special δ-transitions. We stipulate four well-formedness rules that formalise when δ-transitions may occur. For instance, no δ-transition may be followed by an output transition, since this would contradict the meaning of quiescence. Key in our work is the treatment of divergence: a divergent path leads to the observation of quiescence if and only if it is fair, i.e., models a reasonable execution. We use the notion of fairness from Input-Output Automata (IOAs) [6], based on task partitions.

We show that well-formed DQTSs are closed under parallel composition, determinisation and action hiding. In this way, they constitute a compositional theory for quiescence. Additionally, we formally explain how to obtain a DQTS from an existing IOA by a process called *deltafication*, and show that deltafication is commutative with parallel composition and action hiding. The addition of divergence (and correspondingly fairness) brought about a more involved process of deltafication and action hiding (which may introduce divergence), requiring a novel algorithm for detecting divergent states. We provide this algorithm, which allows us to check well-formedness on a given DQTS as well. Finally, we redefine the ioco conformance relation based on DQTSs, allowing it to be applied in the presence of divergence and hence demonstrating the most important practical benefit of our model for testing: a more general class of systems can be handled.

A preliminary version of this work, already providing a fully formalised framework for dealing with quiescence as a first-class citizen, but not yet supporting divergence, appeared as [7].

Overview of the Paper. Sec. 2 introduces the DQTS model, and Sec. 3 presents our well-formedness rules. Sec. 4 then provides operations and properties for DQTSs. In Sec. 5 we describe an algorithm to determine divergent states, and Sec. 6 discusses how to apply DQTSs in the ioco framework. Finally, conclusions and future work are presented in Sec. 7. Due to space limitations, we refer to [8] for proofs of all our results.

2 Divergent Quiescent Transition Systems

Preliminaries. Given a set L, we use L^* to denote the set of all *finite sequences* $\sigma = a_1 a_2 \ldots a_n$ over L. We write $|\sigma| = n$ for the *length* of σ, and ϵ for the *empty sequence*. We let L^ω denote the set of all *infinite sequences* over L, and use $L^\infty = L^* \cup L^\omega$. Given two sequences $\rho \in L^*$ and $\upsilon \in L^\infty$, we denote the *concatenation* of ρ and υ by $\rho\,\upsilon$. The *projection of an element* $a \in L$ *on* $L' \subseteq L$, denoted $a \upharpoonright L'$, is a if $a \in L'$ and ϵ otherwise. The projection of a sequence $\sigma = a\,\sigma'$ is defined inductively by $(a\,\sigma') \upharpoonright L' = (a \upharpoonright L') \cdot (\sigma' \upharpoonright L')$, and the projection of a set of sequences Z is defined as the sets of projections.

We use $\wp(L)$ to denote the *power set* of L. A set $P \subseteq \wp(L)$ such that $\varnothing \notin P$ is a *partition* of L if $\bigcup P = L$ and $p \neq q$ implies $p \cap q = \varnothing$ for all $p, q \in P$. Finally, we use the notation $\exists^\infty$ for 'there exist infinitely many'.

2.1 Basic Model and Definitions

Divergent Quiescent Transition Systems (DQTSs) are labelled transition systems that model quiescence, i.e., the absence of outputs or internal transitions, via a special δ-action. They are based on the well-known Input-Output Automata [9,6]; in particular, their task partitions allow one to define fair paths.

Definition 2.1 (Divergent Quiescent Transition System). *A* Divergent Quiescent Transition System *(DQTS) is a tuple* $\mathcal{A} = \langle S, S^0, L^I, L^O, L^H, P, \rightarrow \rangle$, *where* S *is a set of states;* $S^0 \subseteq S$ *is a non-empty set of initial states;* L^I, L^O *and* L^H *are disjoint sets of input, output and internal labels, respectively;* P *is a partition of* $L^O \cup L^H$; *and* $\rightarrow \subseteq S \times L \cup \{\delta\} \times S$ *is the transition relation, where* $L = L^I \cup L^O \cup L^H$. *We assume* $\delta \notin L$.

Given a DQTS $\mathcal{A}$, *we denote its components by* $S_\mathcal{A}, S^0_\mathcal{A}, L^I_\mathcal{A}, L^O_\mathcal{A}, L^H_\mathcal{A}, P_\mathcal{A}, \rightarrow_\mathcal{A}$. *We omit the subscript when it is clear from the context.*

Example 2.1. The SA in Fig. 1b is a DQTS.   □

Restrictions. We impose two important restrictions on DQTSs. (1) We require each DQTS $\mathcal{A}$ to be *input-enabled*, i.e., always ready to accept any input. Thus, we require that for each $s \in S$ and $a \in L^I$, there exists an $s' \in S$ such that

$(s, a, s') \in \rightarrow$. (2) We require each DQTS to be well-formed. Well-formedness requires technical preparation and is defined in Sec. 3.

Semantically, DQTSs assume progress. That is, DQTSs are not allowed to remain idle forever when output or internal actions are enabled. Without this assumption, each state would be potentially quiescent.

Actions. We use the terms label and action interchangeably. We often suffix a question mark (?) to input labels and an exclamation mark (!) to output labels. These are, however, not part of the label. A label without a suffix denotes an internal label. Output and internal actions are called *locally controlled*, because their occurrence is under the control of the DQTS. Thus, $L^{\mathrm{LC}} = L^O \cup L^H$ denotes the set of all locally controlled actions. The special label δ is used to denote the occurrence of quiescence (see Def. 2.10). The task partition P partitions the locally controlled actions into blocks, allowing one to reason about fairness: an execution is fair if every task partition that is enabled infinitely often, is also given control infinitely often (see Sec. 2.2).

We use the standard notations for transitions.

Definition 2.2 (Transitional Notations). *Let $\mathcal{A}$ be a DQTS with $s, s' \in S$, $a, a_i \in L$, $b, b_i \in L^I \cup L^O$, and $\sigma \in (L^I \cup L^O)^+$, then:*

$$
\begin{aligned}
s \xrightarrow{a} s' &=_{\mathrm{def}} (s, a, s') \in \rightarrow \\
s \xrightarrow{a} &=_{\mathrm{def}} \exists s'' \in S . s \xrightarrow{a} s'' \\
s \xrightarrow{a}\!\!\!\!/\; &=_{\mathrm{def}} \nexists s'' \in S . s \xrightarrow{a} s'' \\
s \xrightarrow{a_1 \cdots a_n} s' &=_{\mathrm{def}} \exists s_0, \ldots, s_n \in S . s = s_0 \xrightarrow{a_1} \cdots \xrightarrow{a_n} s_n = s' \\
s \xRightarrow{\epsilon} s' &=_{\mathrm{def}} s = s' \; or \; \exists a_1, \ldots, a_n \in L^H . s \xrightarrow{a_1 \cdots a_n} s' \\
s \xRightarrow{b} s' &=_{\mathrm{def}} \exists s_0, s_1 \in S . s \xRightarrow{\epsilon} s_0 \xrightarrow{b} s_1 \xRightarrow{\epsilon} s' \\
s \xRightarrow{b_1 \cdots b_n} s' &=_{\mathrm{def}} \exists s_0, \ldots, s_n \in S . s = s_0 \xRightarrow{b_1} \cdots \xRightarrow{b_n} s_n = s' \\
s \xRightarrow{\sigma} &=_{\mathrm{def}} \exists s'' \in S . s \xRightarrow{\sigma} s''
\end{aligned}
$$

If $s \xrightarrow{a}$, we say that a is enabled in s. We use $L(s)$ to denote the set of all actions $a \in L$ that are enabled in state $s \in S$, i.e., $L(s) = \{ a \in L \mid s \xrightarrow{a} \}$. The notions are lifted to infinite traces in the obvious way.

We use the following language notations for DQTSs and their behaviour.

Definition 2.3 (Language Notations). *Let $\mathcal{A}$ be a DQTS, then:*

- *A finite path in $\mathcal{A}$ is a sequence $\pi = s_0 a_1 s_1 a_2 s_2 \cdots s_n$ such that $s_{i-1} \xrightarrow{a_i} s_i$ for all $1 \leq i \leq n$. Infinite paths are defined analogously. The set of all paths in $\mathcal{A}$ is denoted $paths(\mathcal{A})$.*
- *Given any path, we write $first(\pi) = s_0$. Also, we denote by $states(\pi)$ the set of states that occur on π, and by $\omega\text{-}states(\pi)$ the set of states that occur infinitely often. That is, $\omega\text{-}states(\pi) = \{ s \in states(\pi) \mid \exists^\infty j . s_j = s \}$.*
- *We define $trace(\pi) = \pi \restriction (L^I \cup L^O)$, and say that $trace(\pi)$ is the trace of π. For every $s \in S$, $traces(s)$ is the set of all traces corresponding to paths that start in s, i.e., $traces(s) = \{ trace(\pi) \mid \pi \in paths(\mathcal{A}) \wedge first(\pi) = s \}$. We define $traces(\mathcal{A}) = \bigcup_{s \in S^0} traces(s)$, and say that two DQTSs $\mathcal{B}$ and $\mathcal{C}$ are trace-equivalent, denoted $\mathcal{B} \approx_{\mathrm{tr}} \mathcal{C}$, if $traces(\mathcal{B}) = traces(\mathcal{C})$.*

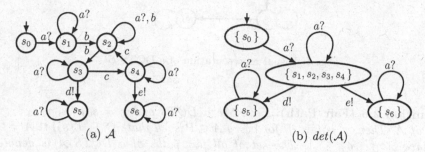

Fig. 3. Visual representations of the DQTSs $\mathcal{A}$ and $det(\mathcal{A})$

- For a finite trace σ and state $s \in S$, $reach(s, \sigma)$ denotes the set of states in $\mathcal{A}$ that can be reached from s via σ, i.e., $reach(s, \sigma) = \{ s' \in S \mid s \overset{\sigma}{\Longrightarrow} s' \}$. For a set of states $S' \subseteq S$, we define $reach(S', \sigma) = \bigcup_{s \in S'} reach(s, \sigma)$.

When needed, we add subscripts to indicate the DQTS these notions refer to.

Definition 2.4 (Determinism). A DQTS $\mathcal{A}$ is deterministic if $s \overset{a}{\rightarrow} s'$ and $s \overset{a}{\rightarrow} s''$ imply $a \notin L^H$ and $s' = s''$, for all $s, s', s'' \in S$ and $a \in L$. Otherwise, $\mathcal{A}$ is nondeterministic.

Each DQTS has a trace-equivalent deterministic DQTS [10,11]. Determinisation is carried out using the well-known subset construction procedure. This construction yields a system in which every state has a unique target per action, and internal transitions are not present anymore.

Definition 2.5 (Determinisation). The determinisation of a DQTS $\mathcal{A} = \langle S, S^0, L^I, L^O, L^H, P, \rightarrow \rangle$ is the DQTS $det(\mathcal{A}) = \langle T, \{ S^0 \}, L^I, L^O, L^H, P, \rightarrow_D \rangle$, with $T = \wp(S) \setminus \varnothing$ and $\rightarrow_D = \{ (U, a, V) \in T \times L \times T \mid V = reach_{\mathcal{A}}(U, a) \wedge V \neq \varnothing \}$.

Example 2.2. The DQTS $\mathcal{A}$ in Fig. 3a is nondeterministic; its determinisation $det(\mathcal{A})$ is shown in Fig. 3b.   □

2.2 Fairness and Divergence

The notion of fairness also plays a crucial role in DQTSs. The reason for this is that parallel composition may yield unreasonable divergences. For instance, if the DQTS in Fig. 4 is the composition of a system consisting solely of an internal a-loop and a system outputting a b precisely once, the progress assumption on the second component tells us that at some point we should observe this b-output. Therefore, we want to prohibit the divergent path $\pi = s_0 \, a \, s_0 \, a \, s_0 \ldots$.

The following definition stems from [9,6,12], and states that if a subcomponent of the system infinitely often wants to execute some of its actions, it will indeed infinitely often execute some. Note that finite paths are fair by default.

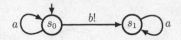

Fig. 4. Visual representation of a DQTS $\mathcal{B}$

Definition 2.6 (Fair Path). *Let $\mathcal{A}$ be a DQTS and $\pi = s_0 a_1 s_1 a_2 s_2 \ldots$ a path of $\mathcal{A}$. Then, π is fair if, for every $A \in P$ such that $\exists^{\infty} j . L(s_j) \cap A \neq \varnothing$, we have $\exists^{\infty} j . a_j \in A$. The set of all fair paths of a DQTS $\mathcal{A}$ is denoted fpaths$(\mathcal{A})$, and the set of corresponding traces is denoted ftraces$(\mathcal{A})$.*

Unfair paths are considered not to occur, so from now on we only consider fpaths$(\mathcal{A})$ and ftraces$(\mathcal{A})$ for the behaviour of $\mathcal{A}$.

Example 2.3. Consider again the DQTS $\mathcal{B}$ in Fig. 4. The infinite path $\pi = s_0 a s_0 a s_0 \ldots$ would not be fair if $P_{\mathcal{B}} = \{\{a\}, \{b\}\}$, as the b-output is ignored forever. It would however be fair if $P_{\mathcal{B}} = \{\{a, b\}\}$.   □

We can now formally define divergence: fair infinite internal behaviour.

Definition 2.7 (Divergent Path). *Let $\mathcal{A}$ be a DQTS and $\pi \in$ fpaths$(\mathcal{A})$ a fair infinite path. The path π is divergent if it contains only transitions labelled with internal actions, i.e., $a_i \in L_{\mathcal{A}}^{H}$ for every action a_i on π. The set of all divergent paths of $\mathcal{A}$ is denoted dpaths$(\mathcal{A})$.*

Example 2.4. Consider the DQTS $\mathcal{A}$ in Fig. 3a with $L_{\mathcal{A}}^{H} = \{b, c\}$. The infinite paths $s_2 b s_2 b s_2 \ldots$ and $s_2 b s_3 c s_4 c s_2 b s_3 \ldots$ are both divergent. Note that divergent traces are not preserved by determinisation.   □

In contrast to SAs, we do allow divergent paths to occur in DQTSs. However, we assume that each divergent path in a DQTS only contains a finite number of states. This restriction serves to ensure that the deltafication of a DQTS, discussed in Sec. 4.1, always results in a correct DQTS. Since DQTSs typically contain a finite number of states, and even in infinite systems divergence often results from internal loops, this restriction is not a severe one.

Definition 2.8 (State-Finite Path). *Let $\mathcal{A}$ be a DQTS and let $\pi \in$ fpaths$(\mathcal{A})$ be an infinite path. If $|states(\pi)| < \infty$, then π is state-finite.*

When the system is on a state-finite divergent path, it continuously loops through a finite number of states on this path. We call these states divergent.

Definition 2.9 (Divergent State). *Let $\mathcal{A}$ be a DQTS. A state $s \in S$ is divergent, denoted $d(s)$, if there is a (state-finite and fair) divergent path on which s occurs infinitely often, i.e., if there is a path $\pi \in$ dpaths$(\mathcal{A})$ such that $s \in \omega\text{-states}(\pi)$. The set of all divergent states of $\mathcal{A}$ is denoted $d(\mathcal{A})$.*

Example 2.5. Consider the DQTS $\mathcal{A}$ in Fig. 3a. The path $\pi_1 = s_1 \, b \, s_2 \, b \, s_2 \ldots$ is state-finite, fair and divergent. Since s_2 occurs infinitely often on π_1, it is divergent; s_1, on the other hand, is not. Whether s_3 is divergent depends on the task partition P. If P contains an element A such that $\{\, c, d, e \,\} \subseteq A$, then $\pi_2 = s_3 \, c \, s_4 \, c \, s_2 \, b \, s_3 \ldots$ is fair and s_3 is divergent; otherwise, it is not.   □

2.3   Quiescence

Definition 2.10 (Quiescent State). *Let $\mathcal{A}$ be a DQTS. A state $s \in S$ is quiescent, denoted $q(s)$, if it has no locally-controlled actions enabled. That is, $q(s)$ if $s \not\xrightarrow{a}$ for all $a \in L^{\mathrm{LC}}$. The set of all quiescent states of $\mathcal{A}$ is denoted $q(\mathcal{A})$.*

Example 2.6. States s_0, s_5 and s_6 of the DQTS $\mathcal{A}$ in Fig. 3a are quiescent.   □

Divergent paths in DQTSs may yield observations of quiescence in states that are not necessarily quiescent. Consider the DQTS $\mathcal{B}$ in Fig. 4. State s_0 is not quiescent, since it enables output b. Nevertheless, this output is never observed on the divergent path $\pi = s_0 \, a \, s_0 \, a \ldots$. Hence, quiescence might be observed in a non-quiescent state (here, if π is fair). After observing quiescence due to a divergent path, the system will reside in one of the divergent states on that path.

3   Well-Formed DQTSs

To be meaningful, DQTSs have to adhere to four well-formedness rules that formalize the semantics of quiescence. As indicated before, we assume all DQTSs to do so.

Definition 3.1 (Well-Formedness). *A DQTS $\mathcal{A}$ is well-formed if it satisfies the following rules for all $s, s', s'' \in S$ and $a \in L^{\mathrm{I}}$:*

Rule R1 (Quiescence should be Observable): if $q(s)$ or $d(s)$, then $s \xrightarrow{\delta}$.
This rule requires that each quiescent or divergent state has an outgoing δ-transition, since in these states quiescence may be observed.

Rule R2 (Quiescent state after quiescence observation): if $s \xrightarrow{\delta} s'$, then $q(s')$.
Since there is no notion of timing in DQTSs, there is no particular observation duration associated with quiescence. Hence, the execution of a δ-transition represents that the system has not produced any outputs indefinitely; therefore, enabling any outputs after a δ-transition would clearly be erroneous.
   Note that, even though the δ-transition may be due to divergence, it would not suffice to require $q(s') \lor d(s')$. After all, $d(s')$ does not exclude output actions from s', and these should not be enabled directly after a δ-transitions.

Rule R3 (No new behaviour after quiescence observation): if $s \xrightarrow{\delta} s'$, then $traces(s') \subseteq traces(s)$.
There is no notion of timing in DQTSs. Hence, behaviour that is possible after an observation of quiescence, must also be possible beforehand. Still, the observation of quiescence may indicate the outcome of an earlier nondeterministic choice, thereby reducing possible behaviour. Hence, the potential inequality.

Rule R4 (Continued quiescence preserves behaviour): if $s \xrightarrow{\delta} s'$ and $s' \xrightarrow{\delta} s''$, then $traces(s'') = traces(s')$.

Since quiescence represents the fact that no outputs are observed, and there is no notion of timing in the DQTS model, there can be no difference between observing quiescence once or multiple times in succession.

In [13], four similar, but more complex, rules for *valid* SAs are discussed. However, these did not account for divergence.

Note that, by definition of divergent states, rule R1 does not require δ-transitions from states that have outgoing divergent paths on which they occur only finitely often. This simplifies the deltafication procedure, as will be made clear in Example 4.1. Also note that a path of a DQTS may contain multiple successive δ-transitions. This corresponds to the practical testing scenario of observing a time-out rather than an output more than once in a row [2,3].

Since SAs are derived from IOTSs, and we assume that these IOTSs correctly capture system behaviour, we find that SAs are 'well-formed' in the sense that their observable behaviour (including quiescence) corresponds to that of realistic specifications. Since we also desire this property to hold for well-formed DQTSs, the above rules have been carefully crafted in such a way that well-formed DQTSs and SAs are equivalent in terms of expressible observable behaviour. The following theorem characterises this core motivation behind our design decisions: it shows that every trace in a DQTS can be obtained by starting with a traditional IOTS and adding δ-loops as for SAs, and vice versa. Hence, except for divergences, their expressivity coincides.

Theorem 3.1. *For every SA S there exists a well-formed DQTS $\mathcal{D}$ such that $S \approx_{\mathrm{tr}} \mathcal{D}$, and vice versa.*

Verifying rule R1 requires identifying divergent states; in Sec. 5 we provide an algorithm to do so. Rule R2 can be checked trivially, while R3 and R4 in practice could be checked heuristically. For R3, verify whether $s \xrightarrow{\delta} s'$ and $s' \xrightarrow{a?} s''$ imply $s \xrightarrow{a?} s''$, and for R4, verify whether $s \xrightarrow{\delta} s'$ and $s' \xrightarrow{\delta} s''$ imply that $s' = s''$.

4   Operations and Properties

4.1   Deltafication: From IOA to DQTS

Usually, specifications are modelled as IOAs (or IOTSs, which can easily be converted to IOAs by taking $L^{\mathrm{H}} = \{\tau\}$ and $P = \{L^{\mathrm{LC}}\}$). During testing, however, we typically observe the outputs of the system generated in response to inputs from the tester; thus, it is useful to be able to refer to the absence of outputs explicitly. Hence, we need a way to convert an IOA to a well-formed DQTS that captures all possible observations of it, including quiescence. This conversion is called *deltafication*. It uses the notions of quiescence, divergence and state-finiteness, which were defined for DQTSs, but can just as well be used for IOAs (interpreting them as non-well-formed DQTSs without any δ-transitions). As for DQTSs, we require all IOAs to be input-enabled.

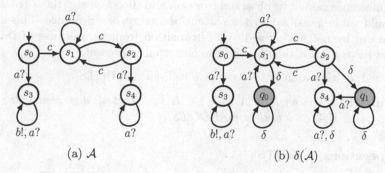

(a) $\mathcal{A}$ (b) $\delta(\mathcal{A})$

Fig. 5. An IOA $\mathcal{A}$ and its deltafication $\delta(\mathcal{A})$. Newly introduced states are grey.

To satisfy rule R1, every state in which quiescence may be observed must have an outgoing δ-transition. When constructing SAs, δ-labelled self-loops are added to all quiescent states. This would not work for divergent states, however, since divergent states have outgoing internal transitions and possibly even output transitions (as in Fig. 4). So, a δ-labelled self-loop would contradict rule R2.

Our solution is to introduce a new state qos_s for every divergent state s, which acts as its *quiescence observation state*. When quiescence is observed in s, a δ-transition will lead to qos_s. To preserve the original behaviour, all inputs that are enabled in s must still be enabled in qos_s, and must lead to the same states that the original input transitions led to. All these considerations together lead to the following definition for the deltafication procedure for IOAs.

Definition 4.1 (Deltafication). *Let* $\mathcal{A} = \langle S_A, S^0, L^I, L^O, L^H, P, \to_A \rangle$ *be an IOA with* $\delta \notin L$. *The* deltafication *of* $\mathcal{A}$ *is* $\delta(\mathcal{A}) = \langle S_\delta, S^0, L^I, L^O, L^H, P, \to_\delta \rangle$. *We define* $S_\delta = S_A \cup \{ qos_s \mid s \in d(\mathcal{A}) \}$, *i.e.,* S_δ *contains a new state* $qos_s \notin S_A$ *for every divergent state* $s \in S_A$ *of* $\mathcal{A}$. *The transition relation* $\to_\delta$ *is as follows:*

$$
\begin{aligned}
\to_\delta = \to_A \ &\cup \ \{ (s, \delta, s) && \mid s \in q(\mathcal{A}) \} \\
&\cup \ \{ (s, \delta, qos_s) && \mid s \in d(\mathcal{A}) \} \cup \{ (qos_s, \delta, qos_s) \mid s \in d(\mathcal{A}) \} \\
&\cup \ \{ (qos_s, a?, s') \mid s \in d(\mathcal{A}) \ \wedge \ a? \in L^I \ \wedge \ s \xrightarrow{a?}_A s' \}
\end{aligned}
$$

Thus, the deltafication of an IOA adds δ-labelled self-loops to all quiescent states. Furthermore, a new quiescence observation state qos_s is introduced for every divergent state $s \in S$, alongside the required inputs and δ-transitions.

Note that computing $q(\mathcal{A})$ is trivial: simply identify all states without outgoing output or internal transition. Determining $d(\mathcal{A})$ is more complex; an algorithm to do so is provided in Sec. 5.

Example 4.1. See Fig. 5 for IOA $\mathcal{A}$ and its deltafication, given $P_\mathcal{A} = \{\{b, c\}\}$. Hence, s_1 and s_2 are divergent, and q_0 and q_1 quiescence observation states. Note that s_0 has an outgoing divergent path, while in accordance to rule R1 it is not given an outgoing δ-transition. The reason is that, when observing quiescence, our progress assumption prescribes that the system can only reside in s_1 or s_2.

Hence, quiescence cannot be observed from s_0, and therefore also the a-transition to s_3 should not be possible anymore after observation of quiescence. This is now taken care of by not having a direct δ-transition from s_0. Because of this, no trace first having δ and then having the $b!$ output is present.   □

As expected, deltafication indeed yields a well-formed DQTS.

Theorem 4.1. *Given an IOA $\mathcal{A}$ with $\delta \notin L$ such that all divergent paths in $\mathcal{A}$ are state-finite, $\delta(\mathcal{A})$ is a well-formed DQTS.*

4.2   Operations on DQTSs

We introduce several standard operations on well-formed DQTSs. First, we define the well-known parallel composition operator. As usual, it requires every locally controlled action to be under the control of at most one component [6].

Definition 4.2 (Compatibility). *Two DQTSs $\mathcal{A}$ and $\mathcal{B}$ are compatible if $L_{\mathcal{A}}^{O} \cap L_{\mathcal{B}}^{O} = \varnothing$, $L_{\mathcal{A}}^{H} \cap L_{\mathcal{B}} = \varnothing$, and $L_{\mathcal{B}}^{H} \cap L_{\mathcal{A}} = \varnothing$.*

Definition 4.3 (Parallel Composition). *Given two well-formed compatible DQTSs $\mathcal{A}$ and $\mathcal{B}$, the parallel composition of $\mathcal{A}$ and $\mathcal{B}$ is the DQTS $\mathcal{A} \parallel \mathcal{B}$, with $S_{\mathcal{A}\parallel\mathcal{B}} = S_{\mathcal{A}} \times S_{\mathcal{B}}$, $S_{\mathcal{A}\parallel\mathcal{B}}^{0} = S_{\mathcal{A}}^{0} \times S_{\mathcal{B}}^{0}$, $L_{\mathcal{A}\parallel\mathcal{B}}^{I} = (L_{\mathcal{A}}^{I} \cup L_{\mathcal{B}}^{I}) \setminus (L_{\mathcal{A}}^{O} \cup L_{\mathcal{B}}^{O})$, $L_{\mathcal{A}\parallel\mathcal{B}}^{O} = L_{\mathcal{A}}^{O} \cup L_{\mathcal{B}}^{O}$, $L_{\mathcal{A}\parallel\mathcal{B}}^{H} = L_{\mathcal{A}}^{H} \cup L_{\mathcal{B}}^{H}$, $P_{\mathcal{A}\parallel\mathcal{B}} = P_{\mathcal{A}} \cup P_{\mathcal{B}}$, and*

$$
\begin{aligned}
\rightarrow_{\mathcal{A}\parallel\mathcal{B}} = \ & \{\, ((s,t), a, (s',t')) \in S_{\mathcal{A}\parallel\mathcal{B}} \times ((L_{\mathcal{A}} \cap L_{\mathcal{B}}) \cup \{\delta\}) \times S_{\mathcal{A}\parallel\mathcal{B}} \mid \\
& \quad s \xrightarrow{a}_{\mathcal{A}} s' \wedge t \xrightarrow{a}_{\mathcal{B}} t' \,\} \\
\cup \ & \{\, ((s,t), a, (s',t)) \in S_{\mathcal{A}\parallel\mathcal{B}} \times (L_{\mathcal{A}} \setminus L_{\mathcal{B}}) \times S_{\mathcal{A}\parallel\mathcal{B}} \mid s \xrightarrow{a}_{\mathcal{A}} s' \,\} \\
\cup \ & \{\, ((s,t), a, (s,t')) \in S_{\mathcal{A}\parallel\mathcal{B}} \times (L_{\mathcal{B}} \setminus L_{\mathcal{A}}) \times S_{\mathcal{A}\parallel\mathcal{B}} \mid t \xrightarrow{a}_{\mathcal{B}} t' \,\}
\end{aligned}
$$

We have $L_{\mathcal{A}\parallel\mathcal{B}} = L_{\mathcal{A}\parallel\mathcal{B}}^{I} \cup L_{\mathcal{A}\parallel\mathcal{B}}^{O} \cup L_{\mathcal{A}\parallel\mathcal{B}}^{H} = L_{\mathcal{A}} \cup L_{\mathcal{B}}$.

Note that we require DQTSs to synchronise on δ-transitions, as a parallel composition of two DQTSs can only be quiescent when both components are.

It is often useful to hide certain output actions of a given well-formed DQTS, treating them as internal actions. For example, actions used for synchronisation are often not needed anymore in the parallel composition. Action hiding is slightly more complicated for DQTSs than for IOAs, as transforming output actions to internal actions can lead to newly divergent states. Still, whereas in SAs this was forbidden, in DQTSs it is allowed. Consequently, after hiding, new quiescence observation states may have to be added for newly divergent states.

Definition 4.4 (Action Hiding). *Let $\mathcal{A} = \langle S_{\mathcal{A}}, S^0, L^I, L^O, L^H, P, \rightarrow_{\mathcal{A}} \rangle$ be a well-formed DQTS and $H \subseteq L^O$ a set of outputs, then hiding H in $\mathcal{A}$ yields the DQTS $\mathcal{A} \setminus H = \langle S_H, S^0, L^I, L_H^O, L_H^H, P, \rightarrow_H \rangle$, with $L_H^O = L^O \setminus H$, $L_H^H = L^H \cup H$, and $S_H = S_{\mathcal{A}} \cup \{\, qos_s \mid s \in d(\mathcal{A} \setminus H) \setminus d(\mathcal{A}) \,\}$. Finally, $\rightarrow_H$ is defined by*

$$
\begin{aligned}
\rightarrow_H = \ \rightarrow_{\mathcal{A}} \ & \cup \{\, (s, \delta, qos_s) && \mid s \in d(\mathcal{A} \setminus H) \setminus d(\mathcal{A}) \,\} \\
& \cup \{\, (qos_s, \delta, qos_s) && \mid s \in d(\mathcal{A} \setminus H) \setminus d(\mathcal{A}) \,\} \\
& \cup \{\, (qos_s, a?, s') && \mid s \in d(\mathcal{A} \setminus H) \setminus d(\mathcal{A}) \wedge a? \in L^I \wedge s \xrightarrow{a}_{\mathcal{A}} s' \,\}
\end{aligned}
$$

So, similar to deltafication, quiescence observation states are added for all newly divergent states, along with the required input transitions to preserve behaviour.

4.3   Properties of DQTSs

We present several important results regarding DQTSs. First, it turns out that well-formed DQTSs are closed under all operations defined thus far.

Theorem 4.2. *Well-formed DQTSs are closed under the operations of determinisation, parallel composition, and action hiding, i.e., given two well-formed and compatible DQTSs $\mathcal{A}$ and $\mathcal{B}$, and a set of labels $H \subseteq L_{\mathcal{A}}^O$, we find that $det(\mathcal{A})$, $\mathcal{A} \setminus H$, and $\mathcal{A} \parallel \mathcal{B}$ are also well-formed DQTSs.*

Next, we investigate the commutativity of function composition of deltafication with the operations. We consider the function compositions of two operations to be commutative if the end results of applying both operations in either order are trace equivalent. After all, trace-equivalent DQTSs behave in the same way. (Note that this is not the case for IOAs or IOTSs, as trace-equivalent variants of such systems might have different quiescence behaviour.) We show that parallel composition and action hiding can safely be swapped with deltafication, but note that deltafication has to precede determinisation to get sensible results. This is immediate, since determinisation does not preserve quiescence.

Proposition 4.1. *Deltafication and determinisation do not commute, i.e., given an IOA $\mathcal{A}$ such that $\delta \notin L$, not necessarily $det(\delta(\mathcal{A})) \approx_{tr} \delta(det(\mathcal{A}))$.*

Consequently, when transforming a nondeterministic IOA $\mathcal{A}$ to a deterministic, well-formed DQTS, one should first derive $\delta(\mathcal{A})$ and afterwards determinise.

Deltafication does commute with action hiding and parallel composition. In the following theorem we use $\setminus_I$ to denote basic action hiding for IOAs, and $\setminus_D$ to denote action hiding for DQTSs (conform Def. 4.4).

Theorem 4.3. *Deltafication and action hiding commute: given an IOA $\mathcal{A}$ such that $\delta \notin L$ and a set of labels $H \subseteq L_{\mathcal{A}}^O$, we have $\delta(\mathcal{A} \setminus_I H) \approx_{tr} \delta(\mathcal{A}) \setminus_D H$.*

Theorem 4.4. *Deltafication and parallel composition commute: given two compatible IOAs $\mathcal{A}$, $\mathcal{B}$, such that $\delta \notin L_{\mathcal{A}} \cup L_{\mathcal{B}}$, we have $\delta(\mathcal{A} \parallel \mathcal{B}) \approx_{tr} \delta(\mathcal{A}) \parallel \delta(\mathcal{B})$.*

The above results allow great modelling flexibility. After all, hiding and parallel composition are often already applied to the IOAs that describe a specification. We now showed that after deltafication these then yield the same well-formed DQTSs as in the case these operations are applied after deltafication.

5   Algorithm for Detecting Divergent States

We present an algorithm to detect divergent states in an IOA or DQTS. This is vital for verifying conformance to well-formedness rule R1, and for deltafication, since additional states have to be added for all divergent states in the

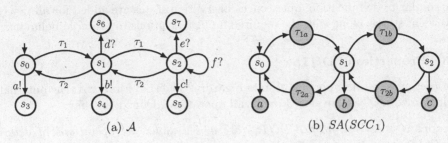

(a) $\mathcal{A}$ (b) $SA(SCC_1)$

Fig. 6. An IOA $\mathcal{A}$ and the Streett automaton $SA(SCC_1)$

original IOA. Recall from Def. 2.9 that a state s is divergent if there exists a fair divergent path on which s occurs infinitely often. Consequently, we need to find a fair cycle that starts at s and consists of only internal transitions. The presence of 'internal' cycles can be determined using Tarjan's well-known and efficient strongly connected components (SCCs) algorithm [14].

One way to efficiently verify fairness is to utilise Streett automata [15], which form a variation on Büchi automata [16]. The acceptance condition for a Streett automaton depends on pairs of sets of states (E_i, F_i) (called Streett pairs), that together form the acceptance component Ω. An ω-word is accepted with $\Omega = \{(E_1, F_1), \ldots, (E_k, F_k))\}$, if there exists a corresponding run that, for each j, only visits a state from F_j infinitely often if it visits a state from E_j infinitely often. This acceptance condition corresponds nicely with our notion of fairness.

Given an internal cycle $\pi = s_0 a_1 s_1 a_2 \ldots a_n s_0$ with $a_i \in L^H$, let $L(\pi) = \{a_1, a_2, \ldots, a_n\}$ be the set of actions executed on the path π, and $L^{LC}(s_i)$ be the set of locally controlled actions enabled at a state $s_i \in states(\pi)$. Because we require every divergent path to be state-finite (see Def. 2.8), these sets can always be calculated. If the cycle π is to be fair, then for every component $A_i \in P$ such that $A_i \cap L^{LC}(s_i) \neq \varnothing$ for some $s_i \in states(\pi)$, there must be an action $a_i \in A_i$ such that $a_i \in L(\pi)$. By introducing additional states that, when visited, represent the fact that a particular locally controlled action is executed, we translate this fairness condition to a nonemptiness check on a Streett automaton.

To clarify this construction, assume we wish to obtain the deltafication of the IOA $\mathcal{A}$ shown in Fig. 6a given $P = \{A_1, A_2, A_3\}$, where $A_1 = \{a, \tau_1\}$, $A_2 = \{b, \tau_2\}$, and $A_3 = \{c\}$. First, we calculate the SCCs of $\mathcal{A}$, while only considering the internal transitions; in this case, there is only one: $SCC_1 = \{s_0, s_1, s_2\}$. To illustrate the conditions for an internal cycle to be fair, consider $\pi = s_0 \tau_1 s_1 \tau_2 s_0$. Since $L^{LC}(s_0) \cap A_1 = \{a, \tau_1\}$ and $L^{LC}(s_1) \cap A_2 = \{b, \tau_2\}$, it follows that for π to be fair, there must be actions $a_i \in A_1$ and $a_j \in A_2$ such that $a_i \in L(\pi)$ and $a_j \in L(\pi)$. This indeed is the case for π, i.e., it is fair.

However, we do not know a priori that the fair path π exists. To find it, consider Fig. 6b. There, we introduced intermediate 'transition' states (marked grey) for every locally controlled transition in and leading out of SCC_1. For state s_0 to be visited infinitely often, it follows from $L^{LC}(s_0) \cap A_1 \neq \varnothing$ and $L^{LC}(s_0) \cap A_2 = L^{LC}(s_0) \cap A_3 = \varnothing$ that there must be actions $a_i \in A_1$ that are executed infinitely often as well. Hence, one of the states a, τ_{1a}, τ_{1b} of $SA(SCC_1)$ must be visited infinitely often if s_0 is. For s_1, in addition, actions from A_2 must occur infinitely often. Finally, for s_2 similar reasoning applies. All this yields $\Omega = \{(E_1, F_1), (E_2, F_2), (E_3, F_3), (E_4, F_4), (E_5, F_5)\}$, where $(E_1, F_1) = (\{a, \tau_{1a}, \tau_{1b}\}, \{s_0\})$, $(E_2, F_2) = (\{a, \tau_{1a}, \tau_{1b}\}, \{s_1\})$, $(E_3, F_3) = (\{b, \tau_{2a}, \tau_{2a}\}, \{s_1\})$, $(E_4, F_4) = (\{b, \tau_{2a}, \tau_{2a}\}, \{s_2\})$ and $(E_5, F_5) = (\{c\}, \{s_2\})$. As mentioned earlier, an accepting run in $SA(SCC_1)$ must satisfy all Streett pairs in Ω. Consequently, if such an accepting run exists, then it immediately follows that a fair internal cycle exists in $\mathcal{A}$. Such a nonemptiness check can be carried out efficiently using an optimised algorithm by Henzinger and Telle [17].

However, a fair internal cycle only gives us a subset of all divergent states. To find all of them, we need to verify for every state if a fair internal cycle exists that contains that particular state. Therefore, if we wish to check if, e.g., state s_0 is divergent, we need to extend acceptance component Ω with an additional Streett pair to obtain $\Omega_{s_0} = \Omega \cup \{(\{s_0\}, SCC_1)\}$. This way, we ensure that internal cycles in SCC_1 are only considered fair if they also contain state s_0. Hence, $SA(SCC_1)$ has an accepting run with acceptance component Ω_{s_0} if and only if s_0 is divergent. In a similar way, we can construct $\Omega_{s_1} = \Omega \cup (\{s_1\}, SCC_1)$ and $\Omega_{s_2} = \Omega \cup (\{s_2\}, SCC_1)$ to check whether s_1 and s_2 are divergent, respectively.

Based on the above, we give an algorithm (Fig. 7) to determine divergent states. For clarity, we range over all states s and check nonemptiness using their acceptance condition Ω_s. A trivial improvement would be to, when a fair cycle is found, mark all its states as divergent and refrain from checking Ω_{s_i} for them.

Complexity. We discuss the worst-case time complexity of this algorithm given a DQTS with n states, m transitions and k partitions.

First note that the size of the acceptance condition of the Streett automaton for an SCC of n' states and m' transitions is worst-case in $O(n'k + n'm')$. After all, each of the n' states yields at most k Streett pairs (yielding the term $n'k$). Moreover, all Streett pairs corresponding to a state, together contain at most all states that represent transitions, of which there are m' (yielding the term $n'm'$).

The time complexity of `construct_streett_automaton(C)` is bounded by the size of the acceptance condition, and hence is in $O(n'(k + m'))$ (with n' and m' taken from C). As the function is called once for each SCC of the system, the total contribution of this function to the full algorithm is in $O(n(k + m))$. Additionally, Tarjan is called once, adding $O(n + m)$. Finally, in the worst-case scenario, the Henzinger/Telle algorithm, which is in

$$O(m \min\{\sqrt{m \log n}, k, n\} + n(k + m) \min\{\log n, k\})$$

as shown in [17], is called once for each state. Together, this yields

$$O(n(k + m) + (n + m) + n(m \min\{\sqrt{m \log n}, k, n\} + n(k + m) \min\{\log n, k\}))$$

Under the reasonable assumption that k is bounded, and after simplification, we find that the worst-case time complexity is in $O(n^2 m)$.

---

algorithm determine_divergent_states **is**
  input: IOA $\mathcal{A} = \langle S, S^0, L^{\mathrm{I}}, L^{\mathrm{O}}, L^{\mathrm{H}}, \rightarrow \rangle$
  output: $d(\mathcal{A})$: a set containing all divergent states of $\mathcal{A}$

  $d(\mathcal{A}) := \varnothing$

  // Use a modified version of Tarjan's algorithm to determine $SCCs(\mathcal{A})$
  $SCCs(\mathcal{A}) :=$ the set of all SCCs of $\mathcal{A}$ that are connected with internal transitions

  for each $C \in SCCs(\mathcal{A})$
      // Build the Streett automaton $SA(C)$ corresponding to SCC C
      $\langle S_{\mathrm{SA}}, \rightarrow_{\mathrm{SA}}, \Omega \rangle :=$ construct_streett_automaton(C)

    for each state s in C
      // Add an additional Streett pair to ensure s is on any accepting cycle
      $\Omega_s := \Omega \cup (\{s\}, Sc)$

      // Use the algorithm by Henziger and Telle to check the emptiness of $SA(C)$
      if $SA(C)$ has an accepting run with acceptance component Ω_s
          $d(\mathcal{A}) := d(\mathcal{A}) \cup \{s\}$
    end for
  end for

  // Auxiliary function to construct the Streett automaton $SA(C)$, alongside acceptance
  // component Ω, for the given SCC C
  function construct_streett_automaton(C)
      input: SCC $\bar{C} = \langle S_{\mathrm{SCC}}, L^{\mathrm{I}}, L^{\mathrm{O}}, L^{\mathrm{H}}, P, \rightarrow_{\mathrm{SCC}} \rangle$
      output: a Streett automaton $SA(C) = \langle S_{\mathrm{SA}}, \rightarrow_{\mathrm{SA}}, \Omega \rangle$

    $S_{\mathrm{SA}} := S_{\mathrm{SCC}}$
    $\rightarrow_{\mathrm{SA}} := \Omega := $ ts_map $:= \varnothing$

    // First construct the Streett automaton
    for each $(s, a, t) \in \rightarrow_{\mathrm{SCC}}$ such that $s \in S_{\mathrm{SCC}}$ and $a \in L^{\mathrm{LC}}$
      // We need to insert a transition state for the transition (s, a, t)
      let $ts_{(s,a,t)} \notin S_{\mathrm{SA}}$ be a new state
      $S_{\mathrm{SA}} := S_{\mathrm{SA}} \cup \{ts_{(s,a,t)}\}$

      if $t \in S_{\mathrm{SCC}}$ **then** $\rightarrow_{\mathrm{SA}} := \rightarrow_{\mathrm{SA}} \cup \{(s, a, ts_{(s,a,t)}), (ts_{(s,a,t)}, a, t)\}$
                     else $\rightarrow_{\mathrm{SA}} := \rightarrow_{\mathrm{SA}} \cup \{(s, a, ts_{(s,a,t)})\}$

      let $A \in P$ be the component such that $a \in A$
      ts_map$(A) := $ ts_map$(A) \cup \{ts_{(s,a,t)}\}$
    end for

    // Now construct the acceptance component Ω
    for each $s \in S_{\mathrm{SCC}}$
      // Add a new Streett pair for every component whose actions are enabled in s
      for each $A \in P$ such that $s \xrightarrow{a}_{\mathrm{SCC}}$ for some $a \in A$
          $\Omega := \Omega \cup \{(\text{ts\_map}(A), \{s\})\}$
      end for
    end for

    return $\langle S_{\mathrm{SA}}, \rightarrow_{\mathrm{SA}}, \Omega \rangle$
  end function

Fig. 7. Algorithm for detecting divergent states

6   DQTSs in a Testing Context

Our main motivation for introducing and studying the DQTS model was to enable a clean theoretical framework for model-based testing. Earlier, the TGV framework [5] already defined ioco also in the presence of divergence. Although this was an important first step, it is not completely satisfactory in the sense that quiescence observations may be followed by output actions; this is counterintuitive to our notion of quiescence. Now, we illustrate how DQTSs can be incorporated in the ioco testing theory without having this problem.

The core of the ioco framework is its *conformance relation*, relating specifications to implementations if and only if the latter is 'correct' with respect to the former. For ioco, this means that the implementation never provides an unexpected output (including quiescence) when it is only fed inputs that are allowed by the specification. Traditionally, this was formalised based on the SAs corresponding to the implementation and the specification. Now, we can apply well-formed DQTSs, as they already model the expected absence of outputs by explicit δ-transitions. In addition, since DQTSs support divergence, using them as opposed to SAs also allows ioco to be applied in the presence of divergence.

Definition 6.1 (ioco). *Let $\mathcal{A}_{impl}, \mathcal{A}_{spec}$ be well-formed DQTSs over the same alphabet. Then, $\mathcal{A}_{impl} \sqsubseteq_{ioco} \mathcal{A}_{spec}$ if and only if*

$$\forall \sigma \in traces(\mathcal{A}_{spec}) . \ out_{\mathcal{A}_{impl}}(\sigma) \subseteq out_{\mathcal{A}_{spec}}(\sigma),$$

where $out_{\mathcal{A}}(\sigma) = \{a \in L^O \cup \{\delta\} \mid \sigma a \in traces(\mathcal{A})\}$.

Since all DQTSs are required to be input-enabled, it is easy to see that ioco-conformance precisely corresponds to traditional trace inclusion over well-formed DQTSs.

This improved notion of ioco-correspondence can be used as before [4,18], at each point in time during testing choosing to either try to provide an input, observe the behaviour of the system or stop testing. As long as the trace obtained this way (including the δ actions, which can now be the result of either quiescence or divergence) is also a trace of the specification, the implementation is correct.

Note that the implementation and specification do not necessarily need to have the same task partition. After all, these are only needed to establish fair paths and hence divergences. This is used during deltafication, to determine which states are divergent. Although this influences ioco conformance (since it induces δ transitions), the conformance relation itself is not concerned with the task partitions anymore.

7   Conclusions and Future Work

In this paper, we introduced Divergent Quiescent Transition Systems (DQTSs) and investigated their properties. Also, we showed how to detect divergent states in order to construct the deltafication of an IOA, and discussed its complexity. Like SAs, DQTSs can be used to describe all possible observations of a system, including the observation of quiescence, i.e., the absence of outputs. Hence, DQTSs are especially useful to model specifications of reactive systems in the context of model-based testing. DQTSs for the first time allow the modelling of systems that exhibit divergence and explicit quiescence.

There are two advantages of using DQTSs rather than SAs for model-based testing. First, DQTSs allow more systems to be modelled naturally, as convergence is not required. Second, DQTSs are stand-alone entities whose properties have been investigated thoroughly. Hence, DQTSs are a formal and comprehensive theory to model and analyse quiescence, even in the presence of divergence.

We have shown that DQTSs are equally potent as SAs in terms of expressible observable behaviour, and that DQTSs can be used as a drop-in replacement for SAs in the ioco framework. Furthermore, we have proven that well-formed DQTSs exhibit desirable compositional properties. Consequently, composite systems can be represented as the parallel composition of smaller subcomponents.

Future Work. The action hiding operation for the DQTS model is quite complex, as outlined in Def. 4.4. To improve this, it might be useful to investigate a different strategy to mark quiescent and divergent states, e.g., using state labels. Also, ioco-based model-based testing tools like TORX internally still use the SA model to represent the specification of the system under test, and an SA-like model to represent the actual test cases. Hence, such tools should be adapted to utilise the improved ioco framework based on DQTSs. Work is currently already underway to adapt the TORX tool. Finally, it would be interesting to see if our notions could be phrased in a coalgebraic setting.

References

1. Vaandrager, F.W.: On the relationship between process algebra and input/output automata (extended abstract). In: Proceedings of the 6th Annual Symposium on Logic in Computer Science (LICS), pp. 387–398. IEEE Computer Society (1991)
2. Tretmans, J.: Test generation with inputs, outputs, and quiescence. In: Margaria, T., Steffen, B. (eds.) TACAS 1996. LNCS, vol. 1055, pp. 127–146. Springer, Heidelberg (1996)
3. Tretmans, J.: Test generation with inputs, outputs and repetitive quiescence. Software - Concepts and Tools 17(3), 103–120 (1996)
4. Tretmans, J.: Model based testing with labelled transition systems. In: Hierons, R.M., Bowen, J.P., Harman, M. (eds.) FORTEST. LNCS, vol. 4949, pp. 1–38. Springer, Heidelberg (2008)
5. Jard, C., Jéron, T.: TGV: theory, principles and algorithms. International Journal on Software Tools for Technology Transfer 7(4), 297–315 (2005)
6. Lynch, N.A., Tuttle, M.R.: An introduction to input/output automata. CWI Quarterly 2, 219–246 (1989)
7. Stokkink, W.G.J., Timmer, M., Stoelinga, M.I.A.: Talking quiescence: a rigorous theory that supports parallel composition, action hiding and determinisation. In: Proceedings of the 7th Workshop on Model-Based Testing (MBT). EPTCS, vol. 80, pp. 73–87 (2012)

8. Stokkink, W.G.J., Timmer, M., Stoelinga, M.I.A.: Divergent quiescent transition systems (extended version). Technical Report TR-CTIT-13-08, University of Twente (2013)

9. Lynch, N.A., Tuttle, M.R.: Hierarchical correctness proofs for distributed algorithms. In: Proceedings of the 6th Annual ACM Symposium on Principles of Distributed Computing (PODC), pp. 137–151. ACM (1987)

10. Sudkamp, T.A.: Languages and machines. Pearson Addison Wesley (2006)

11. Baier, C., Katoen, J.P.: Principles of Model Checking. The MIT Press (2008)

12. De Nicola, R., Segala, R.: A process algebraic view of input/output automata. Theoretical Computer Science 138, 391–423 (1995)

13. Willemse, T.A.C.: Heuristics for ioco-based test-based modelling. In: Brim, L., Haverkort, B.R., Leucker, M., van de Pol, J. (eds.) FMICS 2006 and PDMC 2006. LNCS, vol. 4346, pp. 132–147. Springer, Heidelberg (2007)

14. Tarjan, R.E.: Depth-first search and linear graph algorithms (working paper). In: Proceedings of the 12th Annual Symposium on Switching and Automata Theory (SWAT), pp. 114–121. IEEE Computer Society (1971)

15. Latvala, T., Heljanko, K.: Coping with strong fairness. Fundamenta Informaticae 43(1-4), 175–193 (2000)

16. Farwer, B.: ω-automata. In: Grädel, E., Thomas, W., Wilke, T. (eds.) Automata, Logics, and Infinite Games. LNCS, vol. 2500, pp. 3–21. Springer, Heidelberg (2002)

17. Henzinger, M.R., Telle, J.A.: Faster algorithms for the nonemptiness of Streett automata and for communication protocol pruning. In: Karlsson, R., Lingas, A. (eds.) SWAT 1996. LNCS, vol. 1097, pp. 16–27. Springer, Heidelberg (1996)

18. Timmer, M., Brinksma, E., Stoelinga, M.I.A.: Model-based testing. In: Software and Systems Safety: Specification and Verification. NATO Science for Peace and Security Series D, vol. 30, pp. 1–32. IOS Press, Amsterdam (2011)

Author Index